DUBLIN UNIVERSITY MAGAZINE, 1875.   WOODBURY MECHANICAL PROCESS.

Wilde (aged 59). A photograph published in the *Dublin University Magazine* (1875),

Books published
by Duffy Publishing

Fifty Years Behind the Counter
by
Kevin Duffy

Light hearted biography of his fifty years in the
retail business in the west of Ireland.
Depicts life as it was in a rural town from 1946.
Very enjoyable.
Published in 2001.
€11.40

Wilde's Lough Corrib

A facsimile reprint of Sir William Wilde's
documentary on the antiquities around
the Lough Corrib countryside.
Published in 2002.
€30.00

The Boyne and The Blackwater

Wilde's documentary on the antiquities in
the Boyne Valley area — being also a facsimile
of the original written in 1849.
Published in 2003.
€30.00

Kevin Duffy,
Headford, County Galway.
Phone 093-35449 · Fax 093-35565
E-mail: k.duffy@iol.ie

THE BEAUTIES OF THE BOYNE

AND

BLACKWATER.

Beauties of
The Boyne
and
The Blackwater

William Wilde

Kevin Duffy
Headford, County Galway
2003

First published in 1849
by McGlashan & Gill, Dublin.

Reprinted 2003 by Kevin Duffy,
Headford, County Galway.
E-mail: k.duffy@iol.ie

Introduction © Kevin Duffy
Foreword © Dr. Peter Harbison

Printed in Dublin by Betaprint

A catalogue record for the book is available
from the British Library.

ISBN 0-9540034-2-X

TO

THE RIGHT HONOURABLE

THOMAS BABINGTON MACAULAY,

THIS VOLUME

IS DEDICATED,

IN TESTIMONY OF THE ADMIRATION AND RESPECT OF

THE AUTHOR.

INTRODUCTION

Having successfully reprinted Sir William Wilde's book *Lough Corrib: its Shores and Islands — with Notices of Lough Mask* in the spring of 2002, it was only natural that his previous book *The Beauties of the Boyne and the Blackwater* (1849) would also be welcomed back onto the the book-shelves.

Both books are classics in their own right and trace the history, the archaeology and the antiquities of their respective regions. From being book collectors' items — the two are now available to our readers at affordable prices.

Wilde was a noted antiquarian in his day, and his talents were as varied as his other achievements. In choosing to write about The Boyne Valley, he realized the vast wealth of Irish history in the region — Castles, Forts, Abbeys, Tumuli and Round Towers are strategically positioned along its banks. Newgrange and to a lessor degree — Knowth and Dowth have only in recent years become world famous. Yet, our friend Wilde, explored all of these from within and without in his day and realized their significance and he has embellished them with beautiful woodcut engravings for posterity.

He also gives a graphic unbiased account of the Battle of the Boyne (1690) and includes a map of the Battlefield showing the position of the opposing armies.

The Boyne basin area is literally strewn with an extraordinary amount of these ancient monuments. After all, Tara in pre-Christian times was the home of the Irish High Kings and their Burial Grounds are spread out over the area. It was here too, that St. Patrick commenced his introduction to Christianity in Ireland.

For anyone, apart from the tourist, this book will be of immense benefit to those who are interested in our Irish heritage and there is no better guide-book that I know of, which will give such detailed and accurate information on practically every monument of interest strecthing from Clonard, through Donore, Trim, Navan, Slane and finally Drogheda where the Boyne meets the sea.

Sir William Wilde has been described as 'one of the most the most remarkable *savants* of the nineteenth century — and one of the greatest Irishmen of his time'. Praise indeed and no doubt well worthy of it — we owe a lot to this great man.

Kevin Duffy
Headford, County Galway

FOREWORD
to the reprint
by
Doctor Peter Harbison
Royal Irish Academy

Be it for historical reasons, the Boyne has been the focus of more attention in recent centuries than almost any other Irish river, and has also been fortunate in having a whole volume devoted to it by no less a person than Sir William Wilde (1815-1876). Wilde is all too often thought of as having been merely the father of Oscar but, while not as well known internationally, he was, in fact, a man of broader genius than his brilliant playwright son. This is best appreciated by anyone passing his house at Number 1, Merrion Square in Dublin, where his attainments are listed are listed as follows on a beautiful oval plaque placed between the two large ground-floor windows:

SIR WILLAIM ROBERT WILLS WILDE, 1815-1876
Aural and Opthalmic Surgeon, Archaeology,
Ethnologist, Antiquarian, Biographer, Statistician,
Naturalist, Topographer, Historical, Folklore.

Who, then or now, could lay claim to achievements in more than a few of those fields? Wilde could well have been awarded the old Irish title of '*samildánach*' (all-capable), and be successfully labelled as one of Ireland's last and greatest polymaths.

Born in Castlerea, Co. Roscommon, as the son of a local doctor, he occasionally accompanied his father on his horseback rounds, where he got to know the local people and the Gaelic they still spoke — an accomplishment which stood him in good stead many years later when working on the census returns. He followed in his father's medical footsteps and received his licence from the Royal College of Surgeons at the ripe young age of twenty-two. For his health's sake, he took the post of ship's doctor on the large private yacht of a Glasgow magnate, which brought him southwards along the Atlantic coast and into the Mediterranean, and provided him with material for his first book *Narrative of a Voyage to Madeira, Teneriffe & Along the Shores of the Mediterranean*, which appeared in 1840. Further study and continental travel made him author of a very different kind of book entitled *Austria: Its Literary, Scientific & Medical Institutions*, published in 1843. On returning to Ireland, he opened a practice in Dublin as an eye and ear specialist, where he developed techniques and instruments which still bear his name, and treated all and sundry, often free gratis and for nothing, when he felt that his patients could not afford to pay.

His twenties coincided with the burgeoning work of the Ordnance Survey that was staffed by such eminent Irish literary scholars as O'Curry and O'Donovan. Its great archaeologist was George Petrie, with whom Wilde did a survey of the old kingly crannog at Lagore in County Meath in 1839. Ten years later he dedicated to Petrie and O'Donovan the first edition of his third, and probably best-known book — *The Beauties of The Boyne and its Tributary, The Blackwater*. The famous English historian Thomas Babington Macaulay was so impressed by Wilde's description of Tara in it that he asked the author to guide him around this venerable royal site and Wilde, never a man to miss an opportunity of appearing in exalated company, dedicated the second edition to Macaulay when it appeared a year later.

It is no wonder that Macaulay was impressed. Nothing like this book had ever been seen in Ireland before. It must also have made a deep impression on his Irish contemporaries, who doubtless used Wilde as their guide on expeditions to tour around the valley of what is arguably Ireland's most famous river — a reputation which Wilde himself had helped to enhance. Certainly, they could have had no better cicerone. His opening chapter — described as a 'rhapsody' by Colm O'Loughlainn who did an abbreviated reprint for the centenary in 1949 — is a *tour-de-force*, and unsurpassed in its introductory description of the river. Encompassing the breadth of the valley's history, archaeological sites, literary echoes as well as fuana and flora — and, of course, the Battle of the Boyne — the entire book is written with an elegance that is full of wisdom and knowledge, yet poetic in its lyricism and boundless enthusiasm. He even quotes a stanza by Speranza, the romantic nationalist poet who wrote a glowing review of the book in *The Nation* and who, under her real name, Jane Elgee, was later to become his wife.

Wilde's style is easy-going, flowing — like its subject — at a gentle pace, yet unobtrusively bringing in everything on and around the river's banks that has a bearing on the history of the counties through which it flows, or whose boundaries it meets, Kildare, Offaly, Meath and Louth. The book, however, is not confined to the Boyne itself. It also introduces us to the tributaries that boost it's volume seawards, prime among them, the Blackwater, which helps Wilde embrace important centres like Kells, which has such an important role to play in the nation's cultural history.

Kings Billy and Seamus may have made the Boyne famous, but Wilde may be said to have been the first to have really put its whole valley on the literary map, and to have encouraged people to visit its important tumuli like Newgrange, abbeys like Bective, castles like Trim, and towns like Drogheda. In this, too, he must be seen as having produced of the first and greatest of Irish nineteenth-century guidebooks, written in a masterly prose whose occasional purple passages show him being carried away by the beauty of his surroundings. The book is enhanced by woodcuts by George Hanlon based on drawings by W. F. Wakeman who, himself, must have been inspired by Wilde to go on and write his own much-valued guide to Irish antiquities, which went through many editions in its day.

More than a century and a half after its first appearance, Wilde's *The Beauties of the Boyne & the Blackwater* remains as fresh and bubbling with youthful curiousity and enthusiasm as when it was first written. Of course things have changed — modern agriculture, transport, housing and industry have all affected the landscape — but much still remains unaltered, and Wilde's words unlock the timeless beauty and fascination of the Boyne basin that has attracted mankind to its fish-rich waters and fertile hinterland for more than a hundred generations.

To be taken by the hand by Sir William (who was just plain William when he wrote this book) is to have our eyes opened to what is still around us, but which most of us don't have time to stop and see. It is a salutary lesson in more ways than one to slow down and follow in his footsteps, to join him — as in a canoe or a coracle — as he wends the way downstream from the source to the sea, building up the magic of his surroundings as he goes along.

Wilde went on to publish a medical text-book on eye and ear surgery in 1853, to undertake the mammoth task of producing a catalogue of the collection of the Royal Irish Academy (1857-1861), and to provide valuable and innovatory statistical observations and conclusions on the decennial censuses from 1841 to 1871, the last of which so sapped his energies that he died before he could complete his work on it. But almost a decade before his death in 1876, he had been able to return to his Roscommon roots to write yet another successful travel book *Lough Corrib: its Shores and Islands, with Notices of Lough Mask*. For the man and the woman in the street unaware of Wilde's published expertise in medical, statistical and archaeological matters, *Lough Corrib & The Boyne* represent the height of his popular literary achievements, and it is appropriate that Kevin Duffy should should now now make both of them accessible again by means of facsimile reprints which will help the modern traveller to re-create Wilde's wonderment and enjoyment of the areas covered by the two books which link Ireland east and west as if through a multi-coloured rainbow.

AMENDED PREFACE

TO

THE FIRST EDITION.

———◆———

THE materials for this book were collected during excursions, made from time to time, to the Boyne, for health, amusement, or instruction. With a desire to illustrate some of the scenery and antiquities of my native land, fragments of the original rough sketches were published in the Dublin University Magazine, among the series of " Irish Rivers," now appearing in that periodical. Although the space allotted to such subjects in a serial did not permit of lengthened descriptions of any of the places of note which fringe this river's banks, the interest which had been awakened by those rapid sketches of the Beauties of the Boyne was such as to induce the Publisher to request that I would again visit the great river of Meath, make further observations, collect additional information, include the Blackwater, and publish the materials thus obtained, in the form of an illustrated Hand-book for these charming but hitherto neglected streams.

It may be regarded as a boast, but it is nevertheless incontrovertibly true, that the greatest amount of authentic Celtic history in the world, at present, is to be found in Ireland; nay more, we believe it cannot be gainsaid that no country in Europe, except the early kingdoms of Greece and Rome, possesses so much ancient written history as Ireland. It

is, however, generally speaking, unknown; heretofore it has
neither been appreciated nor understood; until very lately the
great mass of Irish historic manuscripts was scattered and inaccessible.   Many of these have, within the last few years, been
collected together, and several have been translated into English
and published; others are in course of publication, but in forms
which (though no doubt the very best) are not within reach of
the general reader, neither would they be always understood or
valued by such.   To popularize these—to render my countrymen familiar with facts and names in Irish history—has been
one of the objects I have had in view in the historic portion
of this work.   Materials for books of this description are now
so abundant that the chief difficulty is in selection.

Throughout the following pages I have alluded to the want
of a correct Irish history, and the neglect of such histories of our
country as we possess.   I would here again (because I do not
think it can be done too often) revert to this subject. The Board
of National Education,—with whose scheme of instruction, so
far as it goes, I agree, and many of whose books I very much
admire,—while they teach the history of Kamtschatka, and the
geography of the Andes, never once allude, in their system of
education, to the national history of the people they are employed to teach.   Nor need this be wondered at, when I
mention the fact that an eminent publisher of my acquaintance
having some few years ago, in the issue of a popular, and, to
my mind, a very unprejudiced abridgement of Irish history,
written a circular to the different schoolmasters in Ireland,
calling their attention to this little work, was answered by some
of those who deigned to honour him with a reply, that the time
devoted by their pupils to the study of history of any kind
was barely sufficient for those of Greece, Rome, and England!
How long will parents and guardians submit to this? That

Irish history is looked upon as a fable by many ignorant persons is not surprising; but that the ordinarily educated—and, above all, that the learned of any country—should be unacquainted with the materials of our Irish history, is a lamentable fact, and shows either want of knowledge, or utter indifference to the subject.

I was forcibly reminded of this a short time ago, in casting my eyes over that very beautiful book, Macaulay's " Lays of Ancient Rome," in the preface to which, when speaking of the early literature and metrical romances on which the history of most nations is founded, the great modern historian very justly says: " A man who can invent or embellish an interesting story, and put it into a form which others may easily retain in their recollection, will always be highly esteemed by a people eager for amusement and information, but destitute of libraries. Such is the origin of ballad poetry,—a species of composition which scarcely ever fails to spring up and flourish in every society, at a certain point in the progress towards refinement. Tacitus informs us that songs were the only memorials of the past which the ancient Germans possessed." And so the author passes in review the early "poetic literature" and " ancient lays" of the various nations of the earth; the Gauls, the primitive Teutonic and Celtic races of the European continent, the Danes and Anglo-Saxons, the Welsh and Scottish Highlanders, the Servians and Peruvians, the people of Persia and Turkomania, the Sandwich Islanders, the Etruscans and Castilians, the ancient Greeks, and even the inhabitants of Central Africa, whose bards have sung, and whose traditions have perpetuated the story of their early history;—all, except those of the neighbouring island, Ireland, find a place in the preface of the work we allude to.

But worse than this, the last historian who has attempted

to compile and arrange the annals of our country, knew little
or nothing of those rich sources of knowledge in the ancient
Gaelic manuscripts from which alone our history can be obtained.   Thus remarks Mr. O'Donovan, in his preface to The
Battle of Magh-Rath, which, with the name of the monarch
who fought it, is not even once alluded to in Moore's History
of Ireland: " Mr. Moore is confessedly unacquainted with the
Irish language; and the remains of our ancient literature were,
therefore, of course inaccessible to him. That great ignorance
of these unexplored sources of Irish history should be found
in his pages is, therefore, not surprising; but he ought to have
been more conscious of his deficiencies in this respect than to
have so boldly hazarded the unqualified assertion, that there
exist in the Irish annals no materials for the civil history of
the country."

The scientific, as well as the literary and archæological character of our country, has not fallen off of late years; our University and our schools of medicine have borne an honourable
part in the advance of astronomy, mathematics, and medicine.
Three new colleges have been lately established.   The greatest telescope, the most scientific magnetic observatory, and
the first atmospheric railway, were constructed in Ireland.
A survey, the most accurate in its details, and the most extensive in its objects, that any country in Europe has yet been
submitted to, has just been completed; and the last enumeration of the people has been, with justice, pronounced by the
London Statistical Society, " a model for a census."   Unfortunately for the country, either from the indifference of minis-
ters, the unjust economy which the English Exchequer has ever
pursued towards Ireland, or from some mismanagement at home,
—perhaps from a little of each or all,—the memoirs of the
Irish Ordnance Survey have—I would hope only for the pre-

sent—been abandoned. As, however, the materials which have
been collected for them are the property of the country, and
are a necessary portion of her history, they must some day,
sooner or later, meet the light. Without those materials, and
sources of information—which, I may remark, could not
have been collected or procured by private means or individual exertion—the various works relating to ancient Irish
history, which have of late years issued from the press, never
would have appeared in their present extensive form.

The Board of Works has of late done good service, particularly to the inland navigation of the country; and our agricultural and industrial resources have also, within the last few
years, received an impulse which we would ardently antici-
pate may be both permanent and extensive.

In the last ten or fifteen years much has been done to develope
the literary resources of this country. The Royal Irish Academy, the old chartered patron of Irish literature and antiquities, has awoke from the apathetic slumber in which it
remained during the early part of this century, when papers
and communications were admitted into its Transactions, of
which, some were not founded on fact, and others, by the
crude and fanciful theories of their authors, brought upon us
the ridicule of other European nations; while, at the same
time, it permitted some of our oldest and best records, and
most valuable antiquities, to pass into another country. Of
late, however, a zeal and an enthusiasm, and, we would hope,
a nationality, unparalleled in the history of any other Irish
institution, has been infused amongst its members and its
Council, and it has amply redeemed its past indifference,
by creating a museum of Celtic and early Christian antiquities, unexampled in the British isles, and only surpassed
(if it be surpassed) by that of Copenhagen, which is, how-

ever, inferior to our's in this respect, that the same historic
references do not exist there with regard either to the Pagan
or Christian antiquities, but particularly the latter, which are
also less numerous and interesting. And although the Pagan
antiquities at Copenhagen are much more numerous than our's,
it does not appear that the types of form or structure are
much more diversified than those which the museum of the
Irish Academy possesses. Why has the catalogue of this, our
national collection, been so long delayed? Why is not each
new specimen of interest figured in the Proceedings of the
Academy, and its description thus widely distributed among
the public? We know that many valuable acquisitions have
been gained by visiters calling accidentally at the museum;
many more would, we feel convinced, find their way into this
collection, if some general and popular means existed of
giving an account of those which are there already. The
miserable pittance which is doled out to this noble institution
by Parliament, may be used as a reason against this project;
but, while we acknowledge the full effect of all this, we would
suggest that wood-engraving, which is quite applicable to all
purposes of antiquarian delineations and is now remarkably
cheap, should be extensively employed; and as most of the
antiquities have already been drawn at the expense of the
Academy, even fifty pounds a year would do much towards
illustrating them.

By Dr. Petrie's great work upon the Ecclesiastical Architecture and Round Towers of Ireland, the Academy has widely
extended its fame, and the first great impetus has been given
to the true eclectic investigation of Irish history and antiquities. But not by deep archæological research alone, but
by his popular sketches in the Penny Journals, has Dr. Petrie
generated a taste, and created a school of Irish Archæology.

He should have written this book; his profound knowledge of Irish history and antiquities,—his intimate acquaintance with the subjects of which it treats,—his graphic powers of description, and his surpassing abilities as an artist, all combine to render him better suited for the task than any other man living. Because he has not done so I have ventured, *sed longo intervallo*, to describe the scenery presented along the Boyne and the Blackwater, to direct public attention to their antiquarian remains, and to popularize their annals and history.

We have lately had a proof of the growing interest which is taken in the antiquarian department of our Academy, not only by our own, but by other nations. The Danish government sent over Mr. Worsaae, a gentleman of distinguished merit, great shrewdness of observation, and most captivating manners, to investigate and report upon our collection. With a becoming spirit of liberality, the Academy presented to the Royal Society of Northern Antiquaries, through the person to whom I have just alluded, a splendid series of drawings, illustrative of our finest antiquities, and also several specimens of the antiquities themselves, of which duplicates existed. In return, that learned body have lately presented a collection of Danish antiquities to the Academy. This is, I believe, the first instance of good feeling between the Irish and the Danes which our annalists have as yet been able to record.

In the historic department, the Irish Archæological Society has done more to elucidate the annals and records of our country than had been effected during the previous century. Private individuals and enterprising publishers are likewise engaged in this good work. The publication of the Annals of the Four Masters by Messrs. Hodges and Smith is the greatest acquisition ever made to Irish history. The Celtic Society has also done the state some service, and promises well in this department of research. We are, moreover, happy to find that this body does not consider itself a mere transcriber, translator, and commentator on the written labours of the past; but has also constituted itself a conservator of those monuments and architectural remains which the Vandalism of modern commissioners would destroy. Some of these gentlemen, we regret to say, possess little knowledge of, and less taste and interest in, those relics that teach the antiquary, mark the historic era, or adorn the landscapes of our native land.

The nonsensical fancies of Vallancey and his school of imaginary antiquaries have long since been dispelled by the labours of Petrie, O'Donovan, Hardiman, Todd, Eugene Curry, Reeves, Graves, and other modern investigators.

Strangers even who lately visited our soil have become infected by the general feeling of enthusiasm which has pervaded all classes and parties and some of them have ably and generously devoted the pages of their periodicals to the elucidation of Irish history and antiquities.*

Her Majesty Queen Victoria, with her illustrious consort, has just visited this portion of her dominions, and by their coming amongst us, have done more to put down disaffection, and elicit the loyal feelings and affections of the Irish people, than armies thousands strong, fierce general officers, trading politicians, newspaper writers, and the suspension of the Habeas Corpus Act, &c. &c. Let us hope that her welcome visit will be soon repeated.

I have now but to express my obligations to those kind friends who have assisted me in the compilation of the historic and antiquarian portion of this work. First, to my excellent friend, John O'Donovan,—whose labours in the cause of

---

* See the Historical Tableaux, in numbers 160 and 162 of Chambers's Edinburgh Journal for 1847.

Irish Archæology are already so well known to the learned in Great Britain, and which are so frequently referred to in this book, that it seems scarcely necessary to allude to them here; —who has assisted me largely, and devoted much time and attention in the revision of proofs, and in pointing out the sources from which I might gain illustrative materials. I know no man possessing the same amount of knowledge, gleaned with the same labour and research, who is more liberal of it than Mr. O'Donovan; and to this every one who has been engaged, either in strict archæological research, or, like myself, in popularizing our history, must bear testimony.

The Very Reverend Richard Butler, Dean of Clonmacnoise, has also placed me, as regards this work, under many obligations. His long residence at Trim, of which he has become the historian, and his intimate acquaintance with the ancient history of the county of Meath, render him better fitted for the task of a critic upon a book treating of the Boyne, than any other living antiquary; and in the same generous manner as Mr. O'Donovan, he has, as he always does, assisted those who require the aid of his matured judgment and extensive reading.

I have to express my obligations to Mr. George Smith, the enterprising publisher of so many works connected with the history of Ireland, for permission to examine and extract from the early portion of that part of the Annals of the Four Masters, now in course of translation by Mr. O'Donovan. With the Editor's permission, he placed the unpublished sheets of that great work at my disposal.

Indeed, without the assistance of so many generous as well as learned friends, I could not have produced this work in its present form. I do not profess to be an antiquary or an historian; other avocations of a professional nature occupy more of my time than the acquirement of strict and exact archæological knowledge would permit; but I have endeavoured, with the assistance of my friends, and by means of such sources of information as were readily at hand, while I popularized our history and sketched our scenery (chiefly as a source of healthful relaxation from more fatiguing pursuits) to present nothing to the reader that was not strictly true. Had more time been devoted to the subject, this might, perhaps, have been made a better book, but we doubt whether it would be more suited to the purpose for which it is intended.

With the exception of the illustration upon the first page, and the woodcut at page 67, which were drawn by Mr. Grey, and the drawings by Mr. Connolly, engraved at pages 38, 40, and 195, all the illustrations of this work have been sketched, and afterwards drawn on wood by Mr. Wakeman, who is already so favourably known both as an artist and an antiquary, by his useful Handbook of Irish Antiquities, and who combines great artistic skill with a peculiar knowledge of the salient points of the antiquities or ruins he may be engaged in illustrating. I am likewise indebted to Mr. Wakeman for much local information, which his residence on the banks of the Boyne for the last two years enabled him to collect.

Mr Hanlon, the wood-engraver, has also borne no inconsiderable part in the illustrations of the Beauties of the Boyne. And last, though not least, whatever pleasure or profit the fireside reader or the tourist may derive from the perusal of this little book, is chiefly due to the enterprise of its spirited publisher, Mr. McGlashan.

21, WESTLAND-ROW,
    August 1849.

PREFACE

THE SECOND EDITION.

To this Second Edition of the Beauties of the Boyne and Blackwater I have added a full and succinct account of the battle fought at Oldbridge, in 1690, generally known as "The Battle of the Boyne;" and have, I think, given a clearer and fairer account of that memorable transaction, which is so intimately connected with the history of Europe at the time, than has heretofore appeared. I have also, since the issue of the former edition, visited and carefully examined the ruins of the celebrated monastic establishments at Mellifont and Monasterboice; I have had several accurate sketches made of them, and I have also added full letter-press descriptions of these places. The Index has also been made much more copious. I have considerably increased the Itinerary, and given several new routes, suited to tourists limited for time. These additions, together with some minor alterations throughout the work, have considerably increased its pages, and it likewise contains eleven new illustrations, making in all eighty-four woodcuts.

Dublin, 21, Westland-Row,
August, 1850.

CONTENTS.

— ✦ —

CHAPTER I.

THE RIVER'S SOURCE AND HISTORY.

CHAPTER II.

FROM CARBURY TO CLONARD.

CHAPTER III.

CLONARD, AND THE BOYNE TO TRIM.

b

CHAPTER IV.

TRIM.

CHAPTER V.

FROM TRIM TO NAVAN.

CHAPTER VI.

THE BLACKWATER.

CHAPTER VII.

THE BOYNE FROM NAVAN TO SLANE.

CHAPTER VIII.

THE ROYAL CEMETERY OF BRUGH-NA-BOINNE.

CHAPTER IX.

THE ETHNOLOGY OF THE ANCIENT IRISH.

CHAPTER X.

THE BATTLE-FIELD OF OLDBRIDGE.—DULEEK.

CHAPTER XI.

DROGHEDA AND ITS ENVIRONS.

LIST OF ILLUSTRATIONS.

TO THE BINDER.

ITINERARY.

———◆———

THE following directions with respect to the best mode of seeing the beauties of the Blackwater and Boyne will be found useful to the tourist.

The River Boyne may be visited, and its various objects of interest examined, comfortably, in three days. The Blackwater will require a fourth; and a distinct route from Navan to Virginia, along its banks, is given at p. xxiii. of this Itinerary. As railways now approach the river at three different points,—at Enfield, Navan, and Drogheda,—tourists can return to Dublin, if they wish, each night, or, proceeding continuously down the river, they can divide the journey into three portions, sleeping the first night at Trim, the second at Slane, and the third at Dublin, as neither Navan nor Drogheda as yet present the very best accommodation.

The most ready mode of access to the Boyne's source, at Carbery, in the county of Kildare, is to proceed from the Broadstone, Dublin, in one of the early morning trains which starts by the Midland Great Western Railway, to Enfield, which can be reached in about an hour and a half. Here outside jaunting-cars can be hired at the rate of sixpence per mile for two persons, or one can be hired for the day, or by the job. From seven shillings and sixpence to ten shillings per day, with a *douceur* to the driver, will generally satisfy, but in every instance a special bargain should be made with the carman before starting. The tourist should first proceed to Carbery, distant about six miles, where the hill and Castle of Carbery should be visited, and afterwards the source of the Boyne, at Trinity Well, in the adjoining demesne of Newbery. About a mile and a half from Enfield, the Edenderry road through Carbery crosses the Blackwater rivulet, one of the tributaries of the Boyne; then the neat little village of Johnstown, and between that and Carbery we pass Mylerstown church and castle, about a mile to the right of the road. This latter

c

may be visited by those who have time to spare, and who had left Dublin by the early morning train.

From Carbery to Edenderry is not quite four English miles. Except the old castle, which is difficult of access, there is very little to delay the tourist in this town. Two roads—one direct to the Hill of Carrick, the other, the most circuitous, by Monasteroris, Kinnafad, and Grange—lead downward, to Ballybogan. The former is the shorter, the latter by far the most interesting. From Edenderry to Monasteroris is not quite two miles; from thence to Kinnafad a mile, and by the Castle of Grange to the Hill of Carrick two and a half miles more. The next point of interest is Ballybogan, four miles distant from Carrick, and eight from Edenderry. Here two roads, one on each side of the Boyne, lead to Clonard. If the tourist intends to return to Dublin the same night, the northern road upon the left bank of the river, by which the ruins of Ticroghan castle and chapel may be visited, will be found not only the most interesting, but the shortest. From Ballybogan Bridge to Clonard is two miles. Having visited the moat and the site of the ecclesiastical ruins adjoining, the tourist can either continue on to Trim, which is about twelve English* miles distant, by crossing to the right bank of the river, at the Boyne Aqueduct, or he can return by the Great Western road, over Leinster Bridge, to the railway station at Moyvalley, which is about four miles distant; and, taking the evening up-train from Mullingar, return to Dublin the same night. If the latter course is pursued, the tourist should proceed by railway to Moyvalley the second day; then visit Clonard; and thence proceed down the river by Trim to Navan, where a branch of the Drogheda railway will take him up to Dublin in something more than two hours.

Trim, and the Boyne from thence to Navan, one of the most interesting portions of the excursion, can be visited in a day, by taking a car from Enfield either direct to Trim, or by Dangan and Laracor: and proceeding from Trim, by Newtown and Scurlogstown, to Bective. Here we have again to make choice of roads; on the one side we have Clady, and on the other Assey, Riverstown, Bellinter, and Tara.

To follow the route in detail from Trim downward, the most pleasing points of view will be gained by proceeding on the right bank of the river, then crossing over to visit the ruins of Newtown, about a mile distant, returning to the right bank, and proceeding to Scurlogstown, Trubly, and the Bridge of

---

* In this neighbourhood, and about Navan, distances are still counted in Irish miles.

Bective, distant from Trim four miles and a half, and from Navan three and a half miles. Here we cross to the left bank, and having seen the Abbey, proceed upon the same side to visit Clady, which is not a mile distant, and returning by the same route to Bective Bridge, follow the road upon the right bank to Riverstown Castle, and thence ascend the hill of Tara, which being seen, it will be found most advisable to proceed to the bridge of Bellinter, and cross over to the left bank, and then, passing through the demesne of Ardsalla, visit Cannistown. We next cross the Boyne at Athcarne Bridge, in order to see the font at Johnstown, described at page 130, about half a mile distant. It is then optional to proceed to Navan by the road upon the right bank of the river, by which one of the best views of Athlumney Castle can be gained, or to return again to Athcarne Bridge.

At Navan the tourist will decide whether he visits the Blackwater then, or makes a separate excursion to it afterwards. Cars can be hired to proceed by Kells to Virginia. The tourist will find it best in so doing to proceed up the river by Liscarton Castle, upon the left bank, to Kells, where the coach-road crosses to the right bank, and, having visited St. Kieran's church and well at Castle-kieran, the most distant point of interest upon the Blackwater, and to return by Teltown, Donaghpatrick, and Rathaldron, to Navan, by the left or northern road. Coaches, however, proceed daily to Kells and Virginia, at both of which places cars can be procured to return to Navan. The examination of the Blackwater, by any of these means, will occupy an entire day. Tourists can leave Dublin by one of the early trains and go by Drogheda to Navan, from whence public conveyances proceed by Kells to Virginia; or cars can be hired at either of these places to visit the Blackwater, and return in time to catch the up-trains from Navan to Dublin.

From Navan to Kells is nine English miles; from Kells to Castlekeiran three; and to Virginia from the latter place nine miles.

From Navan to Slane we have again a choice of roads : the most advisable plan will, however, be found to visit Donaghmore church and round tower, which is about a mile from Navan, on the left bank of the river, and then, returning to Navan, either procure a boat to proceed to Slane, or walk along the rampart or track-way of the canal. If neither of these two latter modes are feasible, Slane, being distant from Navan about six Irish miles, may be reached by either the eastern or western road; upon the former we have Ard-mulchan and Beauparc, and upon the latter, Donaghmore, Dunmoe, Stackallan, Baronstown, and Slane demesne. A narrow by-road, about three-quarters of a mile long, leads down from the main road to Dunmoe. Boats, however, can generally be procured by timely notice, and they can be taken with facility as far as New Grange, where cars should be sent from Slane or Drogheda to take tourists on to the railway stations at either of these places.

Slane hotel will be found a very desirable residence for those who can spend a few days in visiting the charming scenery of this part of the Boyne, and excursions may be made from it to Navan, Tara, Trim, and the places intermediate, as well as to Kells, Duleek, the mounds of New Grange and Dowth, the field of the Battle of the Boyne, Mellifont, and Monasterboice.

From Slane to Drogheda, a distance of seven miles, the road upon the left bank of the river presents most objects of interest. The tourist should visit in succession, Knowth, New Grange, and Dowth, which can be reached by a by-road branching off near the first of these monuments. Having seen these antiquities and those in Netterville Park adjoining, we proceed by the little bridge over the Mattock river, and join the Slane road again near the ford of Oldbridge. Having examined the battle-field, should time permit, or that the tourist had slept at Slane upon the previous night, a detour may be made from Oldbridge, by the road leading up through King William's Glen to Mellifont, about one and a half mile distant; from thence to Monasterboice three, and having seen the latter, one can easily get upon the great northern road, and reach Drogheda, which is distant from Monasterboice four miles, time enough to get to town by the last train.

Cars may be obtained at the Drogheda terminus to visit any of the places in the vicinity, as Donore, Mornington, Maiden Tower, Termonfechen, and Duleek; but there will soon be a station near where the railway passes the latter.

To those interested in antiquarian researches the following route will form a pleasant day's excursion. Pack up a luncheon. Start for Drogheda by the mail train at 10 o'clock, P. M.; this reaches its destination at ten minutes past 11 o'clock. Hire a car for the day; cost about seven or eight shillings, including driver. Proceed along the river to the Obelisk at Oldbridge, where the scene of the battle of 1690 and the "Boyne Water" may be examined, particularly from the rising ground adjoining the corner of Townley Hall demesne. Drive on as far as the road leading to Dowth, and then return. Pass up King William's Glen, and proceed by Tullyallen to Mellifont, which one ought to reach by 2 o'clock. Having seen that ancient place, drive by the old road across the country to Monasterboice, and return to Drogheda by 5 or 6 o'clock, and while tea is preparing at the hotel or the station house, examine some of the ruins in Drogheda described at pages 306 to 309. The train to Dublin starts at 8 o'clock.

We would advise those desirous of making a careful examination of the battle-field, and going over the ground contested on the 1st of July, 1690, to go up the river to Oldbridge by boat from Drogheda, which can be easily effected if the tide is in, or to have a boat in waiting there; and, having examined the site of the English position on the south side of the Boyne, to cross over opposite the Obelisk, where a car from Drogheda should be in readiness. Then proceed up the hill, through the battle-field, to Donore, or, as the people here call it, "*Done Over*," from the ruined church of which the position of the Irish army can be best seen, and a tolerably accurate idea formed of the skirmishing ground near Rosnaree. From Donore cross down to Duleek by the hill to Cruzrath. Duleek is well worthy of a couple of hours' examination. Next proceed up the hill to Bellewstown, and from this by the Naul to Balbriggan, to meet one of the evening trains to Dublin.

To devote a day to the examination of the great cemetery of Brugh-na-Boinne, the tourist should proceed by rail to Slane, hire a car there, and visit in succession Knowth, New Grange, Dowth, and Netterville, and then, crossing over to Monknewtown, get back to Drogheda in time for the evening train. Fraser's admirable "Hand-Book for Travellers in Ireland," and the Monthly Time Bills of the railways, will be found of great service.

d

THE BOYNE.

CHAPTER I.

THE RIVER'S SOURCE AND HISTORY.

INTRODUCTION.—THE BEAUTIES OF THE BOYNE; ITS SCENERY AND HISTORIC INTEREST; ITS ARCHÆOLOGICAL REMAINS. — DESCRIPTION OF THE ANCIENT KINGDOM OF MEATH; ITS HISTORY AND TOPOGRAPHY. — THE PLAINS OF BREGHIA.—THE ENGLISH CONQUEST.—DEARVORGAIL, THE HELEN OF THE IRISH ILIAD. — THE PALE. — GEOGRAPHICAL DESCRIPTION OF THE RIVER.—THE SOURCE, ORIGIN, AND DERIVATION OF THE BOYNE.—TRINITY WELL; ITS LEGENDS AND ANTIQUITIES.—THE STORY OF BOAN AND DABELLA.

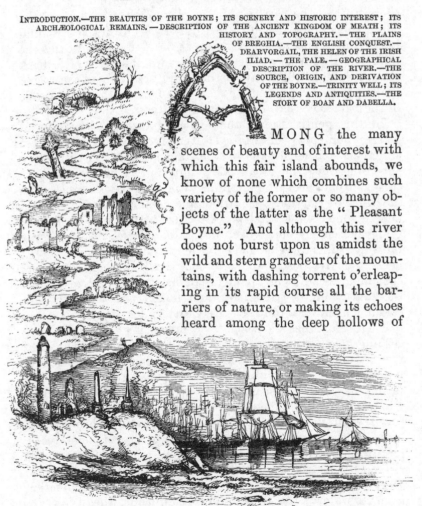

MONG the many scenes of beauty and of interest with which this fair island abounds, we know of none which combines such variety of the former or so many objects of the latter as the " Pleasant Boyne." And although this river does not burst upon us amidst the wild and stern grandeur of the mountains, with dashing torrent o'erleaping in its rapid course all the barriers of nature, or making its echoes heard among the deep hollows of dark-wooded dells, but pursues the quiet, even tenor of its way, through a flat but rich and fertile country, winding by "its own sweet will" through broad savannahs and by green inches, where the calm ripple of its placid waters disturbs not the song of the mavis; still it possesses charms and beauties, and that, too, without a rival in this or perhaps any other country. Slow, calm, and tranquil in its early course, the mower whets his scythe in the deep meadows by its brink, and the reaper gathers the corn from the very margin of its waters; the swift and the martin skim over its clear surface, and the robin sings in the ancient thorn that rises out of the adjoining hedge-row. The very may-fly, as it lights upon it, breaks the mirror of its surface. The wide-spreading circles which mark the springing of the trout, or the timid breathing of the roach, are all, save the flapping of the water-hen, or the easy paddle of the baldcoot, that disturb its placid bosom.

In this gentle stream there is no inequality—no roar of waters nor spray of cataract; it is not boisterous nor yet sluggish; neither broken by the sudden rapid, nor calmed by spreading into the broad lake; but, pure and undefiled, it springs from the crystal fountain of the living rock,—its source sanctified by religious veneration, and commemorated in legend and in song; serene and peaceful, like a true philosopher, it glides noiselessly on, in deep but calm repose, bestowing the blessings of fertility on the counties through which it flows; bearing on its bosom the intercourse which socializes man; enriching, beautifying, and civilizing, it receives in return the homage of its tributaries, and finally mingles with that eternity of waters, the sea. As Clutterbuck says of his story, in "The Fortunes of Nigel," "commencing strikingly, proceeding naturally, ending happily,—like the course of a famed river, which gushes from the mouth of some obscure and romantic grotto, then gliding on, never pausing, never precipitating its course, visiting, as it were, by natural instinct, whatever worthy objects of interest are presented by the country through which it passes." Winding through the heart of the ancient kingdom of Meath, green homesteads, picturesque villages, peaceful hamlets, and thriving towns rise on its banks; the hand of man has turned its power to good account, and mills and factories draw their animation from its waters; the freights of foreign lands, the luxuries of far-distant countries, are borne on its stream towards the interior, and the produce of our own soil and the industry of our people is carried downwards on its tide. Deep hanging woods and rich plantations of noble parks and extensive demesnes, where the willows dip into its calm waters, and the oaks and elms of centuries are mirrored in the wave beneath, stretch for miles along its course, where

"Slow, and in soft murmurs, nature bade it flow."

Towards its centre, and as it nears the sea, its banks become more elevated, their outline more picturesque. Here, rising abruptly from the water's edge, their castled crags, bending over the stream, remind us of the scenery that characterizes the Rhine between Cologne and Mayence; in other places, sloping gradually from the river, their sides are clothed with foliage of the deepest, darkest green, piled up in waving leafy masses to their very summits, so that the sun itself is hidden (except at noon) in many places from its dark waters. The summits of many of these verdant banks are crowned by ruins of castles, towers, and churches, feudal halls, and high baronial keeps, still noble even in their decay, and forming, as they are cut clear and sharp against the azure blue beyond, pictures in the landscape, unsurpassed in grace and beauty by any in the land. In the broad lawns that here and there interpose between these verdant banks and steep o'erhanging precipices, we find the noble mansions of some of the highest of our nobility, and many of the most memorable ecclesiastical remains—the cell of the hermit, the cloister of the monk, and the cross of the pilgrim —that Ireland, rich as she is in relics of the past, can boast of. Ancient stone circles, massive cromlechs, and numerous green mounds, raised by our Pagan ancestors, some clothed with velvet sward, but others fringed with young plantations, are thickly interspersed among the more attractive objects that catch the eye, as it descends upon the limpid surface of the Boyne. Highly cultivated lands, richly ornamented seats, and a population, generally speaking, more comfortable, more intelligent, and more advanced in civilization than the majority of our peasantry, may fill up the outline we have faintly and briefly endeavoured to draw of the general characteristics and present appearance of this celebrated river; and though Spencer has not sung its praises, nor Raleigh gossiped upon its banks, it has been hallowed by events the most interesting in our country's annals. So memorable in ancient history, and so rich in monuments of the past is it, that we fear not to assert that the history of Ireland might be written in tracing its banks. Many a broad smiling plain through which it flows, now green with waving corn, or perfumed and decorated by the wild flowers of a pasture land, or by some delicate female hand cultivated into the elegant garden, in the bowers of which the birds of spring are singing, was once the scene of mortal strife, and crimsoned with the blood of warriors, where the clang of battle, the shout of the victorious, the groan of the dying, and the prayer of the suppliant, alone were heard. Scarcely a ford upon this river but was disputed in days gone by ; every pass was a Thermopylæ; the bardic annals teem with descriptions of its battles ; the fairy lore of other days yet lingers by its tranquil waters; and scarcely a knoll, or mound, or rock, or bank in its vicinity but still retains its legend. The peasant even yet paddles his corragh, or frail canoe of skins, across its waters, and many of the superstitious rites and customs of our ancestors are still observed by the people of that district. How time runs on, and science widens the circle of her power, yet man and many of his customs remain the same for centuries;—on one side of the bridge of Drogheda may still be seen the wicker corragh, with its horse-skin covering, the same in design and execution, perhaps, as floated there a thousand years ago; and on the other we find the latest invented and most improved screw-steamer!

The plains of Midhe, and the flowery fields of Breghia, through which the Boyne flows, appear to have been the first cultivated in Ireland; and it is more than probable that one of the earliest waves of population which reached our island passed up the stream of this great river, and that the aborigines settled amidst the wooded hills and deep alluvial plains upon its banks, and have left their bones in the numerous barrows and tumuli still remaining upon its shores. Beyond all doubt, the earliest undoubted kings of Erin reigned upon its banks, where also the earliest laws were framed, the earliest poems sung, and the most profound druidical mysteries celebrated. Soldiers and sages, bards and brehons, have commemorated many of its localities ; the romance of Irish history is laid amidst the scenery of this river, and much of the imagery of our earliest poets was drawn from this fertile source. Christianity entered Ireland through this sacred stream; Patrick first landed at the Boyne's mouth, and raised the beacon of the cross at Slane; his first sermons were preached, and his first conversions took place

" Where, in delightful streams,
The Boyne, the darling of the ocean, flows."*

Foreign invaders, the Dane and the Norseman, first entered this kingdom on its waters. The earliest abodes of learning, and the most renowned schools of Christian philosophy which our annalists record, had their seats by its margin; parliaments and councils were held in its castles; and kingdoms—in battles fought by kings—were lost and won upon its banks.

These are not the fanciful speculations of the enthusiastic but imaginary writers of the last century; the monuments speak for themselves, their architecture tells their date and purpose ; many of the historic annals which relate these circumstances, formerly difficult of access, and known or capable of being understood but by a few, have been recently published in the English tongue, and have satisfied even the most incredulous as to their antiquity and authenticity. It is acknowledged by all capable of forming an opinion on the subject, that the history of Ireland has yet to be written, but the materials for it are now being collected, and rendered accessible and instructive, by competent authorities, with an interest and an enthusiasm, and, moreover, with a critical regard to the simple and unbiassed statement of the authors, alike honourable to the country, and creditable to those engaged in the production of these works. We are not vain enough to boast of, nor credulous enough to believe, all that is related in many of the early Irish manuscripts, no more than we place implicit faith in all that is told in the great Grecian Epic, or that historians have set down in the primitive histories of other kingdoms; but we receive them as shadows of great historical events, and as highly characteristic of the manners and customs of the times and people they describe. And it may be here remarked, that so far from critical investigation or research

* " In regione BREG prope fluvium pulcherrimum et fertilem Boyn."—
Ussher, Primord., p. 850.

invalidating the testimony of our early Irish bards and annalists, it has been found, and every day's experience confirms
the fact, that the more we collate, examine, and compare, manuscript with manuscript, author with author, and both with
those monuments and antiquities which have still remained
undefaced, and the more we test them with contemporaneous
history, the more the shadow will be found to correspond with
the substance of the truth they figure.* This is the age of
true eclectic investigation. The country, notwithstanding all
her present poverty and privation, is not only ripe for its reception, but cries loudly for her history. It is a fact strange
but true, that either from prejudice, apathy, or indifference,
while the histories of Greece, Rome, England, and Scotland,
are taught, or at least boys are compelled to read them, at the
schools for the sons of the Irish gentry and middle classes, the
history of Ireland, such as it is, is never heard of.

In the historical remarks which we purpose introducing in
order to illustrate the Boyne, it cannot be expected that, in a
popular work of this description, we should break the text
and stay the narrative by interlarding its pages with critical
references to all the various sources of Irish history from which
we have drawn these materials. Neither is it our intention
to describe minutely all the geographical relations, and various
industrial resources of this river; but to present a series of
picturesque views from those points in which its scenic beauty
is most remarkable, and particularly to draw the attention of
the tourist and young antiquary to those localities which are
memorable for their historical recollections, or venerated for
their archæological interest; and, as we have already stated,
no other river in Ireland affords the same scope for the study
of these objects, combined with the same variety and extent of
pastoral inland scenery, of such depth of colour, and such grace
of outline, as the Boyne, for at least thirty miles of its course.

In proof of our assertion, with regard to the numerous monuments upon the Boyne, we may remark, that from Trim to
Drogheda we have traces of every epoch of Irish history, from
the ante-historic period, the date of which carries us back to

---

* We know no better proof of this statement than Mr. Petrie's Essay on
the History and Antiquities of Tara Hill, published in the Transactions of the
Royal Irish Academy, vol. xviii. part ii.

the primæval occupation of this island, and which is indelibly
marked by the Pagan cromlech, the rude cell and altar, and
the stone chamber or kistvaen with its surrounding mound,
containing rude earthen urns, the incinerated bones, the shell
ornaments, and stone weapons of our Firbolg and Tuatha De
Danaan ancestors,* together with their circular raths and
intrenched military forts, of which we have examples in the
mounds and tumuli at Carbery, Clonard, Ardmulchan, Newgrange, Dowth, Knockminaune, and Brugh-na-Boinné. Here
we may linger,

> " By the cromlech sloping downward,
>   Where the Druid's victim bled,
> By those towers pointing sunward,
>   Hieroglyphics none have read,
> In their mystic symbols, seeking,
>   Of past creeds and rites o'erthrown,
> If the truths they shrined are speaking
>   Yet in litanies of stone."—*Speranza.*

The sacred well from which the river flows, with its half-
fabulous legends, serves to connect the earliest historic period
with preceding times, and marks a period shrouded in mystery
and Druidism.

Tara, with its Lia Fail, or oracular stone, and its grassy
mounds, stands alone, the crowning place of its kings, the fo-
rum of the sages, and the banqueting hall of the nobles of Erin,
at least eighteen centuries ago. Then follow the early Christian buildings, the oratories and small missionary churches,
sculptured crosses, carved fonts, and round towers, as at Monasteroris, Clonard, Donaghmore, and St. Eark, till such primitive buildings rose into the more stately edifices, churches,
and monasteries of Slane, Trim, Bective, and Drogheda. The
baronial halls of the Anglo-Normans and proud castles of the
Pale stretching along its banks, and commanding every ford
and pass,—as at Carbery, Trim, Athlumny, Dunmoe, and
Castle-Dexter,—mark another era, and tell of the extended
sway of the De Lacys, Husseys, Berminghams, Plunkets,
Cusacks, Barnwells, Flemings, Prestons, Petits, Tuites,
D'Arcys, and other English chieftains, from the time of the
invasion to the age of Elizabeth. Although we do not find

---

* For a description of the *Firbolgs* and *Tuatha De Danaans* see the ethnological inquiry at the end of this volume, after the account of Dowth.

any well-authenticated architectural remains of the O'Melaghlins, the ancient monarchs of Meath, still remaining, their
written history enables us to note with tolerable precision the
strongholds and fortresses, as well as the sites of the abbeys
and churches founded by this memorable and ill-fated race,
—ruins that still remain,—the foot-prints of history,—with

> ——— " Ivied arch and pillar lone,
> Pleading haughtily for glories gone."

The various holy wells sheltered by the ancient oaks and
thorns, and alike venerated by the Druid priest and the early
Christian saint and pilgrim, occur in spots so calm, so lone
and peaceful, that religious veneration is there awakened, even
in the most apathetic.

The town of Drogheda notes a memorable era in the time of
Cromwell, and its numerous military and ecclesiastical remains
extend over a period of undoubted authenticity for at least
one thousand years. The site and story of the " Battle of the
Boyne," on that memorable occasion when, for the last time,
two kings fought for the sovereignty of these realms, brings us
down to a date almost within the memory of man; while the
monster meeting at Tara, the last great effort of O'Connell
and the "moral force Repealers," occurred but a few years ago.
And yet with all this we know of no river that has been more
neglected by writers, and no scenery that is less known within
the same distance of the metropolis, than that which the Boyne
presents for the greater portion of its course. The modern
writers upon Ireland have one and all carefully avoided it.
Inglis encircled Ireland, but "did" the Boyne while the northern
mail whirled him over the bridge of Drogheda. Barrow no
sooner approached its waters than he fled from them in dismay. The "Angler in Ireland" appears to have omitted it by
particular desire; and with the exception of Mr. and Mrs. Hall's
account of its appearance at Trim, it has remained unnoticed
and undescribed by all modern systematic writers upon the
scenery of this portion of the British dominions.

Dr. Petrie, who first drew attention to its beauties in a
short paper published in the last volume of those valuable
records of Irish history, the Penny Journals, thus graphically describes a portion of this river: " It is of a character
as beautiful as could be found anywhere, or even be ima-

gined. Scenery of this class, of equal richness, may be often found in England, but we do not know of any river's course of the same length in which natural beauty so happily combines, or in which so many interesting memorials of past ages could be found. Scattered in rich profusion along the banks of this beautiful river, we find the noblest monuments of the various races of men who have had sway in Ireland. It is on its luxuriant banks, amid so many instructive memorials of past ages, that the history of our country, as traced in its monuments, could be best studied."

Nor will our readers cavil at this broad assertion, when they remember the various remains which we have enumerated, and the great and numerous historic events to which we have alluded: while, from among the ruins with which it abounds, and underneath the very sod turned up by the spade of the labourer, in the vast and fertile plains of Leinster traversed by the Boyne, a mine of Irish antiquities has been, and is daily being worked, which has largely assisted to stock the museums of our own and other countries. Stone weapons, hatchets, knives, and arrow-heads of various shapes and sizes; bronze celts, swords, and spear-heads; terra-cotta vases; golden torques, rings, bracelets, and ornaments of great value, and of the most beautiful forms; musical instruments of brass; rings, pins, and fibulæ of silver; knives, swords, axes, shears, and domestic utensils of iron; combs and pins of bone and wood; besides other warlike, culinary, or decorative implements and ornaments of the early people of Ireland, have been here found in rich profusion. Here, moreover, may the naturalist speculate on the various races of the extinct animals of this country,— the gigantic elk, almost peculiar to Ireland, the antlered stag, the noble wolf-dog, the different varieties of horned cattle and domestic animals, whose remains are found in its bogs and marshes; or of fowl and other small animals occasionally discovered among the incinerated bones in the urns and tumuli: where also the ethnologist may procure ample means for study and speculation. Shrines, bells, and croziers of the most chaste form and moulding, to many of which an undoubted authentic history is attached, have likewise been discovered in this rich locality. If the remains of plants and animals, fixed in the enduring rocks, mark for the geologist epochs of time, convulsions of nature, transition periods, and great physical

revolutions on the surface of our globe, how much more do
the weapons, ornaments, and tombs with their contents and
architectural remains, afford the antiquary and historian a
means of ascertaining, with much greater precision, their historic epochs, and of forming an acquaintance with the habits,
manners, and customs, the religion, arts, music, sports, and
warfare, of the people to whom such antiquities belonged.

Moreover, along the Boyne and its tributaries may the angler
enjoy good sport, with both trout and salmon, and the bota-
nist reap a plenteous harvest of some of the richest and rarest
plants peculiar to the inland districts of Ireland.

Let us wander together by the banks of the Boyne, when the
sun is high in heaven, when the warm air of summer is around
us, the trees still green with the foliage of spring, and musical
with the notes of birds, and the kine stand in the ford, splash-
ing in the stream which quietly ripples by them; then, when
the cuckoo revels in the grove, and the rail crakes in the meadow, while the perfume of the thorn still lingers about the
hedge-rows, and the dragon-fly is flitting to and fro among the
flaggers by the water's edge, let us wend our way along its
peaceful margins. Such has been the character of the scene,
and such the impressions made upon us, when the notes from
which this little work has been compiled were written down;
and as such we would present it to our readers, and describe
it from our summer recollections, when piles of the richest
foliage were shadowed in the deep pools of the placid waters,
when the lark carolled high above us, and the long calm twi-
light of midsummer, with all its poetic associations, induced
us to linger amidst these lovely scenes of beauty, fairy legend,
and historic interest.

As the season has advanced the scene is changed over all the
land; the corn has been gathered in, and now stands in well-
built stacks round the snug homestead; the stream has filled up
its brinks, and spread partly into the adjoining meadows, while
its surface is ruffled by the fitful gusts of the October blast,
or thrown into bubbles by the heavy patter of the passing
shower of this autumnal April. The various shades of green
which decked the forest and plantation have given place to the
glowing orange, or the more sombre russet tints of umber and
sienna; the haws have crimsoned the hedges, and the leaves
are falling fast, and rustling into nooks and crannies for shelter;

occasional gleams of bright sunshine give, at times, a glow of warmth to the landscape, but they nevertheless forebode the shower, or herald in the rainbow. A few of the early trees have already become stripped of their foliage, and form graceful studies for the student of nature, who, if he would excel in painting trees with their foliage on, should study the anatomy of the leafless branches with as much care as the figure-painter devotes to the dry bones of the skeleton. The lapwing wheels and *peeweets* over the dreary moor, and clouds of field-fares and starlings appear in the distance, as if gathering for the winter's campaign.

But whether it be early spring, with all its morning freshness and elasticity, or sultry summer, or yellow autumn, there is still the same sylvan beauty, the ever-changing tints which the green foliage, the graceful undulation of surface, the glancing river, and the picturesque ruin, impart to the landscape of the British Isles, nowhere else to be met with, whereon the eye never wearies, the mind never palls, and of which the memory never loses sight.

As this is the great river of Meath, a few observations on that ancient province may not be out of place. Under the denomination Meath, Meth, Mide, Media, or Meidhe, and in part that of Magh-Breagh, was formerly included a far wider and more extensive territory than that comprised in the present county of this name. The district included under this title is one of the most level and fertile in the kingdom, and originally stretched from the interior of the island to the sea; hence Camden and other English writers derive its name of Media. Ptolemy places the Laberus, or ancient central castle and city of this kingdom, in the territory of Meath; but antiquaries are as yet undecided whether the present Kells, Tara, or Killaire Castle, occupies the site of that memorable spot; though Tara seems obviously the place intended by the great geographer, whose transcribers and commentatators in all probability mistook the word Taverus for Laberus.

There is an ancient tradition handed down through our manuscripts, that the Firbolgs, or Belgæ, as they have been termed, first settled in this locality; and it is not at all improbable that a rude and primitive people, living by hunting and fishing, such as we may suppose the early inhabitants of this country were, would, upon their arrival on the north-eastern

shores of Ireland, seek the interior through the noble stream
that traversed this great plain, where the woods and forest
glades afforded plenty of game, the waters abundance of fish,
and, in process of time, as civilization advanced, its fertile limestone soil returned a plenteous crop, and its luxuriant pastures
produced numerous herds of cattle. The old writer, Bartho-
lemeius Anglicus, as quoted by Camden, described it as " A
soil which yields plenty of wheat and pastures, well stocked
with herds, abounding with fish, flesh, and other provisions,
butter, cheese, and milk, and well watered by rivers; the situation of it is delightful, and the air healthy. The woods and
marshes in its extremities defend its approaches, and from the
number of people, the strength of its castles and towns, and
the peace which it enjoys in consequence thereof, it is commonly called *The Chamber of Ireland.*"

The first fortified houses and stone buildings that we read
of were in Meath.* The earliest chronological era to which the
most veracious of the modern Irish historians refer, is about
the middle or towards the end of the second century, when
Tuathal Teachtmar, one of the Scotic or Milesian Pagan monarchs, reigned at Tara. He erected Meath into a fifth province, as mensal lands or appanage for the monarchy, by taking
in portions from each of the other four; hence the Irish historians derived its name of Meidhe—a neck—on account of its
being formed by necks taken from the surrounding districts or
provinces. The fact of the Gospel having been first preached
and received in Meath is a proof of its civilization, in comparison with the other parts of the island at that period; and the
immediate reception and rapid extension of the Christian doctrine among the kings and nobles assembled on the banks of
the Boyne on St. Patrick's arrival, speaks loudly for the state
of education in Ireland at that time.† If the Gospel came to

---

* By this we do not mean *castles*. One of the earliest castles erected in
Ireland of which there exist any remains is believed to be Caislean na Kirka,
or the Hen's Castle, upon a rock in the upper lake of Lough Corrib, one of the
wildest and most picturesque spots in Ireland. Some portions of the ruins of
this building still remain. We have slept there when a boy. See an account
of this castle by Dr. Petrie, in the Irish Penny Journal, for July 25, 1840.

† Patrick certainly first preached in Meath, and probably the earliest great
conversion to Christianity took place there; but it should be here remarked, that
it has been the boast of the Munstermen (at least for the last thousand years)

Ireland in the fifth century, and was received, as it is stated
to have been, and as we have every reason to believe it was,
then, indeed, the tone of the bards and annalists who describe
the high state of the arts, and who place such noble sentiments
in the mouths of our kings and chieftains at that time, is not
as vaunting as some critics have supposed.

The province or kingdom of Meath, as established by Tuathal,
extended from Dublin to the Shannon, and from the centre of
Ireland to the sea, and included both east and west Meath,
with portions of Dublin, King's County, Longford, and Cavan.
A part of it was then styled Magh Breagh, "the magnificent
plain," or the Campus Brigantium of Dr. O'Conor and other
authors. The Owen Ree (King's River), now called the Rye-
water, was the boundary of this region on the one side, and
the Casan, in Louth, on the other. It is thus described in an
old Irish rann:

> " From *Lough-bo-deirg* to Birr,
> From the Shannon east to the sea,
> To Cumar Chluana-Iraird,
> And to Cumar Cluana aird."

The ancient manuscripts are very rich in the topographical
descriptions of this district. It was the seat of Irish monarchy
for some centuries after its erection into a province, and one of
our oldest coins is that of Aedh, King of Meath. There were
four royal palaces of great note and celebrity in this province
in ancient times, at Tara on the Boyne, Tailten on the Blackwater, Tlachtga on the Hill of Ward near Athboy, and Uisneach
in Westmeath.

Sylvester Giraldus Cambrensis thus describes this portion
of the Pentarchy: "There arrived in Ireland five brethren that
were valiant and martial gentlemen; to wit, Gandius, Genan-
dius, Sagandus, otherwise named Gangandus, Rutheragos, or
Rutheranus, and Slanius, These five, perceiving that the
country was not sufficiently peopled, were agreed, as it were,
to cast lots, and to share the whole realm between themselves.

that they were the first Irish believers in Christ, and that the Cross was originally raised in Ireland (where it still stands) on the strand of Tra-Kieran, on
the island of Cape Clear. This Munster tradition has been preserved in the
Books of Lecan and Ballymote, and given to the world by Ussher, Harris,
Dr. Smith, and a host of other writers.

The four elder brethren severing the country into four parts, and being loth to use their youngest brother like an outcast or step-son, condescended that each of them should, of their own portion, allot to Slanius a parcel of their inheritance, which being as heartily received of Slanius as it was bountifully granted by them, he settled himself therein, and of that portion it took the appellation of Media, Meeth. The four parts meet at a certain stone at Meeth, near the castell of Killaire, as an indifferent meare to sever the four regions."* And in another place the same authority describes this stone as "Umbilicus Hiberniæ, quasi in Medio in Meditullio terri positus." This large rock is still to be seen on the hill of Uisneach, near Killare, county of Westmeath, and is now called Cat-Uisnigh by the natives. And in the additions which Hooker has made to the first portion of the work of the English chaplain, we read: " Meth, in Latine Media, is one of the five portions of Ireland, according to the first division. It is the least portion, being but of eighteene cantreds, but yet the best and most fertile, and lieth for the most part all within the English Pale: and ever since the conquest of king Henrie the Second, hath beene subject and obedient to the English laws and governement : and bicause it lieth as it were in the navill and bowels of the land, it taketh the name accordinglie, being called *Media*, which is the middle;" and he adds: " There was no prince sole governour of this, as was of the other portions; bicause it was alwaies allowed and allotted to the monarch, whom they called *Maximum Regem*, or *Regem Hiberniæ*, as a surplus towards his diet." This latter, however, like many other statements of the same authorities, is to be received with caution.

Slanius, it is said, soon enlarged his dominions, so that he obtained the monarchy of Ireland. "This Slanius is entombed at a hill in Meeth, which of him is named Slane."

In subsequent times, and up to the date of the English invasion, the five provinces were thus possessed: the O'Melaghlins ruled in Meath; the O'Conors in Connaught; the Mac Murroughs (afterwards called Cavanaghs) in Leinster; and the O'Briens in Thomond or Munster.

To this day Meath is the great grazing ground of Ireland; in it are to be found the most extensive sheep-walks and pas-

---

* See Giraldus's *Topographia Hibernica*, translated by Stanihurst.

ture lands; the finest horned cattle, with the exception of those of Roscommon, are bred in Meath ; and its vicinity to the metropolis and the sea has always afforded it a ready home consumption, and an easy mode of transit to the English markets. Its crops are generally so luxuriant, and its land so fertile, that it has been asserted that if it were all grown in corn it would feed and might form the granary for the whole of Ireland. Its natural capabilities, and particularly its flat level surface, must have rendered it easy to retain when once possessed by an invading army, and easy to colonize by an industrious people. The fertility and riches of Meath more than once excited the cupidity of the roving Northmen ; and several incursions of the Danes are enumerated in the Annals, but particularly that of Turgesius, in the ninth century. Naturalists have been at some pains to discover from whence or through what breeds the present improved English race of short-horned and other highly esteemed varieties of domestic oxen have been obtained, and indeed the question is not yet decided; this fact, however, is certain, that in the bogs and marshes of Meath, at Dunshaughlin, not far from the river Boyne, numerous remains of the ancient animals, both wild and domestic, which formerly existed in this country, have been discovered, and particularly those of oxen, which for beauty of head and horn might vie with the finest modern improved breeds of England, notwithstanding all the pains and expense that have been gone to in bringing them to their present state of perfection; and yet there can be little doubt of those bones, to which we have referred, having lain beneath the surface for many centuries.*

The early population of Meath must have been very great; but, owing to the "clearance system" which has long existed in this county, and produced those extensive pasture lands to which we have alluded, it is now much less, in proportion to its cultivateable land, than that of any county in Ireland, and, therefore, in several parts of it, the amount of labour is unequal to the demand. The peasantry are handsome, well made, stout, and healthy, but more serious and taciturn than those in

---

* See an account of these remains by the Author of this book, in the Proceedings of the Royal Irish Academy, vol. i. p. 420; and in Mr. and Mrs. Hall's Ireland, where the heads of these cattle are figured, vol. ii. p. 393.

the mountain districts of our island; and, as might be expected, the admixture of races is here so great, that the ethnologist is puzzled to make out Celts from Saxons, or distinguish Milesians from those retaining any vestige of the primitive tribes, as may be done in other parts of the island. The colour of their frieze is a light grey, contradistinguished from the blue of the west, and the dark brown of the south; the costume of the females has of late become less national than in other parts of the kingdom; and as civilization extends, the English broadcloth is worn by great numbers. Some twenty or thirty years ago, before the large flax-mills and factories were established on the Boyne, the female attire was more picturesque and less diversified. In the flourishing days of the linen trade, when the fields waved with the beautiful bells of the flax, and pipers played at the camps and princkums* in all the villages, most of the females, young and old, were then employed in spinning, and dressed in black felt hats, like the Welsh of the present day, green linsey-woolsey gowns, and red flannel petticoats. When their occupation ceased, on the establishment of the flax-mills, and the decline of the linen trade, this dress was abandoned, perhaps from the means of procuring it being withdrawn, but also owing in a great measure to the breaking up of the clanship which then existed amongst the spinners, who used to meet in numbers at the farmers' houses, and work, and dance, and sing, almost without intermission, for several days together.

Native music and poetry are not found to flourish on great plains, such as Meath, as luxuriantly as they do in the hills and dells of more elevated regions; yet the lasses of the Boyne are by no means as sombre and phlegmatic as the men; and songs, tales, fairy legends, country dances, and planxties, with wandering bards, and shanaghies and their tales of pishogues, thivishes, and superstitions, together with blind pipers and lame fiddlers, are not wanting to enliven the dull, tedious evenings of winter, from Kells to Maiden Tower.†

* A word applied, in some parts of the west of Ireland, to a merry-making.

† The Meathmen, who were very Irish in the last century, used to boast that they spoke better Irish, and had more poets, minstrels, and men of genius among them, and that they were more lively and energetic than the boors of Leinster, whom they always defeated at hurling, boxing, wrestling, and other athletic exercises. Up to about fifteen years ago, the men of Meath used to

Passing over the occupation of Meath by a line of heroes that certainly were not, when the foregoing topographical descriptions were given, a "royal ragged race of Tara," and the early monarchs and chieftains, from Con of the Hundred Battles, the venerable Cormac Mac Art, Niall of the Nine Hostages,* and Finn Mac Cumhaill, the Fingal of Mac Pherson's Ossian, whose history, as exhibiting the state of civilization in Ireland, as well as the habits, manners, and customs of the people in their times, is well worth the attentive study of our readers; we arrive at the days of the O'Melaghlins, who were kings in Meath at the time of the English invasion, when a daughter of that royal line, Dearvorgail, the faithless bride of Brefney, and the Helen of the Irish Iliad, was seduced by the ill-fated Dermot Mac Murrough, King of Leinster:

——— " Oh, degenerate daughter
Of Erin, how fallen is thy fame ;
And through ages of bondage and slaughter
Thy country shall weep for thy shame."

The English monarch deposed the rightful O'Melaghlin, and made a grant of the fair province of Meath to Hugh de Lacy, one of the fiercest of the soldiers of Strongbow, with, according to some authorities, the title of Lord Palatine. The Boyne's bank became, in after years, the boundary of "The English Pale ;" and numerous castles and strongholds rose along it, occupied by the Anglo-Norman families already enumerated. In the reign of Henry VIII. Meath was divided into east and west.

Notwithstanding our promise not to enter too minutely into the subject of Irish history, or break the text by constant references to authorities, we cannot prevent ourselves, though

---

exhibit their powers in wrestling matches with the men of Kildare and Dublin in the Phœnix Park. We often witnessed these encounters, which resembled the *Dornghal*, or boxing-battle, of Bri-Eile, described in the Annals of the Four Masters, A. D. 468.

The last great patron of Irish wrestling was the witty and eccentric Brennan, the writer of the Milesian Magazine, generally known among the lower orders as the " wraslin-doctor," while among his professional brethren he was commonly denominated " Turpentine Brennan," who used to preside over and sometimes partake in the wrestling matches which took place on a Sunday morning at the Broadstone harbour.

* From Niall sprung the two great clans of the northern and southern Hy Nialls, who figure so conspicuously in our Irish history.

at the risk of detracting from the interest of the romance, relating a few truths—at least, a few well-authenticated historic facts—connected with some of the *dramatis personæ* of the English invasion.   The day has gone by when the fable and fact of history could be presented to the reader indiscriminately; and Irishmen, in particular, so often accused of expressing themselves in superlatives, jumping at conclusions, and drawing so largely upon their imaginations, should endeavour, while they popularize their history, to present nothing, even in a guide-book, but what is strictly founded on good authority. The elopement of Dearvorgail (or Dearvorgailla, which means in Irish "the true pledge") with Dermot Mac Murrough is generally believed to have been the sole cause of the English invasion; but this is questionable; at least the subject requires to be further investigated, although there can be little doubt but it rendered the king of Leinster more obnoxious to O'Rourke and his connexions, the O'Conors of Connaught, than he had previously been, and probably hastened the catastrophe. O'Rourke was blind of one eye, and, at the time of the elopement, must have been as old as Dermot at least, and, consequently, several years senior to his wife, who, we know to a certainty, was born in the year 1108, and was therefore in her forty-fourth year in 1152, the date of her and our misfortune. At this time Dermot was in his sixty-second year! and appears from all accounts to have been of a most unamiable disposition and ungainly person.   Giraldus Cambrensis, who must have seen him frequently, thus describes him (we quote from Hooker's translation): " This man, from his verie youth, and first entrie into his kingdome, was a great oppressor of his gentlemen, and a cruell tyrant over his nobles, which had bred him great hatred and malice. Dermot Mac Morough was a tall man of stature, and of a large and great bodie, a valliant and a bold warrior in his nation ; and, by reason of his continuall hallowing and crieing, his voice was hoarse.   [*Ex crebro continuoque belli clamore voce raucenosa, &c.*]   He rather chose to be feared than loved.   He would be against all men, and all men against him."   After the battle of Ossory, it is recorded that when the heads of the slain were brought before him by the soldiers of Robert Fitzstephen, " among them there was the head of one whom especiallie and above all the rest he mortallic hated.   And he taking up that by the heare and eares with his teeth most horriblie and cruellie bit awaie his nose and lips."* Speaking of O'Rourke, the same author writes, that when he heard of his wife's flight, he "was forthwith marvellouslie troubled, and in great cholor, but more grieved for shame of the fact than for sorrow or hurt, and therefore was fullie determined to be avenged."

O'Rourke was on a pilgrimage at Croagh-Patrick at the time, and not at Lough-Dearg, as has generally been stated; and the Irish historians inform us that the Princess of Brefney left her husband's roof, and fled with the King of Leinster, taking with her her ornaments and her cattle, with the knowledge and even at the instigation of her own brother, O'Melaghlin, son of the King of Meath. The Annals of the Four Masters inform us that "Dearvorgilla (i. e. the wife of Tiernan O'Rourke), daughter of Murrough O'Melaghlin, died in the monastery of Drogheda [Mellefont], in the eighty-fifth year of her age." A. D. 1193.† It should be remembered also that Mac Morough was not expelled from his kingdom for several years after.

Civil wars, family feuds, and the rivalry and jealousy of clans and chieftains, seem, therefore, to have had as marked an influence on the destiny of our unhappy country at that time, as the jealousy of husbands and lovers.

Some observations upon a subject to which frequent reference will be made in the course of this work, may here be found useful. The boundary of the English Pale or territory towards the north and west was chiefly, in later times, formed by the river Boyne, which will account for the number of border castles built upon its banks; but it is difficult to define this line with any degree of accuracy, for it constantly varied, being from time to time narrowed or increased as each party prevailed, so that it has been said that at one period long after the so-called conquest, the King's writ would not run for twenty square miles. In Stanihurst's additions to Giraldus Cambrensis we read, that, "when Ireland was subdued by the English, diverse of the conquerors planted themselves near to Dublin and the confines thereto adjoining; and so, as it were, inclosing and impaling themselves within certeine lists and territories, they

* This description forcibly reminds us of a similar scene in Dante's *Inferno*, where Ugolino is found gnawing the skull of his enemy Ruggieri.

† See Dr. O'Conor's *Prolegomena ad Annales*, Part ii. p. 146.

teased awaie the Irish, insomuch as that countrie became mere
English, and therefore it was termed the English Pale; which,
in ancient time, stretched from Dundalke to Catherlagh or Kil-
kennie. But now [in 1584], what for the slacknesse of march-
uors and encroching of the Irish enemie, the scope of the English
Pale is greately impaired and is cramperned and coucht into
an od corner of the countrie named Fingall, with a parcel of
the king his land Meeth, the counties of Kildare and Louth,
which parts are applied cheeflie with good husbandrie, and
taken for the richest and civelest soiles in Ireland." The extent of English territory north-west of Dublin, particularly in
Meath, may be learned from the several grants made at different times to Anglo-Saxon nobles and ecclesiastics; as, for instance, the grant of Meath to Hugh De Lacy by Henry II. ;
De Lacy's grant to Gilbert De Nugent; and Walter De Lacy's
grant to the Bishop of Meath in the reign of Henry III., all
of which have been published by Dean Butler,* and the two
latter of which are in the collection of our friend Sir William
Betham.

From the Statute of Kilkenny, lately published by Mr. Hardiman, in the Irish Archæological Society's publications, we
learn in a note by that learned author, that "in the reign of
Henry VII. the influence of the English extended little farther
than four counties; and so straitened were they that it was
found necessary to protect them from the incursions of the Irish
by a ditch raised along the borders of the Pale. For this purpose
an Act was passed in the celebrated Parliament held at Drogheda
in A. D. 1494. As this curious Act has been passed over in si-
lence by Cox, and has never been printed, I take the following
extract from the original roll, preserved in the Rolls Office,
Dublin: ' As the marches of four shires lie open and not fen-
sible in fastness of ditches and castles, by which Irishmen do
great hurt in preying the same: it is enacted that every inhabitant, earth-tiller, and occupier in said marches, i. e. in the
county of Dublin, from the water of Anliffy to the mountain
in Kildare, from the water of Anliffy to Trim, and so forth to
Meath and Uriel, as said marches are made and limitted by an
Act of Parliament, held by William Bishop of Meath, do build

* See some notices of the castle of Trim, collected from various authorities;
1840.

and make a double ditch of six feet high above ground, at one side, or part which mireth [meareth?] next unto Irishmen, betwixt this and next lammas, the said ditches to be kept up and repaired as long as they shall occupy said land, under pain of forty shillings; the lord of said lands to allow the old rent of said lands to the builder for one year, under said penalty. The Archbishop of Dublin and the sheriff of the county of Dublin, the Bishop of Kildare and the sheriff of the county of Kildare, the Bishop of Meath, and the sheriff of the county of Meath, the Primate of Armagh and the sheriff of the county of Uriel [Louth], be commissioners within their respective shires, with full power to call the inhabitants of said four shires to make ditches in the waste or *Fasagh* lands without the said marches.' This was a low state for *conquerors* to be reduced to after more than three centuries possession. The question of *conquest* is now of little consequence, but the integrity of history is at all times important, and it is therefore to be hoped that this subject, which can only be cursorily glanced at here, may attract the attention of some of our learned associates, who are versed in the history and antiquities of their native land."*

The Boyne rises in the barony, and near the little village of Carbery, in the county of Kildare, about seven miles south-east of Enfield,† and four from Edenderry, at Trinity Well, in the demesne of Newbury, 289 feet above the level of the sea; one of those holy wells so numerous in Ireland, and to which so much interest, historical as well as superstitious, is attached. Running westward for a few miles, it reaches the King's County, and then becomes the boundary for a short distance between that part of Leinster and its parent county, draining in its course the surplus waters of the adjacent great Bog of Allen. Leaving King's County upon its north-western bank, it touches Meath near Castle-Jordan, and forms the boundary between that county and Kildare, till it reaches Ashford, below the bridge of Clonard. In this portion of its course it receives the Yellow River and Milltown stream, and, where

---

* See also the Rev. M. Kelly's Notes to Cambrensis Eversus, in the Celtic Society's recently published edition of that work.

† Formerly and correctly called Innfield, the field of the Royal Oak Inn. It is the nearest railway station, on the Midland Great Western or Mullingar line, to the Boyne's source. See Itinerary at the commencement of this work.

it enters Meath, the rivulet bearing the local name of the Blackwater, from Kildare, and the Kinnegad and Deel rivers, from Westmeath. Below Ashford it is crossed, at the Boyne aqueduct, by the Royal Canal and the Midland Great Western Railway, and from this point to a few miles above Drogheda it traverses the fertile plains of Meath, which county it divides into nearly equal parts. Passing onward in the same easy course, it reaches the celebrated town of Trim, and then Navan, where it receives the Blackwater from Cavan, which is there nearly as large as the Boyne itself, and, flowing onward by Slane to the borders of the south of Louth, near Oldbridge, the Mattock River empties itself into it a short distance above Drogheda. It enters the Irish Channel below that town by a broad, shallow estuary, having the county of Louth on its left or northern bank, and that of Meath on the right or southern. Following its various windings, from its source to the sea, opposite to the Maiden Tower below Drogheda, it measures about seventy miles on the Ordnance Map, and its general direction is from south-west to north-east. While the river pursues its sluggish and circuitous course through the county in which it rises, and also where it borders a small angle of the King's County, it is but an insignificant stream, interesting alone from the remains which still exist upon its banks. Not far from Edenderry it is crossed by Boyne bridge, bearing the road from that town to Clonard. Some gentlemen's seats also diversify the landscape, but, generally speaking, the stream is, in Kildare, very insignificant, and the country through which it passes low and marshy, yet, both in this county, as well as in the upper portion of Meath, the Boyne is remarkably tortuous in its course, and constantly broken with islands, a peculiarity not uncommon to rivers running through so flat and monotonous a country as this. It is to the last stages alone that the description, which we have already attempted, of its scenic beauty, applies. Looking at the course of the river on the map, it will be seen that it forms a segment of a circle, and, taken with the Blackwater, it makes the shape of the letter Y.

Three great natural divisions present themselves to the topographer of the Boyne: first, from its source to Clonard; secondly, Clonard to Navan; and, thirdly, from thence to the sea; each presenting characters peculiar to itself.

Let us now follow its various windings in detail, and, besides its natural beauty, observe what objects of interest, either for their antiquarian or historic importance, present themselves in our track. In so doing, we shall avail ourselves largely of every possible source of information: books of all sorts, ancient and modern, old records and recent investigations, popular works and old black letter tomes, Irish manuscripts, oral traditions, and scientific researches, dry historical details, and critical dis-- sertations, the Archæological and Celtic Societies' publications, the Ordnance Maps, the public records, ancient ecclesiastical documents, the old Chancery rolls, State Papers, the inquisitions and deeds of forfeiture, the reports of commissioners, parochial and county surveys, the ploughman's song, the Penny Journals, the calliagh's legend, the stories and superstitions of modern shanaghies, ancient ballads, and bardic tales,—each and all shall be here, as they have ever been on such occasions, pressed into the service, and used when opportunity offers.

It cannot be expected, however, that in a popular book of this description, which is chiefly written for tourists, our sources of information should be constantly referred to, after the manner of a strictly archæological work; no more than the materials of which other popular publications have been composed, were stated by their authors to have been derived from sources accessible to all, but only known to a few, learned in Irish history and antiquities. Having prepared ourselves for the subject, we have endeavoured to present our readers with a faithful description of this river, by traversing its banks, or floating down its placid waters, and repeatedly visiting all those scenes of sylvan beauty or rural comfort, all those Pagan relics, feudal remains, and monastic monuments, along its margins, which we have attempted to describe.

The origin and derivation of the word Boyne is involved in the same obscurity as that which surrounds the true meaning of most ancient terms, either in our own or in the early classical literature, and, like them, has occupied the attention and elicited the speculations of the learned, and the unlearned also. By Ptolemy, on whose map of Ireland we find this river figured, it is called Bovinda, or Buvinda; Cambrensis writes it Boandus; and Ware thus speaks of it: " The old name of this river is not quite lost, for it is at present called the Boin; and, by Necham, the Boand in Meath. It takes its name, as some think, from the word Boan, which, both in British and Irish,

signifies *swift*." In Grace's *Annales Hiberniæ* it is written,
" Boundi Fluvii."

" Our countryman, Necham," says Camden, " sings thus of
it:—

> " ' Ecce Boan qui Trim celer influit, istius undas,
> Subdere se salsis Drogheda cernit aquis.' "

Which he thus translates:—

> " Swift flows the Boyne to Trim, then makes his way
> To join at Drogheda the briny spray."

The Necham here quoted was Abbot of Cirencester, and died
in 1217.

As might be expected from the foregoing portion of this
sketch, the Irish manuscripts, annals, and poems, are exceedingly rich in references to, and descriptions of, the Boyne; indeed more so than to any other Irish river, of which we might
give numerous instances, but shall reserve them till we come
to speak of the river in detail. The Boyne, Boinn, or Boan,
has several names in our ancient literature, many of which,
however, may be referred to the following legend—one which
Ovid would have enlarged into a charming metamorphosis—
which is preserved both in prose and verse in two of the oldest
MSS. in the Library of the Royal Irish Academy, the Books of
Lecan and Ballymote; and is copied and repeated in several
of the Irish romances. Many of our Irish rivers have their
source in holy wells, and there are few, if any of them, without their legends.

The well of the Blessed Trinity, at which the Boyne rises, is
at the foot of the hill of Carbury, anciently called Sidh Nechtain, the fairy hill of Nechtain. There was a celebrated poet and
king of Leinster, called Nechtain, or Nuada-Neacht, in the first
century, who had a secret well in his garden, one of the miraculous virtues of which was, that any one who approached it,
except the monarch and his three cup-bearers, Flesg, Lesg,
and Luam, was instantly deprived of sight, their eyes bursting, as the manuscripts describe it. Female curiosity, however, was not to be disappointed, and Boan, the queen, was
determined to test the mystical powers of its waters; she,
therefore, arrogantly, not only approached the well, and defied
its powers to mar her beauty, but passed three times round it

to the left, as was customary in several of the ancient incantations.* Upon the completion of the third round the charm was broken, the spring rose, and three enormous waves burst over the hapless lady, mutilating her sadly, and, says the original, "breaking one of her eyes;" she then fled toward the sea, to hide her deformity, but the waters, now loosened from their source, still followed, til! she reached the Inbher, or present mouth of the river. This Boan was the mother of Aengus Mac An Daghda, a celebrated Tuatha De Danaan chieftain, of whom we shall have to speak hereafter, and who is thus referred to in an old Irish poem, enumerating the fairy palaces of Ireland:

> " I visited that glorious dome that stands
> By the dark rolling waters of the Boyne,
> Where Aengus Oge magnificently dwells."

Dabella, the lapdog of Boan, shared, it is said, the fate of its mistress, and was swept out on the rushing waves of the Boyne to the sea, where it was transformed into the rocks since called Da Billian, which rise above the water at the Boyne's mouth. Notwithstanding the watery grave thus assigned by the poet Kenneth O'Hartigan, in the Book of Ballymote, to the wife of Nectain, her monument is recorded by the ancient poets and topographers among those of the great royal cemetery of Brugh na Boinné. Thus in the *Senchas na Relec*, or History of the Irish Cemeteries, we find enumerated: " The grave of Boinne, the wife of Nechtain; it was she took with her the small hound called Dabilla, from which Cnoc Dabilla is called." So many versions of this story have come down to us, that, without attaching any credence to the legend, we are forced to receive the fact of the name of the river having been derived from an Irish princess named Bóinn, Boan, or Boann. Similar legends are related of the origin of Lough Neagh, and several other lakes and rivers.

The well is famed for its medicinal virtues, and there is a *Pattern*, or *Patron*, still held there on Trinity Sunday.

It is said that Bo was the original name of the river, and that where it meets the river Finnabhainn, of Sliabh-Guaire,—

---

* For a particular account of this " unhallowed round" see Toland's Druids, p. 143; and Martin's Description of the Western Islands of Scotland, p. 20.

in all probability the Blackwater,—near Navan, is the place properly called Boan. Righ is also one of the ancient names of the Boyne, and means the wrist or fore-arm. It is thus explained. Boan, the wife of Nectain, wore her wrist adorned with bracelets and other ornaments, with which she rewarded poets or rhymers ; and in one of the ancient manuscripts of the Brehon laws, still preserved in the library of our University, we find the following notice of this princess: "The righ of the wife of Nuada was covered with rings of gold, for bestowing them on poets:" and this explains how the word Righ came to be applied to the river Boyne, in some of our old poems and metrical romances. This river, probably after Boan was drowned in it, took the name of her *Righ*, or fore-arm, because of the inspiration which its beauties imparted to the poets of after ages.*

Livy says the Tiber was first called the Albuda, and continued to be so till Tiberius was drowned therein. The river Eithne, now the Inny, in Westmeath, is accused of having drowned Eithne, the daughter of King Eochy Feileach, and wife of Conor Mac Nessa, King of Ulster. Many other instances of the names of rivers being derived from distinguished persons might be adduced.

* See also Dr. Petrie's Inquiry into the Origin and Uses of the Round Towers of Ireland, pp. 103, 113.

CHAPTER II.

FROM CARBURY TO CLONARD.

CARBURY; ITS ANCIENT HISTORY, HILL, AND CASTLE.—GENEALOGY OF THE DUKE OF WEL-
LINGTON.—THE BOYNE'S PROGRESS THROUGH THE KING'S COUNTY.—EDENDERRY.—RUINS OF
MONASTERORIS.—THE BERMINGHAMS.—ALTERATION OF ENGLISH INTO IRISH NAMES.—RETURN
TO KILDARE.—KINNAFAD CASTLE.—A BATTLE FIELD; THE MEN WHO FOUGHT THERE, AND
THEIR WEAPONS.—GRANGE.—THE HILL OF CARRICK; ITS CHURCH, WELL, AND CASTLE.—VIEW
OF THE PLAINS OF LEINSTER.—TOBERAULIN.—LADY WELL.—IRISH HOLY WELLS.—BALLY-
BOGAN; ITS CHURCH AND PRIORY.

THE Hill of Carbury, which rises to a considerable height
above the surrounding plains, forms a conspicuous object from
all sides; and the ruins of the ancient castle, which still rest
upon its north-eastern shoulder, are some of the finest of their
kind in Ireland, and form a most imposing object as we approach
from Enfield. The elevation, the total want of surrounding
wood, and the tall, graceful chimneys and gables of the modern
or Elizabethan portion of this edifice, give it an air at once
tasteful and commanding.

The accompanying sketch, taken from the south-east, affords
a very good idea of the style, magnitude, and general extent of
this once noble building, which is now a complete ruin; the
length of the line of the southern wall figured above is alone

100 feet, and the general view of the castle, upon our first approach, with its chimneys, narrow pointed gables, and large stone-sashed windows, is that of one of the best specimens of the castellated mansions of about the time of James I., which we know of in this country, combining lightness, taste, and comfort, with strength and durability. The eastern front, which measures sixty feet, still remains with several of its mullioned windows, even yet quite perfect, and upon a gentle slope leading down from its walls on this side may still be traced the vestiges of a garden, with a few of its flowers, now wild and neglected, mingling with the rank fiorin-grass with which it is surrounded. In fact everything about this ruin bears evidence of ladies fair as well as valiant knights having inhabited it. Such is the impression made by this ruin from a glance at its external face, particularly from the point of view from which the drawing figured on the other side was taken; but upon a closer inspection, and an internal examination, we perceive from the character of the masonry, the massive walls, the deep, stone-roofed donjons, the principal of which runs for eighty-five feet underneath the great keep, from south to north, the manifest antiquity of the entire of the western end, and the general arrangement of the whole, that the present ruin consists of the remains of structures very much older than the early part or middle of the sixteenth century; indeed some of them would appear to be as old as the twelfth century, and there are remains of walls of great thickness, built with rubble masonry, and grouted, extending even beyond the confines of the present ruin to the north-west. The modern additions all exist on the opposite side, and their later date is at once manifest. Four of the chimneys, three of which are in the eastern front, have sixteen sides, and are like some of the chimneys of English castles, built about the year 1530, being beautifully wrought and moulded at top. Owing to the various additions at different ages, the plan of Carbury Castle is very irregular, and its history, which will be found somewhat farther on in this chapter, will in some measure account for the various erections manifested in the ruins. A short distance from the castle we find a modern burial-ground, chiefly occupied with the remains of members of the Pomeroy family.

Toward the summit of this beautifully verdant hill of Carbury, which rises gradually from the surrounding plains, and leading southward from the castle, we meet with some ancient pagan remains of considerable extent; and still more southwards, towards the Edenderry road, we light upon the old church and graveyard of Temple Doath, or Caille, probably the site of the ancient church of St. Muadnat, Virgin, mentioned by Colgan.* This is a fairy hill, as its Irish name implies, and its Pagan remains seem to have escaped the attention of our modern antiquarians. It appears to have been the Tara of north Leinster, and is well worthy of attention.† Upon its top we find a small sepulchral mound, and to the north-west of this two remarkable military forts or raths, both very perfect, and one of considerable extent; but they are not even marked in the Ordnance Map, accurate as it is in all other respects.

We know of no locality so celebrated as the barony and hill of Carbery or Carbury, about which there has been so much discussion, and concerning which there is still so much discrepancy among Irish writers.‡ There are at least four districts of this name in Ireland, all celebrated in history, ancient and modern. Carbery, in the county of Cork, a scene in which has been commemorated in Dean Swift's poem of " Carberiæ Rupes ;" Carbery, in Longford, where we still find Sliabh Cairbre, and in which the magnificent moat of Granard stands; Carbery, in Sligo, where Drumcliff is situated ; and that now under examination in Kildare. The investigation carried on by Mr. O'Donovan and his assistants in connexion with the Ordnance Survey,§ has, however, thrown new light upon the subject, and settled the question of the topography of that

* *Acta Sanctorum*, p. 339.

† The Tara of ancient Leinster was Dun-Aillinne, near old Kilcullen, where the largest *fort* in that province is still to be seen.

‡ From the difficulty attending the investigation, the same discrepancy has crept into the topographical notes to the earlier volumes of our modern societies, the Archæological and Celtic. See notes to the *Leabhar-na-g Ceart*, or Book of Rights; and the references to Carbury in The Battle of Magh Rath, pp. 138 and 148. See also The Tribes and Customs of Hy-Fiachrach, pp. 276, 474 ; and also the Miscellany, p. 144, *n.*, all translated and annotated by Mr. O'Donovan, and published by the Irish Archæological Society.

§ But for the information acquired during that great national work, the records of which are preserved in the Ordnance Office at Mountjoy Barracks, Phœnix Park, it would have been quite impossible for the editors of the various historic and archæological works which are now being produced in Ireland, to have written those full and critical topographical notes with which these works abound.

Carbury most celebrated in ancient Irish writings, and decided
that this barony in Kildare was the *Cairbre Ui Ciardha* of our
most trustworthy historians, and that particularly alluded to
by the Irish poets, O'Dugan and O'Heerin, of whom the former
flourished in the latter part of the fourteenth, and the latter
in the beginning of the fifteenth century, and gave topographical and historical descriptions of some of our most memorable localities.* O'Dugan says that O'Kiery (now Keary) was
lord of this territory, and the only chief of the descendants of
Niall of the Nine Hostages, king of Ireland in the fifth century, located in Leinster. The translation of the passage referred to runs thus:

> " O'Kiery o'er Carbury of the Clergy,
> Of the tribes of Niall of the Nine Hostages,
> There are but themselves (i. e. O'Kierys) there to the east,
> Of the descendants of Niall in Leinster."

This locality has many interesting historical recollections
connected with it, too long, however, for insertion here.
O'Heerin, the topographical historian and poet, contemporary
with the celebrated Giolla Isa Mor Mac Firbis, thus alludes
to it:

> " Over Carbury of Leinster of the plains
> Rules O'Keary of the red-bladed swords,
> The scion of Almhain, without scarcity in the east,
> By whom battles were kindled round Croghan."

The castle of Carbury was originally built by the family of
Bermingham, the descendants of Pierce De Bermingham, one
of the early English settlers in Ireland, of whom some account
is given a little farther on, in the description of Monasteroris.
It suffered greatly at the time of the civil wars in Ireland, particularly during the fifteenth century, and was constantly the
scene of strife in those forays which took place between the
English barons within the Pale and the western Irish chieftains. In 1447 " Castle Carbury was re-edified by the lord
ffurnival" (Furnival). In 1466 Meath was the seat of war,
and in one of the skirmishes between Teige O'Conor and the
Earl of Desmond, the latter was taken prisoner and conveyed

---

* O'Dugan died in 1372, and O'Heerin in 1420. See also the Abbé
Mac Geoghegan's Account of the Rebellion of Carbre, History of Ireland,
vol. i. p. 200.

by that chieftain, his captor and kinsman, to Castle Carbury,
together with several of the English nobles and ecclesiastics.
The celebrated Red Hugh O'Donnel, when laying waste Meath
and Leinster in 1475, " demolished and burned Castle Carbury
and Ballymeyler." So late as 1546 we read that " the plains
of Cairbre and Castle Carbury were plundered and burned"
by some of the Irish insurgents, particularly the O'Kelly's,
the O'Maddens, and O'Conors. The mode in which this out-
rage was punished by the high legal functionary of the Government is highly characteristic of the time. " When," say the
Annals, " the Lord Justice, Anthony St. Ledger, heard of this,
he came into Offaly and *plundered* and *burned* the country as
far as the Togher of Cruoghan;" and again, " the Lord Justice
came a second time into Offaly, and remained fifteen days in
the country, plundering and spoiling it, burning churches and
monasteries, and destroying crops and corn." These notices,
from authentic history, afford us some idea of the state of this
country in the middle of the sixteenth century; and of the mode
taken by its governors to suppress crime, and to gain the affections of the Irish chiefs and people. The modern part of the
present castle must have been erected long since these days,
probably in 1548, and appears to have fallen gradually into
decay. After the Berminghams it passed into the possession
of the Cowleys, an English family, the great ancestors of the
Duke of Wellington.* From whatever side we approach, it

* The Hero of Waterloo boasts that he has not a drop of Irish or Milesian
blood in his veins, and so far as the old Irish stock is concerned, he certainly
has not (except perhaps a slight collateral rill through the Cusacks of Cushinstown), no more than many other noblemen and gentlemen connected with
Ireland, whom the *Times* calls Celts. For the following pedigree we are indebted to our learned friend, John O'Donovan:

" I. *Sir Henry Colley*, or Cowley, son of Walter Cowley, Esq., Surveyor-
General of Ireland (patent 5th November, 1548), was evidently the last builder,
re-edifier, or modifier of Castlecarbury. He was a captain in the army of
Queen Elizabeth, and a Privy Councillor in Ireland. He married Catherine,
daughter of Sir Thomas Cusack of Cushinstown, county of Meath, and had by
her Sir George Colley of Edenderry, who became extinct in the male line, and

" II. *Sir Henry Colley of Castlecarbury*, who was Constable of the Fort of
Philipstown, Seneschal of the King's County, and Providore of the army, in the
year 1561. He married Anne, the daughter of Adam Loftus, Archbishop of
Dublin and Lord Chancellor of Ireland, by whom he had,

" III. *Sir Henry Colley of Castlecarbury*, who married Anne, daughter and
heiress of Christopher Peyton, Esq. He died in 1637, leaving,

" IV. *Dudley Colley, Esq., of Castlecarbury*, Member of Parliament for

*

forms a noble picture, and such is its elevation that it can be seen upon a clear day from Poul-a-Phouca, in the county of Wicklow.

From the summit of this hill of Carbury, which is one of a series of gentle elevations that rise out of the extensive plains of Leinster, we gain a most commanding and extensive prospect, extending over the counties of Dublin, Kildare, Meath, Carlow, Westmeath, King's and Queen's Counties, with the hills of Allen, Carrick, Balrennet, Edenderry, and Croghan, standing up

Philipstown, in the first Parliament after the restoration of Charles II. He died in July, 1674. He married Anne, daughter of Henry Warren, Esq., county of Kildare, by whom he had many children, and among others his son and heir,

"V. *Henry Colley, Esq., of Castlecarbury,* who died in 1700; he married Mary, daughter of Sir William Ussher, of Dublin, and had Henry Colley, Esq., whose issue became extinct, and,

"VI. *Richard Colley, Esq.,* who, according to O'Connell, ' used to be picking potatoes after the crows in the county of Meath.' He succeeded in 1728 to the estates of his cousin, Garrett Wellesley, Esq., of Dangan, county of Meath, the head of an Anglo-Irish family of ancient respectability, and assumed the name and arms of Wellesley. He was elevated to the peerage of Ireland the 9th of July, 1746, by the title of Baron Mornington. He married, in 1719, Elizabeth, daughter of John Sale, Esq., Registrar of the diocese of Dublin; and, dying in 1758, left,

"VII. *Garrett,* second Baron of Mornington, who, on the 20th of October, 1760, was raised to the dignities of Viscount Wellesley of Dangan Castle, and Earl of Mornington. He died in 1781. He married, on the 6th of February, 1759, Anne, daughter of Arthur, first Viscount Dungannon, and had,

"VIII. 1. *Richard, Marquis Wellesley.*

" 2. *William, Baron Maryborough.*

" 3. *Arthur, Duke of Wellington.*

" 4. *Gerald Valerian, D. D.,* Chaplain to King William IV.

" 5. *Henry, Lord Cowley.*

" 6. *Anne,* married, first, to the Hon. Henry Fitzroy; secondly, to Charles Culling Smith."

See also Dean Butler's notes to Grace's Annals of Ireland, p. 47, where it is stated that the Wellesleys were descended from the standard-bearer of Henry II. See also the notice of Laracor. in chapter iv. of this work.

Many distinguished generals and military men of high renown and true Milesian blood have, however, figured in foreign service. Among these may be mentioned the following, taken without selection from a host of other illustrious names :

Trophine Gerard, Compte et Marquis de Lally Tolendal (Tulnadaly, near Tuam), peer of France and minister of state : so illustrious during Napoleon's time. His father and grandfather were equally distinguished in the service of the French Kings.

General Charles Count O'Donell, of the Austrian service, who was mortally wounded in the battle of Neresheim, in October, 1805.

Henry O'Donnell, Conde d'Abesbal, general in the Spanish service, who distinguished himself at the famous siege of Gerona in 1809. See Napier's His-like so many acropoles amidst the deep pasture and meadow-lands rich beyond description, and diversified by green hedge-rows and occasional plantations, which stretch along the Boyne as far as the eye can reach; with the ruins of some of the ancient castles of the Anglo-Normans bursting through the surrounding foliage. Towards the north-east, on the approach from Enfield we see the tall tower of Mylerstown castle, another stronghold of the Berminghams* already referred to; and in the parish

tory of the Peninsular War, and Annals of the Peninsular War, vol. ii. p. 272.

Marshal Mac Donald, of the Connaught sept, so renowned during Napoleon's wars.

Don Carlos O'Donnel, general in the Spanish service during the Peninsular war. See Annals of the Peninsular War, vol. iii. p. 147.

Leopold O'Donnel, Count de Lucena, General Governor of Cuba in 1848.

Maurice Count O'Donnel of Tirconnell, a general in the Austrian service. Now living.

Count Manus O'Donnell, major-general in the Austrian service, who died in 1793.

Connell Count O'Donnell, field marshal in the Austrian service, who commanded the imperial army at the battle of Torgan, after Count Daun was wounded. He died in 1771.

John Count O'Donnell, a general in the same service. He was the brother of the foregoing.

Alexander Count O'Reilly, generalissimo of His Catholic Majesty's forces, captain-general of Andalusia, and civil and military governor of Cadiz, about the year 1786.

Andrew Count O'Reilly, general of cavalry in the Austrian service, who died in 1832.

We have also, in the service of the Autocrat of Russia, two distinguished members of the house of West Breffney, ever ready to crush democracy and republicanism : Joseph Prince O'Rourke, general-in-chief in the Russian empire ; and Patrick Count O'Rourke, a colonel in the same service.

There are also in the Austrian service several of the Kavanaghs of Dermot Mac Murrough's race.

Among the descendants of the ancient Irish on the Continent may also be enumerated, fighting on the side of imperialism, Captain Daniel O'Connell O'Connor Kerry, in the Austrian service, who was commandant of Lodi in August, 1848.

See also the Military History of the Irish Nation, comprising a Memoir of the Irish Brigade in the Service of France. By the late Matthew O'Conor, Esq. Dublin, 1845.

There also some distinguished Irish officers in the Hungarian army at present, and among others Field Marshal Guyon (O'Guihin or Gahan), a native of Rathkeale, in the county of Limerick.

* The tourist should consult the map, and also the itinerary, from time to time, as he follows the various windings of the Boyne. Upon leaving Enfield,

of Ardkill, about a mile from the adjoining village of Carbery,
the foundations of another castle, of which not even the name
now remains; and the site of another fortress is pointed out
near the mill in the parish of Clonkeen, midway to Edenderry:
all showing the military importance of this district in former
times. Edenderry, and the castles of Kinnafad and Carrick,
form prominent objects as the eye sweeps round from south to
west. Although the Boyne is said to rise at Trinity Well, a
small stream which empties itself into it, and which may be
considered the true source of the river, rises in an adjoining
bog or marshy ground to the north of Carbury,—a branch of the
great bog of Allen which extends towards the east,—and creeping round the base of the hill to the neighbouring demesne of
Newberry, passes under a small bridge upon the Enfield road,
as we enter the little village of Carbery adjoining.

As it would be impossible (even did it possess sufficient interest) to follow the various windings of the infant Boyne
from its source to Clonard, where the stream enlarges sufficiently to permit of navigation for small row-boats, we must
take to the road, and avail ourselves of as many way-side
points of interest as the ordinary modes of travelling permit.

Our next resting-place is Edenderry, "the height or brow of
the oaks," about midway between which and Carbery we cross
the river by a small bridge,* forming the boundary between Kildare and King's County, which we now enter. It is a neat, well-
built, and remarkably clean town, belonging to the Marquis of
Downshire ; but possesses little worthy of inspection to the
antiquarian tourist except the castle of the Blundells, the
ancestors of its present noble possessor, which crowns its
wooded height, and the remains of a silver-mine adjoining.† As
we leave the town, on the road to Monasteroris, the next point
of attraction, we pass through a suburb of small cottages, with
well-tended gardens in front of them, characterised by a degree
of care, neatness, cleanliness, and, above all, by an appearance
of industry and thrift quite unusual in Ireland. These cot-

the nearest railroad station to the Boyne's source, after passing the little village of Johnstown, Mylerstown castle can be seen about a mile to the right of
the road to Carbery. It is worth inspection.

  * Rather by two bridges, for the stream-way of the Boyne has been lately
altered here by the Board of Works.

  † For a description of Edenderry, see Fraser's admirable "Hand Book for
Travellers in Ireland." Dublin, 1849.

tages are given by the Marquis of Downshire to industrious tradesmen and labourers at a shilling a year rent. The general appearance of comfort in this district at once bespeaks the encouraging landlord and the admirable care of the resident agent. The peasantry are a remarkably fine, stalwart race, and the females particularly handsome. A very admirable road, through a well-cultivated country, takes us nearly parallel with the Boyne to our next resting-place; a collection of ecclesiastical ruins, about two miles distant from Edenderry, our route still continuing through the King's County.

Monasteroris, the locality just referred to, consists of the remains of a small church with a double belfry, built, probably, about the fourteenth century, and surrounded by an ancient grave-yard; to the east of this, in one of the adjoining fields, we find the ruins of a castellated monastery, the walls of which are of great strength and thickness; and not far off, placed upon a mound which bears all the evidence of being artificial, and was probably an ancient tumulus, we observe the basement of a square dove-cot or pigeon-house, a usual appendage to the houses of the English ecclesiastics in Ireland. The accompanying sketch, taken from the south, affords a tolerably good idea of this interesting group of ruins.

Monasteroris, in Irish, *Mainister-Feorais*, the Monastery of Mac Forais, or Mac Pierce's Monastery, is celebrated in our mediæval history, and the references to it in the works of that period are numerous and interesting. The manner in which

this name arose is peculiar and worthy of remark.   Pierce De
Bermingham was one of the early English settlers, and received
a large grant of land in Leinster.   The surname was dropped by
the Irish-speaking people, and the Christian name, Pierce, or
Peter, translated into Gaelic, as Horish, or Feorais, a name which
the descendants of the Berminghams still bear to the present day.
The Clan-Feorais—the tribe-name of the family of Bermingham—applied the Irish appellation to their territory, which was
coextensive with the barony of Carbury, and extended along the
Boyne, both in Kildare and King's County, as far as the borders
of Meath.*   In process of time this Anglo-Norman stock became more Irish than the Irish themselves ; they joined with
the O'Conors of Offally, and other Irish chieftains, and made
fierce war upon the English settlers within the Pale at different times.   We have an account of the cause of one of these
wars, given us by Dudley Firbisse: " That warr was called
the *warr of caimin*, that is, an abuse that was given to the son
of the Chiefe of the Berminghams (Hibernice, to Mac Ffeorais,
his son), in the great court in the town of Ath-truim, by the
Thresurer of Meath, i. e. the Barnwall's sonn, so that he did
beate a caimin (i. e. a stroke of his finger) upon the nose of
Mac Fforais, or Bermingham's son, which deede he was not
worthy of, and he entering on the Earle of Ormond safe guard ;
so that he stole afterwards out of the town, and went towards
O'Conor Ffaly, and joined together ; and it is hard to know
that ever was such abuse better revenged than the said Caimin ;
and thence came the notable word (*Cogadh an Caimin*)."†
During this war the Berminghams and O'Conors " preyed and
burnt a greate part of Meath."

Sir John de Bermingham, Earl of Louth, founded an abbey
in the year 1325, for conventual Franciscans, at Totmoy, in
Offaly, the ancient name of this territory; and from the Irish
name of this chieftain it was called Monaster-Feoris.   In 1511,

---

* See the Annals of the Four Masters, A. D. 1151, 1446, &c. ; also the Annals of Ireland in the Miscellany of the Irish Archæological Society, from p. 202
to p. 234 ; also Archdall's *Monasticon;* see also O'Donovan's Dissertation on
Irish Names, in the Irish Penny Journal, 184, edited by Dr. Petrie, and published by Gunn and Cameron, Dublin.

  For the possessions of John Bermingham here, in 1625, see the published
Inquisitions, *Lagenia*, Kildare, 6 Car. I., and No. 92, Car. I.

  † *Caimin* (a stroke of the finger), i. e. a fillip on the nose.

Cahir O'Conor, Lord of Offaly, was slain near this Monastery. It was a place of considerable strength, as the remains of the building still testify, and sustained a lengthened siege by the Earl of Surrey, Lord Lieutenant of Ireland, when he marched into Offaly at the time of his expedition against the O'Moores of Leix, who, with other Irish chieftains, had invaded the borders of the Pale.* At the time of the suppression of religious houses it was granted to Nicholas Herbert.

Following the road which leads from Edenderry to Clonard, we again cross the Boyne, and re-enter Kildare, at the little bridge of Kinnafad,—*Ceann-atha-fada*, "the head of the long ford,"—where the river is still inconsiderable, but the streamway has been widened, and its banks straightened, so that it here resembles a small modern canal. On crossing the bridge we get a view of the castle of Kinnafad, another stronghold of the Berminghams, which stands in an adjoining meadow, and of which the accompanying is a faithful sketch.

It is a large, square, block of building, measuring forty-seven feet by thirty-one on the outside, the external walls being still quite perfect. It appears, from its few and narrow windows, as well as its general design, to have belonged to an earlier era than the modern part of the castle of Carbury, when strength influenced the builder more than attention to comfort.

Although the river is but inconsiderable for the first few miles of its course, still, from the difficulty of crossing it except at certain points, these were generally defended with great

* Harris's History of Dublin, p. 290 ; also Archdall's *Monasticon*, p. 403.

care and forethought. Thus at every ford and pass, or bridge, if such existed at the time, some castle was erected. This was in all probability the cause of the position of Kinnafad Castle, which stands beside a shallow in the river, which the local traditions say was often the scene of fierce conflict.

A few months ago, in deepening the bed of the river, and in some places altering its course altogether, so as to cut off the angles and render its stream-way straighter, as we already observed, near Edenderry, the workmen dug up here some human remains, as well as those of a horse, and several weapons of exceeding interest indeed. Through the kindness of a friend, we are enabled to have some of these figured in this work.*

The remains consisted of the skeleton and iron shoes of a horse, several portions of human skeletons, and two very perfect skulls. With these were found divers iron and bronze weapons, — a circumstance of considerable interest, for although it was rumoured that such

had been very frequently found together, no well-authenticated instance of it has been heretofore recorded. These weapons, which are here represented, consist of,—No. 7, a very perfect straight, short sword of iron, the most beautiful of its kind yet discovered; it is twenty-two inches and a half

* Mr. Murray of Edenderry, Lord Downshire's agent.

long; the blade, which measures upwards of seventeen inches, is very narrow in the middle and towards the handle, but, increasing suddenly towards the top, it forms a very obtuse point, an inch and a quarter broad. A sword of the same character, but not so perfect, was found in the excavations lately made in the Shannon. Some swords of the same type, but shorter, and with parallel edges, were a few years ago found at Dunshaughlin. See page 15. Ancient iron swords are much rarer than bronze ones; until very lately there was scarcely one to be found in any of our collections ; we have now four distinct forms of them:—that just described, which is the rarest; a shorter, sharp-edged sword, very like the ancient Roman; the heavy, broad-bladed sword, with a narrow and ornamented handle, supposed to be Danish; and the long, straight iron sword, which varies in size in different specimens, and of which a fragment of one found at Kinnafad is figured here, No. 8. This is evidently of later date than any of the others.

The brazen sword-blades found in Ireland may be classed under two heads: the long, narrow, straight one, tapering from the handle to the point, like the modern small sword; and that with a broad belly, swelling towards the end, resembling the ancient Grecian or Phœnician.* With the two iron swords here figured were found two very perfect spear-heads also of iron, Nos. 1 and 6, and with such small sockets that we are at a loss to know what description of wood, except perhaps yew, was used for their handles. The brazen weapons found in connexion with these consist of the blade of a dagger, No. 2, and two bronze hatchets, commonly called *celts*, Nos. 3 and 5, a sort of war-axe, which was fastened on the end of a curved stick. That figured as No. 5 is a particularly fine specimen, and ornamented on the sides. The other is remarkable from its exceeding lightness, showing the great quantity of tin of which the antique metal in this instance is composed. The cut No. 4 shows one of the horse-shoes. It is peculiar in shape, remarkably oval, and

---

* Specimens of all these antiquities will be found in the Museum of the Royal Irish Academy, which is open to every person desirous of becoming acquainted with these subjects; and the able Curator of which, Mr. Clibborn, the best public officer which any institution ever possessed, takes delight in showing the collection to strangers. Those intending to visit the Boyne, or any other locality of archæological interest in Ireland, should first visit the great national collection at the Academy.

convex on the under side, as may be learned from the position of the small cocks and the nail groove, showing that it was intended for the field, not the road. That bronze and iron weapons have not been more frequently found together is to us a matter of surprise, for they must have been long in use together, and we have reason to believe bronze weapons were used to a very late period indeed.

It is, we think, a fair inference, to suppose that all these weapons were employed by the belligerents who fell at the pass of Kinnafad: can we form a conjecture as to who they were? Upon the races of men who fell in this encounter we certainly can speculate with some degree of plausibility. In the ethnological inquiry, at chapter ix. of this work, the question of the early races of Irishmen is discussed; there it will be seen that we have strong evidence in support of the idea that two races, totally distinct in feature and form of head, formerly existed in this country, and probably fought for the mastery;—a long-headed people, with thick, narrow crania, low foreheads, projecting noses, deep, square orbits, high cheek-bones, prominent mouths, and narrow chins,—probably the first settlers or original stock, low in intellect, dark-haired, strong-bodied, hardy, and courageous. The other a round or globular-headed race, with features not so marked, but evidently possessing more intellect,

and who were probably the conquerors of the former. Examples of both races, particularly the former, may still be found among some of the modern Irish. Two such heads—well-marked specimens of their kind—were found, along with the weapons and antiquities described, at Kinnafad. They are represented in the accompanying wood-cuts. The long head is quite perfect, and has a sword-cut on the crown. The base of the skull and face has been broken off the specimen of the globular head. Is it unnatural to suppose that these people fought with the weapons by which their remains were found surrounded?

It is now more than five years since we first drew attention to this subject, and promulgated the idea as to the two races which originally inhabited this country ; and it is pleasing to find that every instance of human remains since discovered in Ireland is confirmatory of the views we then put forward.*

Upon the northern side of the river, in the King's County, there is little worthy of inspection, except the ruined castle of Clonmore, not far distant from the Yellow River, a stream which empties itself into the Boyne, about midway between Edenderry and Clonard, and forms the boundary between the King's County and Meath.

We are now upon the right bank of the Boyne, passing, by a smooth and admirably kept road, through deep meadows, bordered by luxuriant hedge-rows, particularly of white thorn, which blooms here in great beauty. About a mile from Kinnafad castle, and half a mile from the Boyne, the road passes by the castle of Grange, a fortalice of a somewhat later age than that just described, and a part of which is still inhabited by one of the Tyrrells, a family of repute in the ancient kingdom of Meath. We have not been able to discover any references to either of these two buildings in the historic annals, and it is probable their history has not been preserved in the rolls of time.

We next ascend the sloping hill of Carrick,—one of those high places in the great plains of Leinster which we already saw from the hill of Carbury. From the top of this elevation we again obtain a most commanding and extensive prospect of the well-wooded and highly-cultivated plains of Meath and King's County, forming one vast undulating sea of green;— a truly glorious land, rich and fair; gazing upon it we wonder not at the tenacity with which our fathers clung to it, nor

---

* See a Lecture on the Ethnology of the Ancient Irish, delivered at the College of Physicians in 1844, and originally published in the Dublin Literary Journal.

at the efforts made by the invaders to possess it; neither can we wonder at the peasant's love for it;—we are now only astonished how poverty, misery, and starvation even unto death, can exist in any corner of the island with such a garden as this within it.*

This hill, though not mentioned in history, that we have been able to discover, must, not only from its situation, but from the traditions in the neighbourhood,—the rock denominated the Witch's Stone, and some slight vestiges of architectural remains upon its summit (probably those of a hermit's cell),—have been a place of note in very ancient times, antecedent to the date of the ruins which at present exist upon it. It is said that a considerable town once stood at the base of its north-eastern side, where there is now a vast limestone quarry. The extensive woods of Ballindoolan stretch down from its summit towards the north, and upon the south-eastern brow of the hill adjoining, the more direct road to Edenderry, we find another group of ruins, the church and castle figured upon the opposite page.

The hill of Carrick (the Rock), which very much resembles that of Carbury, and commands a similar extent and beauty of prospect, derives its name from a large block of trap rock, called "the Witch's Stone," which stands upon its northern brow, just over the great limestone quarry. It is evidently the same kind of stone as the large mass of trap which is to be found about ten miles off, near Philipstown, to the south-west of this hill; but whether it is a boulder, and was carried to this spot—which is in the general direction of the great current which appears to have transported the beds of limestone gravel throughout Leinster—by natural means; or was transported there by art for some sacred purpose in early Pagan times, as we know was frequently the case, it is difficult to say. Upon the lower Boyne, near the hill of Dowth, we meet masses of compact basalt, fully as large, which must have been transported there by artificial means. The legend is, that a witch cast this stone from the hill of Croghan, at some of our early saints, and that it alighted here. This is a favourite and widely spread legend in the north of Europe; in Scotland we find it preserved

---

* While we write, we understand there are 1800 paupers in the Workhouse of Edenderry! There must have been something wrong in the system which produced all this misery in the neighbourhood of such a fertile country.

in the story of the Devil throwing the hill of Dumbuck, Dumbarton rock, and Ailsa Craig, after St. Patrick, when he was flying into Ireland.

Some mischievous quarryman split this witch's stone, by blasting it, a few years ago. For this wanton act he was obliged to leave that part of the country.

Near the summit of the hill there is pointed out " the Mule's Leap," when running off with a saint from the Church of Carrick. Eight holes, marking, it is said, the places of the mule's feet, and showing a distance of about ten yards between the place from which it sprung and where it alighted, are still to be seen, and it is said that no grass ever grows upon these footprints. The locality is worth observing, not for the nonsensical story of the mule, but because there is evidence of some masonry —probably the foundation of an ancient oratory—existing between the two sets of footmarks.

As this castle still bears the local name of Carrick-Oris, we have a proof stronger than conjecture that it was erected by the Berminghams. It was originally a tall, oblong square tower or keep, a portion of the southern end of which is yet perfect, measuring about thirty-two feet in length. From the extent of the ruins upon the northern side, it must have been nearly ninety feet long: the walls are upwards of four feet thick. This was the court of Pierce Bermingham in 1305, and consequently the seat of the " treacherous baron," so bitterly complained of by O'Neill and the Irish chieftains in their Remonstrance to Pope John XXII.*

In the Annals of the Four Masters, A. D. 1305, and also in James Grace's Annals of Ireland,† we learn the circumstance of the massacre which occurred here, and which earned for the inhospitable owner of the castle the opprobrious title bestowed on him by the Irish chieftains in 1315.

Murtagh O'Conor, King of Offaly, and his brother Calwagh, with twenty-nine of their companions, were slain here by Jordan Comin, and Sir Pierce Mac Feorais, the latter of whom had invited them to a feast on Trinity Sunday at his castle, "*apud Carricke in Carberia.*" In Mageoghegan's translation of the Annals of Clonmacnoise, the murder is thus alluded to: "A. D. 1305, Murtagh O'Connor of Offallie, Mulmorrey, his brother, and Calvagh O'Connor, with twenty-nine of the choicest of their family, were treacherously killed by Pyers Birmyngham, within the Castle of Carrickffeorus." In the Remonstrance just alluded to it is said: "The instant they stood up from the table he cruelly massacred them, and sold their heads at a dear price to their enemies; and when he was arraigned before the King of England, the present king's father, no justice could be obtained against such a nefarious and treacherous offender." Can we wonder at the Irish people acknowledging the power, and seeking the interference of the Pope, when they could not obtain redress nearer home?

This Pierce Bermingham was the progenitor of the Mac Feoris.‡ These references serve to fix the site of a very memorable locality hitherto unnoticed.

The adjoining Anglo-Irish church appears to be of a date coeval with that still remaining at Monasteroris,—probably the end of the thirteenth century,—one of those long, low buildings, with a belfry in the western gable, and small, narrow, pointed windows in the sides, of which we have so many examples remaining. This church is forty-six feet long and twenty-two broad in the clear. The eastern and southern walls are still standing, and two small, narrow windows, deeply

---

* See Memoirs of Charles O'Conor, of Belanagare, pp. 59, 74.

† Edited for the Irish Archæological Society, by Dean Butler. See p. 48, n. ᵉ.

‡ See, in addition to the remarks on this name, Dean Butler's History of Trim Castle, p. 31.

splayed on the inside (one square and the other circular-headed), and evidently different in date, and the cut stones of which were probably used in some earlier building, as well as a small almery, exist in the latter. The door was in the northern wall of the chancel, and a small, narrow window, now built up, a little to the left of the centre, remains in the eastern gable, which latter rises into a very perfect double belfry.

There are several traditions and some curious remnants of superstitious usages yet remaining attached to this locality. The peasantry used to show a large stone, with some indentations in it resembling the print of the hand, which they said was lifted by St. Columbkill. Not long ago, people were in the habit of carrying away from hence portions of the clay of a priest's grave, and using it as a cure for several diseases, a practice formerly in much repute, particularly in the west of Ireland.*

A few hundred yards below the ruins on the hill of Carrick, in the angle formed by the junction of the roads leading to Edenderry and Carbery, we find the holy well of Tobercro, or *Tober Crogh-neeve*, the Well of the Holy Cross, a beautiful spring shaded with flowering briars and wild white roses. Although it is now totally neglected, and its site scarcely known even by the neighbouring peasantry, it was once highly venerated, and its virtues greatly esteemed. The water runs into the Boyne through the adjacent valley. See page 53.

There are two roads leading along the river towards Clonard, on the Kildare side: the lower sweeps through the valley; the upper, that which we have chosen in our present excursion, on account of the commanding prospect which it affords, winds over the hill of Carrick, which we have just described. Proceeding northward towards the Boyne, we pass through a noble country with enclosed paddocks, fringed with well-grown timber, and exhibiting an admirable state of cul-

---

* This practice, which may to some of our readers appear as extraordinary as it is disgusting, is nevertheless frequently resorted to up to the present time. We have known persons in a respectable rank of life to boil the clay taken from the grave of Father O'Connor, in the abbey of Roscommon, upon milk, and drink it, for the cure of several diseases; and an account has been given by Dr. Pickells of Cork, of a female who, it was said, became seriously diseased from having swallowed the larvæ of beetles and other insects, in making use of a similar remedy.—See the Transactions of the College of Physicians in Ireland, vols. iv. and v. Also, "Our Fellow Lodgers," by Rev. Robert Walsh, M. D. Dublin, 1847.

tivation. Two objects claim our attention: upon the right hand side of the road, the site of an ancient castle, of which nothing now remains but a cairn of stones; and a little farther on, Tober-aulin, or "the Beautiful Well," another sacred spring shaded by graceful thorns, near which we again join the lower road, which runs parallel with the river as we approach it at the bridge of Ballybogan. Here, at a place called Glyn, where three roads meet in an open space shaded by trees,—one of those calm, peaceful, homestead spots, so frequently met with in England,—we find "Lady Well," a fountain dedicated to "the Blessed Virgin," and a very memorable spot in days gone by. It immediately adjoins the road, and is shaded by a splendid sycamore tree, to which a few votive offerings might, in former days, be seen attached. A fair and *Patron* is held here in harvest.

Holy wells abound in this locality, and assist to feed the growing stream, so that the river becomes doubly consecrated, not only by the ruins of sacred edifices which cluster upon its banks, but through the waters which flow into it from so many hallowed springs. Besides the Well of Trinity, and these two just mentioned, we have Tobercro, and also Carbury Well, and not far from the point where the Yellow River pours its waters into the Boyne we have upon the Kildare side the Well of Tobernakill;—six in all, baptizing the infant Boyne.

The peasants' faith in the *Blessed Well* has ceased; the last remnant of it, at least in the midland counties of Ireland, was obliterated by the famine.

> "Old times are changed, old manners gone."

The days of rounds and penance, of vows and votive offerings, of charm and miracle, of pilgrim and boccagh, of fun and frolic, faction fight and whiskey, which took place at the *Patron* (i. e. the patron saint's day) at our holy wells, are past and gone; and, once omitted, these rites, ceremonials, and pastimes of the people, are seldom or never restored. There is scarcely a holy well in Ireland, the waters of which, independent of the general efficiency of the *station* performed there, either as a penance or in redemption of a vow, but is celebrated for its cures of particular diseases ; and this at which we rest, with the other wells upon the Upper Boyne, were famed far and wide for their sanitive efficacy. Most of our holy wells were objects of veneration, perhaps of worship,

long prior to the spread of Christianity in Ireland, when the
Pagan altar, the sacred grove, and Druid priest, were their
general accompaniments; and, therefore, it cannot be wondered
that so many unchristian rites and ceremonies should still
attend the practices observed there by the uneducated.

———— " This may be superstition,
But even the faintest relics of a shrine,
Of any worship, wake some thoughts divine."

Each holy well generally bears the name of some saint, upon
whose festival day the *Patron* is celebrated; and each has its
legend, often of great interest both in a historical and topographical point of view. Ancient thorns, or gnarled ash trees, clad
with the propitiatory offerings of the pious, bend over their clear
waters; a certain number of oval or circular stones, used as a
sort of beads, generally surround their margins, and a quantity
of white pebbles are scattered over the bottom of each; while in
many instances a pair, or more, of sacred trout are allowed to remain unmolested in these still pools. Like other shrines of religious veneration, the virtues of our holy wells are subject to va-
riation, remaining for years inert, and then breaking out afresh,
upon the recital of a recently performed miracle by some cun-
ning boccagh, or neighbouring publican: when, in defiance of
the threatenings of the Church, the exhortation from the altar,
and frequently of the personal influence of the Roman Catholic
clergyman on the spot, scenes of superstition, riot, and debauch-
ery ensued, which would now be scarcely believed if we ventured to relate them. These wells were often not only chary of
their powers, but very fickle in their dispositions, frequently
changing their localities, from their waters having been pro-
faned by the irreligious or diseased, and springing up next
morning in a different spot ; or, like the Boyne in more miraculous times, bursting forth from their rocky prisons, and
overwhelming in their waters their sacrilegious polluters. The
pilgrim was allowed to drink at the well itself, but he was not
permitted to wash, except in the stream which flowed from it;
and most of the instances of the change of locality among our
holy wells is attributed to some diseased person having been
bathed in their waters, and for which offence the saint's dis-
pleasure has been generally manifested.

We require a book upon the holy wells of Ireland. Such

a work would be instructive, amusing, and popular. If illustrated by a good artist, capable of feeling such subjects, and
drawing them with fidelity,—a Petrie or a Burton,—it would
greatly assist the study of the antiquary, and such embellishments would afford the fireside reader a series of some of the
most charming scenes which this country possesses. Amidst the
wildest glens, among the most savage rocks, on bare mountain
tops, surrounded by savage grandeur, or located by the quiet
homestead in the cultivated plain; embosomed among aged trees
in the sequestered valley; o'ershadowed by the ruined church
or abbey wall, or guarded by the ancient sculptured cross; with
the drooping thorn, or the ragged ash, hung with the offerings
of the pilgrim, stretching its arms over the crystal fountain;—
these venerated spots may be found in abundance; and with
some " Blind Girl" or burly boccagh kneeling by their waters,
the artist will find subjects for his pencil of surpassing interest.
And the author in his description of these ancient and romantic sites of religious veneration or medical superstition,—by
inquiring into their Pagan origin, recounting the legends attached to each, so illustrative of ancient manners, and elu-
cidating popular traditions which are becoming hourly obscured; in telling something about the saint to whom each
is dedicated, and of the rites and ceremonies, the *rounds*,
prayers, and all the formulæ (generally self-imposed) which
are there gone through, by the pious pilgrim, the devout
penitent, the faithful valetudinarian, or the paid representa-
tive, together with some notices of the humours, fights, and
frolic of the *Patron*, its tents and pipers, beggars, rogues, and
gamblers,—could not fail to interest his readers.*

---

* A little work was produced some years ago, called " The Holy Wells of
Ireland," from which title the reader might suppose that some, if not all, the
subjects alluded to in the foregoing passages were treated of. Such, however,
is not the fact. It is a mere tirade against Popery, for which purpose alone it
appears to have been compiled. Its descriptions are almost entirely made up
of extracts from the works of Inglis, Cæsar Otway, Carleton, Crofton Croker,
and other modern Irish writers.

The Annals of the Four Masters, now in process of translation and annota-
tion by O'Donovan, and which, when complete, will form the great ground-
work for all future Irish histories, contain numerous descriptions and accurate
references to the origin and names of our Irish wells; and the great local and
topographical knowledge of the learned commentator renders these accounts
of immense value. Cambrensis and his commentators, Holinshed and Richard

The materials for a work of this description abound in such quantities that the only difficulty is in selection. Almost every barony possesses several holy wells. The Lives of the Saints, and the Irish Annals and early histories, are profuse in their references to our " blessed wells;" but it is only by visiting these spots upon *patron* days, by culloguing with the neighbouring shanaghies, and by appearing to give credence, in addition to tobacco, to the priestess of the well, that the legendary lore of such can be acquired, or their traditional romance preserved.

In the Irish ballad poetry of the last few years we find several charming songs upon our holy wells; in particular we would instance those by our friend, Samuel Ferguson, Esq.,

Stanihurst, may be consulted, particularly with reference to the legendary tales and mode of performing stations at Patrick's Purgatory and other holy wells and places of religious resort in their day; as also Camden, Hanmer, and other writers of that time; but it must always be borne in mind with what prejudices these writers were possessed, for what end and under what influence they wrote, as well as the exceeding ignorance of the Irish language which they exhibit. Dr. Lynch's Cambrensis Eversus, lately translated and commented on by the Rev. Matthew Kelly, and published by the Celtic Society, should be carefully consulted. All the publications of our Archæological Society abound with materials which might be made use of with effect, particularly the translation of Nennius, by the Rev. Dr. Todd and the Hon. Algernon Herbert, especially that portion of it upon the " Wonders of Ireland, according to the Book of Glendalough." Dr. O'Conor's third letter, published in his *Columbanus ad Hibernos*, contains many interesting particulars on the subject of Irish well-worship, and will show our English readers what the opinions of an educated and intelligent Irish Roman Catholic priest were on the subject. Richardson's " Great Folly, Superstition, and Idolatry of Pilgrimages in Ireland," published in 1727, should be read; and also Barnaby Ryche's very scarce " Description of Ireland, 1624," where the reader will find many curious matters connected with our vulgar superstitions generally, and the holy wells of Dublin in particular. The manuscript letters preserved in the Library of the Ordnance Survey, contain much valuable information. The Dublin and Irish Penny Journals afford notices of many blessed wells; and in the last volume will be found a most charming paper on the subject, by Petrie, under the head of " St. Senan's Well." We have to express our great obligation to Mr. Hackett of Middleton, and to Mr. Windele of Cork, for having furnished us with several interesting topographical descriptions and a quantity of legendary lore connected with this subject.

We have written this note in the hope of eliciting further information, as well as directing attention to this curious subject; and should we find leisure and inclination to continue the " Irish Popular Superstitions," two parts of which have already appeared in the Dublin University Magazine (Nos. for May and June, 1849), we will devote a chapter to our blessed wells.

and also ones by Mr. Fraser and Mr. Teeling;* but most of
the poems upon these our sacred fountains assign to them a
fairy origin, an idea not by any means popular among the
people, who are generally acquainted with the saintly legends
attached to them; by what patriarch of the Irish Church they
were blessed or cursed; what miracles they have wrought; on
what days they are to be resorted to; and what prayers are to
be repeated at them;—circumstances never connected with the
fort or rath, the cave, or hill, or glen,—the true fairy ground.

The following lines, characteristic of the Irish people's religious belief in blessed wells, have been forwarded to us by a
lady, while these pages were passing through the press:

> " Thou chosen spring of sacred gift!—
>   By prayer and penance blest!—
> Here, on thy knee-worn margin, let
>   My wand'rings find a rest.
> I would not pass thee heedlessly,
>   Or deem, with scoffing thought,
> That God hath, thro' thy hallow'd drops,
>   No healing wonders wrought.
> With solemn pause I gaze upon
>   Thy surface calm and pure,
> Recalling days when simple souls
>   In faith found simplest cure!
>
> " Who knows thou art unsanctified,
>   And hast no salving pow'r?
> Let me, at least, revere thee now,
>   In thy deserted hour.
> Perchance, when angry justice frown'd
>   On sinning sons of earth,
> The Virgin's interposing tears
>   First gave thee heav'nly birth?
> Or were thy waters angel-stirr'd,
>   For humble suff'rers' weal?
> Be blessed still!—and may I too
>   In thee my sorrows heal!"

To return to the stream of our discourse. The sedgy, sluggish river is here crossed by the first bridge of any note which
we meet with upon the Boyne, and leads to Ballybogan, " the

* See The Spirit of the Nation; the Book of Irish Ballads, by D. F.
M'Carthy; The Ballad Poetry of Ireland, by C. G. Duffy; the Poems of
Thomas Davis, &c.

town of O'Bogan," an insignificant village upon the northern
side of the river.

Upon this, the Meath side, and a little to the north-west of
the bridge, are the ruins of one of the largest churches and
monasteries, except those of Trim, Slane, Bective, or Drogheda,
which we meet with in our downward course; and if indeed
the domiciliary buildings (of which nothing but the foundations
now exist) were in proportion to the church, the former must
have been very extensive, for the latter is of great magnitude.
The accompanying engraving, taken from the south-east, shows
all that now remains of the church or priory of Ballybogan,
which is pleasingly situated in a rich meadow, surrounded by
trees, on the river's bank. The church was originally cruciform,
but the transept has been entirely destroyed on both sides. The
nave and choir measure 193 feet in the clear, and are twenty-
six feet broad. So very little architectural decoration is to be

found, either in the walls which are still standing, or among
the surrounding rubbish, that we cannot believe it was ever
highly decorated. Over the western entrance there was a tall,
narrow window, without mullions or cross-bars, the arch of
which, as well as those of the east window, exhibit the transition from the circular to the pointed style. In the northern wall
of the choir three sedilia, with trefoil arches, yet remain; and
attached to the outer wall of the chancel, upon the same side,
there is a very curious little building, apparently a vestry or
robing-room.

This priory was almost exclusively English. It is mentioned

only twice by the Four Masters ; once, in the year 1446, in recording the interment of Tany, son of Maoilin, who was interred in the monastery of *Baile-ui Bhogain;* and again, the year following, when we read of a great plague which raged in Meath, Leinster, and Munster; and by which it is related that several hundred priests died; among the rest the Prior of Ballybogan.*

Archdall has collected with great care some curious notices of this monastic edifice, which was founded in the twelfth century by Jordan Comin,† under the invocation of the Holy Trinity, for canons of the order of St. Augustine, and was originally called "The Priory de Laude Dei." By an inquisition taken in the year 1399, "it was found that John O'Mayller, a mere Irishman, and of the Irish sept of the O'Mayllers, enemies to our Lord the King, was instituted to the priory of the Blessed Virgin of Ballybogan; but Richard Cuthbert did on the same day make due proof that the said priory was not under the invocation of the Virgin Mary, but dedicated to the Holy Trinity, and that he was the lawful prior thereof. Cuthbert was accordingly restored to the temporalities."‡ From the well of Ballybogan, or Lady Well, being dedicated to the Virgin, it is not improbable that there may have been some earlier monastic buildings here under the same invocation, and that hence arose the dispute just referred to.

In 1404 King Henry IV. granted certain lands belonging to the prior of Ballybogan, in the county of Dublin, to one William Stokynbrygge. Dudley Firbisse records the burning to the ground of this priory about the middle of the fifteenth century. The last prior was Thomas Bermingham, and the following inventory of his possessions has been preserved upon the surrender of his church property to Henry VIII., in 1537.

---

* We might add here some notice of the different plagues, famines, and pestilences, from which this country has suffered during the last 1000 years, and show that the very same misery under which we have so lately laboured is but a repetition of similar calamities which existed in early years, but that we fear to extend this little work to too great a length. A history of our Irish plagues and famines would be useful in a medical, a sanitary, and an historical point of view. The materials are most abundant.

† Was this the Jordan Comin who assisted at the massacre of the Irish chieftains at Carrick, in 1305 ? If so, this priory must have been founded in the thirteenth century.

‡ *Monasticon Hibernicum,* p. 514.

Besides the cloister, kitchen, &c., there were attached to the priory "twenty-four messuages, four gardens, one orchard, one curtilage and an haggard within the precincts of the said priory; also the manor of Ballyboggan, containing one hundred and sixty messuages, one hundred and sixty gardens, a watermill, six eel-wiers, eighty acres of arable land, one hundred and forty of meadow, one thousand of pasture, forty of wood, forty of underwood, and six hundred of moor in Ballyboggan, of the annual value, besides all reprises, of 8*l.* 6*s.* 8*d.* ; sixty messuages, forty gardens, three hundred and twenty acres of arable, two hundred and forty of pasture, forty of meadow, eighty of underwood, and three hundred of moor, in Herreyeston alias Ballykill, of the annual value, besides all reprises, of 40*s.* ; one hundred messuages, sixty gardens, forty acres of arable land, ninety-six of meadow, six hundred and forty of pasture, one hundred and sixty of wood, and three hundred and sixteen of moor, in Knockangoll, Ballykesty, and Cardoneston, of the annual value, besides all reprises, of 50*s.* ; and sixty messuages, forty gardens, two hundred and forty acres of arable, three hundred of pasture, two hundred and forty of moor, and two hundred of underwood, in Kyllnedobbragh and Kyllaskelyin, of the annual value, besides all reprises, of 50*s.*"* From this recital we learn somewhat of the vast possessions held by the Church in Ireland before the Reformation. The greater portion of the lands of this monastery, together with those of Clonard, were granted by Henry VIII. to Sir William Bermingham, afterwards created Lord Carbery; and the reversion of the monastery, with certain of the estates, were bestowed on Edward Fitzgerald in the latter part of the reign of Elizabeth.

Ware's Annals inform us that in 1538 a crucifix which was held in great veneration was here publicly burned; and *Tober-Crogh-neeve*, or the Well of the Holy Cross, at the foot of the hill of Carrick, mentioned at page 45, may, perhaps, have derived its name from some connexion therewith. At the same time the reformers burned the celebrated image of the Virgin Mary at Trim, and St. Patrick's Staff (crozier) at Dublin.

The abbey and surrounding lands at present belong to Lord Lansdowne, who has most creditably placed several buttresses

* *Monasticon Hibernicum,* p. 515.

against the northern wall, which was in a falling condition some years ago. The prospect from the abbey, though tame, is particularly pleasing. Looking up the Boyne upon the Kildare side, the planting of Rahin demesne stretches along a gentle elevation which slopes gradually from the river's edge, and the country rises in successive undulations to the woods of Ballindoolin and the hill of Carrick, while toward the west we get a glimpse of the hill of Croghan, in the King's County.

Our next point of interest is Clonard, to which two roads, one on each side of the Boyne, lead from the bridge of Ballybogan. The southern will be found most interesting to the tourist, as it passes through a pleasingly-diversified country, not remarkable either for its cultivation or its amount of population,—which is here, indeed, particularly thin,—but for the number, variety, and graceful form of the swelling undulations through which we pass. To this part of the country may be applied the simile which has been elsewhere used with respect to Tipperary, that it resembles a swollen sea which had become suddenly consolidated. A circular earthen fort, of the military class, belonging to the times before stone buildings were much in use, may be seen upon the south-eastern shore of the Boyne, in the townland of Ballycowan, not far from the high road, and can be visited by those who feel particularly interested in the examination of such remains; but as we shall direct attention to other similar structures, of greater magnitude and more accessible, upon the lower portions of the river, it is here unnecessary to do more than point out its site.

CHAPTER III.

CLONARD, AND THE BOYNE TO TRIM.

CLONARD.—DESCRIPTIONS OF CÆSAR OTWAY.—THE BATTLE OF 1798.—ANCIENT SEAT OF LEARN-
ING.—HISTORY OF ST. FINIAN.—THE ABBEY, MONASTERY, AND ROUND TOWER.—DISASTERS
AND DESECRATIONS, ANCIENT AND MODERN.—ANTIQUE FONT AND LAVATORY.—RECOVERY OF
AN ECCLESIASTICAL STOUP.—THE PAGAN REMAINS AT CLONARD.—THE MOAT AND FORT ; SPE-
CULATIONS ON THEIR ORIGIN AND USES.—THE BATTLE-FIELD OF RATHCORE.—THE BATTLE OF
IOLG-BOINNE.—TICROGHAN.—DONORE CASTLE.—THE BOYNE TO TRIM.—TRIMBLESTOWN.

CLONARD, at which we have now arrived, is the first spot of
great and undoubted historic and ecclesiastical celebrity which
we meet with on the Boyne, and deserves a more lengthened
notice than any of the foregoing. The great western road here
crosses the river by Leinster bridge, a remarkably flat, well-
built structure.

Our lamented friend, Cæsar Otway,—a most graphic describer of Irish scenery, the most charming of companions,
and one of the most genuine, true-hearted Irishmen that ever
lived, and whose powers of description were such that, to use
the expression of an Edinburgh reviewer, " Give C. O. an old
stone, a green field, and a gossoon, and he will make a book out
of it,"—noticed this spot in his " Tour in Connaught" in 1832,
and, as we affect to be little more than gleaners in this work,
we hesitate not to transcribe some of his impressions of the
place at that period.

" The Boyne water flows lazily here, amidst sedge and reeds,
—appearing but the dark drain of an immense morass—the
discharge of the waste waters of the bog of Allen. A strong
position in time of war—Lord Wellington knows it well : he
has often had his soldier eye upon it, his paternal mansion Dangan being not far off to the right, near Trim. How different
was the young, fun-loving, comical, quizzing, gallanting Captain Arthur Wellesley, when residing in his shooting-lodge
between Summerhill [Trim] and Dangan, from the stern,
cautious, careworn Fabius of the Peninsular war ; the trifling,
provoking, capricious sprig of nobility, half-dreaded, half-
doated on by the women, hated by the men,—the dry joker, the
practical wit, &c.,—from the redoubtable warrior of Waterloo

—the great prime minister of England. He who achieved a greater moral victory than that of Mount St. Jean, when, neutralizing and overcoming political and religious animosities, he set at rest a question that had vexed the world for nearly three centuries.* The Boyne, then, is not here that lovely, picturesque water which it becomes when it sweeps under the wood-crowned banks of Beau-parc, winds under the limestone bluffs of Slane, washes the castle of the Marquis of Conyngham, or meets the tide

> " ' At Oldbridge town,
> Where was a glorious battle :
> When James and William staked a crown,
> And cannons they did rattle.' "

But there was a battle at Clonard also; unhappily, however, in it both sides were our own countrymen. To the right of Leinster-bridge, on the old road, are the ivy-mantled remains of a massive wall, a porch, and a portion of a turret, all that now exist of the memorable dwelling where the brave yeomen under Lieut. Tyrrell, in 1798, made so gallant a stand against a large force of insurgents, some hundred and fifty of whose bodies are buried beneath a small mound in one of the adjoining fields.† The defence of this little Hougomont was, perhaps, one of the most striking instances of determined courage on the part of the loyalists that has been recorded during the whole of that ill-starred, most unmeaning, and most ill-conceived rebellion. At the time of this engagement,—the 11th of July,—the peasantry who took part in the "rising" had become tolerably well organized and accustomed to arms, and had then unfortunately seen too much blood spilled, so that they did not, at that time, present the unguided rabble mass which they appeared some six weeks earlier, at the commencement of that disastrous campaign. After the defeat at Whiteheaps, a large portion of the insurgents, under Parry, Kearns, Holt, and the two Byrnes, fled into Kildare, and in their progress attacked the little garrison of yeomanry at Clonard, con-

---

* This description of Clonard appeared originally in the Dublin Penny Journal. See vol. i. p. 150. The sentence immediately preceding the reference to this note was omitted in the published " Tour in Connaught." Why?

† This little mound, which lies between the Ballybogan road and the river, has never been tilled since, and is now covered with gooseberry bushes.

sisting at the time of but twenty-seven persons, two of whom, sons of Mr. Tyrrell, were mere boys. The place to be defended resembled, in a remarkable manner, that portion of the field of Waterloo to which we have already likened it, consisting of a dwelling-house, then occupied as a barrack, and surrounded by a court-yard and garden, enclosed by a high wall, on one side of which there was a turret commanding the bridge and great western road; in front was the river, on the left a mill-race, and behind it some wooded rising ground. The advance of the besiegers was so rapid that the gate of the court-yard was closed with considerable difficulty. After several hours' hard fighting, during which the slaughter of the rebels was immense, and the courage, both of the besiegers and besieged, severely tested, the garden was lost; and thus the Tyrrell yeomanry became divided. The insurgents then turned their chief attention to the turret, from which they had sustained the hottest fire. The six men whom it contained, thus cut off from their fellows, drew up the ladder and ascended to its topmost story, and fought so determinedly, and fired so effectually, that it is stated twenty-seven of the assailants were killed within and about the ground floor of it during this portion of the contest. The attacking force, finding it impossible to gain access through the floor, at last lighted a quantity of straw within and around the turret, and literally smoked out its occupants. While it was enveloped in smoke and flames, two of the band attempted to rush through the crowd of assailants, but were instantly shot; yet the other four, leaping from one of the upper windows, escaped to their comrades in safety. Still the conflict raged for six hours without intermission; the valour of the handful of determined spirits within the barracks continuing unsubdued, the vengeance of the attacking party remaining unsatiated; till at five o'clock in the evening the siege was raised by the arrival of twenty-one additional men from Kinnegad, when Mr. Tyrrell and his party sallied forth, and drove the insurgents from the garden with great loss. God avert such fearful scenes from being again enacted in our land ! and—shall we not add ?—forgive the rulers who could, by misgovernment, drive, or the selfish leaders who could seduce, the people into a similar condition !*

* See Sir Richard Musgrave's History of the Irish Rebellion, and the Me-

Within the enclosure of Tyrrell's mansion may be seen a very perfect ancient tumulus.

The name of this celebrated spot, Clonard, or Cluain Ioraird, has been translated by Ware, Vallancey, and other topographers, "the Retirement on the Western Heights:" but this meaning is very questionable, for there are no heights, or even hills, in this locality, to which such could refer. Cluain, which is the general prefix to the names of our churches and bishops' sees, means a lawn, an insulated meadow, or level, fertile plain, surrounded by a bog or marsh; in fact a kind of oasis, as we know is the general appearance of such localities in Ireland; and Ioraird is a proper name: we have examples of this in Cluain Mac Nois, Cluain Coner, Cluain Dolcain, &c.* Clonard was once the most distinguished bishop's see in Meath, perhaps it would not be exaggeration to say in the kingdom; and its cathedral may be conjectured to have been one of the very first erected in Ireland, and was probably coeval with Clonmacnoise, and the original buildings at Armagh. It is well known to have been one of the most distinguished seats of learning of which the Irish historians can boast. Ware informs us that St. Finnian, Finen, or Finbar, who must have been one of the immediate successors of St. Patrick, was created first Bishop of Clonard in 520, "where he also opened a school, which, by his care and industry, produced many men of eminent sanctity and learning, among whom were the two Kierans, the two Brendans, the two Columbs (namely, Columb Kill, and Columb, the son of Crimthan), Laserian,

moirs of Joseph Holt, General of the Irish rebels in 1798, edited by T. Crofton Corker, Esq., 1838, who adds in a note: "The Kinnegad infantry [Tyrrell's corps] received for their conduct, in cutting down the rebels on this occasion, the *soubriquet* of 'the Slashers;' and a lively melody, still popular in Ireland, was named 'The Kinnegad Slashers,' in complimentary commemoration of the achievements of that corps at Clonard." Three celebrated ladies in that neighbourhood were also called "The Kinnegad Slashers." Holt acknowledges that he commanded 3000 men at Clonard, and that number was only a portion of those engaged. The rebel loss was upwards of 150. The leaders at Ballingarry should have studied the history of Irish rebellions more attentively.

* See Petrie's Essay on the Round Towers, and O'Brien's Irish Dictionary. But it is stated by Archdall that the original name of Cluain Ioraird was *Ross-Finnchuill*, "the Wood or Shrubbery of the White Hazel," an appellation which we can readily suppose was highly characteristic of this spot in early times.

the son of Nathfrach, Cainec, Moveus, and Ruadan. And as St. Finian's school was not 'improperly a sacred repository of all wisdom,' as the writer of his life tells us, so he himself got the surname of 'Finian the Wise.'"* To this ancient seat of learning resorted students, not only from all parts of the British isles, but also from Armorica and Germany; so that at one time it is said they numbered about 3000. The venerable Bede, it is said, bears testimony, not only to the instruction delivered at Clonard, but to its fame for hospitality towards the students of the many nations who resorted there; and Colgan, Ussher, Sir James Ware, and the learned Dr. Lanigan, have collected materials, and inserted in their writings the life of this distinguished philosopher and divine, who was also one of the most celebrated commentators on the Holy Scriptures of his age. One of the hymns anciently sung at his festival begins thus:

> " Regressus in Clonardiam,
> Ad Cathedram Lecturæ,
> Apponit diligentiam
> Ad studium Scripturæ."†

There is some discrepancy as to the date of his decease, but the best authorities acknowledge that it occurred between the years 548 and 563.

After the establishment of Christianity in Ireland, several bishoprics were created in Meath, namely, Clonard, Damliag or Duleek, Ceananus now Kells, Trim, Ardbracken, Dunshaughlin, Foure, Slane, and others; but in the beginning of the twelfth century, all these, except Duleek and Kells, were united to form the see of Clonard.

It appears from our monastic annals, that St. Kieran the younger, commonly styled the son of the carpenter, the founder of Clonmacnois, and who was born in 506, bestowed the territory of Clonard, which was his patrimony, on St. Finian, whose character and descent is thus recorded by Mac Geoghegan, who has paraphrased Colgan and Ussher: "St. Finian, or Finan, sometimes also called Finbar, son of Fintan, a subtle philosopher, and profound theologian, was first Bishop of Clonard: he was of the noble race of the Clanna Rorys, and his

---

* Ware's Irish Bishops, p. 136. † Ware's Writers of Ireland, p. 13.

piety added new lustre to his birth. Having been baptized
by St. Abban, he was placed under the guidance of St. Fortkern, Bishop of Trim, where he remained till the age of thirty
years, continually profiting by the instructions of this holy
bishop. He afterwards went into Britain, and became attached
to St. David, Bishop of Menevia in Wales, by whom he was
particularly beloved for his piety and learning. He remained
thirty years in Britain, where he founded three churches.
Having returned to his own country, and being consecrated
bishop in 520, he established his see at Clonard, on the river
Boyne, in Meath, where he founded a school, or university,
celebrated for the great concourse of students, amounting
sometimes to 3000, amongst whom were a great number of
subjects celebrated for their sanctity and learning."*

Dr. Lanigan writes,—his parents were Christians, " and
sent him towards the Church of Roscor, to be there baptized
by Bishop Fortkern. The women who were carrying him were,
it is said, met on the way by the priest, St. Abban, who, having inquired whither they were going, and what was their er-
rand, undertook to baptize him, which he did at a place where
two rivers unite into one." From this and other passages bearing a like interpretation, we are inclined to think the early
Irish Christians employed *immersion* as their mode of baptism,
and some of our very oldest fonts, particularly one still remaining in the churchyard of Tallaght, in the county of Dublin, would appear to have been constructed for that purpose.

At a later period the abbey was dedicated to St. Peter, but
what the original buildings were we can now but conjecture, probably a missionary chapel, a few monastic cells, and
a cloictheach, or round tower. There was also a derthech,
or penitentiary, the burning of which, in the eleventh century, has been recorded. We have constantly wondered
that no trace of a round tower had been discovered in this
sacred spot; but we learn from the Annals of Clonmacnoise
and the Four Masters, that the cloictheach, or steeple of
Cluain Ioraird, fell to the ground in the year 1039. Archdall
understands this to be the steeple of the church, and so indeed
it was, though a separate building from it. For upwards of
a thousand years the annals of Clonard have come down to us;

* Mac Geoghegan's History of Ireland, vol. i. p. 402.

and, although scattered through various works, they are now well known, and the majority of them have been collected with great industry by Archdall, in his Monasticon Hibernicum, in which work he also relates the nobleness of birth, distinguished philosophy, and eminent piety and learning of the founder. The library was burned in the year 1143. Is it too great a stretch of the imagination to suppose that that very copy of the psalms, in the handwriting of St. Columbkille, contained in the splendid silver shrine called the *Cathach* of the O'Donnells, now in the Museum of the Royal Irish Academy, was written in this very library? So early as 665, we read of regular professorships having existed there. Besides those who resorted thither as students, it seems that several pious laymen retired to this secluded spot, to spend the remainder of their days in contemplation and repose. From this sanctuary and abode of wisdom, undoubtedly, sprang much of the learning both of Britain and the continent. The far-famed Iona, from whence arose

> " That fire which lit creation in her youth,
> That turned the wandering savage into man,
> And showed him the omnipotence of truth,"

derived its religion and its architecture from Clonard.*

Numerous disasters befell this place. It was pillaged and in part destroyed no less than twelve times, on five of these occasions by the Danes. The church and adjoining buildings were fourteen times consumed by fire; indeed, this destructive element appears to have marked these structures for its particular fury, for we read that, in 1045, " the town of Clonard, together with its churches, was wholly consumed, being thrice set on fire within one week." In 1136, " the inhabitants of the Breney (Brefney) plundered and sacked Clonard, and behaved in so shameless a manner, as to strip O'Daly, then chief poet of

---

* In that most meagre and incorrect historical account of Iona, by Mr. Maclean,—the only guide-book, we are sorry to say, with which travellers visiting that sacred isle are furnished,—he has the ignorance and bad taste to say : " In the year 563, one Colum M'Felim M'Fergus, latinized Columba, a *Scotsman*, set out from Ireland in a currah, and landed at Kebudæ," &c. Now, the birthplace and parentage of St. Columb are both well known, and are mentioned in all the lives of this saint ; nay, the very passage in Adamnanus, to which he refers, is quoted incorrectly ; but we need not wonder at this in an author who embellishes his title-page with a veritable *Gaelic* quotation from Ossian !

Ireland, even to his skin, and leave him in that situation; and amongst other outrages, they sacrilegiously took from the vestry of this abbey a sword, which had belonged to St. Finian, the founder." It was sacked and plundered by Dermot Mac Murrough, and his English allies, in 1170. The English settlers appear, however, subsequently to have located themselves in the town of Clonard, which must then have been considerable, and they are even mentioned as having rebuilt some of the edifices. Besides the abbey of Regular Canons, there was also a nunnery, endowed by O'Melaghlin,* to which, in after times, immense revenues and very extensive lands were attached.

In 1206, Simon Rochford, an Englishman,—for English ecclesiastics ruled in Ireland then, as well as now,—who assumed the title of Bishop of Meath, removed the episcopal chair from Clonard to Newtown, near Trim, where he founded the celebrated abbey of Augustinian Monks. Clonard is frequently mentioned in the Annals of the Four Masters, and all the ecclesiastical histories of Ireland, and some of the most distinguished Irish prelates are said to have been buried there.† There was also a castle at Clonard, erected by Hugh de Lacy, but, unless Ticroghan be the spot, even its foundations have long since been obliterated.

Amongst the legendary lore attached to this abbey, is a tale of Columba, the son of Crimthan, having been seen late one night in his cell, when his lamp had expired, reading the sacred volume by a light which emanated from the tips of his fingers, as he passed them over the leaves before him.

At the beginning of this century, and indeed till a very modern date, the ruins of some of the many buildings which once adorned this memorable locality were in existence. Archdall thus describes them: " The entrance into this abbey, on the west side, was through a small building, with a lodge

---

* This name, which is written in half-a-dozen ways by the Irish, Latin, and English annalists, means Mael-Sechnal, the attendant or servant of Sechnal, the patron saint of Meath.

† We would direct the attention of any of our Irish antiquaries who may be travelling in the Highlands of Scotland to the churchyard of St. Finian, at Otter, in which will be found some exceedingly curious and highly sculptured tomb-stones, the workmanship of which is evidently of Irish origin.

over it, which led into a small court ; to the right of this
court stands the kitchen and cellar, and over them the dormi-
tory, ranging with the river, and overlooking the garden,
which sloped from thence to the water's edge ; opposite the
entrance was another small apartment, and adjoining it,
the refectory, which was carried for some length beyond the
square, and joined the choir, a large and elegant building, most
part of which still remains, and the windows are finished in a
light Gothic style. On the south side of the altar, fixed in the
wall, is a small double arch, in the old Saxon manner, and divided by a pillar through which iron bars were fixed. This
is supposed to have been the founder's tomb. There are many
remains of walls adjoining the other parts of the abbey, but in
so ruinous a state that little information can be gleaned from
them. At a little distance from the east window, in the burial
ground, stands a small chapel, in which is a table monument,
ornamented with the effigies of a man and a woman, in a praying posture, and dressed in the ruff of Queen Elizabeth's time;
the sides are adorned with many coats of arms,—that of the
family of Dillon is most conspicous."*

We have thus described Clonard from whatever research we
have been able to devote to the subject ; but of all the magnificence of all these buildings not even a trace now remains.
It is with difficulty their former situation can be made out.
The Christians have, after numberless burnings, sackings, and
plunderings, for upwards of a thousand years, at last succeeded
in completely obliterating every vestige of these Christian edifices, the tombs and temples of their ancestors, while some
pagan remains, erected centuries before the introduction of
Christianity into Ireland, attract our attention from the
Boyne's banks, and point out the locality sought for. Here,
upon the Trim road, the village of Clonard stands, and in connexion with it the modern church and graveyard. This latter, and the fields adjoining, were the site of the ecclesiastical
remains, but it would appear from the ancient references that
the monastical and scholastic buildings extended down towards
the western bank of the river for some distance. Three stones
are all that can at present be discovered of the vast range

* Archdall's *Monasticon;* also Gough's additions to Camden, and Seward's
Topography, &c., &c.

of buildings, and the numerous decorations and ornaments
which so lately existed here. One of these is a head, probably a fragment of a corbel or bracket, inserted into the
wall of the present church tower, over the door. The second
is a baptismal font, that figured in the annexed cut, which was
probably too heavy to be carried away, or useless in the erection of the modern ugly structure adjacent, and too massive to

be broken with facility. It is still preserved, and has been placed
in the parochial church.   It is one of the finest, and perhaps,
of its kind, one of the oldest in Ireland, and, being of very
hard, compact, grey limestone, or marble, it is still in most wonderful preservation. It is three feet high, and stands on a square
pedestal, the upper portion of which is highly ornamented
with floral decorations, in eight compartments, and divided by
a moulding from the basin, which is formed out of a separate
stone, the lower part of which corresponds in the number of
its sides with the upper part of the shaft ; but four of the
panels contain figures of angels, the remaining ones being
filled with the representations of trees or shrubs.   The basin
is octagonal in shape, two feet one inch in diameter, and highly

sculptured externally, with figures in relief, representing the Flight into Egypt, the Baptism in the Jordan, St. Finian, St. Peter, and various grotesque figures of monks of the Augustinian order; which latter show that it was carved since the days of Walter De Lacy, on the rebuilding of the monastery in 1175. The principal figure in the foregoing engraving, that of a bishop with a crozier, is supposed to be that of the founder, St. Finian. As may be seen by referring to the cut, some of the panels are divided per pale, and each small compartment contains a figure. The carvings on this curious relic are well worthy of inspection, and are a rude pictorial representation of scriptural and Irish monastic history and hagiology. The bowl of this font is very deep, and measures about twenty inches across, a sufficient size to permit of immersion, which, it is more than probable, was the form of baptism employed by the early Irish Church. There is an aperture in the bottom of it.

The third stone to which we alluded is a square trough, probably the lavatory of the ancient monastery. It is rude and undecorated, with a cavity two feet two inches long, by twenty-one inches wide, and about fifteen inches in depth. It remained, until we had it taken up, very lately, almost completely buried in the grave-yard, near the present church tower. Like several other hallowed stones, such as piscinas, bolt-holes, and steps or bases of crosses, which are met with on the sites of many of our old churches and religious houses, peculiar superstitious reverence attached to this ancient washing basin as long as it remained over ground. Like the " Deer-stone" at Glendalough, it was said to have contained water at all times, and to this water peculiar properties were attributed by the peasantry; it was believed to cause the illness and death of geese and all animals which drank it, and it was sought for as an infallible remedy— one of the hundred infallible cures—for warts.[*]

At what precise period during the present century those time-honoured ruins at Clonard were completely effaced, or to what base uses they were applied, it is now difficult to say. The chief dilapidation certainly occurred within the last five-and-twenty years. Ruins such as these are the landmarks of

---

[*] See the Author's articles on Irish popular superstitions, in the Dublin University Magazine, already referred to, and in the London and Edinburgh Monthly Medical Journal for June, 1849.

F

our history, transmitted to us through "ages of sorrow and shame," from a brighter and more glorious era, and are fully as interesting and as valuable to the Irish people as the stately edifices of Westminster or St. Paul's are to the English. Whatever government, political or ecclesiastical, rules this country, should be taught, by the voice of public opinion, to preserve our architectural remains and antiquities; and neither vestry clerk, parish bumpkin, itinerant architect, nor titled commissioner, should be permitted to remove one stone of those sacred piles, which are not the property, and do not belong to this parish or that proprietor, but appertain by right to the country at large.

We had a lamentable instance of the desecration of monuments, the dilapidation of ancient structures, and the complete obliteration of the records of several well-marked historic eras, in the spoliation of the church of Lusk, not far from this city, a few years ago; and not many months past a similar attempt was made to destroy the monuments in the old church of St. Audoen's, in Dublin. Where will paternal love, or filial piety, the adoration of a husband, the mourning of a friend, or the grateful homage of a country, erect the tomb or carve the tablet, to the memory of the hallowed, though not forgotten dead, if such memorials are, within the lapse of a few years, by the vote of a vestry, or the dictate of a commission, to be hurled from their niches, broken, scattered through the surrounding grave-yard, or turned into sharpening-stones by the masons and artisans employed in erecting modern ungainly buildings, in the construction of which the materials of a church some five or six centuries old are often "thrown into" the contractor's agreement?

But, above all, the people themselves should be taught to reverence and respect these remains, and not (as we have frequently observed), destroy them, by removing some of their beautifully carved stones to form lintels and cornices for their wretched cabins, the surrounding filth and misery of which contrast but too mournfully with the relics of ancient grandeur in their vicinity.

Among the remnants of ecclesiastical remains belonging to the cathedral of Clonard, which have been discovered or preserved, one unique object of interest deserves our especial notice. The Kinnegad river winds by this spot, and in some improvements lately made for the purpose of deepening the bed of that stream, a nest of curious antiquities was discovered. They consisted of a bucket, composed of small oaken staves, in which were packed some thin brazen culinary vessels; one of those long brass Dutch boxes, well known to the curious in such matters, containing some silver coins of the reign of Elizabeth; some of the "brass money" of James II., and several copper coins of the reign of William and Mary, dated as late as 1694, which latter serve to mark the time of the interment of these relics. But the object of most interest is a small bucket or Stoup, of oak, about six inches high, and beautifully hooped or bound with a thin filagree of brass; the handle, which is also brass, is affixed by loops and clasps, which contained precious stones, and were decorated in the

form of some of those carvings, so characteristic of early Irish art, both in the engraving and adorning of ornaments, and the embellishment and illumination of manuscripts. It is altogether an exceedingly light, chaste, and elegant fabric, and was, in all probability, used in the service of the cathedral, perhaps for carrying round the holy water.* Utensils of this kind, both household and ecclesiastical, are alluded to in the Brehon laws. Were we to offer a conjecture, we would say that after the battle of the Boyne, when Dutch boxes were common in Ireland, these relics were removed from the Abbey, and hidden, or dropped by accident, in the locality where they were found.

---

* See a picture, by Shoreel, in 1520, in Shaw's Dresses and Decorations of the Middle Ages, vol. ii., given in the Glossary of Gothic Architecture. This interesting relic figured above belongs to Dr. Barker, of Gardiner's-row, in this city, in the vicinity of whose family estate it was found, and to whom we are indebted for permission to publish the accompanying engraving. With laudable zeal he has deposited it, with the other objects of interest found in the same locality, in the great national collection of the Academy, where the public have an opportunity of seeing them, and where they are carefully preserved. The public generally, and even our fellow-citizens, do not seem to appreciate this noble collection, where, besides the articles intrinsically the property of the Academy, several interesting family relics have been deposited for safety and the purposes of exhibition.

We now turn to those Pagan remains which already attracted our attention, and to which we lately directed our steps from the Boyne's banks. About half a mile beyond the bridge of Clonard, near the church, and consequently on the left bank of the river, rises one of the most picturesque green moats of the many that border this noble stream. On its summit a most picturesque ash flourishes in great luxuriance. That tree has a particular charm for us; we remember it some fifteen years ago, when its commanding position attracted our attention, as we first wended our way from the far west towards Alma Mater; and season after season as we passed it, returning to the home of friends, and the glens and mountains in the sterner and more romantic, but less historic lands washed by the wide Atlantic, we watched the growth of its graceful, wide-spreading boughs with no common interest.

This large tumulus, the great bulk of which is probably formed of small stones, but the surface of which is now a verdant greensward, rises in steps caused by the gradual slipping of the alluvial soil. In circumference it measures 433 feet round the base, and at the top, which is flat and truncated, 168 feet. Its perpendicular height is upwards of fifty feet. Some excavations were made both at top and bottom upon its northern aspect, by treasure-seekers, some years ago.

Circular mounds of this description are of two kinds, mili-

tary and sepulchral, and it is often difficult, without an examination of the interior, to distinguish to which class some of
them belong; but this point we shall discuss as we advance
among the larger and more numerous collection of these
monuments on the lower Boyne. This at Clonard appears
to be a barrow, or tumulus, and probably covers a stone chamber, or a cromlech, containing the remains of some distinguished Irish chieftain. In numberless instances we find architectural remains of more recent date, and coming within the
historic period, occurring in the immediate neighbourhood of
these mounds; and not far from this moat once stood the celebrated school, abbey, and cathedral, which we have already
described. It would appear that the odour of sanctity still
lingered round the spot hallowed by the dust of the noble
dead, or commemorated by the battle-field of heroic times, and
that on the national acceptance of a new religion and another
system of Government, of policy, or warfare, Christian edifices,
civil and ecclesiastical, arose round their Pagan predecessors.

Independent of this great mound beside the town of old Clonard, the entire of the vicinity is studded over with mounds,
forts, and raths, of various shapes and sizes; there is one, however, in particular, a short distance to the north-west of the
great tumulus, to which we would especially direct the attention
of the tourist, on account of its importance, and the peculiarity
of its structure, as distinguished from the sepulchral mounds
in its neighbourhood. This rath or dun, which is evidently
one of the military class, formed an ancient fort or encampment, and was capable of containing as many as 200 men; it
consists of an external fosse, encircling a raised ditch, or circular earthen wall, within which we find a level platform,
elevated somewhat above the surrounding plain, but not so
high as the earthen circle which encloses it. A broad entrance,
through which a modern carriage might enter, exists upon
its eastern side.

In some instances there is a double wall of circumvallation;
and cases might be enumerated, in which sepulchral mounds,
cromlechs, and tumuli, exist in the centre of these military enclosures. Several of these ancient forts contain a central subterranean chamber, and circular passages, in all probability for the
purposes of security, and to serve as granaries; and beside the
rude weapons and ornaments occasionally discovered in their

vicinity, quantities of animal remains, particularly of goats and oxen, have been found within and around these enclosures.

Between this ancient camp and the great mound, in the low ground through which the Kinnegad or Blind River flows, have been dug up, from time to time, numerous Irish antiquities, brazen celts, spears, fibulæ, and also quantities of charcoal, slag, and such material as would indicate the previous existence of some foundry or smelting establishment. But looking down from the tumulus upon the surrounding flat country, and examining the situation and appearance of this great rath, we are strongly inclined to believe that the ancient name of the place is derived from it. It fully answers the meaning of the term Cluain, an insulated meadow, a sort of oasis rising out of a bog or morass, and, as we already remarked, bore the name of a man, probably some early Irish warrior;—is it too speculative to suppose that of the person buried in the great sepulchral moat, figured at page 68? Sometimes these raths or cashels are formed of stone, and in some rare instances they enclose Christian churches and monastic remains; but, besides the difference in material and contents, these circumstances in no wise prove their Christian origin, for it is acknowledged that Christian edifices have been erected, within these enclosures, within the historic era.

There has long existed an opinion among the reading and middle classes in this country, that these raths are of Danish origin; but, though still described as such by some of the peasantry, no person of any antiquarian knowledge now believes them to be any other than Pagan structures, erected by the Firbolg, Tuatha De Danaan, Scotic, or Milesian population, and constructed long prior to the first Danish invasion of Ireland. Conversing with an old man at Bective lately, we asked his opinion of these remains: " Ough," says he, " sure it's well known they were med by the Danes, who, when they were nearly bet all out, and grown mighty wake entirely in the counthry, lived under ground in thim same forths."

Besides the very general belief that exists even among the upper classes of society—an opinion, by the way, chiefly ascribable to the writings of Sir Thomas Molyneux—of the Danish origin of these raths, a certain degree of superstitious reverence attaches to them in the minds of the peasantry, by whom they are often styled " fairy raths" and fairy circles, and are believed

to be now inhabited by, if not originally the handiwork of the
"gentry" or "good people," whose music is said to be often heard
within their enchanted precincts, in the calm summer evenings;
and this superstition is strong against their Danish origin.*
Although by no means inclined to foster these rude and early
prejudices of our people, still we respect them, inasmuch as
they have for centuries thrown a magic spell around these enchanted halls, which few were hardy enough to attempt to
break. Until very lately, scarcely a peasant in the land would
put his spade into one of these mounds or circles; and we
have known blood spilled in attempting to force the people to
demolish an ancient rath. Sometimes this spoliation arises from
ignorance, or want of patriotism, in our farmers and gentry, but
often from mere curiosity, or in order to manure or level the land,
and frequently, to our own knowledge, for the mere purpose
of "breaking down prejudices," and showing the people that
no ill-luck or misfortune could possibly occur from their destruction. So much for the veneration for our national monuments; so much for the reverence for the dust of our ancestors!
It does not bespeak either education, taste, or patriotism, thus
wantonly to obliterate these footprints of our early history.

While we speculate upon the construction, the uses, and the

* Giraldus Cambrensis calls some of them Danish; but, after the publication
of Sir T. Molyneux's Discourse on "Danish Mounts, Forts, and Towers," this
idea was chiefly propagated by Hugh Boy M'Curtin, whose dissertation was
widely circulated among the native Irish.

In no place in the Irish histories do we read of the remains at Tara, Emania,
Tailte, or Croghan, &c., being attributed to the Danes, or called Danes' forts.
In the autograph letter of Thady O'Roddy, published in the Irish Archæological Society's Miscellany, p. 124, we have the following common sense view of
the case, written by an intelligent Irish antiquary in 1517:

"For the Carnes, or heaps of stones, in several parts of Ireland, some of
them were heaped as monuments in memory of battles fought in such a place,
some made in memory of some eminent persons buried in such a place, some
of them layed over some corps, as the Romans did: *Aggere cinctus.*

"For the forts called the Danes forts, its a mere vulgar error. For these
forts (called Raths) were entrenchments made by the Irish about their houses.
For we never had any stone worke in Ireland till after St. Patricke's coming,
aº Christi 432, the 5th yeare of the reign of Laogary Mac Neill. And then we
began to build churches, &c., of stone. So that all our kings, gentry, &c., had
such raths or forts about their houses, witnes Tara forts, where the kings of
Ireland lived, Rathcroghan in Connaught, etc."

By "stone worke," Dr. Todd, the learned editor of this Tract, very justly remarks in a note, that the author must mean that "we had no buildings of

historic era of these raths, duns, lises, or ancient fortresses and encampments, which have given names to so many places in Ireland, we must carry the mind back to a very early period in the colonization of this island, when a great portion of the country was thick wood and impassable morass; when the population did not exceed, if indeed it even amounted to two millions; when the warfare of the country consisted in the desultory incursions of some neighbouring chief; and the weapons of the belligerents were flint arrows, sling-stones, and stone and bronze hatchets and celts, with, in a little later period, short brazen swords, like those found on the field of Cannæ. We should then, in all probability, have found a half-civilized tribe or clan, or portion of a clan, intrenched within one of these raths,—which was further strengthened by a strong wooden palisade, erected on the outer embankment,— with their flocks grazing on the neighbouring plain, and their habitations constructed of timber, within the circle of the great enclosure.

As several other military forts, and one in particular, the great ring fort on the lands of Dowth, will claim our attention as we descend towards the sea, we shall refer to these structures in another locality.

It is very remarkable, as we already observed, how frequently we find some of the earliest Christian remains in the vicinity of Pagan mounds, tumuli, and other similar ancient structures, as if the feeling of veneration remained round the spot; and, though the grove of the Druid was replaced by the cashel of the Christian, still the place continued to be respected, and the followers of the early missionaries raised their churches and laid their bones in those localities hallowed by the dust or renowned by the prowess of their ancestors. Until within the last three centuries, which may be styled the dark ages of Ireland, each succeeding generation appeared to vie with its predecessor in the elegance and the beauty of its architecture. The pillar-stone, enlarged and decorated, grew into the sculptured cross; the hermit's cell became the cloistered monastery; the small belfry within the rude cashel

stone cemented with lime and sand mortar before the introduction of Christianity; for the Cahers or Cyclopean stone forts, built without cement, are as old as any of the earthern raths."

rose into the stately tower; the simple missionary church of early times grew into the florid cathedral; and individuals, as well as nations, strove to show their piety in the religious edifices which they erected, and their patriotism and ancestral veneration in the tombs and monuments which they adorned. These holy feelings continued alive and warm in the breasts of the nobles, churchmen, and chieftains of Ireland, even through ages of wild misrule; in the days of foreign invasion, when the plundering Northmen pillaged, burned, and destroyed, and a conquering neighbour fomented civil disagreements and domestic strife; when might, not right, was law; when the soldier's stalwart arm, and the churchman's moral power,—the bannered or the mitred tyrant,—swayed in turn the destinies of our people; before peace, with its accompaniments of security, wealth, and commerce, flourished in the land; e'er national schools offered education to the peasantry,—centuries antecedent to the creation of Art Unions and national Architectural Institutes, and long prior to the date of modern commissions,—church architecture obtained an eminence in Ireland which it has never since equalled. These reflections were forcibly impressed upon us in some of our excursions along the Boyne, where, beside the ruin of some light and elegant early church, with its leaning door-posts, its round chancel arch, and triangular-headed windows, its carved imposts, and sculptured piscinæ, and all those details which, though simple and inexpensive, preserve the rules of taste and architecture, we find some ugly, inarchitectural, modern, white-washed or yellow-washed structure, with its sentry-box for a belfry, and cold, damp, unpainted interior, erected at an expense far exceeding that which the construction of a building, similar to the original, would have cost. The church at Clonard affords a lamentable instance of our position. We neither belong to the schools of Rome nor Oxford, but we do hope to see the day when an Irish parish church, for a congregation of some fifty persons, will be constructed on the model of some of the early churches, the creed of the occupants of which was, perhaps, as pure and as free from the middle age corruptions as that now believed by the portion of the population professing the reformed faith.

A new era has taken place in the vicinity of this memorable locality, an event which the wildest visionary of that far-famed school of philosophy, who sauntered along " The Boyne of Science," could not by any possibility have even speculated upon. An aqueduct carries the Royal Canal over the stream a short distance below this; and at the same point the river is crossed by the Midland Great Western Railway, by which our readers, instead of being, as of old, tugged along in a dirty tub through a muddy ditch, at a rate little exceeding two miles and a half an hour, can spin over the Boyne with comfort and security at a rate of twenty miles an hour at least.

In the cuttings that were made along the banks of the canal, between Enfield and Clonard, for the progress of the railway, a most interesting battle-field was opened at Rathcore, in the townland of Newcastle, county of Meath, and such a quantity of human bones exposed, that the entire bank was literally white with them. They were found in every possible position, but had evidently been thrown into a large pit, without order, and not surrounded by any form of sepulchral monument. The most superficial part of this ossific stratum was scarcely two feet beneath the surface: and along with these bones were found some iron spear-heads, hatchets, and other weapons, which incline us to believe that these remains may be those of the gallowglasses, or heavy Irish soldiery employed in this country from the tenth to the end of the fifteenth century. Such, however, may be the speculations which men will yet form when similar exhumations occur on the fields of Cressy, Poictiers, or Agincourt, or, in a few centuries to come, perhaps even Waterloo. Some of these weapons have been placed in the national collection of the Academy.

The Annals of the Four Masters have afforded us the following references to this locality :

"A.D.799.—Hugh Oirdnidhe (monarch of Ireland) collected a large army, and marched into Leinster ; and he devastated Leinster twice in one month. He again raised the whole of the men of Ireland, except those of Leinster, both lay and clerical, and marched to Dun-Cuair, on the confines of Meath and Leinster ; Connmach, the Coarb of Patrick, accompanied by the clergy of the northern, or Conn's half of Ireland. The clergy were displeased at being called on expeditions at all. They complained of their grievance to the King ; and the King, Hugh, said that he would abide by the decision of Fothadh-na-Canoine [Fathadh of the Canon] in the matter. And it was on that occasion that he [Fathadh] gave the judgment which relieved or exempted the clergy from expeditions or hostings ever after." Dun-Cuair is the same as Rath-Cuair, the modern Rath-Core.

" A. D. 800.—Hugh Oirdnidhe went to Cuar, and divided Leinster between the two Muireadhachs, viz., Muireadhach, son of Ruadhrach, and Muireadhach, son of Brian."

" A. D. 815.—Hugh Oirdnidhe, King of Ireland, went out with a great army to Dun Cuar again, and divided Leinster between the two grandsons of Bran."

There is in this locality a remarkable winding of the river, styled in ancient writings " the sweep of the Boyne," where it spreads out into a considerable expanse, and the spot is memorable in Irish history. In the year 765, the seventh of Niall, the Annals of the Four Masters, in recording the various battles which took place in the east of Ireland, give us an account of " the battle of Bolg-Boinne" (the belly of the Boyne), " against the men of south Breagh," in which certain Irish chieftains were slain. The hostile belligerents appear to have been the Leinstermen.

About a mile beyond the bridge of Clonard, towards the west, we find the ruins of the old fortress of Ticroghan, or Queen Mary's Castle, as it is sometimes styled; it can be seen from the Ballybogan road, upon the left bank of the river, and may be visited in that route. We cannot, however, stop to record the annals of every feudal or monastic pile that attracts our attention in this passage down the Boyne; but we may here remark, that Lord Ormonde retired to this castle from Trim, in 1649, shortly before the siege of Drogheda, and that, " after a well-regulated defence," it was surrendered by Lady Fitzgarret, in 1650, to Colonel Reynolds and Colonel Huetson.[*] In its vicinity some remains of the walls of an ancient church and a burial ground, which formerly contained an antique font, also exist; but even within our own memory portions of the walls of the castle have been torn down to supply building materials. De Lacy built a castle at Clonard, but, if this was not it, we cannot find any trace of it.

* The peasants in the neighbourhood relate a story that the siege was about to be abandoned when the besiegers discovered that the soldiers in the fortress were firing silver bullets; encouraged by this proof of the extremity in which the beleaguered were, the Parliamentary forces continued the attack with renewed energy, and soon succeeded in reducing the castle.

We now commence the second great division of the Boyne, extending from Clonard to Navan. In the first portion of this division, from Clonard to Trim, a distance of about ten miles, the characteristics of the river vary little from those which we have described; slow, deep, and tortuous, it winds on its placid course, through deep, alluvial meadows, to the bridge of Stonyford, over which the road from Mullingar to Trim crosses to the southern bank. For the next four miles of its course there is little to attract attention; the banks are low, and the country exceedingly flat, and liable to yearly inundations from the overflow of the river, several of which have been recorded by the Annalists. This stream has not been made any use of, either for the improvement of the country or commercial purposes. There is scarcely one boat upon it for many miles of its course, and the only fish it affords here are pike, perch, and eels. The fish of the Boyne have been celebrated in ancient story; but these were, we have reason to believe, salmon, which now at least are seldom caught so high up. On the original proposal of making a canal along the Boyne, it was intended to have rendered the river navigable as far as Clonard, but the canal never was completed further than Navan, although it remains half finished as far as Trim. A river of such magnitude, and with such facilities, running from the very heart of the kingdom, and through the granary of the island, to a good sea-port, and remaining, for such a length of time, in the upper portion of its course, nearly as when the first migrations of the human family passed up it, certainly speaks badly either for the government of the country or for the native enterprise or industry of the people: perhaps both are to blame. The bed of the river is being now deepened, and some interesting relics have been discovered in it; among the rest, a most beautiful and most perfect gallowglass axe, the finest of the kind ever found; it is in the Museum of the Royal Irish Academy.

In the demesne of Killyon, on the northern bank of the river, about midway between Clonard and Trim, are the ruins of an old church and friary, originally founded by St. Liadhan or Liedania, the mother of St. Kieran of Saighir, who is still the patroness of this parish. From some of the Inquisitions and Burke's *Hibernia Dominicana* we learn that the Dominican monks of Trim retired to the Friary of Donore, as it is

sometimes called. The two walls which now remain are pictu-
resquely situated on a sloping ground, surrounded by some patriarchal ash trees; and nearly opposite these, on the southern
bank, at Lion's Den, in the townland of Castle Ricard, we find
the crumbling walls of an old battlemented house. Two very
perfect tumuli, one near the church of Castle Ricard, also occur
in this locality.

Below the friary, on the northern bank, the square border
castle of Donore, here represented, forms a conspicuous object,

as its ruins are in better preservation than most of the other
castles of the Pale, particularly those on the northern side
of the river. We have not been able to collect any accurate
information with reference to this building, which does not
appear to be older than the fifteenth century. It was probably built by some of the Anglo-Norman soldiers, who spread
themselves over the fertile valley of the Boyne for two or
three centuries after the English invasion. There are several
Donores, both in Meath, Westmeath, and Kildare; and two of
these—McGeoghegan's castle, in Westmeath, and Donore Hill,
from whence James beheld his defeat at the Boyne—are memorable localities.

The next bridge we meet is that of Inchmore, near which the
Kildare Blackwater empties itself, and beyond it that of Sca-
riff, below which latter the river is broken into a great
number of islands, and intersected by weirs. The road
approaches to within a few yards of the stream at this

point; and here the true sylvan beauty of the Boyne com-
mences, a circumstance of which the neighbouring proprietors
seem to be aware, for now every mansion, lodge, or cottage, seems proud of its locality, and we find the elevated,
sloping, wooded banks here, studded with Boyne views, Boyne
banks, and Boyne lodges, one of the latter of which is located
at the next bridge we meet with, Derrinydaly. The country
through which the river passes to this point is light in
soil, very thinly populated, and chiefly used as meadow or
pasture land, a circumstance owing partly to the yearly inundations. Below Derrinydaly the stream passes the demesnes
of Newhaggard and Trimblestown, still preserving the same
tortuous course, slow in progress, and constantly broken
into islands, some of which are planted with considerable taste.
On the right bank of the river, in a bold sweep, with which it
encloses the ground of Roristown and Newhaggard, we find a
large oval military fort, with a small souterrain in its western
face; and a similar description of fort may be observed about
a mile from the Boyne, on its northern side, near the coach
road from Trim to Athboy.

The castle and chapel of Trimblestown, the residence of the
Barnewall family, and which gives title to the present baron,
are about a mile from the Boyne, in a direct line. Trimblestown castle was fortified during the war of 1641, and for
the ten following years. General Jones attacked it in 1647,
when it surrendered to the Parliamentary forces. This is
the first demesne of any magnitude, and the first noble residence, which we meet with on the Boyne's bank; and we regret to say, that it is too true a picture, and too well-marked
a type of many similar residences in the country, forsaken
and neglected, a perfect ruin, yet still imposing even in its
decay; its high embattled walls and massive towers, which
formerly rose above the surrounding woods, exhibit one of the
finest specimens of domestic architecture of the fifteenth century in the kingdom. The family cemetery, in the small ruined
chapel in the neighbourhood, is worthy of inspection.*

---

* For some notices of the late Lord Trimblestown see Memoirs of Richard
Lovell Edgeworth. A drawing of Trimblestown Castle, by Petrie, forms the
frontispiece to the second volume of the " Excursions through Ireland."

CHAPTER IV.

TRIM.

WE now approach Trim from the west, but the views of its ruined towers, its steeples, and its abbeys, are, from this side, far inferior to those gained on every other approach. To see Trim aright the tourist must approach it by the Blackbull road from Dublin, when all the glorious ruins which crowd this historic locality, and which extend over a space of above a mile, burst suddenly upon him : the remains of St. John's Friary and castellated buildings at the bridge of Newtown ; the stately abbey of St. Peter and St. Paul a little further on, raising aloft its tall, light, and ivy-mantled windows, the neighbouring chapel, with its sculptured tombs and monumental tablets ; the broad green lawns, through which the Boyne winds, between that and Trim ; the silver stream itself, gliding smoothly onward with unbroken surface ; the grey massive towers of King John's castle, with its outward walls and barbican, the gates, and towers, and bastions, the fosse, and moat, and chapel ; the Sheep-gate and portions of the town-wall ; and, towering above all, the tall, commanding form of the Yellow Steeple, which seems the guardian genius of the surrounding ruins. All these beauteous objects, with the ancient church tower, the town itself, the Wellington testimonial, and the modern public buildings, form a combination of scenery and an architectural diorama such as we have rarely witnessed. We have also this additional charm in the views of Trim, that, look at this place as we may, its noble ruins are ever forming new combinations, fresh groups of beauty and of interest, singly or collectively: in all the varying aspects caused by atmospheric changes ; in glaring sunshine playing upon their massive walls; with the heavens overcast, and the drifting shower half revealing some of their turrets and gables;

with the calm subdued light of evening softening every object in the landscape; or the silver moontide throwing into shadow every dark recess and deep cathedral niche ; with the stream that winds among them now burnished as a golden mirror, now dark and gloomy, with scarce light upon it to reflect the ruins that are usually mirrored in its calm waters.   In each and all of these we have ever found new sources of admiration, new themes for the painter's art, the poet's feeling :

> ——————" Here you stand,
> Adore and worship when you know it not ;
> Pious beyond the intention of your thought,
> Devout above the meaning of your will."

Among the other beauties of the ruins of Trim are the tableaux which each group form when seen from one of the others; thus appear the castle and the Yellow Steeple with the town of Trim, when framed in the beautiful Gothic window of Newtown Abbey; thus may Newtown or the Yellow Steeple be seen from the interior of the castle; and other views of a like character, and formed in a similar manner by some surrounding arch or window, might be cited.

But we rave of scenes that we have admired, instead of conducting our readers through the town of Trim, and over these ruins in detail. Well, then,—of all the modern towns in Ireland, of our acquaintance, we know few to vie with Trim in dirt, laziness, and apathy; and of all the ruins in the country, we cannot call to mind any more carefully kept or better preserved from decay than these.   This preservation of the ruins of Trim is chiefly to be ascribed to the energy and zeal of Dean Butler, the vicar, who has taken immense pains not only to collect a great body of information on the subject of Trim, but also to bring to light and preserve many of its antiquities.   The Dean possesses a fine collection of coins, found among these ruins, and has printed and published some notices of the castle and church at Trim, collected from various authorities.   These little publications, which, we confess, we would rather have seen in a less dry and more popular form, contain, we believe, the greatest amount of information, in the fewest possible words, of any works we ever read.   They are chiefly composed of annals, collected from various ancient re-cords, and arranged in a chronological form, extending—the ecclesiastical notices from 433 to the present century, and the military from 1128 to 1689. We have availed ourselves largely of these researches in the present notice, particularly in the description of the military remains of Trim.

It would seem as if the modern inhabitants—perhaps degenerated by the causes which have ever acted in demoralizing small corporations, and owing in part to the unfortunate circumstances of a plurality of landlords, or wanting the stimulus of the warder's bugle, and the exciting scenes when De Lacy's lancers and mailed warriors careered through their narrow streets, when the standard of royalty proudly waved from the tall towers of their castle, and the mitred abbot and stole-girt priest, with all the gorgeous paraphernalia of the Church, paraded their dull town—have sunk down into apathy and listless indifference. According to the last Census, the population of Trim amounted to 2269 persons, 1124 males, and 1145 females. It has the honour of being the county town, and possesses a gaol, a fever hospital, a poor-house, barrack, courthouse, and a school under the Incorporated Society endowed by Richard first Baron Mornington; and it has been ornamented with a testimonial pillar, erected by the gentry of Meath to the honour of the Hero of Waterloo, who spent some of his early days at Dangan, in this neighbourhood, and who represented this borough the first time he sat in Parliament.

We cannot say much for the accommodation of Trim ; but we are bound to acknowledge every possible desire to afford comfort and civility. A little more care, and a little more cleanliness, added to the civility which it at present affords, would make the Trim hotel a very desirable residence during a tourist's stay. A coach passes between this town and Dublin twice in the day, and the Navan Railway on the one side, and Midland Great Western on the other, bring the tourist within little more than an hour's drive of the scene we are describing. The immediate suburbs, like all those surrounding ancient monastic remains, exhibit great richness and fertility. Before it enters the town the Boyne widens considerably, but becomes exceedingly contracted while passing beneath the ancient castle. It is crossed by a narrow bridge not unlike that of Drogheda.

The ancient name of that place was Ath-Truim, " the Pass or Ford of the Elder Trees;" and a ford, or shallow in the river, a short distance above the bridge, and within the extent of the

G

old fortifications, was probably the site of this pass, for above, and particularly below it, the river is very deep.

Although we have no evidence of the military importance of Trim before the arrival of the English in the twelfth century, there is high authority for believing it to be "one of the oldest, if not the very oldest, of the Irish episcopal sees;" and consequently it had an abbey or conventual church, which, it appears, was used, like the round towers of old, as an occasional place of refuge and defence to the small Christian community which had collected around it. "Colgan informs us that so early as the year 432, St. Patrick founded here an abbey of canons regular, dedicated to the Virgin Mary, built on a piece of ground given for that purpose by Fethlemid, the son of Laoghaire [Felimy, or Phelimy, son of Leary], and grandson of Niall."* The first bishop of this see was St. Loman, the nephew of Patrick, who was succeeded by Forcherne, the grandson of King Laoghaire, who was said to have been baptized by Patrick himself.

"A. D. 433. When Patrick, in his holy navigation, came to Ireland, he left St. Loman at the mouth of the Boyne, to take care of his boat forty days and forty nights; and then he (Loman) waited another forty, out of obedience to Patrick. Then, according to the order of his Master (the Lord being his pilot), he came in his boat against the stream, as far as the ford of Trim, near the fort of Feidlimid [Felimy], son of Loiguire [Leary]. And when it was morning, Foirchern, son of Feidlimid, found him reciting the Gospel; and, admiring the Gospel and his doctrine, immediately believed: and, a well being opened in that place, he was baptized by Loman, in Christ; and remained with him until his mother came to look for him; and she was made glad at his sight, because she was a British woman. But she likewise believed, and again returned to her house and told to her husband all that had happened to her and her son. And then Feidlimid was glad at the coming of the priest, because he had his mother from the Britons,—the daughter of the King

---

* Archdall, *Monasticon Hibernicum.*

We have been asked why we have not reduced our terrible, unpronounceable Irish names into something English, that people can read. This has, we feel, in a great part arisen from the Irish people being totally unacquainted with their history; and until they become familiar with their country's history, those Irish names must, indeed, sound harsh and grating in their ears.

of the Britons,—namely, Scothnoesa. And Feidlimid saluted Loman in the British tongue, asking him, in order, of his faith and kindred, and he answered, 'I am Loman, a Briton, a Christian, a disciple of Bishop Patrick, who is sent from the Lord to baptize the people of the Irish, and to convert them to the faith of Christ; who sent me here according to the will of God.' And immediately Feidlimid believed, with all his family, and dedicated (*immolavit*) to him and St. Patrick his country, with his possessions, and with all his family; all these he dedicated to Patrick and Loman, with his son Foirchern, till the day of judgment. But Feidlimid crossed the Boyne, and Loman remained with Foirchern in Trim, until Patrick came to them, and built a church with them, twenty-two years before the foundation of the Church of Armagh."—*Tircehan*, as quoted by *Ussher, Primordia*, 853.*

It must be remembered, that the Britons had Christianity preached to them two centuries previously. The Church of Armagh here referred to stood on the north side of the river, and belonged to the see of Armagh.

The original abbey, which was dedicated to the Virgin Mary, stood, in all probability, upon the picturesque site of the Yellow Tower which in after ages was erected here, and is stated to be " the most lofty remnant of the Anglo-Norman architecture now existing in Ireland." It was originally a square steeple, or abbey tower, of gothic architecture; it is now upwards of 125 feet high, and consists of one perfect and two partial walls, which, thus leaving it open on the west, exhibit a series of stories in its interior. It was, in all probability, like many of the other early monastic remains, and the round towers in particular, used as a place of security and defence; and its great height and commanding position may have caused it to be employed as a watch-tower over the surrounding country. Although the buildings of St. Mary's Abbey adjoining have been removed, a considerable portion of their site can be traced. There is a tradition that Cromwell battered down a portion of this tower; but we do not find any further authority for this assertion than mere local history; and there is scarcely a ruin along the Boyne, from this to Drogheda,

---

* See some notices of the Church of St. Patrick, Trim, by the Rev. Richard Butler, Dean of Clonmacnoise.

which is not said to bear evidence of his cannon. Gough, indeed, in his additions to Camden, on the authority of the *Gentleman's Magazine* for 1784 (where there is a figure of this tower), asserts that one half of the Yellow Steeple " was demolished by Oliver Cromwell, against whom it held out a considerable time, as a garrison; a quarter of it being blown up by Cromwell, the top overhangs several feet;" but considerable dilapidations have occurred in it since then. The accompanying illustration represents the Sheep-gate of Trim, and the Yellow Steeple in the distance.

This abbey of St. Mary's, to which the "Yellow Steeple" was attached, together with the other abbeys of Trim, always maintained the most friendly intercourse with the Court of England, and particularly favoured the house of York.* The De Lacys are said to have re-edified and endowed it.

---

* The abbots of Trim, and the barons in its neighbourhood, particularly favoured the impostor, Lambert Simmel, who was ridiculously crowned in Christ Church, Dublin, as Edward the Sixth of England.

A cloictheach, or round tower, formerly existed at Trim, the burning of which by Conor O'Melaghlin, in 1108, and by Conor Feargal O'Lochlinn, in 1127, is mentioned in several of the Irish Annals. Like Clonard, the ecclesiastical buildings at Trim suffered various conflagrations; but neither our space, nor the character of this work, permit us to follow out the well-recorded annals of this or the other abbeys and monastic remains along our track,—consisting of notices of the celebrated persons who flourished or were interred in them, poets, priests, and warriors, mail-clad barons and palmer knights, holy nuns and pious monks; the various miracles wrought in these monasteries; the plunderings, seizures, and dilapidations they sustained; the records of the privileges which they enjoyed, and the broad lands they occupied; together with the offerings of the devotional, and the various plagues (from which Meath suffered so frequently and so severely) ;—which form the records of these establishments,—highly interesting, no doubt, in their way, but merely valuable to us for the epochs which they mark, and the historic facts which they attest.

The Grey Friary of Observantines stood by the water's edge, near the site of the present court-house, but all trace of it has been long since completely effaced.

The Black Friary of the Dominicans was founded by Geoffrey de Geneville, Lord of Meath, in 1263, to which he subsequently retired on the accession of Roger de Mortimer, his heir in right of his wife in that territory. Several Parliaments were held here, in one of which, in 1446, it was enacted that the Irish should cut their beards according to the English fashion, and not wear yellow shirts. Some meagre remains of this friary still exist near the site of the abbey-gate, on the northern side of the town, and without the ancient wall. It is much to be regretted that more of the history of the illustrious founder of this abbey has not come down to modern times. Geoffrey de Geneville, or De Joinville, was of noble birth, a native of Champagne, and brother to the celebrated Jean de Joinville, the companion and historian of St. Louis. Geoffrey was a most distinguished statesman, and the confidential friend of Edward I., by whom he was employed in most of the great diplomatic affairs of England at that time, both at home and abroad. About the middle of the thirteenth century he joined the Crusaders, and remained for some time in the Holy Land. After his return in

1273, he was appointed Lord Justice of Ireland; and in virtue of his wife, Maude, sister to Gilbert de Lacy, he became possessed of a large portion of the great Palatinate of Meath. After a most eventful history, he died on the 19th of October, 1314, in the Black Friary, which he had founded. Dean Butler, the historian of Trim, thus graphically alludes to this distinguished character:—"It is to be lamented that our notices of the varied life of this great man are so meagre that we cannot fill up the outline of the young noble of Champagne wooing his wealthy bride in the court of England, retiring with her to her great seignories in Ireland, and joining with her in founding a religious house;—joining in a crusade to the Holy Land; administering for a short time the government of his adopted country; busy for years in the councils and campaigns of the bold and politic Edward I. ; and closing his career by the resignation of his lordship of Meath to his youthful granddaughter and her ambitious husband, and ending his days in the habit of a Dominican, in the cloister which he and his wife had built fifty years before. The following verses are quoted from I know not what monkish author, in the *British Magazine*, x. 670. The person to whom they relate had, like Geoffry, been a Crusader; and they give a beautiful picture of such a life as Geoffry de Geneville may have led in our Black Abbey:

" ' Ipse post militæ bursum temporalis,
    Illustratus gratia doni spiritualis,
    Esse Christi cupiens miles specialis,
    In hac domo monachus factus est claustralis.

" ' Ultra modum placidus, dulcis et benignus,
    Ob ætatis senium candidus ut cygnus,
    Blandus et affabilis, ac amari dignus,
    In se Sancti Spiritus possidebat pignus.

" ' Nam sanctam ecclesiam sæpe frequentabat,
    Missarum mysteria lætus auscultabat,
    Et quas scire poterat laudes personabat,
    Ac cælestem gloriam mente ruminabat.

" ' Ejus conversatio dulcis et jocosa,
    Valde commendabilis et religiosa,
    Ita cunctis fratribus fuit gratiosa.
    Quod nec gravis exstitit nec fastidiosa.'

"We may easily suppose that the old Crusader, who had been employed in the wars and embassies of the time, had tales

of travel and of danger which would make him a very accept-
able companion in a monastery; and we may imagine, as he
roamed about it,—

> " ' Hic per claustrum quotiens transiens meavit,
> Hinc et hinc ad monachos caput inclinavit,
> Et sic nutu capitis eos salutavit,
> Quos affectu intimo plurimum amavit.' "

There were also a nunnery and a Greek church at Trim,
which latter has been supposed to afford some evidence of a
Grecian people settling in Ireland.   Sir James Ware says: " I
confess, indeed, that there remain some small traces of the ancient Grecians having been in this country, in a church at
Trim, in Meath, called *Græcorum Ecclesia;*" but as the only
foundation for this supposition merely consists in the name,
it may as likely have been given from some peculiarity in the
doctrines or form of worship of those who frequented it, or from
some similarity in its architecture to the Grecian or Pelasgic
type, as we now speak of Grecian, Cyclopean, Roman, Saxon,
or Norman masonry in some of our early churches. The question is still an open one.

The military buildings of Trim next claim our attention.

We have neither space nor inclination to enter into the
much-mooted question as to whether the Irish possessed castles and military fortifications of that nature, prior to the arrival of the English, in the twelfth century.   Besides the
raths to which we have already alluded, they certainly had several very ancient fortresses, or circular duns of Cyclopean
masonry, with walls of immense thickness, containing circular
passages within them, and erected on highly defensible and
commanding situations,—on rocks, islands, promontories, and
isolated blocks of massive rock, on the level plains, like the
ancient acropoles of the Greeks and Orientals, or on natural
mounds in the midst of swamps and morasses ; but these
were constructed without mortar or cement. Several such
acropoles are already well known, and their sites determined.
The use of lime cement, and the accurate adjustment of the
stones according to certain rules of masonry, were, however,
well known to, and extensively employed by the Irish, centuries
before the arrival of the English in this country, of which we
have innumerable examples in the round towers, missionary

churches, and early ecclesiastical buildings, centuries before
the conquest; and we may well suppose that, with such a
knowledge of architecture, the Irish chieftains and their architects and artisans would have erected castles of defence and
security for life and property, against the inroads of the neighbouring tribes, during those centuries of civil war with which
this country was distracted, as well as against the descents of
the plundering Dane and fierce Northman, during the ninth,
tenth, and eleventh centuries at least. But, besides these speculations, we have positive historic assurances of the use of lime
cement in the ancient Irish palaces; and we have authentic
records of castles after this fashion having been built, particularly by the O'Conors of Connaught, antecedent to the English invasion of Henry II. The castles of Galway, Dunlo (now
Balinasloe), and Colooney, in Sligo, were built in 1125. Tur-
lough More O'Conor, monarch of Ireland, built the castle and
bridge of Athlone in the summer of 1129, called the dry summer. The castle of Tuam, called "*Castellum Mirificum*," built
by Roderic O'Conor, was also long prior to the date of the
Invasion.*   The castle of Cullintragh in Meath, the stronghold of O'Melaghlin, was demolished by Roderick, son of Tur-
lough O'Conor, in 1155, and in the same year O'Melaghlin in
retaliation destroyed the fortress and bridge of Athlone. That
such buildings bore no comparison in strength, skill, or extent to those erected by the English here, there can be also little
doubt. One can easily account for the almost total obliteration
of these remains, while the relics of ecclesiastical architecture,
many of which were constructed without lime or mortar, still
remain. With regard to the first, every circumstance combined
to dilapidate them, and the great superiority of the fortresses
and castellated mansions of the English, in a short time rendered the Irish strongholds useless ; while the most powerful
of all feelings,—religious veneration,—a feeling common to the
conquerors and the conquered, continued to preserve the latter, if not from desecration, at least from total annihilation;
and the more distant from the theatre of war, and the scene of
the early Anglo-Norman colonization, the more perfect have
these sacred relics been preserved, and the longer have the

* See also note at page 12.

ancient manners, habits, and customs of our people been retained.*

We do not think the term " Saxon," so frequently employed
in modern Irish writings referring to this period, is correct.
The colonization was Anglo-Norman. We find that the families who became Anglo-Irish clans here were chiefly Norman, viz. : Butlers, Burkes, Barrys, Fitzgeralds, De Lacys, De
Courcys. Many Welsh families settled here also, as Joyces,

---

* We cannot forbear mentioning the following circumstance as corrobora-
tive of this opinion. Shortly after the British Association met in Dublin, in
1835, we spent a week in the island of Achill, and there witnessed some
scenes and modes of life which it could scarcely be credited were passing at
one end of this small kingdom, while at the other the savans of Europe and
America were met to discourse on science. There are several villages in
Achill, particularly those of Keeme and Keele, where the huts of the inhabitants are all circular or oval, and built for the most part of round, water-
washed stones, collected from the beech, and arranged, without lime or any
other cement, exactly as we have good reason to suppose the habitations of
the ancient Firbolgs were constructed ; and very similar to many of the ancient monastic cells and oratories of the fifth and sixth centuries, which religious veneration and the wild, untrodden situations where they are located,
have still preserved in this country. Those of our readers who have ever
passed the Minaune or Goat's Track, on the towering cliff that rises above the
village of Keele, with the glorious prospect of Clew Bay and the broad swell
of the western Atlantic before them, and have looked down upon the pigmy
dwellings, resembling an Indian wigwam, scattered over the beach beneath,
may call to mind the scene we describe. During the spring, the entire population of several of the villages we allude to in Achill, close their winter dwellings, tie their infant children on their backs, carry with them their loys, and
some corn and potatoes, with a few pots and cooking utensils, drive their cattle
before them, and migrate into the hills, where they find fresh pasture for their
flocks; and there they build rude huts, or summer-houses, of sods and wattles,
called booleys, and then cultivate and sow with corn a few fertile spots in the
neighbouring valleys. They thus remain for about two months of the spring
and early summer, till the corn is sown ; their stock of provisions being exhausted, and the pasture consumed by their cattle, they return to the shore,
and eke out a miserable and precarious existence, by fishing, &c. No further
care is ever taken of the crops ; indeed they seldom even visit them, but return in autumn, in a manner similar to the spring migration, to reap the corn
and afford sustenance to their half-starved cattle. With these people it need
scarcely be wondered that there is annually a partial famine.

Spencer relates that the Irish, like the ancient Scythians, " kept their cattle
and lived themselves the most part of the year in *Boolies* [cow-houses], pas-
turing upon the mountain and waste wild places, and removing still to fresh
land as they have depastured the former." Several laws were made to prevent
this indiscriminate grazing on the borders of the Pale. See also the Statute
of Kilkenny in the Archæological publications, p. 41.

Barretts, Walshes; but we had no early chieftain of the "Saxon race," which appears to have been less warlike than the Normans. The Saxons had no castles of stone at any time, and they had few laws. The truth is, they were an inferior *buddagh* race, and their history has been made too much of by modern writers. We had no Saxons here till the reign of Elizabeth, except some farmers in Forth and Bargie, and a few *villani* or buddaghs who followed the fortunes of the great Anglo-Norman warriors, and settled in Meath and elsewhere; but these were mere *serfs*. It was Cromwell who poured the great flood of Saxon blood into Ireland.

There is no evidence of the existence of a castle, or any military building, at Trim, anterior to the date of the English invasion. If the O'Melaghlins, the original monarchs of Meath, possessed a stronghold here, no record of it has come down to modern time. As we have already stated, Henry II. bestowed, for the service of fifty knights, the fertile territory of Meath upon the celebrated Hugh de Lacy; who fixed on Trim as his residence, and built there, about the year 1173, a strong castle, surrounded by a deep moat, into which it is most likely the water of the Boyne was conducted. Having established his power and authority in this part of the kingdom, the Norman baron departed for England, leaving his stronghold at Trim in the custody of Hugh Tyrrell.

" To destroy this castle, Roderick O'Connor, King of Connaught, assembled a large army; and Tyrrell, having despatched messengers to Earl Strongbow, beseeching him to come to his aid, and finding himself too weak to resist the multitudes brought against him, he abandoned the castle and burned it. The Irish king, having thus obtained his object, returned to his own country; and Earl Strongbow, who was advancing to the relief of Trim, meeting on his way with intelligence that the castle was burned, marched on, and when he came there he found neither castle nor house to lodge in ; wherefore he made no stay, but pursued the enemy, and fell upon their rear, of whom 150 were slain; which done, he returned to Dublin, and Hugh Tyrrell to the ruined castle of Trim, to re-edify the same before Hugh De Lacy's return out of England.

" Giraldus Cambrensis says, that, ' on hearing of this inroad of Roderick into Meath, Raymond le Gros, although the news reached him at Wexford the day of his marriage with Basilia, sister of Earl Strongbow, marched the next day to oppose him, not being overcome either by love or by wine; that Roderick, who had had previous experience of his valour, retreated at his approach; and that Raymond repaired the castles of Meath, that is to say, of Trym and of Duleek, which had been wasted by Hugh Tyrell.' "

The tragical end of the first English lord of Meath is already well known: he is said to have been murdered by an Irish labourer, while directing some work at the castle which he was building at Durrow, in the King's County. De Lacy having stooped forward at the moment, the man nearly severed his head from his body, at a single blow, with a sharp axe, which he had concealed for the purpose beneath his clothes.

Such is the version of this affair pawned upon the world by the Jesuit Campion, and copied by Hanmer, Harris, and has even been repeated by Moore; passing, like any story of the present day, from hand to hand, till it is now generally received as authentic history. Keating, it is true, endeavoured to rectify the error, but he was not attended to. The fruitful source of this, like innumerable other false statements in the works of writers upon the history of Ireland, has been their total ignorance of the language in which these statements were written, and their trusting (even if honest) to incorrect translations or garbled extracts.

In the Archæological and Celtic publications we perceive the dawn of a clearer, if not a brighter day for true Irish history; but the morning of that day has been ushered in by the publication, by Mr. O'Donovan, of the great work of Irish history, generally known as the "Annals of the Four Masters," so often referred to in this little work.

The true story is this. About the middle of the sixth century, Columbkille having obtained a grant of land from a chieftain named Brendan, in the King's County, at a place called Dair-Mahg, or the "plain of the oaks" (now Durrow), erected there a monastery, which subsequently became very celebrated. Well, some centuries after, comes the English baron, Hugh De Lacy, — the acknowledged destroyer of churches, — and erects his castle beside it, and even with some of the very materials, it is said, of the ancient abbey, which he destroyed. This naturally excited the wrath of the rightful heirs, the descendants of the ancient lord of Dair-Mahg, the renowned Brendan.

These were, the O'Caharney, chief of Teffia, well known under
the soubriquet of Sinnach, or " The Fox," and O'Brien, chief
of Brawney.   Now, as may be shown from *unquestionable* authorities, the man who slew De Lacy was no Irish labourer,
but a young soldier of the household of O'Caharney, who was
remarkably swift of foot.   The fact is recorded in the " Annals
of Ulster," the " Annals of the Four Masters," and also more
fully in the " Annals of Kilronan," from which latter we quote
the following account:

   " A. D. 1186.—Hugo de Lacy went to Durrow, to make a
castle there, having a countless number of the English with
him, for he was King of Meath, Brefny, and Oriel, and it was
to him the tribute of Connaught was paid, and he it was that
won all Ireland for the English.   Meath, from the Shannon to
the sea, was full of his castles and English followers.   After
the completion of this work by him, that is, the erection of the
castle of Durrow, he came out to look at the castle, having
three Englishmen along with him.   Then came there one youth
of the men of Meath up to him, having his battle-axe concealed,
namely, Gilla-gan-innaher O'Meyey, the foster-son of the Fox
(O'Caharney) himself, and gave him one blow, so that he cut
off his head, and he fell, both head and body, into the ditch of
the castle."—*Annals of Kilronan, T. C. D.*"*

And the Four Masters take up the narration of this event,
and inform us that Gilla-gan-innaher escaped by flight into
the neighbouring wood of Kilclare, where the Irish chieftains
were awaiting him.

What a prolific theme for the novelist the stirring dramatic
events of this period of Irish history would prove,—what a romance a Sir Walter Scott would have made of the whole story
of the English invasion, and this incident in particular ; and
until some great historical novelist arises, Irish history and Irish
scenery and manners will not be known, and consequently not
valued, by the educated classes, either here or in England.

   * See also the Annals of the Four Masters, A. D. 1186, with O'Donovan's
note thereon.
   It is a remarkable circumstance, that almost on the very spot on which
Hugh de Lacy was slain, Lord Norbury, the late possessor of Castle Durrow,
or Durrow Abbey, as he styled his new mansion, was murdered a few years
ago; and it is said that he also interfered with the rights appertaining to the
adjoining abbey.

De Lacy's body was detained for several years by the Irish, who then attacked the castle, but it was at last restored, and buried with great solemnity at Bective Abbey, while his head was carried to Dublin, and interred in the Abbey of St. Thomas, in the tomb of his wife, Rosa de Monmouth. This division of the remains of the unfortunate De Lacy gave rise to a fierce dispute between the two abbeys, as to which should possess both, and the controversy arose to such a pitch that the matter was referred to the supreme Pontiff at Rome. It was finally decided that the body should go along with the head; and it is supposed to have been removed to Dublin about the year 1205. Gerald of Cambria thus described this remarkable man:

" If you will know what manner of man Hugh de Lacie was, you shall understand his eies were blacke and deepe, and his nose somewhat flat, like that of an ape; and the right side of his face, from the chin upwards, by a mischance, was schrewolie skalled; his neck was short, and his bodie hairie, as also not fleshie, but sinewish and strong compact; his stature was but small, and his proportion deformed; but in construction he was verie sober, trustie, and modest. He was verie carefull in his own private matters, but in causes of government and in all public affairs he was most vigilant and carefull: and albeit he were a verie good souldier, and one of great experience in martial affairs; yet in his sundrie adventures, wherein he was sometimes rash and verie hastie, he sped not alwaies best, nor has the best success. He was verie greedie and covetous of wealth and possessions, but over much ambitious of honours and reputation."

In 1210 King John arrived in Ireland, and spent the second and third days of July at Trim; but although the present castle is called after him, it does not appear that he lodged at any castle at Trim,—if there was one at that time fit for his reception; and his writs are dated " apud Pratum subtus, Trim,"—the field now called the King's Park. What a volume might be written on *royal visits to Ireland;*—by whom made, under what circumstances, with what objects or inducements; what was the condition of the country, what the mode of reception, what the state of manners at the time of each;—from the days of Henry II. to those of Queen Victoria in this present year, 1849.

The present castle of Trim, which has been justly styled the
finest specimen of Anglo-Norman military architecture in Ireland, is generally believed to have been re-erected by Richard
Peppard or Pipard, who, according to the Registry of Clogher,
also built the castle of Donaghmoye, in Farney.* It occupies
within its walls about two acres of ground, and stands on a sloping mound on the right bank of the Boyne, from the banks of
which it presents a noble and commanding appearance. The

great keep or donjon in the centre is a rectangular building,
with massive square towers abutting from each side, and rising
to a height of nearly eighty feet ; some parts of the wall are
twelve feet in thickness. By the arrangement of its ground plan,
it presented, when perfect, a figure of twenty sides, and the external face is still in very excellent preservation, with the exception of the tower facing the town gate, which is said to have
been destroyed by the cannon of Cromwell. Some of the winding staircases, by which the topmost turrets were reached, still
enable the visitor to gain the highest pinnacle, from whence a
view of immense extent and great interest is obtained. Standing here, the eye ranges over many miles of the vast and fertile plains of Meath, with the Boyne sweeping through them,
the various groups of ruins immediately beneath and around,

---

* See some account of the Territory or Dominion of Farney, &c. By
Evelyn Philip Shirley. 4to. London : Pickering. 1845. p. 17.

the hills of Skreen and Tara, the mountains of Kildare and Dublin, the tower of Kells, and, in a word, a territory of which the lords of Trim may well have felt proud. The outer wall, which was surrounded by a deep fosse, through which the waters of the Boyne were originally admitted (thus completely insulating the fortress), is 486 yards in length, and defended by ten flanking towers at nearly equal distances. The gate towards the town, and the barbican, with the remains of their portcullisses, draw-bridges, and all the most approved military inventions of the day, are still in wonderful preservation. On the whole, we know of no castle in Ireland which affords the same scope for the study of the military architecture of the thirteenth century as this, which may justly be classed with those of Conway and Caernarvon. Within the wall, on the river side, we find the remains of a chapel, perhaps that used by the common soldiery; while two niches, resembling piscinæ, in the interior of one of the castle towers, mark the site of a small private chapel within. Adjoining the large chapel near the external wall are the remains of a tower supposed to have been the mint.

Our space, however, will not permit our entering at any length into the details of this noble structure, connected with which we find so many historic occurrences and classic associations. Besides those already enumerated, we cannot forget the pageants and tournaments of the celebrated Earl of Ulster; the imprisonment of the families of the Dukes of Gloucester and Lancaster, during the time of Richard of England's sojourn in this country; the confinement here of the royal hero of Agincourt; its occupation by the De Lacys, the Mortimers, the Verdons, and Cootes, its parliaments and its sieges;—all of which throw a degree of splendour over the ruins of Trim.

But, great as these names and circumstances are, they pass into insignificance when compared with the celebrity which this place has acquired by its connexion with the greatest warrior and statesman of the day. It is generally, but erroneously, believed that the Duke of Wellington was born in or near Trim; but the evidence at present is altogether in favour of Dublin, and the honour of his birth-place is now awarded to the house at present occupied by the Ecclesiastical Commissioners, in Upper Merrion-Street. The Registry of St. Peter's

*

parish, in this city, contains the following entry: "Arthur, son of the Earl and Countess Mornington, born 30th April, 1769." The house where "The Duke" resided for some time at Trim still stands at the corner of Dublin-Gate-street.

The borough of Trim has the honour of having returned the Duke of Wellington, on his twenty-first birth day, to represent it in the Irish Parliament; and, in 1847, the gentry of Meath erected a Corinthian column on the fair-green of this town, to commemorate the military achievements of our distinguished countryman, whose early life and history is so intimately connected with this ancient town.

There were two other castles at Trim besides that just described, the castle of the Nangles and the castle of the Talbots, both of which stand behind the modern town upon the north side of the river and in the neighbourhood of the Yellow Steeple. The latter was built by the celebrated Sir John Talbot, Lord Lieutenant of Ireland in 1415, "The Scourge of France,"

—————— "So much feared abroad
That with his name the mothers still their babes."

This building was until lately the Diocesan School of Meath, when it acquired an additional celebrity from the Duke of Wellington having been for some time at school there. In it also was educated another distinguished Irishman, Sir William Rowan Hamilton, our Astronomer Royal. At present the building possesses little to attract attention except a tablet in the northern wall bearing the Talbot arms, quartered with those of Furnival.

Dangan, one of the seats of the Wellesley family, and where the Duke spent many of his boyish days, is distant about five miles from Trim, but is now completely dilapidated, and has long since passed out of the hands of the Wellesley family.

A locality, however, of still greater interest than that of Dangan, presents itself within two miles of Trim, and one which, like the former (with which it is in a certain degree connected), has been permitted to fall into utter ruin and neglect. We allude to Laracor, the early residence of Dean Swift.

It is a dark, secluded locality, into which one would suppose a breath of the busy world without never entered; a spot more uncongenial to the anxious thoughts and high ambition of the Irish patriot can scarcely be imagined; but he had here other charms and more endearing associations, to which even the votaries of politics and philosophy are not inaccessible. Here Stella and Mrs. Dingley lived, and here they sauntered through the quiet roads with Dr. Raymond, the Vicar of Trim, and with the future author of " Gulliver" and the " Drapier's Letters." Here, on this very bridge which spans the noiseless streamlet, with its sedgy margins of willows and alders, must Swift have often mused; (for who is there that has not mused upon a bridge's battlements when gazing on the current beneath?) Beside this bridge, on the right-hand side of the road, once stood the residence, and around it the well-stocked garden, of the Dean, but the whole is now (or was when we last visited it) an ill-tilled potato garden; yet, without guide or cicerone, we were able to trace, from the recollection of the scene as described in the journal to Stella, the pond and bath which existed in this garden, the boundary of its ancient walls, the site of the very willows, some of whose posterity still exist, which hung over the stream, and beneath which the Dean and Esther Johnson so often walked. Some remnants of the brick wall which enclosed the garden, and the stands on which some bee-hives stood, were discovered a few years ago; but briars and thorns, rank sedge, and luxuriant weeds, are yearly obliterating even the faint traces we refer to. Of the house, a small portion of one of its gable ends is all that now exists; even this, thick and massive as it is, will soon have crumbled away, for, to the disgrace of those connected with the rectory, two wretched cabins have been erected within the site of the walls of Swift's glebe at Laracor.

In front of this residence stands a very perfect sepulchral mound, similar to that which we described already at Clonard, but very much smaller; and beyond this we find the old parish church, to which Swift ran the race with Delany, and where " my dearly beloved Roger" officiated as clerk. Within this Church we find a handsome monument erected to the last Wesley, or Wellesley, who bequeathed his name and his estate to the ancestor of the present Duke of Wellington.

About a mile nearer Trim is pointed out the cottage which Stella and Mrs. Dingley occupied; but this is somewhat apocryphal.

H

We might now conduct our readers over the numerous
other interesting remains which still hallow and adorn Ath-
Truim,—the ancient steeple of its parish church, erected in
1449 by Richard Duke of York,—the remnants of the town
wall, which mark the ancient boundary, with its Sheep and
Water-gates, still wonderfully perfect. We might visit the
site of the meeting of its last parliament, speculate upon the
locality of its mint, or enumerate the various coinages struck
there; we might occupy pages with its annals; the miracles
said to be wrought in its abbeys; the sieges which it sustained;
the plagues with which it was visited; and the conflagrations
which it suffered;—but neither our space nor the object of
this book admit of this.

Somewhat less than a mile below Trim, within a magnificent
sweep of the river, and beside the bridge of Newtown, on both
sides of which they extend, we find a group of monastic remains which, with the exception of the Yellow Steeple, far
surpass any of those now existing at Trim ; the abbey of St.
Peter and St. Paul, with the remains of the ancient cloister;
and the broad parterre, or terrace, which stretched down to the
water's edge, and where the good monks of old quaffed their
wine by the banks of the Boyne, in the calm summer evenings,
before the vesper bell summoned the community to worship.
Unlike the military and ecclesiastical ruins of many other localities in Ireland, choked by the dilapidated buildings of some
wretched dirty town, like the rank weeds of a neglected garden obscuring its urns and statues, those of Newtown-Trim
stand alone and distinct on a swelling bank of the river, whose
stream seems here to linger by them, as if in memory of their
by-gone splendour, and stretch, without even a wall or fence
to break the foreground, over nearly an acre of the richest turf,
and surrounded by the greenest verdure in the broad plains
of Meath.

In 1206 the English prelate, Simon de Rochfort, already
mentioned, founded here an abbey of Canons Regular, of the
order of St. Victor, and removed the episcopal see of Clonard
to this spot. This haughty churchman, who appears to have
enjoyed the confidence and support of the powerful De Lacys,
seems to have possessed almost unbounded sway in the province
of Meath at this period. He abolished several of the minor
bishoprics, and had himself created sole Bishop of Meath,

under which title his successors* sat next in rank to the archbishops, as lords spiritual in the Irish Parliament; and he appears to have assumed an authority over the Irish clergy in
this part of the kingdom, little inferior to that which the newly-
imported Norman barons did over the laity.   His settlement
here, under the very walls of the time-honoured chapels and
priories of Trim, the foundations of Patrick and his immediate
successors, must have been no small cause of offence to the
jealous churchmen of that ancient town; but, like the dust of
their founders, both are now

" Mingled in peace."

The principal ruins consist of the monastery, with its usual
appendages, and the remains of the ancient cathedral of St.
Peter and St. Paul, which is one of the most elegant structures,
and perhaps one of the very earliest specimens of the light
pointed Gothic, in the kingdom.   Portions of the southern
wall, and of the eastern and western ends, still remain. Ivies,

centuries old, of enormous size, yet still of the freshest green,
cluster round and mantle over these ruins, particularly about
the eastern window, which now lies open to the ground, and is

---

* Dr. Lanigan, however, states that, in or " about 1194, died Eugene,
Bishop of Clonard, who, a little before his death, assumed the title of Bishop
of Meath, which his successors have since used ;" the same authority believed
that this title was used by Bishop Idunan, as far back as the year 1096.

some fifty feet in height, affording, in several points of view, those beauteous framings to the neighbouring landscapes to which we already alluded.

> " Where the ivy hangs in masses,
>   Like a clustering mantle thrown,
> And the many-feathered grasses
>   Quiver o'er the sculptured stone.
>
> On the desolation stealing,
>   With a step of mournful grace,
> All the harsher tints concealing
>   Of each ruin's blanching face."

In the walls of a small parish church adjoining are seen the sculptured tomb of one of the mitred ecclesiastics, besides several portions of beautifully carved imposts, flowery capitals, highly decorated mouldings, and other fragments of the abbey, several of which have been, within the last few years, erected there by the same friendly hand which has done so much to preserve the ruins of Trim.

In front of this chapel we find the noble monument of the Dillons, which, with its fine bas reliefs, and its numerous armorial bearings, would take pages to describe. It is the " remains of a tomb erected to the memory of Sir Lucas Dillon, Chief Baron of the Exchequer in the reign of Queen Elizabeth, and the trusted friend of Sir Henry Sidney. It is an altar tomb, with the recumbent figures of Sir Lucas and his lady, Jane Bath, and adorned with the arms of the Dillons, Baths, and Barnewalls, and with a shield bearing two bends.

" Sir Robert Dillon, father of Sir Lucas, was Attorney-General to Henry VIII.; and, at the dissolution of the monasteries, received from that king a grant of the lands of Newtown, where his brother Thomas was prior in 1511. Sir Lucas, in 1568, had a grant of the abbey of the Virgin Mary of Trim, and of the towns of Ladyrath, Grange of Trim, Canonstown, and Rathnally. He was the builder of the house of Moymett, and was the father of the first Earl of Roscommon."

The inscription, which is now defaced, is thus given by Lodge (Roscommon) :

> " ' Militis hic Lucæ Dillonis ossa quiescunt,
> Conciliis Regni summus, Buroq. supremus
> Mense Februarii decimus cum septimus instat,
> Tempora lustrali profusus flumine clausit,
> Terrenos linquens cælestes sumpsit honores."

Much of the adjoining ground is still used as a graveyard, and we regret to see throughout several fragments of the ancient sculpture used as head-stones by the people. This destruction, which has proceeded for so many years in all similar localities in the country, has in no small degree conduced to the dilapidation of several of our finest monasteries. Scarcely a day passes but several of the carved stones, and portions of doors and windows, are rudely torn from their situations, to be placed as head-stones; and some means, though late, should even now be taken to rescue these remains from further demolition. Even the ancient tombstones, many of which contained valuable Irish inscriptions, have been removed, defaced, or broken.[*] The graveyard of Clonmacnoise affords a true and lamentable intance of what we assert; and many of the jambs and window-sills to the wretched cabins in the village of Cong, in the county of Mayo, are formed of portions of the beautifully carved pillars and cut stones of the neighbouring abbey.

Archdall, on the authority of King, relates the history of a desperate murder committed at Newtown in 1307, when several of the friars, rebelling against the prior, killed two or three of their brethren, who endeavoured to oppose their entrance to the cellar. A synod was held here in 1216; and in 1486 one of its priors, Thomas Scurlock, was made Treasurer of Ireland. In

---

[*] On a small tablet in the little church at Newtown we find the following inscription, which, in honour to the learned author, and because some barbarian has recently endeavoured to deface it, we here insert:

> " HAS ANTIQUÆ PIETATIS ET ARTIS RELIQUIAS
> VICINI MONASTERII SS. PETRO ET PAULO DEDICATI
> OLIM ORNAMENTA
> PROSTRATAS DIU ET PENE DETRITAS
> PARIETIBUS HUJUS ECCLESIÆ
> INFIGENDAS CURAVIT R. B. VICAR DE TRIM.
> A. D. M.DCCC.XLII."

1488 its prior received the royal pardon, like those of his brethren, at Trim, for being concerned in the rebellion of Lambert Simnel. Its last prior was Laurence White, who surrendered this priory and its possessions in June, 1533; and three years afterwards this house was suppressed by Parliament, and granted to King Henry VIII., when the establishment was found to consist of " a church, two towers, an hall, storehouse, kitchen, brewhouse, two granaries, a pigeon-house and haggart; also of four messuages, twenty acres of arable land, being part of their demesne on the south side of the river Boyne ; seventy acres of arable land, twelve of pasture, being part of the said demesne on the north side of the Boyne ; and the close, containing an acre of pasture; with three gardens in Newtown : annual value, besides reprisals, one hundred and one shillings and four pence;" besides above 550 acres of some of the finest land in Meath, a castle, several villages, gardens, and messuages, in different parts of the adjoining country. So that this must have been one of the richest monastic establishments in Ireland.[*]

A few hundred yards further on, beyond the old bridge, on the southern side of the river, are the castle-like remains, consisting of a large square keep, immediately adjoining the bridge, with square towers at two of its angles; and somewhat lower down the river, but connected with it by a range of buildings, we meet a second smaller tower. Besides these, the walls of this extensive enclosure contain the ruins of a small chapel, with a beautiful triple window; and also a light circular turret by the roadside, which probably commanded the gate. This must have been always an important post, as it commanded one of the approaches to Trim; and the church militant here could have afforded every necessary protection to the extensive ecclesiastical establishments adjoining. The Hospital or Priory of St. John the Baptist stood here, and some of the remains which still exist within the general enclosure were erected in the thirteenth century for friars of the order of Cross-bearers, or Crouched Friars, a fraternity who wore a cross embroidered on their habit, and devoted themselves to the redemption of Christian captives.

---

[*] The ruins of Newtown form fruitful subjects for the painter. In the exhibition of paintings, at present open in Dublin, may be seen a very charming little sketch of these ruins by Mr. Connolly.

CHAPTER V.

FROM TRIM TO NAVAN.

SCURLOGSTOWN; ITS TUMULUS, CHURCH, AND CASTLE.—TRUBLY.—BECTIVE ABBEY.—INTERMENT OF HUGH DE LACY.—CLADY; ITS SUBTERRANEAN CHAMBERS, CHURCH, AND ANCIENT FOOT-BRIDGE.—THE HOUSE OF CLETTY.—RIVERSTOWN CASTLE.—TARA; ITS HISTORY AND ASSOCIA-TIONS; ITS TOPOGRAPHY.—RATHS.—THE LIA-FAIL.—SKREEN.—HYMN OF ST. PATRICK.—ARD-SALLAGH.—ST. BRIDGET'S WELL.—KILCARN FONT.—ATHLUMNEY CASTLE; ITS LAST OCCUPANT. —NAVAN; RECENT DISCOVERIES THERE.

Passing down the river from Newtown-Trim, its banks assume a more elevated and broken appearance,—now swelling gradually into long, undulating mounds, some of which have been lately planted, and now depressing into broad meadows, while the stream itself quickens its course, and its waters assume a brighter and more limpid character, but still dotted with islands, as in the previous portions of its course. Crowning the hill occupied by Newpark demesne, upon the northern bank, which will be found the most convenient route for the tourist, we find a very perfect circular military fort; and a little further down, upon its southern side, another group of ruins and ancient remains claims our attention, — the old castle, church, and mills of Scurlogstown, which here present from the river's bank an exceedingly picturesque appearance.

In connexion with the neighbouring streamlet and mills, below the latter, in a deep, sequestered nook, formed by one of the niches in the river's bank, we find one of those sepulchral mounds or barrows, so common along the Boyne, and beside it the site from which another was a few years ago removed for the purpose of manuring the adjoining fields. Some of the large flag-stones, which, no doubt, assisted to form the kistvaen, or central chamber, are still resting on the spot.*

A little above the mill may be seen the ancient church,—one of those small early chapels with a circular chancel arch, and a trefoil east window, not uncommon in this part of the king-

---

* This tumulus, the well-marked and extensive remains on the hill of Carbury, the military rath at Clonard, the ancient Pagan remains at Clady, below Bective, the remains of the great rath at Teltown, and that at Donaghpatrick, are the only structures of that nature which we have not found marked on the Ordnance Maps.

dom; and in the adjoining graveyard we lately observed a considerable portion of an ancient stone cross used as a head-stone;—a relic in all probability older than the church itself. This was one of the smallest of our early churches, not being much above thirty feet in length. It is very likely as old as the twelfth century, and was granted to the Abbey of St. Thomas, in Dublin, in the beginning of the thirteenth century, by Walter de Lacy.

The castle of Scurlogs-town, here figured, stands by the roadside, and commands a most extensive prospect around; and though possessing but little architectural adornment, its outline is particularly pleasing. It was one of the strongest-built watch-towers of the Pale, and its having so few external apertures, its massive and gloomy walls, its tall towers, and unbroken battlements, give it such a stern appearance that on passing it one still expects to hear the warder's challenge from its gate. It was built in 1180, by William de Scarlog, one of the Anglo-Norman fiefs of Meath. Its outward wall is still quite perfect, as are also some of its stone floors; it may be considered the type of several other English castles in this part of the country, as, for instance, at Asigh and Trubly, &c.; consisting of a square keep or donjon, with round towers at the diagonal corners; these turrets, having circular stairs in them, were entered by small doors from each of the floors, and they rise somewhat above the height of the square portion of the castle. A perpendicular crack traverses the entire extent of the eastern wall of this building, said to have been caused by the balls of Cromwell, whose progress up the Boyne from Trubly, where he slept the night after the siege of Drogheda, the constable of Scurlog's castle was hardy enough to challenge; but, like many similar recitals of Cromwell's

" crowning mercies" in Ireland, this rests for its authority more upon tradition than written history. Indeed we know nothing more required than an essay upon Cromwell's Irish campaign. Materials there are in abundance, but scattered throughout several works, and contained in State Papers, and other materials, to which, we are quite sure, an author could have ready access; and yet it is one of the most defective portions of modern Irish history.*

We have here another example of the connexion and combination of ancient and modern remains to which we have already alluded:—a pass upon the Boyne, memorable, no doubt, in some ancient Irish saga, as the scene of hostile fray by its banks; a tumulus covering the sepulchre of the slain ; a Christian era antecedent to the Church, marked by the rude cross we spoke of ; the early Church itself telling of the simple purity and religion of our forefathers; the gaunt, warlike form of the ancient castle pointing out the epoch of the great English invasion, and its walls bearing evidence of the Protector's rule.

The next point of beauty is Rathnally, where the banks rise on both sides to a considerable elevation; and here some noble trees in the surrounding demesne, clad in the livery of summer, with the highly cultivated state of the grounds,—the deep, sullen waters of the river,—the calm, Sabbath stillness of the scene, broken only by the cawing of the rooks, and the interrupted craik of the meadow rail,—the long, dark vistas through which the stream winds,—and the picturesque view of the adjoining mills and mansion, form one out of the many charming landscapes which now adorn the Boyne, not here alone, but almost throughout the entire of the remainder of its course.

> " Oh! so green is the grass, so clear is the stream,
> So mild is the mist, and so rich is the beam,
> That beauty should ne'er to other lands roam,
> But make on the banks of *this* river its home."†

Not only is the transition in the scenery of this,—the second division of the Boyne,—well marked, and totally distinct from

---

* Our learned friend Mr. Hardiman has made a collection of all the documents relating to Cromwell in Ireland, and it is hoped that the Irish Archæological Society will have funds sufficient to publish them.

† The Banks of the Lee, by Thomas Davis.

the previously described portion of the river, but the whole appearance of the country changes, and an air of healthy prosperity, marked by the high state of cultivation, prevails, which is in vain sought for between Clonard and Trim.

Mr. and Mrs. Hall, in their charming book on Ireland, speaking of this district, remark : " The hedges are remarkably luxuriant; the trees (of which there is an unusual abundance) are of extraordinary growth; and the fields have at all times and seasons that brilliant green so refreshing to the eye, and so cheering to the mind, when associated with ideas of comfort and prosperity. There is indeed no part of Ireland where the Englishman will find himself so completely at home ; for, added to great natural beauty, he sees on all sides the beneficial results of careful cultivation, and marks, in every direction, the ordinary consequences of industry directed by science; while the poverty and wretchedness that are elsewhere forced upon his attention is here so seldom perceptible, and the clamorous voice of woe 'rarely intruded upon the ear.' "*

Such, in particular, is the character of the scenery at the next point of interest as well as beauty—Trubly,—the river being here also completely shut out by its towering, wooded banks, from the roadside view. On a high, commanding knoll, on the southern bank of the Boyne, we still find in the haggard of its proprietor some remnant of the castle of Trubly, or Tubberville, the ancient seat of the Cusacks, who possessed it as early as the time of Richard II. This originally consisted of a square keep, with circular corner towers, like that of Scurlogstown; the foundations of the former can still be traced, and about twenty feet of one of the latter is yet standing, looking, at some distance, and in some points of view, very like the butt or lower portion of a round tower. This is the castle which Cromwell is reported to have slept in on his march up the Boyne. Adjoining it is another isolated circular tower, erected for a dove-cote, or pigeon-house; it is one of the most ancient and best built structures of that description in the kingdom, and resembles very much the dove-cote in one of the towers in the outer wall of Trim castle.

By an inquisition of 1663, the possessor of Trubly was found

---

* Ireland ; its Scenery, Character, &c. By Mr. and Mrs. S. C. Hall. Vol. ii. p. 373.

guilty of high treason; and in the charter of James the Second, Nicholas Cusack, one of Tyrconnell's captains, who owned this castle at that period, was nominated Portrieve of Trim; but at what period this border fortress was destroyed, whether from storm or by gradual dilapidation, does not appear.

Stanihurst says that in his time the Irish, by which term he must mean the retainers, servants, and villagers in the vicinity, " merely passed the night in these castles; the day was spent in mud walls covered with thatch, adjoining the castle and the bawn, which was surrounded with a hedge and ditch, and into which the cattle were driven in time of alarm. At night there was always a watchman on the top of the castle."

Trubly is three miles from Trim, and about a mile further down the river we again cross the stream, by the bridge of Bective, to visit the noble ruin beside it, which gives name to this locality and title to an Earl. As we approach from Trubly, the southern road cuts through a very fine mound of the sepulchral kind,—indeed one of the largest, though not the highest, on this part of the Boyne,—although diminutive in comparison with those which shall engage our attention lower down. Partly for the gravel and small stones, of which it is for the most part composed, and partly from excavations made by the peasantry seeking for treasure, at various times, the top of this mound has been removed. There exist many legends in the country about this ancient cemetery, kept up by the idle dreams of an imaginative people, and these, coupled with the fact of some antique articles of value having been occasionally discovered there, have conduced, in no small degree, to cause these excavations, and thus to lessen its size. But we have heard of the doings of road contractors,—and the intentions of grand juries also!—with regard to the employment of the stones which form similar structures in other parts of Meath, which should awaken the attention of those whose patriotism (for this really is one of the instances to which that term may at present be applied) is greater than their agricultural or macadamizing speculations. From this mound we obtain a charming prospect of the yellow battlemented walls and lichen-clad cloisters of the abbey; and at a point nearly equidistant from the river, on the opposite bank, may be seen a fine specimen of the military raths or duns of the ancient colony who first passed up and settled upon this river's borders.

From the bridge of Bective, or Begty, situate midway between Trim and Navan, we obtain a pleasing view of the adjoining abbey, upon the left bank of the river. From this
point the ruins present an imposing and picturesque appearance of a noble castellated mansion, rearing high its turrets,
gables, and chimneys, and showing that its architect had both
comfort and security in view. The tints which usually play
upon the walls of Bective are of a richer and more varying
hue than we have ever seen elsewhere. The square grey towers,
gables, and chimneys, rendered in some parts perfectly golden
by the most brilliant orange and yellow lichens, and in parts
festooned with the dark-green drapery of the Irish ivy, rising
out of the light feathery foliage of a plantation of young larch,
and standing in the midst of a field of corn, which stretches
between the ruins and the blue waters of the Boyne, form,
upon a summer's evening, one of the most lovely objects in
nature.

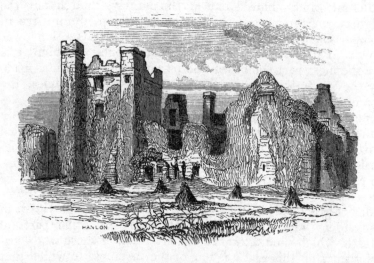

The ruins of this great Cistercian monastery are among the
most perfect in Meath, and enough still remains to enable the
tourist to decide, with a tolerable degree of certainty, upon the
original use of each compartment, and every room and cell in
the building; and as the present proprietor has enclosed them
with a wall, they are less desecrated than most of the ecclesiastical remains in Ireland. It is a fact, strange but true, that

the peasant, who will not (or rather who heretofore would not), for love or money, touch a stone, or remove a mound believed to be of Pagan origin, will wantonly pollute, or, for ordinary building purposes, dilapidate the noblest monastic structure, or the most sacred Christian edifice !

Around the ruins of Bective Abbey a young plantation is yearly obscuring its fair proportions. The dark, wide-spreading yew, the gnarled oak, the stunted elder, or the blasted ash, form fit companions for the crumbling wall and falling arch; but those young trees are anything but suited to the locality, and will, in a short time, completely hide the lower portions of this noble pile. Whether domestic comforts, more than piety and self-mortification, influenced the founders and early tenants of this monastery, or that the condition of the country at the time required a castellated mansion for defence, rather than an edifice erected for the service of religion, it is difficult to say; but certain it is that while we are able satisfactorily to trace the various halls, corridors, kitchens, galleries, courts, dormitories, and cloisters, it is with great difficulty we can decide upon the situation of the church. Two tall, lancet-shaped arches outside the enclosure on the northeastern side, and the remains of a handsome window, which splays outward from the great court of the building, would lead us to conjecture that it must have been situate adjoining that point. Some have, however, supposed that it stood over the gallery which formed the southern enclosure of the courtyard.

This abbey, called in Irish Sendrede, or " the Old Bridge," was founded from Mellifont, in the middle of the twelfth century, by Murchard O'Melaghlin, King of Meath, for monks of the great Cistercian order,* under the title of the Abbey de Beatitudine, and dedicated to the Virgin. The endowment was remarkably rich, the demesne consisting of 245 acres, besides a mill and fishing weir on the Boyne. The lord abbot of Bective sat as a spiritual peer in Parliament, one of the fifteen abbots then entitled to that dignity in Ireland.

There is a remarkable historic incident attached to this ancient house. After the murder of Hugh de Lacy at Durrow, in 1186, an account of which we gave at page 91, the body was

---

* It is the only Cistercian building in Meath. See Grace's Annals, p. 107.

not recovered till 1195, when " the Archbishop of Cashel, Legate of Ireland, and John Archbishop of Dublin, brought from the Irish country the body of Hugh Lacy (who had conquered Meath), and buried it in the Abbey Beatitudine, that is, of Bective; his head they buried in the church of St. Thomas, Dublin."* Now, as this latter establishment had been founded by one of the Anglo-Norman barons, William Fitz-Adelm, a companion of the great Palatine, by whom also it was largely endowed, the brotherhood of St. Thomas claimed the rest of the remains from the monks at Bective. As we already remarked at page 93, a fierce controversy ensued amongst the rival churchmen on this subject, as to which abbey should possess both the relics; and, as in all Irish ecclesiastical disputes, then, as now, the Pope was appealed to for his decision. Innocent III. appointed the celebrated Simon Rochfort, then Bishop of Meath, and his archdeacon, together with Gilebert, the prior of Duleek, to arbitrate between the belligerents, and they awarded the corpse to the monks of St. Thomas, to which place it was accordingly removed. Such was the estimation in which the remains of a viceroy were held in Ireland in the twelfth century!

An arcade of pointed cinquefoil arches, supported by light clustered pillars, decorated with elegantly carved capitals, separates the cloister from the court-yard or quadrangle, on the southern side; and beneath one of these tradition says that the great Lord Palatine was buried. The carving of this colonnade is, from the hardness of the Ardbraccan stone, of which it is built, and the sharpness of the cutting, in fine preservation, and well worthy the attention of the archæological and antiquarian student. On the extreme western pilaster

---

* See Grace's Annals of Ireland. A portion of this abbey of St. Thomas, now Thomas's Court, was remaining within the memory of man. In the incident related above, we have quoted the circumstances as they are set forth in records acknowledged to be authentic; but, at the same time, we are inclined to question the chronology of the documents relied on by Irish historians, for if the body and head of De Lacy were thrown into the ditch, and endeavoured to be concealed by the Irish, it is not likely that they could have been identified nine years after; and the very fact of the head having been removed to Dublin, while the body was carried elsewhere, induces us to believe that the interment of both took place immediately after the murder. It is possible, however, that the body may have been originally interred at the cemetery at Durrow.

we find a figure, cut in relief, of an abbot, and above it a shield enclosing three fleur-de-lis, probably the arms of the prelate interred beneath, for we know that underneath these arcades the ecclesiastics of olden time were wont to place their most venerated dead.

The great tower at the entrance above the porch is still very perfect, and by its loop-holes and battlements shows that the inmates were, occasionally at least, entitled to be considered a part of the church militant. It has been said that a portion of this abbey was erected prior to the date of the English invasion, and that Grecian architects were employed in its construction, but upon what authority we have not been able to discover.

The annals of Bective present us with nearly the same amount of history as those preserved of similar establishments of the same era along the Boyne and elsewhere; and their detail, though highly valuable in eking out the history of the country, would be uninteresting to the general reader; charters, grants of lands, endowments, and forfeitures; bulls of Popes, and letters of kings; excommunications and interdictions; pillagings; disputes with neighbouring powers, rival ecclesiastical establishments, exacting chieftains, or rude military commanders; observances of festivals; solemn interments; the preservation of relics, and the records of the accession and deaths of superiors, forming the great bulk of such materials.

There is a small hamlet near the bridge to which the name of Bective is given; and the family of Taylor derive the title of Earl from this locality.

From Bective to Navan the Boyne sweeps gracefully through a highly cultivated country; and its banks are adorned, throughout the entire length of this portion of its course, by the grounds and plantations of noble parks and demesnes, as those of Balsoon, Bective, Bellinter, Dowdstown, and Ardsallagh. The banks are not high or abrupt, but form pleasing slopes and gentle undulations of surface; here stretching out into broad lawns, and there fringed with aged trees, which, with the handsome mansions of the neighbouring proprietors, give the whole very much the appearance of the inland scenery of England. It is not the peculiar feature of any one of these seats that engenders this idea, but it is the general continuity of style, and the effect which the demesne on one side lends to that on the other, together combining to shut out the surrounding country, which produces this beauty, and that keeps the stream still flowing onward for several miles of its course through a succession of picturesque landscapes in this charming valley.

Near the Navan road, upon the northern bank of the river, not far from the abbey, we find one of those early military raths, so common throughout Meath; and about three-quarters of a mile below Bective bridge, on the same side, upon a small tongue of land which runs out between a tributary streamlet and the river, some very interesting and hitherto almost unnoticed remains, both Pagan and Christian, claim our attention. These consist of the old church and bridge of Clady, and some subterranean structures lately discovered in the immediate vicinity. The church, which is now a complete ruin, was originally a parallelogram, with a projection at the south-eastern side—a sort of transept—and a bell-turret upon the western gable; but although we are able to trace the outline of this building throughout, the only portion of much interest spared by the hand of time is a very beautiful window, in the south chapel, the stone frame-work of which is still very perfect. It consists of two cinquefoiled arches, in the " early English" style, separated by a light shaft. The carvings on the round capitals are rich and tasteful. An aged elder-bush overshadowing and partly protruding through these lights, serves to heighten the effect of the picture, while a patriarchal ash, of gigantic dimensions, spreads its rugged arms over the adjoining graveyard. That many such windows as that we have described must have existed in this church originally, may be learned from the quantity of fragments, exhibiting the same form of mouldings and carving, which are scattered around, or partly sunk in the ground, as head-stones. A hollow stone, apparently an ancient lavatory or a piscina, is still remaining in the enclosure, on the northern side. Mr. Bolton, in whose demesne the church stands, has lately, with laudable zeal, removed the font to his garden, to preserve it from utter demolition, and being literally ground away; for it had been used by the adjoining peasantry for years as a rub or whetstone, as all loiterers in ancient churchyards must be aware has been the fate of many a similar sacred vessel. It is perfectly plain, octagon in shape, and measures two feet five inches in diameter. It is evidently of great antiquity; and the size of its basin rather favours the idea which we already stated when alluding to the font at Clonard, that immersion was, in all probability, the form of baptism employed by the early Irish Christians. Now that Mr. Bolton has enclosed his demesne, and that the same means of access for mere knife-grinding purposes have ceased to exist, we confess we should like to see this relic restored to its ancient and original site.

The accompanying graphic and faithful sketch, will afford the reader a tolerable idea of this interesting group of ruins.

The adjoining stream is crossed by an ancient stone footbridge, about thirty yards in length, and supported by two arches of different shapes. It is about five feet in breadth, and does not appear to have ever had a parapet. It is one of the very few foot-bridges which we have ever seen or heard of in this country; and if it is coeval with the church to which it leads, and which in all probability it is, it cannot be denied that this is the most ancient stone bridge now existing in Ireland.

In an adjoining plantation, and not above a stone's throw from the church, were lately discovered two subterranean chambers. Each of these crypts is formed entirely of un-hewn stones, arranged in the shape of a bee-hive dome, but without mortar or cement, the arch being formed by each tier of stones projecting somewhat within or beyond that beneath, and the summit completed by a large flag, the whole structure being preserved by the pressure and weight of the surround-ing earth, for these chambers are quite below the surface; and it was owing to the accidental circumstance of a cow having pressed in one of the top stones, that a knowledge of their ex-istence was obtained. The first chamber is nine feet broad, and the walls are not indented by either niches or minor crypts. From the floor to the summit measures upwards of nine feet; but owing to the drifting of some fine sand into the interior of these chambers and passages, their apparent altitude is at pre-sent much less. A small quadrangular passage, nine feet in length, two and a half high, and three broad, and roofed with large flag-stones laid upon the flat, runs in a northerly direc-tion to another chamber, exactly similar in every respect, but without any other passage leading from it. From the first chamber, a second gallery branches off in a westerly direction, to a distance of about fifteen feet, where its dimensions increase considerably; but from the roof having fallen in, it is not pos-sible at present to investigate it much further. We under-stand that these chambers were found in this condition when first opened, a few years ago, and did not contain either wea-pons, ornaments, or any animal remains, which could in any way assist us in pronouncing upon their probable use. Still the antiquary will speculate upon the purposes for which such structures were erected, their ages, and the people by whom they were built. They differ from the sepulchral caves in that the dome springs directly from the floor, and not from a course of upright pillars, such as we find at New Grange, Dowth, and elsewhere; and in not possessing niches, or minor chambers, which some of the smallest of these latter do, as that in Net-terville Park, to which we shall presently allude. The stones are also much smaller, and totally devoid of carvings; and the existence of passages from one to the other, as well as these chambers being sunk in the earth, and not surrounded by a distinct mound of clay or stones, serve to distinguish them from those of the sepulchral class. There can be little doubt that they are to be referred to Pagan times, before the use of the arch, or the advantages of mortar, were known, and were probably employed by some of the very early people of this island as places of security, temporary habitations, and granaries, for which latter purpose their dryness well fitted them. The two chambers and the passages just described are, in all probability, but portions of a large collection of other souterrains adjoining; and some elevations of the ground in the neighbouring plantation, which have a remarkably hollow sound, lend probability to this conjecture. It is not unlikely to have been a troglodyte village, used as a granary as well as a hiding-place, by some of our Firbolg or Tuatha De Danaan aborigines. The place is well worthy of further investigation in these days of scientific antiquarian research; and we are sure the proprietor would willingly aid such an undertaking.

Several subterranean chambers and passages, some of them similarly constructed, exist in Connaught and Munster; they are generally formed in the raised embankment, or within the precincts of an ancient fort or rath, and are by the peasants invariably attributed to the Danes, although we have no authority whatever for such a supposition. Within some of these have been found quantities of animal remains, those of goats and oxen in particular, besides quantities of charcoal, and very often small tobacco-pipes. Sir Thomas Molyneux gave a very accurate description of these caves and galleries, upwards of 120 years ago, in his "Discources concerning the Danish Mounds, Forts, and Towers in Ireland."* Most probably a rath existed here in former times, but the planting and the very great alteration of the surface at present prevents its being discerned. A somewhat similar chamber may be seen in the vicinity of Navan, somewhat lower down upon the Boyne. It is figured in Mr. Wakeman's Archæologia Hibernica,† and

---

* Dublin : printed by and for George Grierson, at the Two Bibles, in Essex-street, 1725; and reprinted in Boate and Molyneux's Natural History of Ireland. See also the Author's Memoirs of Sir Thomas Molyneux, in the Dublin University Magazine for 1841, vol. xviii.

† *Archæologia Hibernica :* A Hand-Book of Irish Antiquities, Pagan and Christian, especially of such as are easy of access from the Irish Metropolis. By William F. Wakeman. With numerous Illustrations. Dublin : McGlashan. 1848.

Mr. T. Crofton Croker has given an interesting account of several in the county of Cork.*

Two of the most celebrated Irishmen of early times died on the Boyne's bank: Finn Mac Cumhaill, the renowned warrior, popularly known as Fin-ma-Cool, who was killed with a dart or gaff by a fisherman named Athlach, at Ath-Brea or Rath-Breagha,† and also his father-in-law, King Cormac Mac Art, the grandson of Con of the Hundred Battles, who died from a fish-bone having stuck in his throat. The circumstances attending the death of the latter are here worth recording. He was one of the most renowned, just, and wise of the monarchs of Tara, and is said to have been the third person who accepted Christianity in Erin before the time of Patrick. One of his eyes having been destroyed by the warrior Engus Gaibhuaibhnech, he afterwards generally resided at Acaill (now Skreen), at Kells, or at the *House of Cletty* (Cletigh, Cleiteach, or Cletech), as "it was not lawful that a king with a personal blemish should reside at Tara."‡ Two years after the loss of his eye, he was suffocated, from the bone of a salmon having stuck in his throat, at this House of Cletty, the site of which has not yet been determined by topographers. The name, the situation, and the remains at Clady, afford us, however, some clue to it. In several Irish manuscripts, both in prose and verse, this house is alluded to as being over or above the Boyne ("Cletig supra Boin"), and in the vicinity of Tara, to both of which circumstances this place accurately answers; but furthermore we learn something of its precise locality from the account given of the death of King Muircheartach Mac Earca, nearly two centuries and a half after the time of Cormac. He was burned to death in the House of Cletty, by his mistress Sheen, after the battle of Kirb,—a spot believed to be Assey, upon the opposite side of the Boyne. St. Cairneach, of Tuilen (now Dulane, near Kells), cursed the place, and it was soon after deserted. His prophecy is recorded in the Annals of Tighernach. King Cormac's death took place, according to the Four Masters, A. D. 266, " at Cleiteach, the bone

---

* See the Dublin Penny Journal, vol. iii. p. 350.

† See the Annals of the Four Masters, A. D. 284; and the Annals of Innisfallen, quoted by O'Donovan, in a note to the above.

‡ See History of the Cemeteries in the *Leabhar na h-Uidhre,* a translation of which is given in Petrie's Round Towers.

of a salmon sticking in his throat, on account of the Sibhradh [Genii], which Malgeen, the Druid, had incited at him, after Cormac had turned against the Druids, on account of his adoration of God in preference to them."

The situation of Cletty is described in the historical tale entitled Oighidh Muircheartaigh Mhoir mhic Earca, thus : " Good indeed was the situation of that house over the margin of the salmon-full, ever-beautiful Boyne, and over the verge of the green-topped Brugh." This latter place, is, however, against our theory, but so is it against the situation of Cletty assigned by others to the vicinity of Stackallan Bridge,* and there may have been, and no doubt were, more Brughs or forts than one. This inquiry is well worthy of further investigation.

Below Clady, some high, precipitous banks arise, upon the northern side of the river, near Bective House ; and upon the opposite hill, two sites, of considerable interest, claim our attention,—Balsoon and Asigh or Assey. The former was once the residence of Archbishop Ussher, and its ruined church and ancient graveyard are still worthy of a visit. The latter, called in Irish *Ath-Sighe*, consists of the ruins of a castle, originally constructed upon the type of those at Scurlogstown and Trubly, a square keep, with circular flanking towers at the eastern and western angles.† Like other castles of the Pale, its summit commands a most extended view, including a long reach of the river both above and below this point. On the slope leading down to the river we meet with a small group of ecclesiastical ruins, portions of the walls of one of the early missionary churches: the middle wall, with a square doorway, occupying the place of a choir arch; and some broken fragments of stone mouldings, with a surrounding graveyard. Several noble ash trees, which seem the peculiar growth of the valley of the Boyne, shelter this ruined chapel; and the luxuriant crop of white lichens, which have crept over the walls and adjacent tombstones, give this place an air of great antiquity.

As the Boyne passes through the noble demesne of Bellinter, it is again broken into islands, a group of which, nearly oppo-

---

* See O'Donovan's Note on Cleiteach in the Annals; and also the Banquet of Dun na nGedh, and the Battle of Magh Rath, pp. 19, 20.

† The plan of these Boyne fortresses consisting of square keeps, with circular turrets at the corners, is well shown in the ruins adjoining the Church of Lusk, where an ancient Round Tower is used as one of the flanking towers.

site Mr. Preston's house, are planted with considerable taste. This residence, which was once the seat of the lords of Tara, was designed by Mr. Cassells, and is one of the finest specimens of domestic architecture in this part of Meath. It consists of a large square central building, with a projecting wing on each side, connected to it by a colonnade. The southern road to Navan presents the traveller with a fine view of this mansion and the intervening park.

Turning southward from Bellinter Bridge, as we begin to ascend the hill towards Tara, the castle of Riverstown, about a mile and a half from the Boyne's brink, will be found well worthy of inspection. This was one of the best built castles upon the Boyne; and the remains which still exist, in the perfection of their masonry, and the sharpness and beauty of their lines, still bear witness to the fact. The ruins of this beautiful building show it to have been of the same type as most other castles of the Pale which we have examined, consisting of two portions, an ancient and a modern. The former is a massive square tower, entirely built of cut or hammered stone, with three square turrets at the corners, which batter very much toward the foundation, and at top rise several feet above the principal part of the building. The eastern turret was originally a pigeon-house, and that on the west side contained a spiral staircase which led to a parapet at top. These turrets were lighted by small square windows and loop-holes, and were, as well as the central tower, divided into four floors and an attic. In the wall of each of these turrets we find one of these chimney-like, concealed flues, or upright passages, common in some of the ancient castles, and popularly known among the people as "murder-holes." This part of the castle was inhabited within the last eighty years, and portions of the plaster still remain upon the interior of the walls. The more modern portion abutted against the western wall of the tower, and shows, by the two gable-grooves, which are still visible in the latter, that it was erected or re-edified at different periods; and this conjecture is further supported by the fact of the existence of a large stone-arched keep, still remaining on the north-western side. Portions of the wall of the bawn can still be traced in the surrounding farm-yard.

By whom, or at what precise time, the original castle of Riverstown was built, we have no means of ascertaining, but we know that in the sixteenth century it was in the possession of the Dillons. In the churchyard of Tara may be seen the monument of Robert Dillon of Riverstown, who died in 1595.

In our passage down the river we have heretofore confined our observations and researches to the scenery in its immediate vicinity, and the objects which presented themselves within view of its banks ; for were we to extend the field of our inquiry beyond this limit, we would have to enlarge this work much beyond the dimensions of a guide-book to the Boyne. In fact, it would become, had we sufficient knowledge of the subject, an antiquarian history of Ireland ; and yet, as we stated at the beginning of this work, such might be written from the ruins still remaining in these localities. Thus, were we inclined to draw upon the sources of early Irish history, from documents of undoubted authenticity, referring to Pagan and early Christian times, and to point with certainty to the evidences which existing remains afford of the truth of the topography, at least, set forth in those early records, the bardic histories, which were written in the few first centuries of the Christian era, we might lead our readers from Bellinter Bridge up a gradual ascent which rises on the right bank of the river, about two miles beyond this spot, and, standing on a commanding eminence, point to the grassy mounds of Tara in proof of our assertion. A full description of this celebrated locality would, however, occupy several chapters. Aroused by the enthusiasm which the very name inspires, we might describe at length the royal residences which once crowned this sacred spot, and still point out the foundations of these very structures. We might recount the monarchs who reigned here, Belgic, Scotic, and Milesian, from the days of Slaigne and Dagda, through the royal line of Temur, to the subversion of Paganism, and the introduction of Christianity into Ireland. We might describe the great *Feis Teamhrach*, or assembly of the chieftains ; and while we hold not with superstitious reverence by all the bardic tales and poetic legends handed down to us for some fifteen centuries, except so far as they accord with common sense, or are borne out by collateral evidence, we could point with pride to the just and wise laws which emanated from the house of Ollamh Fodhla ; we could tell of Con, the warrior of the hundred battles ; of the Druid famed for sorcery ; the Brehon wise in judgments ; the Bard who chronicled in

wild and imaginative song the half fabulous events of a semi-
barbarous age; the Kings renowned in story,—the Cormacs and
Nialls, and Dathis: but now

> " No more to chiefs and ladies bright
>   The harp of Tara swells ;
>   The chord alone that breaks at night
>   Its tale of ruin tells."

We might, by merely paraphrasing the translations of authentic Irish history, occupy pages in recounting the deeds of
Patrick, when he converted the Irish monarch and the whole
court at Tara. We might, even now, preach with the sermons, and enliven modern Christianity with the hymns of our
patron saint. We could tell of the cursing of Temur by St.
Ruadhan, and its subsequent desertion. Or again, we might
trace the various raths, and descant upon the wells and pillar-
stones which consecrate this spot. The Lia Fail, or stone of
destiny, supposed to have been removed to Scone, and from
Scone to Westminster, but which is still, it appears, undoubtedly at Tara, would in itself form a text for an entire
chapter upon the civil history of this kingdom; while the name
of St. Adamnan is a fitting proem for an hour's dissertation on
our early ecclesiastical writings, and the colonies which sprung
from this Isle of Saints, even to the far-famed Iona. Or, to
come down to later years, the graves of the croppies, the lyrics
of Tom Moore, and the monster meetings, would lead us far
beyond the limits of this little work. Were we to allow ourselves the latitude we should desire, or, perhaps, the subject
deserves, we would carry our readers to the opposite hill of
Skreen, the ancient Acaill, and while we pointed out, from that
elevated situation, the extensive prospect of the broad lands
and fair mansions, the castles, churches, and monasteries, so
full of interest in themselves, and such embellishments to the
extended landscape within view, with the " Pleasant Boyne"
gliding smoothly by them, we could also tell of the wonders
of the locality whereon we stood, and call to our readers' recollection the legends about the shrine of Columba, and the
history of the battles fought here by the Ostmen of old, and also
refer to its occupation, in more modern times, by the Feypos,
and Cusacks, and Verdons.

For all that is known, or can, in all probability, be known, of the antiquarian lore, historic records, and topographical details, connected with Tara, we must refer our readers to Dr. Petrie's essay upon the history and antiquities of that ancient seat of learning, wealth, and power, which has been published in the eighteenth volume of the Transactions of the Royal Irish Academy. This essay, while it stamped its author as a most profound scholar, acute observer, and a most honest and laborious searcher after truth, with a mind unbiassed by theory, uninfluenced by the dogma of the schools, or the authority of names, has been of immense value to Irish history, not only on account of the sources of learning which it discloses, but for the lesson it teaches to all future gleaners in this field of patient investigation and judicious critical research. If Dr. Petrie had never written another line, or established another truth, this memoir upon Tara would have established his fame, and formed the model from which the history of Ireland may hereafter be framed or worked out.

Strangers, and foreigners speaking the English language, and Irishmen also, visit the site of this regal city; and some carry with them the quarto volume of the Academy's Transactions, as they would one of " Murray's Hand-books," and expect that it will point out at once, and with but little trouble, all the ancient halls and courts, so poetically described in some of the fanciful histories of Ireland. On the one, however, they find nothing but a collection of earthen mounds and grassy undulations, a few time-worn stones, and an old churchyard, crowning the top of rather an unpicturesque hill; and in the text of the other a mass of what is, to them, dry, unintelligible, documentary evidence, partly written in a language the very characters of which they are unacquainted with, and interspersed with quaint old poems, containing names of men and things quite unpronounceable by their vocal organs. Such casual visiters spend an hour at Tara, and some read the commentary upon it, and acknowledge that they are none the wiser; and this we can fully conceive. To understand the one, and effectually to observe the other, requires a certain amount of schooling in the investigation of the sources of history, an eye practised to the forms of ancient remains, and an ear attuned to the language of archæology; but, even with all or any of these acquirements, there is a feeling, an innate feeling, necessary, which no art can teach, no schooling generate; for there *are* hundreds whose valour or patriotism would *not* be aroused on the field of Marathon, nor their piety awakened amidst the ruins of Iona.

The following brief notice of Tara, intended chiefly as an itinerary, may, however, serve to direct the tourist's attention to the objects best worthy of attention in this celebrated locality.

Retracing our steps for a short way from Riverstown, we meet another ruined fortress at the cross-roads of Castletown, and now we commence the ascent of Tara by the ancient road leading to the north, the *Slighe Fan na g-Carbad*, or Slope of the Chariots, which has been mentioned in the old topographical descriptions of this renowned locality. The first object which demands attention is the *Teach Miodhchuarta*, or great Banqueting Hall, the chief monument of all, which runs north and south, a deep excavation, with parallel sides, rising up a gentle ascent of the hill, 360 feet long, and 40 wide, the sides being formed by a raised *mur*, or earth embankment, in which a number of excavations or gaps may be observed, corresponding to the doors which led into the great hall, "the house of the thousand soldiers," the locality where the Feis Teamhrach, or solemn assembly of Tara, was held. Standing at the top or southern extremity of this remain, and bearing in mind the various prose and bardic histories of the Irish annalists, one cannot help reverting to ancient heroic times, and again, in imagination, peopling it with its early occupants. Here sat in days of yore kings with golden crowns upon their heads; warriors with brazen swords in their hands; bards and minstrels with their harps ; grey-bearded ollamhs; druids with their oak-leaf crowns ; learned historians ; wise brehons and subtle lawyers; the physicians; the smiths, artificers, charioteers, huntsmen, architects; the chess-players and cup-bearers, together with crowds of servants and retainers, whose places are all specified in the ancient annals relating to Tara.* Sneer not at the Irishman's veneration for this spot ; the history of its "long-faded glories" is still preserved; the memories of Tara have remained a silver thread in the garment of sackcloth he has worn for centuries.

---

* We wish our space permitted of our introducing here some of the poems of the Book of Rights, describing the feasts at Teamhair, lately published by the Irish Celtic Society. It should be consulted by every visitor to Tara.

Most probably a wooden building covered in at top extended along the earthen elevations still remaining at the sides of this great banqueting-hall. The prospect from this site now is one of the most extensive and beautiful in Meath, and fully as awakening as that wherewith Demosthenes, standing on the Areopagus, aroused the valour of the ancient Athenians.

In the adjoining field is *Rath Caelchon*, and beyond it are the remains of two circular duns, but greatly obliterated by plantations; one of these is *Rath-Grainne*, and the other, together with the small well of Tober Finn, are now scarcely perceptible; none of these, however, are of sufficient importance to require particular notice in a popular description like the present.

Ascending the slope towards the south we gain the top of the hill, crowned by the *Rath-na-Seanadh*, the Rath of the Synods, or the King's Chair, where it is said the tent of Adamnan was pitched, presenting a double wall of circumvallation, the eastern side of which has been cut off by the adjoining churchyard. Upon this rath in particular, it is more than probable, some of the synods at Tara, in Christian times, were held. It is the highest spot upon the hill, being 512 feet above the level of the sea. The two beautiful gold torques, preserved in the collection of the Royal Irish Academy, were found by a boy in the side of this hill some years ago. Immediately adjoining this elevation stands the modern church, the decorated western window of which was removed from the ruins of an ancient ecclesiastical building which existed here within the present century.* Within the enclosure of the surrounding churchyard we find some objects of antiquarian interest, especially a flat pillar-stone about six feet high, supposed to be the shaft of the cross of St. Adamnan, on the eastern face of which is carved, in relief, a rude human figure, about eighteen inches high.† In its vicinity we find a short

---

* There is a view of this church given in Grose's Antiquities, vol. ii. p. 88.

† This small naked figure, with something like horns upon the head, is from its position evidently one of those curious pieces of ancient sculpture, popularly known in some places as *Sheelah Ny Giggs*, frequently found inserted into the walls of some early Christian buildings, and of which there are one or two specimens in the Museum of the Royal Irish Academy. There is one to be seen built into the side wall of the ruined Church at Dowth facing the Boyne. See the description of that building.

pillar-stone, not unlike some of those at New Grange. This is
supposed to be one of the two druidical stones called *Bloc* and
Bluicni, which used to open out to admit the chariot of the
king at his coronation.

Proceeding still southward we pass into the great oval enclosure of the *Rath na Riogh*, the King's Rath or the Cathair of
Crofinn, the most extensive of all the earthen circles at Tara,
measuring upwards of 280 yards in length in its longest dimensions. It is obliterated in several places, but a sufficiency
still remains to point out its site. Immediately within its northern boundary we find the mound of the hostages, *Dumha-
na-Ngiall*, a small circular moat, so named in memory of the
hostages which King Cormac took from the different provinces,
and on which formerly lay the obelistic monolith, believed to
be the Lia Fail, or Stone of Destiny. Nearly in the centre
we meet the triple enclosure of the *Forradh;* and toward the
south-east and immediately adjoining the latter, the *Teach Cor-
maic*, the House of Cormac.

Between the house of Cormac and the rath of the Forradh
existed, it is supposed, the ruins of *Tea-mur*, from which Temur, or Tara, takes its name, in memory of a Milesian queen
called Tea. In the centre of the internal mound of the Forradh stands an upright stele or cir-
cular pillar-stone, which was formerly on the top of the Mound of
the Hostages, but was removed to
this spot in the year 1798, and
erected as a headstone to the grave
of thirty-seven of the insurgents,
who were killed in a skirmish with
the military in this neighbourhood.
Dr. Petrie supposes this stone to be
the celebrated *Lia Fail*, on which
the early Irish kings were crowned,
and which has been generally believed to have been carried to Scotland for the coronation of Fergus
Mac Eark, and afterwards removed

by Edward I. from Scone to Westminster Abbey. The Lia
Fail was the stone so famed in ancient history, which was said
to have roared beneath the Irish kings at the time of their in-

auguration. For the various authorities bearing upon this point, we must refer our readers to the "History and Antiquities of Tara Hill," already so frequently referred to. We fully acknowledge the force of the reasoning of Dr. Petrie on this subject, and admit the validity of his arguments with respect to the history of the Stone of Destiny, and we must believe that it is not that now in Westminster Abbey; but at the same time we are not by any means convinced that this *round pillar stone,* now placed over the croppies' grave, is *the* stone. Perhaps the *flat sculptured stone,* latterly called the Cross of St. Adamnan, may have been it.*

To the east of the Forradh, immediately adjoining the road, is the Well of Neamhnach [*Newnagh*], a beautiful spring, formerly shaded by a magnificent ash tree, the roots of which still stretch over it. The only two other object of general interest to the tourist here are, the *Rath of Laoghaire,* upon the slope of the hill towards the south, in which it is said King Laoghaire was buried in a standing position; and about a quarter of a mile distant, in the same direction, among some trees crowning an adjoining elevation, the great fort called the Rath of Queen Meve, which is very well worth inspection.

From the centre of the Forradh on the one side, and the King's Chair upon the other, we gain most extensive views of the great plains of Meath, extending along the Boyne from the towers of Trim to the wooded heights of Slane; stretching over the course of the Blackwater to the regal hill of Tailtean, to Kells and to the mountains of Cavan; and, towards the southeast, taking in the tower of Skreen and the ancient castle adjoining.

There were several ancient roads leading through and from the royal residence at Tara, but, without entering into the general history and topography of the place, their description would be uninteresting. We regret to say that one of the raths of Tara was removed the year before last, by an inhabitant of Navan, for manure; and we understand a similar act of desecration is meditated towards another during the present harvest. Surely the proprietor of the soil, if acquainted with

---

* This opinion was likewise held by O'Donovan. See his valuable and voluminous letters on Tara, in the Ordnance Library, which we have lately perused.

these circumstances, would interfere to prevent further obliteration of these most interesting historic remains.

While our limits forbid our entering at all upon the records of Tara,—for the account which we could here afford to give would be so meagre, that we feel it would rather obscure than elucidate its true history,—we cannot forbear, in concluding this brief itinerary, quoting, in the subjoined note, the following hymn of St. Patrick, composed, it is believed, at the time he visited Tara, immediately after his arrival in Ireland, and which is supposed to have been sung by the Saint and his attendants as he approached this seat of monarchy surrounded by his Pagan enemies. It is not of so much consequence here, whether it really was composed by Patrick, or not until some two or three centuries after his death; its authenticity as a very ancient document has been fully established, and it exhibits in a remarkable manner the purity of faith of the early Irish Christian Church. It has been published by Dr. Petrie from the celebrated *Liber Hymnorum*, preserved in the Library of Trinity College, Dublin, a manuscript which, in the opinion of Archbishop Ussher, as expressed in a letter to Vossius, was in his time a thousand years old. It is written in the very ancient Irish dialect in which the Brehon laws are preserved, and seems to be oldest Christian Irish document extant.*

---

* The translation is as follows :

"At Temur to day I invoke the mighty power of the Trinity. I believe in the Trinity under the Unity of the God of the Elements.

" At Temur to-day I place the virtue of the Birth of Christ with his Baptism, the virtue of his Crucifixion with his Burial, the virtue of his Resurrection with his Ascension, the virtue of the coming to the eternal Judgment.

" At Temur to-day I place the virtue of the love of Seraphin ; the virtue which exists in the obedience of angels, in the hope of the Resurrection to eternal reward, in the prayers of the noble fathers, in the predictions of the prophets, in the preaching of the apostles, in the faith of the confessors, in the purity of the holy virgins, in the deeds of just men.

" At Temur to-day I place the strength of heaven, the light of the sun, the whiteness of snow, the force of fire, the rapidity of lightning, the swiftness of the wind, the depth of the sea, the stability of the earth, the hardness of rocks between me and the powers of paganism and demons.

"At Temur to-day may the strength of God pilot me, may the power of God preserve me, may the wisdom of God instruct me, may the eye of God view me, may the ear of God hear me, may the word of God render me eloquent, may the hand of God protect me, may the way of God direct me, may the shield of God defend me, may the host of God guard me against the snares

It is with some reluctance that we so soon return to the Boyne ; for at Loch-Gabhair, or Lough-Gower, near Dunshaughlin, a few miles from hence, we could have introduced our readers to some subjects connected with the domestic life and usages of the Irish people, prior to the tenth century, from a vast collection of weapons, domestic implements, and culinary utensils, and even objects employed in the toilet, as well as an enormous heap of animal remains, which were discovered in that locality not very long ago; and have entered, at some length, and from most valuable authentic materials within our reach, into details concerning the races of cattle, and animals of the chase, as well as those used for domestic purposes, at that period in Ireland. But these we also fear to touch on; they are rather without the pale of this guide book ; we cannot at present do more than direct attention to this interesting locality, and to the subjects which these remains illustrate. Perhaps upon some future occasion we may conduct the pilgrims of the Boyne to Skreen and Dunshaughlin.*

Crossing the left bank of the Boyne at Bellinter bridge we enter the noble demesne of Ardsallagh,† now belonging to the

of demons, the temptations of vices, the inclinations of the mind, against every man who meditates evil to me, far or near, alone or in company.

" I place all these powers between me and every evil unmerciful power directed against my soul and my body, as a protection against the incantations of false prophets, against the black laws of Gentilism, against the false laws of heresy, against the treachery of idolatry, against the spells of women, smiths, and Druids, against every knowledge which blinds the soul of man. May Christ to-day protect me against poison, against burning, against drowning, against wounding, until I deserve much reward.

" Christ be with me, Christ before me, Christ after me, Christ in me, Christ under me, Christ over me, Christ at my right, Christ at my left, Christ at this side, Christ at that side, Christ at my back.

" Christ be in the heart of each person whom I speak to, Christ in the mouth of each person who speaks to me, Christ in each eye which sees me, Christ in each ear which hears me.

" At Temur to-day I invoke the mighty power of the Trinity. I believe in the Trinity under the Unity of the God of the elements.

" Salvation is the Lord's, salvation is the Lord's, salvation is Christ's. May thy salvation, O Lord, be always with us."

* See Proceedings of the Royal Irish Academy, vol. i. p. 424, and Annals of the Four Masters, A. D. 675–848.

† Ardsallagh would seem to be an anglicised form of Ard-salach, i. e., the dirty height; but it is more probable that its original form was Ard-saileach, i. e., *altitudo saliceti*, or the height of the sallows or willows, which may possibly have flourished on the high banks of the Boyne here of old.

Duke of Bedford, who has recently erected here a handsome
Elizabethan mansion, in which report whispers he will annually spend some time. In no part of its course does the
river present the same extreme calmness and repose as here.
Widening into deep, still pools, shaded by aged timber, and
fringed with wild plants of gigantic growth, huge colts-foot;
with the modest blue forget-me-not and the little yellow poten-
tilla peeping through their dark umbrageous foliage; long,
topling bulrushes, fragrant meadow-sweet, and broad water-
lilies, stretch in wild luxuriance along the placid banks. Long
avenues of lime trees, and groves of tall grey-stemmed beeches
with arcades of aged yew, give an air of antiquity as well as
grandeur to this handsome park. One almost always expects
to meet some remnant of ecclesiastical buildings where aged
yew trees abound, and accordingly we read that St. Finian
founded the monastery of Escair-branain near this, but at present even the site of that ancient edifice is unknown.

We are not, however, altogether disappointed in our search,
for the holy well of St. Bridget still exists here, in the immediate vicinity of the house, and but a few paces from the river.
Although a modern cut stone pointed arch has by some taste-
less architect been thrown over it, still the thorns and elders
that overhang its pure waters, the mullen, the ground ivy, and
wild geraniums that droop and festoon the adjoining bank, and
the old carved head of St. Bridget, with its plaited hair and
prim formal features,—the very impersonation of a mother
abbess,—all combine to render this once celebrated spot a
pleasing picture. We wish we could say as much for the
house, which looks as if it was in a sort of half mourning, being
built of very dark—almost black—limestone, with all the
quoins, chimneys, and ornamental portions nearly white. Time,
however, may greatly assist to remedy this, and soften the
glaring effect which it now presents, but we greatly fear it
will never add to its height, equalize its proportions, nor mend
the deficiency in many of its details. Still, with all this, it is
a very fine pile of building, and every well-wisher of the country should rejoice to see such mansions rising in the land. The
interior is as yet unfurnished. A series of green terraces,—in
the olden style, when clipt yew trees, quaint statues, and urns,
were their general accompaniments,—lead from the principal
entrance down a gentle slope towards the river side.

The Boyne now turns nearly northwards to Navan. Upon its left bank, about half a mile from the river, and not far from the road leading from Bellinter to Navan, the old church of Cannonstown or Cannistown claims a passing notice, from its picturesqueness, and its affording several beautiful specimens of early Irish ecclesiastical archi-tecture. The circular choir-arch, springing from highly-decorated imposts, the bell tur-ret in the western gable, the nave and east window, with the piscina, afford the tourist and the antiquarian student a good opportunity for stu-dying one of our churches of the thirteenth century; and, in the surrounding grave-yard, rude portions of a cross and a font, now used as head-stones, give additional inter-est to the investigation of the tourist; while some noble ash trees, the usual guardians of our graveyards and ruined churches, greatly assist to heighten the picture of Cannistown.

At Kilcarn, immediately adjoining, the Dublin road is car-ried over the Boyne by a well-built bridge, and continues upon the western bank, between which and the river intervenes a narrow stripe of greensward, while the opposite, or eastern bank, rises abruptly from the water's edge, and forms a pleas-ing wooded rampart from this point to Navan.

Let us cross the river again, and make a little detour of about half a mile from this spot to view the old church of Kil-carn, which derives its name from an adjoining cairn. It is now a complete ruin, claiming attention only from the ancient baptismal font, which was recently exhumed here, but which has been very lately removed into the neighbouring Roman Catholic chapel of Johnstown.* Mr. Wakeman, in his Hand-

---

* The preservation of this beautiful font is due to an intelligent blacksmith, named Walsh, who resides in the neighbourhood, and whose family burial-

K

book of Irish Antiquities, has given the following description
and illustrations of this most interesting relic:

"Placed upon its
shaft, as represented in
the cut, it measures in
height about three feet
six inches ; the basin is
two feet ten inches in
diameter, and thirteen
inches deep. The heads
of the niches, twelve in
number, with which its
sides are carved, are en-
riched with foliage of
a graceful but uniform
character, and the mini-
ature buttresses which
separate the niches were
decorated with crockets,
the bases resting upon
heads, grotesque ani-
mals, or human figures,
carved as brackets. The
figures within the niches

are executed with a wonderful degree of care, the drapery
being represented with each minute crease or fold well expressed. They were evidently intended to represent Christ, the
Virgin Mary, and the twelve Apostles. All the figures are
seated. Our Saviour, crowned as a king, and holding in his
hand the globe and cross, is in the act of blessing the Virgin,

place is in this churchyard. About twenty years ago this font stood in the old
ruined church, and it was the usual practice for the " boys" who came to a
funeral to try who could throw a stone into it with greatest ease and adroit-
ness. Old Walsh, who is " a bit of an antiquary," perceiving the too probable
fate of this beautifully sculptured stone, dug a great hole and buried it within
the precincts of the church, where it remained until he exhumed it, the year
before last, for Mr. Wakeman to make a drawing of it. It is now, as mentioned
in the text, in the chapel of Johnstown, where it has been set up as a holy water
vessel immediately inside the door, but placed so near the wall that a considerable portion of its sculpture is obscured.

who also is crowned, the ' Queen of Heaven.' The figures of most of the Apostles can easily be identified: St. Peter, by his key; St. Andrew, by his cross of peculiar shape; and so on.

They are represented barefooted, and each holds a book in one hand. The font did not, when drawn, rest upon its ancient shaft, nor had it done so in the memory of the old people of

the neighbouring village; but the shaft still remained within the church, and the whole has since been restored."

Immediately approaching Navan, the river makes a bold sweep round the foot of the hill, from which rise up the ruins of Athlumney Castle, the dilapidated towers and tall gables of which shoot above the trees that surround the commanding eminence on which it is placed, while glimpses of its broad, stone-sashed, and picturesque windows, of the style of the end of the sixteenth century, are caught through the openings in the plantation which surrounds the height on which it stands. This beautiful pile consists of a large square keep, with stone

arched floors and passages rising into a tower,* from which a
noble view can be obtained of a clear day: and a more modern
castellated mansion, with square stone-mullioned windows, tall
chimneys, and several gables in the side walls. In the immediate
vicinity is the ruin of a small church of about the fourteenth

century, with a triple belfry in the western gable. In front of
this ancient feudal hall, and immediately crowning the high
eastern bank of the river, on the grounds of Dr. Hudson, the
present owner of Athlumney, an exceedingly perfect and
most gracefully shaped sepulchral mound is placed. If it were
opened under the direction of persons competent to the task, the
antiquary and ethnologist might expect the discovery of most
interesting remains within it.

Of the history of the castle of Athlumney and its adjoining church, there is little known with certainty ; but, standing on the left bank of the Boyne, opposite this point, we
cannot help recalling the story of the heroism of its last lord,
Sir Launcelot Dowdall, who, hearing of the issue of the battle
of the Boyne, and the fate of the monarch to whose religion and
politics his family had been so long attached, and fearing the
approach of the victorious English army, declared, on the news
reaching him, that the Prince of Orange should never rest
under his ancestral roof. The threat was carried into execution.
Dowdall set fire to his castle at nightfall, and, crossing the Boyne,
sat down upon its opposite bank, from whence, as tradition re-

* This fine old tower is now draped with ivy, planted by the hand of Miss
Edgeworth.

ports, he beheld the last timber in his noble mansion blazing and flickering in the calm summer's night, then crash amidst the smouldering ruins; and when its final eructation of smoke and flame was given forth, and the pale light of morning was stealing over that scene of desolation, with an aching and a despairing heart he turned from the once happy scene of his youth and manhood, and, flying to the Continent, shortly after his royal master, never returned to this country. All that remained of this castle and estate were forfeited in 1700. Many a gallant Irish soldier lost his life, and many a noble Irish gentleman forfeited his broad lands, that day. We wish their cause had been a better one, and the monarch for whom they bled more worthy such an honour.*

The inhabitants of Navan, like those of most Irish towns through which a river runs, have turned their backs upon the stream, scarcely a glimpse of which can be obtained from any of its narrow streets. There is here a picturesque weir, and immediately below the bridge which crosses it on the Drogheda road, the Boyne receives the Blackwater, which is there nearly as large as the stream into which it flows. There are also two valuable and extensive flour mills at this point.

As we only engaged to present our readers with scenes of beauty or of interest, we cannot be expected to devote much of our space to a description of Navan!—a dirty, ill-built, straggling collection of houses, boasting the honour of having been *half* a county-town. It contains, however, 5000 inha-

---

* Tradition gives us another, but by no means so probable a story about Athlumney castle, which refers to an earlier date. It is said that two sisters occupied the ancient castles of Athlumney and Blackcastle, which latter was situated on the opposite bank of the river; and the heroine of the latter, jealous of her rival in Athlumney, took the following means of being revenged. She made her enter into an agreement, that to prevent their mansions falling into the hands of Cromwell and his soldiers, they should set fire to them at the same moment, as soon as the news of his approach reached them, and that a fire being lighted upon one was to be the signal for the conflagration of the other. In the mean time the wily mistress of Blackcastle had a quantity of dry brush-wood placed on one of the towers of the castle, which, upon a certain night, she lighted; and the inhabitants of Athlumney perceiving the appointed signal, set fire to their mansion, and burned it to the ground. In the morning the deception was manifest. Athlumney was a mass of blackened, smoking ruins, while Blackcastle still reared its proud form above the woods, and still afforded shelter to its haughty mistress.

bitants, and is not without its wealthy trader and thriving petty merchant. A church, a chapel, an infirmary, a bride-well, workhouse, and fever hospital, constitute its modern erections. It was originally a parliamentary borough, and in olden times was a place of considerable note, having been walled by Hugh de Lacy, and containing an abbey, founded by Jocelyn de Nangle, on the site now occupied by the bar-rack. It is probable that a cross existed in this town ; and, in all likelihood, it stood in the market-place, where all the passing funerals now make a solemn circuit. A friend of our's possesses a portion of a small sculptured cross lately dug up at Navan.

The original name of Navan was Nuachongbhail. The An-nals of the Four Masters afford us an account of a great plundering of Meath, as far as Tara, by the O'Neills and O'Donnells, in the year 1539: "They obtained immense and innumerable spoils on this expedition, for the Irish had not in latter times assembled to oppose the English army that de-stroyed more of the property of Meath than this plundering army; for many were spoils of gold and silver, copper, iron, and every sort of goods and valuables, besides what they took from the towns of Ardee and Nuachongbhail, which they ut-terly plundered on that expedition."* When Lord Justice Leonard heard of this, he collected all the English forces in Ireland, and pursuing the invaders came up with them at Bal-lahoe in Farney, where a battle ensued, in which the Irish were completly routed.†

A branch of the Dublin and Drogheda Railway has lately been extended to this place; it crosses the Boyne upon a series of arches immediately below Athlumney Castle, and in the

---

* In a note upon this word, *Nuachongbhail*, by O'Donovan, in the second volume of the published copy of the Annals, we read : "It appears from the Life of St. Fechin, published by Colgan, that this was the ancient name of the place where the town of Navan, in Meath, now stands : 'Nuahchongbhail est oppidum Mediæ ad ripam Boinnii fluvii a Pontani [Drogheda] decem millibus passuum distans ab Authrumnia quinque.'—*Acta Sanct.* pp. 135, 141.

"In the account of this invasion of the Pale given in the Annals of Kilronan, this town is called an Uaṁ, which is its present Irish name, as pronounced by the natives of Meath. Ware, who seems to have known the ancient and modern names of this place, calls it Navan, in his Annals of Ireland at this year."

† See Some Account of the Territory and Dominion of Farney, by E. P. Shirley, Esq., M. P., already referred to.

cuttings on the eastern side of the river were discovered a
quantity of most interesting antiquities, bridle-bits and horse
trappings of iron, bronze, and silver, rings, buckles, head-stalls,
peytrells, and clasps, &c. ; besides a large collection of bones,
both human and those of the lower animals.* While these
pages were passing through the press, a most extensive souterrain was discovered in the cutting of the railway on the western bank, just under Athlumney, consisting of a straight passage fifty-three feet and a-half long, eight broad, and six high,
branching into two smaller passages which run off at right
angles from it, and ending in two circular bee-hive shaped
chambers, precisely similar to those at Clady, together forming the figure of a cross. The walls of this great cave having risen to a height of about four feet and a half, they then
begin to incline, and the roof is formed by enormous flag-stones
laid across ; these stones are all rough and undressed, and
are placed together without mortar or cement. This extensive cave, so recently discovered, will form an additional object of attraction to the tourist. A few bones of oxen are all
that have as yet been found in it.†

The meeting of the waters of the Boyne and Blackwater at
Navan forms the natural division between the second and
third portions of the former. Let us in the next chapter follow
and describe the course of the latter.

* These antiquities are in the Museum of the Royal Irish Academy; so far so
good. A very perfect human skull, and fragments of two others, were found in this
heap. For these fragments (which are good specimens of the long-headed early
Irish race) we are indebted to Mr. Wakeman. The only perfect head found
was sent out of the country ; it was given to the late Dr. Prichard, immediately before his death, and no account of it has since appeared. We are not
collectors; we have not the least desire to *possess* either bones or brasses; if
such came into our possession we should feel ourselves bound to give them,
sooner or later, either to the national collection of the Academy or to some of
our friends who might have museums; but we confess we feel indignant when
we see things of this class sent out of the country without either drawings,
casts, or models, having been first made of them. Like ourselves, our late
friend Dr. Prichard did not value skulls merely as old bones, so a good cast
of this head found at Navan would have answered all his purposes just as well.

† A somewhat similar cave may be seen in Mr. Metge's grounds, not far distant from Navan.

CHAPTER VI.

THE BLACKWATER.

THE Blackwater runs out of Lough Ramor, or Loch Muinrea-mhar, in the south-eastern extremity of the county of Cavan; it would appear, however, from some notices in the ancient topographies, that the true source of the river was in the hilly district of Sliabh-Guaire, to the north of Virginia. This river resembles in a remarkable manner that to which it is tributary, the Boyne, exhibiting the same even but tortuous course, winding through the same fertile meadows, and its banks presenting similar scenes of sylvan beauty, adorned by the same description of feudal and monastic remains, and commemorated by localities memorable in history and in song; the palaces of Pagan kings; the raths of warriors; the pillar-stones of Druids; the footprints of early Christian saints, their oratories, round towers, and churches, their wells and crosses; and the battle-fields, fortresses, and castellated mansions of more modern times. The entire length of the river, following its various windings from its source to Navan, is about twenty miles; its direction is from north-west to south-east; and the great northern road from Navan to Virginia, through Kells, passes first upon its northern, and then upon its southern bank, for the entire of its course, and so close to it that nearly all the objects of interest, or that are worthy of inspection, on this river, are more easy of access than those on any other which we are acquainted with.

The name Blackwater is applied to several rivers in Ireland, the most celebrated of which is the magnificent Blackwater of

the south.* In the topographical description of the Boyne at
the commencement of this work, we hazarded a conjecture (p.
25), that the river called Finnabhainn [i. e. White River] in the
very ancient histories was no other than that now denominated
the Blackwater of Meath, because it is said to have its source
in Sliabh-Guaire,† a district in the vicinity of Lough Ramor,
to which we have already alluded ; and a small stream which
flows into this lake of Cavan lends support to this idea, and is
in all probability the true source of the river, in the same
manner as the Shannon, though said to rise in Lough Allen, has
its real source in the neighbouring mountain of Sliabh an Ia-
rainn. *Abhainn Sele* was the name of this river till the time of
St. Patrick, who, having cursed it, its waters are said to have
assumed a peculiar dark hue, and it has ever since been known
by its present name of Abhainn Dubh. The circumstance
is thus recorded in a passage in the Tripartite Life of St. Patrick,‡ which likewise serves to fix the situation of Tailtean
or Teltenia: "Prima autem feria venit Patricius ad Talteniam:
ubi regiæ nundinæ et publici regni ludi et certamina quotan-
nis servari solebant. Ibique convenit Carbreum Nielli filium,
et Laogarii Regis fratrem fratrique animi ferociâ et increduli-
tate similem. Huic S. Patricius verbum vitæ prædicaret vi-
amque salutis ostenderet, vir adamantini cordis, non solum
recusavit prædicatæ veritate credere, sed viam vitæ proponenti
machinabatur mortem: et in vicinio fluvio nomine Sele Sancti
viri socios flagellis excepit, quia Patricius eum appellavit ini-
micum Dei."—*Trias Thaum*. p. 129. Colgan adds in a note :
" Fluvio nomine Sele, cap. 4, hodiè fluvius hic Abha-dhubh id
est fluvius niger, appellatur."

We shall have occasion again to refer to this insult offered
by the sons of Carbre and Loeghaire to Patrick, when we come
to describe Teltown.

Lough Ramor, from which the Blackwater flows, is a very
beautiful sheet of water, charmingly irregular, and studded
with islands, several of which, as well as its undulating sides,
are tastefully planted. The lake, which is said to have burst

---

* See Mr. O'Flanagan's charming work on the southern Blackwater.

† See *Leabhar-na-g Ceart*, or the Book of Rights, published by the Celtic
Society, p. 188.

‡ *Trias Thaumaturga*, part. ii. c. 4, p. 173, N. 14.

from Sliabh Guaire,* is about five miles in length, and from a
mile to a mile and a half in breadth. In the year A. D. 845,
King Malachy I., who first broke down the Danish power in
Ireland, attacked and destroyed an island in this lake, on which
a number of Irish outlaws and rebels of Meath, who joined
the Danes against their own monarch, had fortified themselves.
The Irish annals state that these rebels were in the habit of
plundering the districts in the neighbourhood of the lake
"more Gentilium;" and that Malachy destroyed their island,
and put themselves to death. Upon its northern shore stands
the neat little town of Virginia, where the tourist who may
wish to visit the source of the Sele will find admirable accommodation. After a course of about a mile and a half, the
river touches Meath at the barony of Castlekieran, having
the coach-road parallel with, and but a short distance from
it. It now completely enters Meath, through which county
it passes during the remainder of its course. For the
first few miles the only objects of antiquarian interest in its
vicinity are a number of forts and earthen raths, which
crowd upon both sides of the river, and show the military
importance of this locality, as well as its populous condition, in early times. Several of these enclosures are of great
extent, and two which stand upon the immediate brink of the
stream are worthy of note, from the peculiarity of their form,
being perfectly square.

About three miles above Kells, on the southern bank of the
river we meet the first group of interesting antiquarian remains, consisting of the ancient Church of St. Kieran, with the
remains of five termon crosses in its vicinity, four of which are
placed north, south, east, and west of the ruin. The northern
one was erected in a ford in the river, a very remarkable situation for one of these early Christian structures. The base
still stands in its original locality, but the shaft, the arms,
and the top were removed, it is said, many years ago, by some
good Protestant, who, anxious to show his loyalty, as well as
his detestation of such idolatrous structures, threw them into
into an adjoining deep pool in the river. Such is one of the
local traditions, but we shall presently relate another just as
probable.

---

* Annals of the Four Masters, A. D. 2859 ; and see note у, p. 10.

The accompanying illustration represents the cross which exists upon the south side of the church. It is not quite so large as that upon the north, which measures twelve feet in height, although the upper portion (that above the circle) has been broken off. The western cross is very imperfect; one of its arms and a portion of the head having long since been destroyed. The old tradition current among the people here concerning these crosses is, that St. Kieran had a number of them hewn at the quarry of Carrickleck, and brought here to adorn his church. They were the wonder, the admiration, and—alas! that such a sentiment should enter into the breast of Christian saints—the envy also of all the neighbouring saints and church builders. St. Columb, who was then erecting his church and tower at Kells, cast, it is said, a longing eye upon St. Kieran's crosses: he came by night and surreptitiously abstracted at least three of these, which the traditionary legend says are those now remaining at Kells. At last, upon the night that he was taking away the fourth, St. Kieran awoke, and caught him in this very act of petty larceny. Kieran immediately "buckled" in his brother of Kells, just as he was stepping into the ford of the river with the base of the cross on his back; but the latter being the younger and the stronger man, the cross-owner was soon worsted. He wasn't, however, to be bet so asily, so he still held fast by the thief, who, seeing that he could not get off clear with his booty, threw it into the middle of the river, from which it has never since been removed, and where, except during a heavy flood, it is always to be seen.

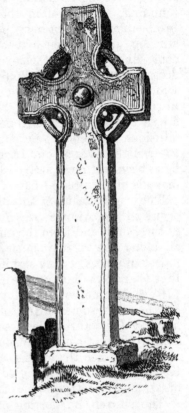

It is hard to hear those slanders of the good St. Columb, or of any saint in the calendar; but still it must be confessed, that, notwithstanding his piety, and what appears to have been a stronger feeling with him, his taste for architecture and church founding, he was often the cause of fierce wars and family broils among his not very peaceable countrymen, constantly stirring up agitation and fomenting rebellion, for which he came under the just censure of his superiors, was obliged to do penance, and was finally, it is said, sent off to Iona, which was then, perhaps, a sort of Norfolk Island, to which unruly Irish saints were transported. These saintly errors are, it is true, but idle rumours, but some way or other dark allusions to them have crept into the Annals, and even into the written lives of our Irish saints, who, after all, appear to have been but men, swayed by like passions with poor sinning mortals of the present day.

The original name of this place, to which frequent references occur in the Annals, was *Bealach-duin*, the "Road or Pass of the Fort," and from the numerous raths in its vicinity, and all along the river, it must have been, like most other Irish names of places, a very significant appellation. Here we read that Ciaran, or Kieran, the Pious, died on the 14th of June, 770; so that, notwithstanding the force of tradition—to which, by the way, some of St. Columb's successors still attach so much value—authentic history enables us, from the positive anachronism of the legend, to acquit the great churchfounder of having stolen the crosses. The spot thus consecrated by St. Kieran was afterwards called *Disert Chiarain*, from which the present barony and parish of Castle-Kieran takes its name.*

The church, no portion of which can be regarded as the original structure founded by St. Kieran, is a small oblong building, erected apparently upon low arches, of a late period of Gothic architecture, and quite devoid of mouldings or or-

---

* See the Annals of the Four Masters at the years A. D. 770, 778, 855, 868, &c., with O'Donovan's notes thereon. These references are to volumes yet unpublished, and for permission to examine which we are deeply indebted to our friend George Smith, Esq. There was a *Patron* held here formerly. O'Clery places the festival day of St. Kieran on the 14th of June, the day of his death. Dean Butler, in his notes to John Dymmok's "Treatise on Ireland," published by the Archæological Society, says Castle-Kieran is sometimes called "Trystel Kieran," and that "there was a church here appropriated to the Priory of St. John the Baptist at Kells."

nament,—a sort of crypt. Its direction is, as usual, east and west. No doorway or window-case remains, to indicate by their style the period to which the church might be referred; but judging from the masonry, which consists of small stones and rubble-work set in an unusually great quantity of mortar, we should consider it an erection of a period not earlier than the fourteenth century. Of the three nearly perfect crosses, one is placed at a short distance to the west of the church, one to the south, and the third and largest, though least perfect, to the north. The base of a fourth is found to the east; so that originally the church must have been placed between four crosses. Unlike the exquisite remains of the same class, at Kells and Monasterboice, these crosses were, except the circle by which the head and arms are connected together, almost totally devoid of ornament or sculpture of any kind.

There is also in the graveyard a fine specimen of the oldest style of monumental stone found in Ireland, but it bears no inscription.

About a furlong's length to the west of the old church may be seen St. Kieran's well, one of the most beautiful holy wells in Ireland, and shaded by a hoary ash tree of surpassing size and beauty, which is faithfully represented in the accompanying graphic delineation. The well is situated on the side of a beautiful and exquisitely green sloping bank, upon which the neighbouring sheep love to congregate. It springs from a limestone rock of considerable extent; and appears first in a small natural basin immediately at the foot of the tree.

Within the well are several trouts, each about half a pound weight. They have been there " as long as the oldest inhabitants can recollect," and, strange to tell, they are said not to have grown an ounce within that period! These fish are held in the highest veneration by the people, who, when the well is being annually cleansed of weeds, carefully preserve the blessed creatures, and replace them as soon as possible.

About ten years ago a report spread over Meath and the surrounding counties, that Saint Kieran's ash tree was bleeding, and thousands of people flocked to the place to witness the wonder, and many brought with them vessels and bottles in which they hoped to carry away a portion of the miraculous fluid. With this it was hoped they might perform cures such as " common doctors" could not even attempt.

> " The holy wells—the living wells—the cool, the fresh, the pure—
> A thousand ages rolled away, and still those founts endure ;
> And while their stainless chastity and lasting life have birth
> Amid the oozy cells and caves of gross material earth,
> The scripture of creation holds no fairer type than they—
> That an immortal spirit can be linked with human clay!
> How sweet, of old, the bubbling gush—no less to antlered race,
> Than to the hunter and the hound that smote them in the chase !
> The cottage hearth, the convent's wall, the battlemented tower,
> Grew up around the crystal springs as well as flag and flower;
> The brookline and the water-cress were evidence of health,
> Abiding in those basins, free to Poverty and Wealth :
> The city sent pale sufferers there, the faded brow to dip,
> And woo the water to depose some bloom upon the lip ;
> The wounded warrior dragged him towards the unforgotten tide,
> And deemed the draught a heavenlier gift than triumph to his side.
> The stag, the hunter, and the hound, the druid and the saint,
> And anchorite are gone, and even the lineaments grown faint,
> Of those old ruins into which, for monuments, had sunk
> The glorious homes that held, like shrines, the monarch and the monk."[*]

The Blackwater, or Owen Duff, as it is called by the peasantry, now winds on towards Kells, the church and round tower of which appear in the distance ; and to the south-west the beautifully verdant hill of Lloyd, with its lighthouse-like

---

[*] The Holy Wells of Ireland, by J. D. Ffraser, in " The Ballad Poetry of Ireland."

observatory, from which a most commanding prospect can be obtained, attracts attention. The river then bends somewhat to the south, and in the splendid demesne of Headford spreads out into a series of small lakes and ponds, partly natural and partly artificial, and encloses several small islands. This noble demesne, belonging to the Marquis of Headford, though possessing no natural features that attract attention, " has in its general appearance a degree of magnificence arising from its extent, unity of design, the richness of the verdure, the long and gently inclined plains into which the surface is naturally disposed, and the arrangement and preservation of the plantations ;"* but the grounds are at present very much neglected, and the long-continued want of a resident proprietor is but too manifest throughout.

Within three-quarters of a mile to the south-west of the river stands Kells, one of the most memorable places in early Irish ecclesiastical history. The modern town is pleasingly situated, and its principal streets present several very charming views of the adjoining ruins, of which the round tower, the beautifully sculptured cross in the market-place, and St. Columbkill's house in the north-western suburb, are the most remarkable. The neighbouring demesne of Headford, with some well-grown timber adjoining, the general graceful outline, and the fertility and high state of cultivation of the surrounding district, all conduce to set off to considerable advantage this little town. The population of this place in 1841 was 4205, located in about 600 houses.

The name by which this town is generally known in early Christian and middle age writings is Ceanannus, head-fort or residence—Kenlis. We read in the Annals of the Four Masters that, a few years prior to the Christian era, King Fiacha-Finnailches erected *Dun-Chuile-Sibrinne*, which Mac Geoghegan, in his translation of the Annals of Clonmacnoise, says was certainly Kells. " It was by this king that the earth was first dug in Ireland that water might be in wells. It was difficult for the stalk to sustain its corn in his reign. Every calf that was brought forth in his reign was white-headed,"†—A. M.

---

* See Fraser's Hand-Book for Travellers in Ireland, p. 494.

† Annals of the Four Masters, with Translation and Notes, by John O'Donovan, Esq. Dublin : Hodges and Smith. Now in process of publication.

3972 to 3991,—and hence the King's cognomen of Finnail-ches, according to the bards. The celebrated Cormac Mac Art is said to have resided for some time at Kells. Dermod, the son of Fergus Kervaill, made a grant of this place to St. Columb, who founded a monastery here about the year 550, and dedicated it to the Virgin Mary. No vestiges of this structure at present exist. There are, however, some architectural remains here, of about that period, of surpassing interest; of these perhaps the most interesting is that figured in the adjoining wood-cut, generally known as St. Columb's House, a small, arched, and stone-roofed building.*

This is supposed to have been used as a small chapel or oratory, as well as a dwelling-house, like what is called St. Kevin's Kitchen at Glendalough, and the house of St. Flannan at Killaloe. Several descriptions of this building have been given.

* The accompanying view of St. Columbkill's house, which will afford the reader a better idea of its appearance than any description of our's, was drawn by Mr. Wakeman, and published in his useful little work, already so frequently referred to.

The following, by Dr. Petrie, is the most accurate: " This remarkable building is, in its ground plan, of a simple oblong form, measuring externally twenty-three feet nine inches in length, and twenty-one feet in breadth, and the walls are three feet ten inches in thickness. It is roofed with stone, and measures in height, from its base to the vertex of the gable, thirty-eight feet; and as the height of the roof and width of the side walls are nearly equal, the gables form very nearly equilateral triangles. The lower part of the building is arched semicircularly with stone, and has at the east end a small semicircular-headed window, about fifteen feet from the ground; and at the south side there is a second window with a triangular, or straight-lined head, about the same height from the ground, and measuring one foot nine inches in height. These windows splay considerably upon the inside. The present entrance doorway of this building, which is placed in the south wall, is obviously not original or ancient; and the original doorway, which is now built up, was placed in the west end, and at a height of eight feet from the ground. The apartment placed between the arched floor and the slanting roof is six feet in height, and appears to have been originally divided into three compartments of unequal size, of which the largest is lighted by a small aperture at the east end. In this chamber is a flat stone, six feet long and one foot thick, now called St. Columb's penitential bed."* The accompanying illustration shows the character of the angular-headed window just alluded to.

When we last visited this house it was inhabited by a miserable, wretched family.

We next turn to the round tower which stands beside the wall of the churchyard, and of which the illustration upon the next page is a very good view.

This tower is a very perfect specimen of those interesting and almost peculiarly Irish structures. It is about 100 feet high, with a door some ten feet from the ground. The top, though not the roof, is still nearly perfect; in it there are

* See Dr. Petrie's Essay on the Origin and Uses of the Round Towers of Ireland. Dublin: Hodges and Smith.

L

four windows, remarkable for presenting examples of the three varieties of such apertures found in round towers, namely, with square, round, and triangular heads.

As the conclusions arrived at by Dr. Petrie, with respect to the origin and uses of the Round Towers of Ireland, cannot be too widely disseminated, or too generally known, and as, moreover, this at Kells, and that at Donoughmore, on the Boyne, near Navan, are, even to the tourist and the popular reader, highly confirmatory of his views, we here insert the general results of his inquiries.

I. " That the towers are of Christian and ecclesiastical origin, and were erected at various periods between the fifth and thirteenth centuries." In support of this position the learned author remarks, that " the towers are never found unconnected with ancient ecclesiastical foundations. Their architectural styles exhibit no features or peculiarities not equally found in the *original* churches with which they are locally connected, when such remain. On several of them Christian emblems are observable, and others display in the details a style of architecture universally acknowledged to be of Christian origin. They possess invariably architectural features not found in any buildings in Ireland ascertained to be of Pagan times.

II. "That they were designed to answer, at least a twofold use, namely, to serve as belfries, and as keeps or places of strength, in which the sacred utensils, books, relics, and other valuables, were deposited, and into which the ecclesiastics to whom they belonged could retire for security in cases of sudden predatory attack." The proofs adduced in support of this are, that "their architectural construction, as will appear, eminently favours this conclusion. A variety of passages, extracted from our Annals and other authentic documents, will prove that they were constantly applied to both these purposes."

III. "That they were probably also used, when occasion required, as beacons and watch-towers. There are some historical evidences which render such a hypothesis extremely probable. The necessity which must have existed in early Christian times for such beacons and watch-towers, and the perfect fitness of the round towers to answer such purposes, will strongly support this conclusion."

Adjoining this round tower is an ancient cross, beautifully sculptured, eleven feet four inches high, the base of which has been very recently uncovered; and within the enclosure of the churchyard, near the belfry, the remains of a second, still larger, the shaft alone measuring ten feet six inches; the third—the great sculptured cross of Kells—stands in the market-place of the town.

The square bell-tower stands distinct and separate from the modern church; it consists of three stories ending in a spire; and some sculptured stones and tablets, probably much older than this structure, are built into its side walls, as well as an ancient inscription in old black letter characters, recording the re-edification of the adjoining church in 1578.*

* For the following literal transcript of this inscription we are indebted to our learned friend, Joseph Huband Smith, Esq. It is on two separate stones:

"The bodie of the churche being in utter rupne and decaie was reedi= fied in anno domini, 1578, et in anno rr Elizabeth xx throghe the dilig— ce and care of the reverende father in God hughe brady byshop of meathe and Sir Thome Garuie archedieacon of the same and deane of christ church dubline bothe of here maiestie is priue consaile Sir Henrie Sidney knight of the nobll ordire being thene lord deputie &c. the said reedifing was begone and seatt forward be the addyse and daly

"carfull travaell of the auncient burgis Nicholas D— then being suffraine of kenllis 2 of Julii anno predicto with other daly furtherens boght the rowff of this c uppon his owin priв chargis God is not unright— at he shuld forget the worke and labour that preceded which love is shewed for his name is sake."

A few miles from Kells (but not sufficiently near to be included in our excursion along the Blackwater) is the old Church of Rathmore, a picturesque ruin, with a most interesting tablet still existing inserted in its walls; and a

The great Cross of Kells, of which we here present our readers with a wood engraving, is one of the most beautiful in
Ireland, and, although not so
tall or massive, may in elegance
of design, in form, and in variety
and perfection of sculpture, and
the richness of ornament, be
classed with the crosses of Monasterboice and Clonmacnoise.
The shaft is eight feet nine
inches high: when perfect, it
must have been nearly twelve
feet high. The width across the
arms is five feet four inches.
The top, which in our large
Irish crosses is often carved in
the shape of a small church or
shrine, has been broken off, but
the base, which is rather larger
than usual, being fifteen feet
in girth, is very perfect, and
well worthy of minute attention. On it may be seen, as
on some of the ancient friezes,
a series of mounted figures, apparently in procession, in good
relief. Both the figures of the
men and horses remind us
strongly of some of the old
Greek and Roman friezes. The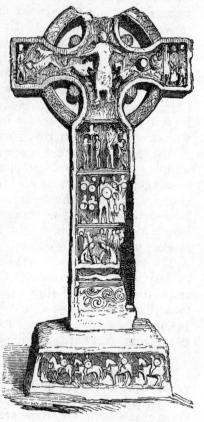
shaft, arms, and circle, are of one entire stone.*

Kells was at one time strongly fortified. The castle, said to
have been erected by Walter de Lacy, stood near the site of the

tombstone erected in 1531, to the memory of Christopher Plunket, son of
Sir Alexander Plunket, who was Lord Chancellor of Ireland in 1492. There
is here also a fragment of a sepulchral cross. See Mr. Huband Smith's communication on the subject in the Proceedings of the Royal Irish Academy for
12th June, 1848, p. 184, vol. iv.

* There is a tradition current that the shaft of this cross was prostrate till
placed upon its pedestal by Dean Swift. Another fact connected with this
cross, still keenly remembered by the inhabitants of Kells, is, that it formed
part of the gallows from which several men were hanged in 1798.

great cross, and one of the towers of the town wall still stand
on the south-western side of the church.

The Annals of Kells would fill a volume such as this; we
can here only allude to a few of the most remarkable historic
events which occurred here. We already mentioned the erection of the early ecclesiastical buildings at Kells by St. Columb. It is recorded that in 806 Cellah, Abbot of Iona,
took refuge here from the Norwegians, and repaired or rebuilt the abbey. Numerous battles were fought, both within
and on the plains around Kells, which sustained several
sieges, and was frequently plundered, sacked, burned, and
destroyed ; its churches robbed, its shrines polluted, its
altars desecrated, its relics stolen; its abbots and monks
murdered, and its soldiers and inhabitants either butchered
or carried off as prisoners by the Irish themselves, by the
English settlers, or by the Danish invaders, for upwards of
nine hundred years. Plague, pestilence, and famine, the sword,
fire, battle, murder, and sudden death, form the chief items in
the records of this ancient and most celebrated place. We read
that Sitric and the Danes of Dublin made great havoc of all
things belonging to this abbey in 1108, and Edward Bruce
defeated Lord Roger Mortimer, and burned the town of Kells
in 1315 ;—and thus might we occupy an entire chapter.

One of the most valuable pieces of antiquity connected with
this place, and which has come down to modern times, is the
celebrated Book of Kells, a most beautifully illuminated Irish
manuscript, still preserved in the library of Trinity College.

Descending the river upon the northern bank we arrive at
Teltown, about midway between Kells and Navan. This is
one of the most celebrated spots in Ireland; perhaps, next to
Tara, it is the most ancient, if not the most notable. An entire
chapter might be devoted to it, describing its topography, trans-
cribing its annals, relating its legends,—Pagan and Christian,—
and giving a detailed account of its battles, sham and real; its
fairs, games, sports, and marriages; these, however, would far
exceed the limits of a guide-book, intended chiefly to direct
the tourist, and point out the scenic beauty, and the memorable localities upon the hitherto neglected Boyne and Blackwater, which is all this little work pretends to. Let the following notice suffice. Upon a green hill sloping gradually
from the water's edge, and rising to a height of about 300

feet, amidst the most fertile grazing lands in Meath, if not in Ireland, may be seen a large earthen fort, about a furlong's length to the right of the road, with a few hollows or excavations in the adjoining lands, apparently the sites of small, dried up lakes ; and to the left of the road, nearly opposite these, parts of the trench and embankments of two other forts, which, judging from the portions still remaining, must have been of immense size, greater even than any of those now existing at Tara. These mark the sites of the early Pagan settlement, and the position of the palace of Tailtean, one of the four royal residences which existed in Ireland in very early times.

The first notice which the Annals record of Tailtean (the name of which is still preserved in the modern Teltown) is, that in the year of the world 3370, in the reign of Lugh Lamhfhada, " The fair of Tailltean was established in commemoration and in remembrance of his foster-mother *Tailte*, the daughter of Maghmor, King of Spain, and the wife of Eochaidh, son of Erc, the last king of the Firbolgs."* This fair continued down to the time of Roderick O'Conor, the last monarch of Ireland, and was held annually upon the first of August, which month derives its name in the Irish language from this very circumstance, being still called *Lugh-nasadh*, or Lugh's fair,—the Lammas day,—to which several superstitious rites and ancient ceremonies still attach throughout the country generally. Upon these occasions various sports and pastimes, a description of Olympic Games, were celebrated, consisting of feats of strength and agility in wrestling, boxing, running, and suchlike manly sports, as well as horse races and chariot races. Besides these the people were entertained with shows and rude theatrical exhibitions. Among these latter are enumerated sham battles and also aquatic fights, which it is said were exhibited upon the artificial lakes, the sites of which are still pointed out. Tradition assigns the site of the fair to that portion of the great rath still existing upon the northern side of the road, and about a quarter of a mile to the north-east of the great fort, or Rath Dubh ;† and here it is said the most remarkable of the Tel-

---

* Annals of the Kingdom of Ireland by the Four Masters.

† None of these localities, with the exception of the great fort and the two adjoining hollows, are marked upon the Ordnance Map. Indeed the remains of Tailtean have been, except by Mr. O'Donovan, in his unpublished letters,

town ceremonies took place—the marriages or betrothals. Upon one side of this great embankment were ranged, it is said, "the boys," and on the other "the girls;" the former ogling, the latter blushing; for human nature is, we suppose, the same at all times and in all places, among our forefathers and mothers at Teltown upwards of a thousand years ago, or in a modern drawing-room, or at a flower-show or review. They then, having had a good view of each other, passed down a little to the south, where there is a deep hollow in the land, evidently formed artificially, probably the ditch of one of the ancient forts, and called *Lug-an-Eany*, where they became separated by a high wall, which prevented their seeing each other. In this wall, say the local traditions, there was a door with a small hole in it, through which each young lady passed her middle finger, which the men upon the other side looked at, and if any of them admired the finger he laid hold of it, and the lass to whom it belonged forthwith became his bride; so that we find a fair and pretty hand, a delicate and taper finger, with its snowy skin and delicately formed nail, were even more captivating among the Irish lads and lasses some twelve hundred years ago than they are at the present day. He took her for better for worse, but the key-hole or wooden ring was not as binding as the modern one of gold; for, by the laws of Tailtean, the marriage only held good for a year and a day. If the couple disagreed during that time they returned to Tailtean, walked into the centre of Rath Dubh, stood back to back, one facing the north, and the other the south, and walked out of the fort, a divorced couple, free to try their luck again at Lug-an-Eany.* What a pity there is no Teltown or Black Fort marriage in the present day! What numbers would take advantage of it!

In the bottom of this hollow there is a well, which in wet weather overflows, and its waters trickle down the adjoining hill towards the Blackwater. Leading nearly southward from this spot we pass down the remains of an ancient paved, but now grass-grown way, called "Cromwell's road," and near

altogether too much neglected. There exists ample material, both from the records and the existing remains here, for a very interesting archæological paper on the subject.

* A somewhat similar custom existed in Wales, and parts of England and Scotland, till very lately. The expression, "a Teltown marriage," is often used in Meath to this day.

where this joins the modern main road there is another hollow, still containing some water, pointed out as the site of one of the artificial lakes. The fair of Tailtean was continued up to about eighty years ago, and some vestiges of the sports, particularly the fighting, existed within the memory of man at a *Patron* which used to be held on the opposite side of the river.*

The Great Fort, or *Rath Dubh*, measures round the outer wall of circumvallation 321 paces, having openings in it nearly due north and south. The height of the surrounding earthen embankment varies from fifteen to twenty feet. Standing in the centre of this great fort we again obtain one of those refreshing views which we have so often attempted to describe when following the course of the Boyne. Looking up towards the north-west, the hill of Lloyd presents a grand and imposing object. Below it the eye rests upon the steeple and round tower of Kells, appearing to rise out of the woods of Headford; while in the extreme distance the round hills of Cavan bound the horizon. Immediately around us is a country of immense fertility and with a gently undulating surface, divided into fields of great size,—that in which we stand contains nearly 100 acres,—bordered by rows of well-grown timber, rising out of tall quickset hedges. There is scarcely a cottage, or even a farmer's house, to be seen. All seems one vast pasture farm, through which the Sele winds in pleasing curves, presenting glimpses of its dark blue waters among the flowery meadows which stretch along its brink. The wooded hill of Foughan rises up beyond it to the south-west, and following its track by the little ruined church of Teltown, by the heights of Donaghpatrick, over the woods of Liscarton, above which the old castle in that locality topples, and by the plantations of Rathaldron, the eye rests upon the hills of Skreen and Tara in the extreme north-eastern distance.

St. Patrick visited the royal residence of Tailtean early in his missionary career, and not merely in the local legends, but in the written Lives of that saint, we meet with abundance of

---

* This meeting and rustic pastime was, we understand, suppressed by the neighbouring magistrates and clergy about thirty years ago, in consequence of the rioting which generally took place there. It is a remarkable circumstance, and confirmatory of the conjecture of its being a remnant of the Teltown sports, that this assembly, though called a *Patron*, was not held in honour of any saint, but upon Lammas Day.

tales and fables regarding the miracles and the wonders which
he wrought here upon the sons and servants of Cairbre, brother
of King Loeghaire.

Many of the legends told of Patrick by the people here are
evidently but paraphrases of his "doings" at Tara. The
Shadrach, Meshach, and Abed-nego story about the fire trial
between the servant of Patrick and the servant of the Druid
gets here a new dress, with new names and "entirely new
scenery, machinery, decorations, and processions." King Loeghaire or Leary (not Cairbre), who was a wonderful Druid
and powerful magician entirely, is the chief personage in the
Tailtean fables. After being defeated in various trials of
skill and necromancy with the saint, who could make no
hand of him at all, Patrick was forced to put him down
into a dark " condemned hole," near the river, called to this
day, " an t-áithghearr go h-Iffrionn," " the short road to
hell," where the heathen king, Loeghaire, is still believed
to be, if he never got any farther. Some fool-hardy people
went a few years ago to lift *mooreen* out of this spot, but
they had scarcely broke the *scraw* that covered the soft surface of the hollow, when a terrible roaring was heard coming up out of the bottom of the earth, and presently a most
vinimous sarpint, with a long mane and a head as big as a
horse, riz up out of the pit, and looked about him; but when
he saw nobody, for all the men had run away, he drew himself down again, and no one ever attempted to make any inquiries after the ould king of the black rath since. But all
that is nothing to what happened at the building of Dona-
patrick Church hard by. Every one knows that Prince Conall
gave the saint one of his beautiful raths there to build a
church upon, and that the workmen engaged in the erection
of it came very short of provisions one hard summer,—just, for
all the world, like the year before last. Well, Loeghaire when
he heard that, sent him a furiously wicked bull that was the
terror of the whole country, and used to be horning and aiting
every body that came next or nigh him,—he was as cross and
as thievish as the ould king himself,—in hopes that he'd finish
the blessed man all out. The baste was sent over to the other
side of the water, and when he saw St. Patrick, he stopt bel-
lowing and snorting all of a sudden, and was as quiet as a suck-
ing calf. ' Kill him,' says the saint; so they made a great feast

of him.   Next day the king came down to the river side, just
walking along mighty easily, letting on as if he didn't want to
know anything about what happened, but hoping all the while
that the bull had made a meal of some of the good Christians.
He wasn't long there when some of the saint's servants bid
him the time of day, and told him how much they enjoyed the
bull, which, we may be sure, was no ways pleasing to his majesty; but to convince him, not only of the truth of the story,
but to give him a taste of his power, St. Patrick ordered his
servants to bring out the well-picked bones, and to tie them
up in the skin, and to throw them into the river to Leary.
That was easy enough, but then comes the miracle.   The
bundle had hardly touched the water, when out of it rose the
bull, well and harty, large as life, bone to bone, and sinew to
sinew, and swam over to the king.   And yet, for all this, history records that the old reprobate died in his mother Church,
and was buried in the hill of Tara, in a standing position, ac-
coutred in his battle dress.   Conversions of old people or
grown up men and women are not as common or as easy as
people imagine.

A short distance above Teltown the river is crossed by
Bloomsbury Bridge; but the tourist will find greater and
more frequent objects of attraction on the northern bank, till
he reaches Donaghpatrick, about a mile and a quarter lower
down.

In the valley, by the water's edge, about midway between
these two places, and beside a broad curve of the river, we
meet the ruins of *Cill-Tailltean*, the little church of Teltown,
which was plundered by Diarmaid Mac Murchadha and the
Danes in 1156, and again by the same prince and the English
in 1170, in their marauding excursions among the rich
churches of East Meath.

We now arrive at Donaghpatrick, which takes its name from
Domnach-Padraig, the ancient church of Patrick, which formerly stood here, on the site now occupied by the modern
parish church.   This was the " *Ecclesia Patricii Magna*," the
Domnach Mor, or great church, sixty feet long, so frequently
alluded to in our Irish hagiology,[*] one of the earliest daimh-
laigs, or stone sacred edifices, erected in Ireland after the in-

---

[*] See Petrie's Round Towers.

troduction of Christianity. It is related in the life of St. Patrick, attributed to St. Evin, and published by Colgan in the *Trias Thaumaturga*, that Conall, the brother of King Loeghaire, who resided here, not only gladly accepted Christianity, and was baptized, but also showed great kindness to Patrick, and gave him his house or rath on which to erect a church; and the outline of this very cashel can still be discerned in the present graveyard. The only other evidence of great antiquity now remaining here, is what appears to be a fragment of a gable tombstone similar to that still existing at Slane, of which we give a drawing, in the description of that place (p. 182). It can be seen just protruding above ground to the south of the present church.

Upon the left of the road, as we approach the church, stands, without exception, one of the very finest raths of the military class to be seen in Ireland. It is of immense size, but, its outline being now obscured by trees and much underwood, it escaped the notice of the Ordnance surveyors, and has not been marked on the map of this part of Meath. It much resembles that at Downpatrick, consisting of a central circular mound, rising gradually out of several circumvallations, or earthen embankments, four of which can still be traced; the great ring fort at Dowth, and the King's Rath enclosing the Forradh at Tara, and Rath Dubh at Tailtean, extend over a greater space; but of its kind there is nothing to compare with this along the Boyne or Blackwater.

It is much to be regretted that earthen mounds of this description should be planted; a graceful tree at top, or a few growing on the sides, add to their picturesqueness; but covering them with trees and underwood quite obscures their form and conceals their purpose. May not this moat have been the celebrated Rath Airthir, the eastern fort, now Oristown; or even the house which the good Conall erected for himself after he so hospitably gave his own to Patrick?

From hence to Navan objects of almost equal interest and beauty present themselves on both sides of the river. The scenery is the same, presenting graceful, well-wooded, swelling undulations of surface, adorned by the seats of resident proprietors, with some interesting antiquarian remains; castles, churches, moats, crosses, occurring in nearly equal numbers, and of similar value on both sides. Upon the south-western

bank we have Liscarton castle, and the ruins of its most beautiful Gothic church; Ardbraccan, and the fine moat of Navan;
and on the north-eastern road, Rathaldron House, and the old
cross of Nevinstown, with a much finer view of the river and
the surrounding country than that which can be obtained from
the opposite side.

The accompanying view presents us with Liscarton castle,
(which is still in part inhabited), and the adjoining dwelling-
house. It is pleasingly situated on a green lawn sloping to
the river: and a short distance to the west of it, surrounded
with trees, stands the church just alluded to, forming in the
shade of the surrounding grove, with its tall, light, pointed
windows, a most charming picture.

This castle appears to have been, from its strength and
extent, of great importance. We know little of its history,
except that in 1633 it belonged to Sir William Talbot, Bart.,
who held it of the king *in capite per servitium militare*. It originally consisted of two large quadrangular towers, connected
together by a large hall, the roof of which no longer exists,
but its position is shown by marks in the wall at either end.
The thatched, modern-looking building shown in the accompanying cut is a portion of one of the towers much reduced in
height. The church is remarkable for the extreme beauty of
its eastern and western windows, each of which consists of one
great light, divided by a shaft branching off on a level with
the spring of the arch into two members, which join the arch-
head about the centre of the curve. An exquisite variety of

tracery, in the decorated style of Gothic architecture, fills the head of both windows, and the mouldings are deep and well executed. Upon the exterior face may be observed well carved human heads projecting from the drip stone. There were two doorways, one in each side wall, near the western end.

The moat of Navan, about a mile and a half lower down upon this side of the river, and which forms such a conspicuous object from all sides, is of the military class, and well worthy of inspection, from its size and its appearing to have been in part formed out of the natural hill.

Upon the opposite bank we have Gibbstown, with its noble approach, and Rathaldron castellated mansion, partly ancient and partly modern, approached by one of the finest avenues of lime trees in Meath, perhaps in Ireland; it consists of a strong, well-built quadrangular tower, of very considerable antiquity, to which a handsome castellated dwelling-house has lately been added. Not far from it, in a field towards the east, we meet the way-side cross of Nevinstown. As Mr. J. Huband Smith has presented the Royal Irish Academy with a detailed description of this relic, we shall here quote his judicious and accurate observations from the published Proceedings of that body:

" One side bears an inscription; the opposite has a shield, with armorial bearings, *party per pale*, nearly effaced. Beneath the dexter side are the initial letters M. C., and, under the sinister, M. D. The height of the shaft is at present three feet six inches above the slab, in which a socket is cut to receive the tenon upon the lower end of the shaft. This slab stands on a low grassy hillock, the remains, doubtless, of an ascent of three or four stone steps, which, when complete, the cross surmounted.

" A restoration of the entire inscription showed that the upper part of the shaft had been broken off, and with it the first line of the inscription. Of what remains the first line is illegible, but the rest is tolerably distinct. It is in the black-letter character of the sixteenth century, the letters being beautifully formed; and (filling up the contractions) it runs thus:

" ' . . . . . Armigeri, et Margaretæ Dexter uxoris ejus ac heredum eorum qui hanc crucem fecerunt anno Domini 1588 quorum animabus propicietur Deus, Amen.'

" This inscription leaves little doubt that this memorial was one of the wayside crosses so generally erected by the piety of individuals about the sixteenth and the preceding centuries, but which the ill-directed zeal of a subsequent period so unsparingly mutilated, and often wholly destroyed. Upon inquiry it proved that a road, leading from Navan to Rathaldron Castle, long the residence of one of the principal branches of the ancient family of the Cusacks, once passed close in front of this cross."

The name of the husband of Margaret Dexter Mr. Smith soon after learned from a manuscript in the possession of Mr. H. T. Cusack. " This MS. is written in French, and entitled 'An Historical Memoir and Genealogy of the ancient and illustrious House of Cusack, of the Kingdom of Ireland.' It appears to have been compiled by the Chevalier O'Gorman in the year 1767. It states that 'Michael de Cusack, lord of Portrane and Rathaldron, married Margaret Dexter, who brought him, as a marriage portion, the castle, town, and lands of Rathaldron. He was ' Greffier' [a term which Boyer translates ' Registrar,' or Keeper of the Rolls] of Westmeath and of Louth in 1553, one of the Barons of the Exchequer in 1580, and died in 1589.' From this it may be safely concluded that the initials ' M. C.' upon the cross are those of ' Michael Cusack,' and that his was the name sculptured on the upper part of the cross, now lost."

CHAPTER VII.

THE BOYNE FROM NAVAN TO SLANE.

DONAGHMORE ROUND TOWER.—BLACK CASTLE.—BABES' BRIDGE.—ARDMULCHAN.—DUNMOE.—
STACKALLAN BRIDGE.—CASTLE DEXTER. — BEAUPARC. — FENNOR. — SLANE CASTLE.—THE
HERMITAGE OF ST. ERC.—VIEW FROM THE HILL OF SLANE.—THE ARRIVAL OF ST. PATRICK.—
NAME AND ORIGIN OF SLANE.—FERTA-FEAR FEIG.—THE MONASTIC AND ECCLESIASTICAL
RUINS.—AN ANCIENT TOMB.

FROM Navan to the Boyne's mouth the river, though intersected
by several weirs, and descending several rapids, has been rendered navigable by means of a canal, affording transit to lighters
of several tons' burden, by which a considerable traffic, particularly of coals and corn, is carried on between this place and
Drogheda. Along the road by this canal and the river the
tourist can walk to Beauparc, or descend, as we have effected
the voyage, in a boat, drawn by a single horse; and this mode
of conveyance we would strongly recommend to our freinds,
not only as the least fatiguing, particularly for ladies, but also
as enabling the tourist to cross the river at pleasure, for it is
only in some places that the canal is necessary.

Immediately on leaving Navan, where the river resumes
its original north-easterly direction, the scene reminds one
strongly of some of the views upon the Dutch canals. The
river here is deep, and its current slow, the force of the water
being retained by a weir lower down. On the left bank stands
Blackcastle, the seat of Mrs. Fitzherbert,—a square, modern
building, designed more for comfort than architectural beauty;
but the grounds, which are naturally picturesque, are well
laid out, and afford many pleasing prospects of woodland
glade and sloping meadow, as we descend the river; and the
wood which skirts the stream throws a cool refreshing shade on
its left bank, for above a mile of its course.

Adjoining the demense of Blackcastle, on the Slane road,
about a mile from Navan, on the western bank of the river,
we pass the group of ecclesiastical ruins figured in the engraving upon the next page,—the round tower and church of
Donoughmore.

The original church, called *Domnach-mor-muighe Echnach*,

*

the great church of the plain of Echnach, is said to owe its
origin to St. Patrick, who gave it to his disciple Cassanus.
As this interesting group of
ecclesiastical remains, which
forms such a charming picture from every side by
which we approach it, has
been accurately described
by Dr. Petrie, and as the
tower itself is in every respect not only one of the
most picturesque in appearance, but one of the most
conclusive as to the Christian origin of these structures in Ireland, we afford
our readers the following
detailed account of it and
the adjoining church, from
the pen of the great au-
thority alluded to, rather

than any description of our own. He has given an account
of this tower in two places,—in the Transactions of the Royal
Irish Academy, where there is a drawing of the doorway, and
in the Irish Penny Journal, from which latter, being the most
detailed, we quote.

Regarding the erection of the great church at Domnach-
mor, we learn from a passage in the Tripartite Life of St. Patrick, that,

" ' While the man of God was baptizing the people called
Luaignii, at a place where the church of Domnach-mor in the
plain of Echnach stands at this day, he called to him his disciple Cassanus, and committed to him the care of the church
recently erected there, preadmonishing him, and with prophetic
mouth predicting, that he might expect that to be the place of
his resurrection; and that the church committed to his care
would always remain diminutive in size and structure, but
great and celebrated in honour and veneration. The event
has proved this prophecy to be a true one, for St. Cassanus's
relics are there to be seen in the highest veneration among the
people, remarkable for great miracles, so that scarcely any of

the visitors go away without recovering health, or receiving other gifts of grace sought for.'—*Tr. Th.* p. 130.

" But though the existing ruins of the church of Donaghmore sufficiently indicate it to have been a structure ' diminutive in size,' its architectural features clearly prove that it is not the original church of St. Patrick's erection, but a re-edification of the thirteenth century, in the usual style of the parish churches erected by the Anglo-Norman settlers within the Pale. Neither can the round tower, though unquestionably a structure of much higher antiquity than the present church, be referred to the time of the Irish apostle, or perhaps to an earlier age than the ninth or tenth century. At all events its erection cannot be ascribed to an earlier date than that of the tower of the church of Kells,—a religious establishment founded by St. Columbkille in the sixth century,—as these towers so perfectly agree in architectural style and mason-work, that they appear to have been constructed by the same architects or builders.

" This very beautiful tower is built entirely of limestone, undressed, except around the doorway and other apertures, and is of admirable masonry. It has two projecting ledges or steps at its base, and six rests for stories, with intermediate projecting stones or brackets in its interior. These stories are each, as usual, lighted by a single aperture, with the exception of the upper one, which has two openings, one facing the east, and the other the west ; and the apertures present all the architectural varieties of form observable in our most ancient churches.* The circumference of this tower, near its base, is sixty-six feet six inches, and its height, to the slant of the roof, which is wanting, is about 100 feet. The wall is three feet nine inches in thickness, and the doorway is twelve feet from the ground. This doorway, which is of very beautiful execution, and, as usual, faces the west end of the church, is five feet two inches in height, and has inclined sides, and a semi-

---

* Since this was written the top of Donaghmore tower has been repaired ; but while we must, with every admirer of the ancient architecture of Ireland, and every one who desires to see those ruins preserved from utter destruction, applaud the motive that induced this reparation, we cannot but regret that more attention was not paid to the form of the tops of other round towers In this modern top there are no windows whatever, an anomaly in Irish round towers.

M

circularly arched top. It is two feet three inches wide at bottom, and two feet beneath the spring of the arch at top. Over the door there is the figure of the Saviour sculptured in relief, partly on the key-stone and partly on the stone over it ; and on each side of the architrave there is a human head, also in relief, as on the doorway of the church of Kells.

" Some antiquaries, in their zeal to support the theory of the Pagan origin and the antiquity of the round towers, have asserted that this doorway is not the original one, but an ' after work.' But there is not the slightest ground for such a supposition, and this sculpture, as a profoundly skilled architectural antiquary, the late Sir Richard Colt Hoare, well observed, furnishes ' a decided proof that these buildings were not (as some writers have conjectured) built by the Pagans.'

" A similar argument against the application of the round towers to the purposes of a belfry, has been grounded on the circumstance of the western front of the church having three apertures for bells above its gable. But it should not be forgotten that this structure has no claim to an earlier date than the thirteenth century, when a variety of bells, and a different mode of hanging them, were brought into use by the Anglo-Norman settlers.

"The church of Donagh-more has been confounded by Archdall and subsequent writers with the ancient church of Domnach-Tortain, also founded by St. Patrick, but which was situated near Ardbraccan."

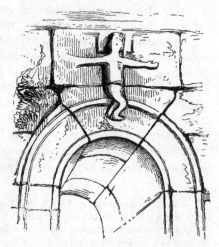

Since the above was written we visited, in company with Dr. Petrie, the round tower of Brechin in Scotland, and had there an opportunity of seeing a very perfect and much more finished representation of the Crucifixion, carved in relief, on the top stone of the doorway; and that tower is probably not older than the tenth century; there is also a hatchment with heraldic devices carved, in relief, on the front of the door-sill.

The foregoing wood-cut is a faithful representation of the figure over the door of Donaghmore tower.

A mile below Navan, there is a large flax factory, which, like other similar establishments, though highly advantageous to the country, is no addition to the picturesqueness of the scenery. Beyond this mill we pass an abrupt bank, called Knock-a-Raymon, in which, a few years ago, a vast quantity of animal remains, and some sepulchral urns in small kistvaens were discovered. It was evidently one of the barrows of the aborigines; and we record the circumstance here, not from any present interest attached to the place, for it is now but a potato garden, but because we feel that the name and locality of every spot of Irish ground, in which such records of our ancestry are discovered, should be carefully noted, in order that the historian and the searcher into the unpublished manuscripts and archives, which are being now, for the first time, properly examined, may be aware of the fact,—for a vast number of these cairns and tumuli are alluded to in the annals referring to the Pagan occupation of this country. Not far from this point, we find the sacred well of Tober Ruadh; and now the right bank spreads out into broad meadows, glowing with the bright yellow blossoms of the butter-cups and may-flowers.

At the first lock upon the canal, an abrupt precipitous hill, the Knockminaune, or Kids' Hill, is crowned by a minor tumulus, the view from the summit of which commands the church of Ardmulchan, and two of the most interesting objects in the beauties of the Boyne,—the round tower of Donaghmore, already described, and the grey massive castle of Dunmoe. Seen from this point, the tall slender tower rising out of the green woods of Blackcastle, and cutting clear and sharp on the horizon, against the blue sky, forms an object of intense interest and beauty in this most charming landscape; and lower down upon the river's bank, the ancient fortress of the D'Arcys stands in gloom and grandeur on a brown and generally verdureless mound, without a tree or a single spot of green to relieve the sombre hue of its high walls and flanking towers.

The contrast between these two memorials of the art and history of this country is very striking, and tells the tale of times to boast of, and also to mourn. The stately, chaste, and simple style of the early pillar, whose age cannot be far from 1000 years, added to the knowledge which we possess of the erection of the original church which once adjoined it, points to the first preaching of Christianity in our island, when a few devout Christians and some of the early fathers of the Irish Church settled round these buildings, and passed a life of pastoral quiet and simplicity; and now, surrounded by patriarchal timber, and reverenced by the people, it remains almost as perfect as when it came from the hands of the mason; and may continue so for centuries yet to come, unless some prying and infatuated antiquary should be allowed to grope under its foundation, for fragments of human bones to decorate museums, or give to the vulgar and uninformed some fancied proof of a theory as unintelligible as it is absurd. Turn to the castle of the D'Arcys,—a thing comparatively of yesterday, marking the boundary of the English Pale: it tells of the worst days of misrule in this unhappy land, where, without conquering the proud hearts, or gaining the warm affections of the Irish, the Anglo-Norman barons, who, with mailed hearts as well as backs,—neither civilizing nor enriching the country,—resided amongst us.* It is now fast falling into decay, and in a few years more will be but a great cairn of stones.

A bridge crossed the Boyne below this point in former days, a single arch of which, upon the right bank of the river, still remains. Before its complete demolition, it went by the name of Farginston's, or " the Robbers' Bridge," tradition says, on account of some noted horse-stealers, in the early part of the last century, having made it their chief resort. The country people also tell us, that Cromwell's army crossed it in its passage up the Boyne; and a village poet, named Courtney, has celebrated this ancient pass in some doggerel rhymes, which still live in the mouths of the neighbouring peasantry. The ancient name was "Babe's Bridge," and that it was one of the

---

* It struck the *Times* Commissioner, who commenced the late crusade against the Irish landlords, that the great majority of them are English, or of English descent. Is it known to the world, that while English settlers have become the proprietors, there never was any extensive importation of English farmers or yeomen into the southern and western parts of Ireland?

earliest bridges upon the Boyne may be learned from James Grace's Annals of Ireland, where we read, that, in the year 1330, "there was also a great flood, especially of the Boyne, by which all the bridges on that river, except Babe's, were carried away, and other mischief done, at Trim and Drogheda."

The next points of interest are, Ardmulchan church upon the right, and somewhat below it, Dunmoe Castle, upon the left. And here the true beauties of the Boyne, its real Rhine-like characters, commence, and crowd upon us for the next few miles of its course. High beetling crags, crowned by feudal halls and ruined chapels,—steep, precipitous banks, covered with the noblest monarchs of the forest,—dells, consecrated to the moonlight dance of sprites and elfins, and rocks, memorable for their tales of love, and legends of the olden time, catch the eye at every turn in this noble stream, presenting new beauties, ever-varying pictures, here in sunshine, there in shade, with charming bits of scenery, which simple prose cannot describe: the painter's art alone can embody, or give an accurate representation of these. We "stop not for brake, and we stay not for stone;" clear and blue the stream runs fast, and we must onward with its course, skimming lightly over its surface, rather inciting inquiry by our remarks, and directing attention in our researches, than attempting anything like an elaborate or detailed description.

The ruins of Ardmulchan (Ard-Maelchon, or Maelchu's height), top one of the highest banks above a bold stretch of the river, and consist of a tall square tower or belfry, and the remains of a church, which stands surrounded by an ancient graveyard, and some walls, believed to be part of one of the castles of the Tyrrells. That this church tower is composed of the material of some earlier building may be learned from the fact of the lintel in one of its upper doors being formed of an ancient sculptured tombstone, as  shown in the accompanying wood-cut. We are well aware that crosses are sometimes found carved on the soffit of the lintel in some very ancient church doors; but they are not of the same description, nor partially concealed, like this at Ardmulchan.

In the year 968, Amlaff Cuaran, with his Danes, and a party of Leinstermen, plundered Kells, and carried off a vast prey of cows, and gained a victory over the southern Hy-Neill at Ard-Maelchon.*

Ardmulchan belonged at one period to the Earl of Kildare. By an inquisition taken in the tenth year of the reign of James I., it was found that in the parish church of St. Mary (Ardmulchan) was a perpetual chantry of one priest, who was constantly to celebrate service therein, and this chantry was a body corporate. It at present belongs to the rectory of Painstown. A very beautiful well below this spot is worthy of attention; and a short distance beyond the church we meet with an ancient military fort, consisting of a circular mound, enclosed with a fosse and rampart. A grove of ash-trees now covers the entire, their tall, slender stems permitting the outline of this ancient relic to be seen at a considerable distance, while their feathery tops form an umbrageous shadow to the whole. Miss Beaufort, in her learned "Essay upon the State of Architecture and Antiquities previous to the landing of the Anglo-Normans in Ireland,"† informs us that a kistvaen or small stone chamber was discovered at Ardmulchan some years back, by a gentleman, in removing an artificial tumulus. It contained several skeletons, urns, and some golden ornaments. Into a deep pool in the river, opposite Taaffe's lock, called Lug-Gorrom, or the Blue Hole, it is said that the bells of this church were thrown at the time of the Reformation.

Dunmoe Castle stands on a commanding eminence, above one of the fords upon the Boyne, and must have been originally a position of considerable strength. The stones, however, with which it is built, are remarkably small, in consequence of which it is yearly crumbling into a shapeless mass of ruins. It is an oblong pile, with circular flanking towers on its river face, which measures seventy-three feet.‡ It was

---

* Annals of the Four Masters.

† Transactions of the Royal Irish Academy, vol. xv. p. 159.

‡ The accompanying sketch, by Mr. Wakeman, is taken from the right bank of the river. In Mr. Thomas Cromwell's "Excursions through Ireland," 1820,

originally built, it is said, by De Lacy, but the present structure bears the evidence of an Anglo-Norman keep of the
sixteenth century. It has had many masters and stood several sieges in its day. During the civil wars of 1641, after the
defeat of the English forces near Julianstown, an Irish detachment was sent to take Dunmoe; but Captain Power, who
commanded it, with a mere handful of men, so long and bravely
resisted his assailants, that the latter had to resort to strata-
gem to take it, and by producing a forged order from the
Lords Justices, Parsons and Borlace, induced its gallant defender to surrender the castle and proceed to Dublin. Oliver
Cromwell, it is said, took a passing shot at it from the opposite
bank of the Boyne, but did not think it worthy of further
notice. The ball which he fired at Dunmoe, or one shown as

such, was, until a very recent period, used as a weight at
a neighbouring crane. This castle was re-edified and inhabited while James II. was in Ireland. Its last lord was
D'Arcy, whose name is now usually associated with it. The

will be found a beautiful drawing, by Petrie, of Dunmoe Castle, vol. ii. p. 79.
Since then it has been considerably dilapidated.

peasantry state that an underground passage leads from it under the Boyne to the opposite bank. Dunmoe was burned in 1799, but a portion of the roof remained within the last thirty years. Within the adjoining enclosure is a small chapel containing the mausoleum of its last lords; it is now a filthy dungeon, exposed to the atmosphere, and strewed with the bones and coffins of the descendants of this once noble family. Some twenty years more, and the traveller will have to inquire for the site of this celebrated castle of the Pale.

> " I walked one day adown the Boyne,
>   From Domnach-Mor to Slaine;
> How rich the fields on every side,
>   In cattle, wood, or grain.
>
> The river flowed in summer pride,
>   And on its banks of green,
> How many a noble ancient home
>   Seemed sent'nelling the scene.
>
> I marked the salmon springing free,
>   Beneath the glittering fall;
> I heard the cuckoo in the glen
>   Repeat her welcome call.
>
> The hare would skip from out the green,
>   And, sporting on the lea,
> Seem mad with joy—with very joy,—
>   O, who so blythe as he?
>
> The nearer kine had left the field,
>   To cool them in mid-stream;
> With glossy sides and switching tails,
>   They stood, and seemed to dream.
>
> The sheep-bells tingled on the hill;
>   And from the mossy wheel
> That flashing plays 'neath old Dunmoe
>   An ancient sound would steal."*

The ruins at Ardmulchan adjoin the direct road between Navan and Drogheda on the southern bank of the river, and the railway passes immediately beside them. This southern road, though it does not here command views of the Boyne, presents many objects of great interest, and passes through a charming

---

* " Vigilantius," in the *Irishman*. One who knows the Boyne well.

country. Leaving Ardmulchan, with its adjoining demesne, on the left, we pass by Hayes, the Meath residence of the present Earl of Mayo; and on the road side between that and Beauparc, we meet two fine raths,—one of considerable extent, and overlooking the river, " the horse fort" near the cross roads leading to Stackallan-bridge, and the other a little further on, at Dollardstown, a most picturesque wooded mount, with a surrounding fosse and ditch. A few trees, such as these upon this mound are rather an improvement; but when raths are covered with low underwood or brushwood, or completely obscured by timber, as at Donaghpatrick and New Grange, we lose much of their scenic effect. Several other raths stand by the wayside between this point and Drogheda; and lower down towards Rosnaree, where the road skirts the river, we obtain views of those great sepulchral pyramids, which form the cemetery of Brugh-na-Boinne, particularly those of Knowth, New Grange, Dowth, and that elegantly shaped little rath which stands in a green meadow within a bold stretch of the river opposite Roughgrange.

Presuming, however, that the tourist has descended the river in a boat, or loitered by one or other of its margins, we would conduct him to our next point of interest, Stackallan, where Broad Boyne Bridge, leading to the Slane and Navan road, crosses the river. In the immediate vicinity is the residence of Viscount Boyne, lately occupied by the Seminary or College of St. Columba. This, like almost every spot of ground along the Boyne and Blackwater, to which a name attaches, has been commemorated in our ancient histories. Its Irish name is Tigh Collain—*Teach-Collan*, the house of Collan, which was, we read, situate in the ancient territory of Ui-Crimhthainn, at present comprised in the baronies of Upper and Lower Slane.*

In the neighbourhood of Stackallan, upon the Slane and Navan road, on the northern bank of the river, there are two

---

* O'Donovan, in his note on the record of the death of " Cethernach, bishop from Teach-Callain," who died on a pilgrimage at Hi, A. D. 1047, writes : " It is curious to remark, that in some of those districts, colonized by the Danes and English, the *Teach* or *Tigh*, of the Irish, was made *Sta* or *Sti*, as in this instance [Stackallan], and in Stickillen, Stagonnell, Stillorgan, in Irish ᴄᴉᵹ Chillín, ᴄeaċ Chonaill, ᴄᴉᵹ Lopcáin." The same learned authority thinks the name should be ᴄeaċ Conáin, *St. Conan's house.* See Annals of the Four Masters, p. 851, A. D. 1047.

trivial objects, still not so uninteresting as to be passed by without a peep into the one and a glance at the other, if only to assist us in making good the promise contained in our first chapter as to the multitude and variety of remains extending along the Boyne. These are Tober Padraig, a blessed well, dedicated to our patron saint, but now neglected and disused, and Baronstown cross, a wayside monumental cross, the pillar or shaft of which, supported by a short pedestal or base, still stands on a small knoll near the road; the head has been broken into fragments, several of which may be seen scattered around. This monument was erected by one of the Dowdalls, the great cross-builders of Meath, of whose memorials of piety and affection two other examples of a similar description may be seen not far off, one in the town of Duleek, and the other at Annesbrook, in its neighbourhood. The shaft of this cross at Baronstown is four-sided, and on each face there is a rather rude and ill-spelled inscription. Upon the western face, beneath a figure of St. Patrick, we read,

" I PRAY YOU, SAINT PATRICK, PRAY FOR THE SOULES OF OLIVER PLUNKET, LORD BARON OF LOUTH, AND DAME JENET DOWDAL, HIS WIFE."

Upon the south front:—

" THIS CROSSE WAS BULDED BY DAME JANET DOWDALL, LATE WIFE UNTO OLIVER PLUNKET, LORD BARON OF LOUTH, FOR HIM AND HERSELFE, IN THE YERE OF OUR LORD GOD" * * * [Probably 1590.]

Underneath a rude image of St. Peter, on the east side:—

" I PRAY YOU, SAINT PETER, PRAY FOR THE SOULES OF OLIVER PLUNKET, LORD BARON OF LOUTH, AND DAME JENET DOWDAL, HIS WIFE."

On the back, towards the north, under a plain shield, similar to that which exists at top of the south front, is the " Hail Mary," and an invocation for the prayers of the Virgin.

A little to the south-east of Broad Boyne Bridge, another military fort (this may be the house of Cletty of the Irish writers), similar to that at Ardmulchan, appears on the right bank. The river here forms a smooth, glass-like sheet of water, and below the bridge affords us one of those striking effects which the weirs upon the Boyne exhibit, of a long unbroken line of liquid, bent into a graceful curve, goldened with the sunshine, as it glides in swift but silent track over the long horse-shoe fall, and then breaks into a million streams—its spray dancing in the sunshine, and its bubbles reflecting all the prismatic colours of the rainbow, as it again springs onward in its course. These charming effects, whether varied by the grey morning's light, or the evening's uncertain haze, or having an air of obscurity thrown over them by the veils of mist which rise and play round the fall, or float like phantoms over the broad surface of the river—here assuming the figure of a stately vessel, there rising into tall, castellated form—creeping under the arches of bridges, re-appearing in an instant; wrapping in their shroud the aged trees, which dip into the waters,—drifting again along the surface, like the broken fragments of some tall iceberg, and suddenly lifted above the mirror on which they play, leaving the surface on which they had appeared to breathe, again unbroken on its outline,—add not a little to keep those scenes in our remembrance. If we stand at sundown on the bridge of Slane, when there is any body of water in the river, on a calm summer's evening, listening to the soothing monotony of the fall, and cast our eyes over the broad reach of the Boyne above, we cannot fail to be struck with the effect which is here attempted to be described.

The broad reach of the river below the bridge at Stackallan has been supposed by some antiquarians to be in the vicinity of *Brugh-na-Boinne*, one, if not the chief of the royal cemeteries, and where the monarchs of Tara were interred of old; but we think the evidence is in favour of a locality lower down beyond Slane, to which we shall presently refer. A deep pool, immediately below the bridge, receives the name of Lugaree, the king's hole, where the river well deserves the name of the "Broad Boyne," which it still retains. Some ancient pagan remembrances and superstitions attached to this locality, up to a very recent date; and, at a *Patron* which used to be held here some years ago, it was customary for the people to swim their cattle across the river at this spot, as a charm against fairies and certain diseases, as in former times they drove them through the Gap of Tara.*

* The same practice is still observed at Newtown-Trim upon the first Sunday in August. St. Sinchea's well, *Tober t-Sinne*, is said to be in the neighbour-

To many of our readers, however, and most of the tourists who may follow our wanderings, or require a guide-book in their excursion, a more interesting subject than ancient customs, or even the tombs of kings, invites us onward; for the wood-crowned heights and leafy banks of Beauparc, one of the most picturesque spots in Ireland, and the noble demesne of Slane, lie immediately before us. Beyond the fall of Stackallan we pass through the most delicious scenery, particularly along the left bank, where groves of noble beech trees and aged chesnuts fringe the heights, and an underwood of laurels, thorns, and sweet-briars mantle upon the undulating surface of the shores beneath, till we pass the mill and bridge of Cruisetown, where (supposing that we have come down in a boat, which is by far the best plan) we commit ourselves to the centre of the stream, and bestow an equal share of our attention upon both banks. Here the river forms a number of sudden curves, each winding presenting us with a new picture more beautiful than its predecessor. The banks spring high and abrupt from the water's edge, so that in some places the massive trees, rising in piles of the most gorgeous foliage, appear topling over us from their summits, and darken the deep smooth pools they overhang. Upon a summer's day an air of calm repose pervades this spot; the very songsters of the grove seem hushed in admiration, and unwilling to disturb the peaceful thoughts which here gradually steal over the beholder. On the right the modern mansion of Beauparc peeps through the never-ending green of tall pines, sycamores, oaks, and elms. On the left the ivy-mantled walls of Castle Dexter raise themselves above the dark plantation, contrasting the times of feudal rule and massive defensive architecture, with its light domestic neighbour of more modern date. The limestone rock, here twisted into a variety of curious contortions, breaks through the surface, and relieves the eye, almost satiated with the endless variety both of colour and foliage. Through occasional openings we obtain glimpses of long vistas, formed by the overhanging boughs, and terminated by glades of turf, on which the sun beams with unusual splendour. The river spreads out, and the sun again glances upon its smooth waters ; the

hood of Broad Boyne Bridge, but, unless that now called on the Ordnance Map Tober Patrick be it, we are not aware of its site.

massive perpendicular rock of Fennor, about which we could tell many a fairy legend and relate many a tale of love, rears aloft its giant form, with its fir-fringed summit and bold grey front, draped with festoons and long tendrils of dark green ivy; and then, as we float downward with the stream, enjoying beauties scarcely known and little noticed in this country, the modern castle of Slane suddenly bursts upon us, occupying a most commanding situation, and appearing, with its sur-rounding wooded hills, the back-ground or extreme distance of a picture framed by the elevated banks of the Boyne, which here spreads out in front of it into a noble sheet of water, for which there does not, at first view, seem any exit.

To visit these different objects of interest in detail;—here is the ruined fortress of Castle Dexter, from which the surround-ing townland of Carrickdexter probably takes its name. The ovens and huge fire-places in this castle attest the good living of its early occupants; but the windows are not so well preserved, neither were they ori-ginally so well made as those at Athlum-ney. Very little is known of the history of this beautifully situated castle, at least that was acces-

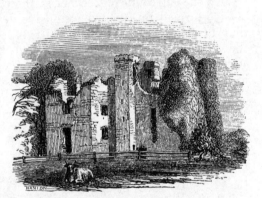

sible to us through the ordinary sources of information. It is said by the people around to have been erected by one of the Flemings, the early lords of Slane, and to have been their ori-ginal residence. From its name, however, we should suppose it to have belonged, if it was not built, by one of the D'Exeter family, some of whom were located in Meath, although the great sept was in Connaught, where they assumed the Irish name of Mac Jordan. In the " Annales Hiberniæ Jacobi Grace, Kilkenniensis," under the year 1312, we read that " Milo Ver-don married the daughter of Richard de Exoniis (Dexter);" and the inscription on the monumental wayside cross at Nevins-town, already mentioned at page 157, assists to throw some light on the history of the Meath branch of this family. The name is also mentioned (as a witness) in the Register of All-Hallows, Dublin, lately printed by our Archæological Society. A story is told that a salmon-trap formerly existed in the river immediately adjoining Castle Dexter, and when a fish was caught its struggles touched a wire connected with a bell in the castle, which gave the cook notice of its capture. A similar tale is, however, told of several other castles and monasteries standing by the brinks of rivers.

Slane Castle, the seat of the Marquis of Conyngham, and memorable in modern times, from its being visited by King George IV., stands on a swelling bank of verdant greensward, rising gradually from the river. It is a large castellated mansion, with towers and embattled parapets, but not boasting much beauty of architectural design. It is principally the surrounding scenery, the combinations of sylvan beauty formed by its own extensive demesne, blending with that of Beauparc, the neighbouring woods of other seats, the charming associations awakened by the ancient ruins standing on the romantic shores of its noble river, and the highly cultivated landscape on all sides, which claim for Slane Castle the eulogiums of its modern describers. Leaving this

modern residence of the lords of Slane, we drift onward, still approaching the northern bank, and land at the church or hermitage of St. Erc, which stands within the demesne, upon the shore immediately below the castle, embosomed within the dark shadows of a grove of ancient yews, one of the most romantic ruins of its date and style in Ireland. Considerable portions of this picturesque building still exist. The accompanying engraving fathfully represents the doorway.

It takes its name from Erc, " the sweet-spoken judge," the first Bishop of Slane, who was consecrated by St. Patrick, and died A. D. 514.* It was afterwards the retreat of Malachi and Donat O'Brien, two hermits, who resided here in 1512. Over the pointed door we find the fleur-de-lis, and upon the inner doorway some rose ornaments, rather unusual in Irish architecture. Within the little chapel is the tomb of the Earls of Drogheda, and upon the walk above the hermitage there lies a handsome sculptured stone, with twelve figures upon it, evidently a portion of an ancient tomb, and well worthy the attentive examination of the antiquarian student.

From the mixture of round and pointed arches, as well as the evident difference in the styles of masonry, it is manifest that this building at St. Erc's was erected or remodelled at two different eras.

* The Annals of the Four Masters say Bishop Erc died upon the 2nd November, 512. " His age was four score years and ten when he departed. This Bishop Erc was judge to Patrick. It was for him Patrick composed this quatrain :

<blockquote>
" ' Bishop Erc,—
Everything he adjudged was just ;
Every one that passes a just judgment,
Shall receive the blessing of Bishop Erc.' "
</blockquote>

In the historical tale of the banquet of Dun na n-Gedh, a composition of the twelfth century, there is a curious reference to this place. King Domhnall, having completed his great fort, or house, determined, as was usual on such occasions, to give a feast, and for that purpose sent forth his stewards to collect every delicacy of the season, for, like many a modern Heliogabulus, " Domhnall did not deem it honourable that there should be in Erin a kind of food that should not be at that banquet."

" And the collectors went forth throughout Meath, in search of the eggs, until they came to a small Duirtheach [hermitage], in which was one woman with a black hood upon her head, and she praying to God. The king's people saw a flock of geese at the door of the Duirtheach; they went into the house and found a vessel full of goose eggs. ' We have had great success,' said they, ' for should we search Erin, there could not be found more goose eggs together in one place than are here.' ' It will not be good success,' said the woman, ' and it will not redound to the happiness of the banquet to which this small quantity of provisions will be brought.' ' Why so?' said they. ' It is plain,' said the woman; ' a wonder-working saint of God's people dwells here, namely, Bishop Erc, of Slaine,* and his custom is to remain immersed in the Boinn, up to his two arm-pits, from morning till evening, having his Psalter before him on the strand, constantly engaged in prayer; and his dinner every evening on returning hither is an egg and a half, and three sprigs of the cresse of the Boinn; and it behoves you not to take away from him the small store of food which he has. But the proud people of the king made no reply to her,—for they were plebeians in the shape of heroes on this occasion,—and they carried away the property

---

* " This is an anachronism, for Bishop Erc, of Slaine, who was contemporary with St. Patrick, died in the year 514 (Ussher's Primordia, p. 442), and this battle was fought in the year 638, that is 124 years after Erc's death !   The probability is, that the original composer of the story had written *Comharba* [i. e. successor] of Erc, of Slaine ; but all the copies to which we have access at present agree in making the saint Erc himself." See " The Banquet of Dun na n-Gedh, and the Battle of Magh-Rath, an ancient historical Tale, now first published from a Manuscript in the Library of Trinity College, Dublin, with Translation and Notes, by John O'Donovan, for the Irish Archæological Society."

of the righteous man and saint, in despite of him [her]. But woe to him to whom this small quantity of food was brought, for a great evil sprang from it afterwards; for Erin was not one night thenceforward in the enjoyment of peace, or tranquillity, or without a desire of evil or injustice, for some time.

" The holy patron, Bishop Erc, of Slaine, came to his house in the evening, and the woman told him how he was plundered. The righteous man then became wroth, and said: ' It will not be good luck to the person to whom this kind of food was brought; and may the peace or welfare of Erin not result from the banquet to which it was brought; but may quarrels, contentions, and commotions be the consequence to her.' And he cursed the banquet as bitterly as he was able to curse it.

" As the king's people were afterwards at the assembly, they saw a couple approaching them, namely, a woman and a man; larger than the summit of a rock on a mountain was each member of their members; sharper than a shaving knife the edge of their shins; their heels and hams in front of them; should a sackful of apples be thrown on their heads not one of them would fall to the ground, but would stick on the points of the strong, bristly hair which grew out of their heads; blacker than the coal or darker than the smoke was each of their members; whiter than snow their eyes; a lock of the lower beard was carried round the back of the head; a lock of the upper beard descended so as to cover the knees; the woman had whiskers, but the man was without whiskers. They carried a tub between them which was full of goose eggs. In this plight they saluted the king. ' What is that?' said the king. ' It is plain,' said they, ' the men of Erin are making a banquet for thee, and each brings what he can to that banquet, and our mite is the quantity of eggs we are carrying.' ' I am thankful for it,' said the king. They were conducted into the palace, and a dinner sufficient for a hundred was given to them of meat and ale. This the man consumed, and did not give any part of it to the woman. Another dinner sufficient for a hundred was given them, and the woman alone consumed it. They demanded more, and another dinner for a hundred was given them, and both of them together consumed it. ' Give us food,' said they, ' if you have it.' ' By our word we shall not,' said Casciabhach, the king's Rechtairè, ' till the men of Erin in general shall come to the feast.' The others then said, ' Evil

N

shall it be to you that we have partaken of the banquet first, for the men of Erin shall be quarrelsome at it, for we are of the people of Infernus.' And they predicted great evils to the multitudes, and afterwards rushed out, and vanished into nothing." This banquet was the cause of the celebrated Battle of Magh Rath.

Not far distant from the Hermitage was Lady Well, but it is now nearly obliterated; and in the wall of the pleasure-ground of the castle may be seen the carved effigy of an ecclesiastic, probably a bishop: and below, a little to the right of the bridge of Slane, stands the old church and ruined castle of Fennor, but they do not possess sufficient interest to require minute examination.

Let us pass under the handsome gate of Slane demesne, through the neat little town adjoining, where, at its comfortable hotel, we may enjoy as bright and generous a glass of claret, and receive as good cheer, as at any similar establishment with which we are acquainted; and then climb the hill which rises immediately over the town. On the western brow of the hill stands a noble circular, entrenched rath, possibly the seat of the palace of the monarch from whom its present name is derived. We are now upon the wooded height which so frequently caught our eye as we passed down the Boyne, and upon the spot so

often referred to in the foregoing descriptions,—Slane, the early residence and the burial-place of King Slanius (see page 14). Ascending the hill, we stand beside a group of ruins, the remains of the church and monastery figured above.

Here, pilgrim, stop; rest on yonder monumental slab, beneath the shadow of that tall, ivy-mantled tower, the belfry of the cathedral—it once was gorgeous with the shrines of Fathers, and illumed by many a flickering taper, though now the hemlock fills its aisles, and the purple foxglove waves its lonely banneret. The ground whereon we stand is sacred,—consecrated by the foot-prints of our patron saint, hallowed by the dust of kings. Look abroad over the wide, undulating plains of Meath, or to the green hills of Louth: where, in the broad landscapes of Britain, find we a scene more fruitful and varied, or one more full of interesting, heart-stirring associations? Climb this tower and cast your eye along the river. Look from the tall, pillar-like form of the Yellow Steeple at Trim, which rises in the distance, to where yon bright line marks the meeting of the sea and sky below the Maiden Tower at Drogheda, and trace the clear blue waters of the Boyne, winding through this lovely, highly cultivated landscape, so rich in all that can charm the eye and awaken the imagination; take into view the hills of Skreen and Tara; pass in review the woods of Hayes, Ardmulchan, Beauparc; look down into the green mounds and broad pastures of Slane; follow the Boyne below you, as it dances by each ford and rapid, to where the great pyramids of western Europe, Knowth, New Grange, and Dowth, rise on its left bank; see you not the groves of Townley Hall and Old Bridge, marking the battle-field of 1690, with the ill-fated hill of Donore, where the sceptre passed for ever from the royal line of Stuart, obtruding its long-remembered tale of civil strife upon us? Duleek stands in the distance. Beyond those hills that border Louth lie Monasterboice, and Mellifont, the last resting-place of the faithless Bride of Brefney. Those steeples and turrets which rise in the lower distance were shattered by the balls of Cromwell; and that knoll which juts above them is the Mill Mount of Drogheda. What a picture have we here, from this Richmond Hill of Irish scenery! What an extensive page of our country's history does it unfold to us! What recollections gush upon us as we stand on the abbey walls of Slane, and take in this noble prospect at a glance! The records and the footprints of two thousand years are all before us; the solemn procession of the simple shepherd to the early Pagan mound; the rude slinger standing on the earthen circle; the Druid fires, paling before the bright sun of Christianity; the cadence of the round tower's bell; the matin and the vesper hymn swelling from the hermit's cell, or early missionary church; the proud galleys and glancing swords of fierce northern hordes; the smoking ruins of church and tower; the shout of rival clans in civil feuds; the lances and banners of Norman soldiers; the moat, and fosse, and drawbridge of the keep, still echoing back the strife of hostile ranks,—the native for his soil, the stranger for his hire; the ford defended, and the castle won; the pilgrim's cross, the stately abbey, and the baron's hall; in church, the stole ejected for the surplice; the town besieged, the city sacked; and then the ratttle, and the roar, and smoke of recent battle; —have, one and all, their epochs, ruins, sites, or history, legibly inscribed upon this picture.

The early Irish name of Slane was Ferta-fear-Feig, the graves of the men of Feig,* and one of the first notices of it which our annals contain relates to a most remarkable epoch in the history of this country. We mentioned that Patrick landed at the Boyne's mouth ; he afterwards passed up that river's bank a day's journey into Meath. Although some months in the island, it is not said that he made any extensive or remarkable conversions to Christianity till the Easter of 433, on the Thursday night before which we read the following account of him, as collected from the various Lives of St. Patrick by Ussher and Colgan, and thus condensed by the learned Dr. Lanigan:—" Having got a tent pitched there (Slane), he made preparations for celebrating the festival of Easter, and accordingly lighted the paschal fire about nightfall. It happened that, at this very time, the King Loeghaire and the assembled princes were celebrating a religious festival, of which fire-worship formed a part. There was a standing law that, at the time of this fes-

---

* Where these graves are has not yet been determined ; perhaps they formed part of the great neighbouring cemetery of Brugh-na-Boinne, for in an ancient MS. in the Library of Trinity College, Dublin, called " Irish Triads," enumerating three of each of the most remarkable objects in Erin,—as the three mountains, the three cataracts, the three plains, and the three rivers,—it is stated that the three darkest *caves* of Ireland are Uaimh Cruachna, i. e. the cave of Croghan; Uaimh Slaine, i. e. the cave or crypt of Slane; and Dearc Fearna, i. e. the cave of Dunmore, near Kilkenny. See also the Annals of the Four Masters, A. D. 928, and the Dublin Penny Journal, vol. i. p. 73. Can New Grange be the cave of Slane ?

tival, no fire should be kindled for a considerable distance all around, until after a great fire should be lighted in the royal palace of Temoria, or Tarah. St. Patrick's fire was, however, lighted before that of the palace, and, being seen from the heights of Tarah, excited great astonishment. On the king's inquiring what could be the cause of it, and who could thus dare to infringe the law, the magi told him that it was necessary to have that fire extinguished immediately, whereas, if allowed to remain, it would get the better of their fires, and bring about the downfall of his kingdom. Loeghaire, enraged and troubled on getting this information, set out for Slane with a considerable number of followers, and one or two of the principal magi, for the purpose of exterminating those violaters of the law. When arrived within some distance from where the tent was, they sat down, and St. Patrick was sent for, with an order to appear before the king, and give an account of his conduct. It was arranged that no one should show him any mark of respect, or rise up to receive him ; but, on his presenting himself before them, Horc, son of Dego, disobeyed the injunction, and, standing up, saluted him, and, receiving the saint's blessing, became a believer."

The subsequent preaching of Patrick at Tara, and its results, are set forth in the various Lives of the saint. A nobler spot on which to raise the beacon of Christianity could not possibly be chosen. The itinerary of St. Patrick up the Boyne might form a guide to the ancient topography of the river.

A cloictheach, or round tower, formerly existed at Slane, and probably stood on the site of the present ecclesiastical ruins, where it must have formed an object of surpassing beauty. It was destroyed by the Danes of Dublin, about the middle of the tenth century. It is alluded to in a great many of the ancient records; the following is, perhaps, the fullest, and at the same time the most intelligible notice of it to the popular reader : " A. D. 948. The cloictheach of Slane was burned by the Danes, with its full of reliques and good people, with Caoine-chair, reader of Slane, and the crosier of the patron saint, and a bell, *the best of bells*." An abbey of canons regular was founded here at a very early date, and Archdall (who was rector of Slane) informs us, on the authority of Mezeray's History of France, that it " was remarkable for being many years the residence of a royal prince; for we find that, in the year 653,

Dagobert, King of Austrasia (part of France), when at the
age of only seven years, was taken by Grimoald, mayor of the
palace, and by his direction he was shorn a monk, "rendered
unfit to hold the reins of government, and banished into Ireland. From oral information we learn that he was received
into this abbey, where he obtained an education proper for the
enjoyment of a throne; he continued here during the space of
twenty years, when he was recalled into France, and replaced
in his government." By what means the author of the Monasticon obtained this latter information, or what oral traditions, referring back for such a length of time, should be
received as history, we cannot now pause to discuss. Among
the several tombs around the abbey the stranger's attention is
pointed to one, said to bear the fleur-de-lis upon it, and this,
"from oral information, we learn" is the tomb of the son of the
King of France !—but any one accustomed to examine such
objects, at once recognises it as the tomb of an Irish ecclesiastic,
being figured with a cross, each arm of which ends in a leaf-
like ornament, and also having upon it a chalice; and beneath
the foot of the cross the name W. J. Kirwan may still be deci-
phered. Several other curious old tombs may be observed
here; one, in particular, to the south of the church, is of a remarkable form, and, in all probability, of greater antiquity than
any Christian tomb in Ireland, except a similarly constructed
one which we are given to understand exists in the churchyard

of Saul, near Downpatrick,
and that to which we already
referred at Donaghpatrick,
a fragment of which occu-
pies a precisely similar position with respect to the adjoining church there. This
tomb at Slane, of which the
accompanying is a sketch,
consists of two large gable-
shaped flags, about three
feet of which rise above
the ground, and separated

by an interval of about six feet. Each of these stones is grooved
exactly like the gable of a house, the grooves appearing to be
intended for the reception of the ends of horizontally inclined

flags which formed the roof. That this is a tomb of great antiquity, and to which peculiar reverence attaches, may be learned
from the fact that, at all the funerals of the lower orders here,
the people, in carrying the corpse round the graveyard, according to ancient custom, invariably lay it down for a short
time at this spot. Within the enclosure of the burial-ground,
and to the north of the abbey, is the well of Tober Patrick,
formerly in great repute, and which the people say not only
rises and falls with the floods of the Boyne, but sometimes has
bits of bulrushes floating in it. This rising and falling of the
water in this holy well is not peculiar; several similar circumstances are related of other holy fountains. (See Nennius).

The noble pointed window, in the highly decorated style
denominated flamboyant, over the round arched doorway in the
western side of the tower, together with the many rare examples of architecture, of great elegance of design, both in the
ruins of the church and the adjoining monastery, not forget-
ting the prim face of a nun, sculptured in a stone, built up in
the wall which now encloses the grave-yard, and the wide
range of prospect obtained by climbing the tower itself, are
well worthy a morning's visit to Slane. The church is somewhat more than 100 feet long by eighteen wide. Within it,
among the nettles and rank weeds, may, if carefully looked
for, be found the ancient font. It is unornamented, octagon
in shape, and the basin, as usual, twenty-two inches in diameter. The ruins of the monastery, which are very extensive,
are quite detached from the church, and to the north-east of it.

In the park of Slane were found, some years ago, those brass
antiquities now in the Museum of the Academy, believed to
be musical instruments, and called crotalins by Walker and
Ledwich, but which were probably fastenings or clasps. By
the shores of the deep meadows through which the Boyne sweeps
here, the curragh of wicker-work, covered with horsehide, may
still be seen. We might stop our course to describe its construction, or speculate on the circumstance of this ancient relic of the
rude early navigators of this river still remaining, in the very
heart of civilization; and step by step might we thus follow the
river's windings from the bridge of Slane to the sea, redeeming,
at every turn, the boast we made of presenting our readers with
a series of tableaux of the most interesting stream in Ireland,
but that more inviting objects, about two miles lower down,
attract attention.

CHAPTER VIII.

THE ROYAL CEMETERY OF BRUGH NA BOINNE.

THE SENCHAS-NA-RELEC.—BRUGH NA BOINNE.—THE INTERMENT OF KING CORMAC.—ROS NA RIGH.—KNOWTH.—THE TUMULUS OF NEW GRANGE; ITS ENTRANCE, PASSAGE, AND CHAMBER.— CRYPTS IN THE INTERIOR.—ANTIQUE CARVINGS.—ANCIENT HISTORY OF THIS MOUND.—DOWTH. —RECENT EXAMINATION OF ITS INTERIOR.—DESCRIPTION OF ITS CHAMBERS AND PASSAGES.— ROSSAN.—CLOGHLEA.—NETTERVILLE.

THERE were several royal burial places in Ireland in early Pagan times, eight of which have been enumerated. In the Senchas-na-Relec, or the History of the Cemeteries, contained in the Leabhar na h-Uidhre, a work compiled at Clonmacnoise, in the twelfth century, we learn that among these chief cemeteries were Cruachan, now Rathcroghan, in the county of Roscommon, where there are still considerable remains; Tailltean, Teamhair Erann, or Tara, and Oenach Colmain; so from these it would appear that the monarchs were sometimes buried in the immediate vicinity, or perhaps within the enclosure of their dwellings, like King Loeghaire, who was contemporary with St. Patrick, and who was interred in a standing position, with his weapons and war dress upon him, in the external rampart of the rath which bears his name at Tara, with his face turned southward, towards his enemies, the Leinstermen.

But by far the most celebrated and extensive of all the Irish cemeteries was that denominated Brugh, or *Brugh na Boinne*, the Burgum Boinne, the fort or town of the Boyne, of which an account is given, not only in the work already alluded to, but in another Irish manuscript of great antiquity, the Dinn-seanchus, a tract contained in the great Speckled Book of Ballymote; and to this place references continually occur in almost every ancient Irish manuscript. This was the great royal cemetery of the Kings of Tara; and from an examination of the various authorities which describe it, as well as the monuments themselves which still exist, it is manifest that Brugh na Boinne was no other than the assemblage of mounds, caves, pillar-stones, and other sepulchral monuments, forming the great necropolis which extends along the left or northern bank of the river, from Slane to Netterville. " The nobles of the Tuatha De Danaan were used to bury at Brugh (i. e. the Dagda, with his three sons, also Lughaidh, and Oe, and Ollam, and Ogma, and Etan, the poetess, and Corpre, the son of Etan), and Cremthann followed them, because his wife, Nar, was of the Tuatha Dea, and it was she solicited that he should keep Brugh as a burial-place for himself and his descendants, and this was the cause they did not bury at Cruachan."* The Lagenians (Leinstermen) of the race of Cathair, were buried at Oenach Ailbhe; the Clann Dedad, at Tara; the men of Munster at Oenach Culi and Colmain; and the Connaughtmen at the Relec na Riogh, at Rathcroghan. The monuments at Brugh are enumerated as "The bed of the Dagda first; the two paps of the Morrigan, at the place where Cermud Milbhel, son of the Dagda, was born; the grave of Boinn, the wife of Nechtan; . . . . . . the mound of Tresc; the grave of Esclam, the Dagda's brehon, which is called Fert Patric at this day; [the monuments of] Cirr and Cuirrell, wives of the Dagda; these two hillocks; the grave of Aedh Luirgnech, son of the Dagda; the cave of Builcc Bec; the monument of Cellach, son of Maelcobha; the monument of the seed of Cinaedh, son of Irgalach; the prison of Liath-Macha; the glen of the Mata, i. e. the Monster, as some assert; the pillar-stone of Buidi, the son of Muiredh, where his head is interred; the stone of Benn, i. e. the monument on which the monster, Mata, was killed; it had one hundred and forty legs and four heads; the Mound of the bones; the Caisel (stone enclosure) of Aengus, &c. &c."

From this description we learn somewhat of the nature of an ancient Irish Pagan cemetery, and of the kind of remains which we are to expect wherever any traces of such still exist, and we shall see presently that this in the neighbourhood which we are now investigating fully answers the description. In the "Genealogies, Tribes, and Customs of Hy-Fiachrach," given in the Book of Lecan, lately translated by Mr. O'Donovan for the Irish Archæological Society, we have some account of the Releg na Riogh, or cemetery of the kings of Croghan in Connaught, in the description of the death and interment of Dathi, whose body, it is said, was carried to battle by Amhalgaidh, as a stimulant to the warriors of his clan and a terror to his enemies. The passage runs thus: "Dungal, Flannghus,

---

* See Translation of the Senchas-na-Relec, in Petrie's Round Towers, p. 101.

Tuathal, and Tomaltach, were the four servants of trust who
carried with them the body of the king.   The body of Dathi
was brought to Croghan, where the kings of the race of Heremon were for the most part interred, where to this day (1666)
the cairrthe dhearg, *red pillar-stone*, remains as a monument
over his grave, near Rathcroghan.   That the body of Dathi
is interred in the middle of Aonach na Cruaghna is attested by
Torna Eigeas, in his poem pointing out the burial-place of the
kings of the race of Heremon to the men of Erin."—p. 25.
From this we learn not only the use of the pillar-stone, about
which, as well as the cromlech (generally but erroneously
called a Druid's altar), speculative and imaginary antiquaries
—who are usually unacquainted with the Irish language or
Irish history—have written so much, and with such an as-
sumption of learning, but also the fact that the graves and
monuments of Irish chieftains were well known 200 years ago.
The cemetery is still to be recognised among the great Raths
at Croghan, and we have often seen the pillar-stone alluded to,
where it stood in a field near the cross-roads of that place, and
was used as a "scratching stone" by the fat cattle that grazed
among the raths and upon the fertile plains of Rathcroghan.
Did our space permit, or if the object for which this book
is written allowed it, we could, from abundant materials now
at hand, record the modes of interment as well as the exact
burial-places of many of the Pagan Irish chieftains and warriors,
together with their mode of death, and many other most interesting particulars connected with this subject.   It is related
that Caeilte, the foster-brother and one of the generals of Finn
Mac Cumhail, killed Fothadh Airgthech in the battle of Ol-
larba, near the Larne, in the county of Antrim, A. D. 285,
with a spear, the *iron* head of which passed through him, and
was left buried in the earth.   The grave of the vanquished is
afterwards recognised by Caeilte, who, it would appear, threw
the spear or dart at his enemy from a rock in the neighbourhood.   He thus describes the locality : " The round stone from
which I made that shot will be found, and east of it will be
found the iron head of the spear buried in the earth; and the
ulidh [cairn] of Fothadh Airgthech will be found a short distance to the east of it.   There is a chest of stone about him in
the earth.   There are two rings of silver and his *bunne doats*
[bracelets!] and his torque of silver on his chest, and there is

a pillar-stone at his carn, and an Ogum is [inscribed] on the end of the pillar-stone which is in the earth, and what is in it is—' Eochaid Airgthech here.' "*

We are now in a position to inquire after the site of Brugh na Boinne, the royal cemetery of " the Fort of the Boyne." About two miles below Slane the river becomes fordable, and several islands break the stream. Here, upon the left, or south-western bank of the river, is the place called Rossnaree, the ancient Ros-na-Righ, or the Wood of the Kings, and upon the opposite swelling bank of the river occur a series of raised mounds, raths, forts, caves, circles, and pillar-stones, bearing all the evidence of ancient Pagan sepulchral monuments, which, there can now be little doubt, was the Irish Memphis, or city of tombs, already so frequently alluded to. The following reference from the History of the Cemeteries, already referred to, will, we think, set the question at rest, and fix the site of Brugh-na-Boinne here, and not, as has been conjectured, at Stackallan. We already mentioned, in describing Clady, that King Cormac Mac Art died at the house of Cletty. His burial is thus detailed: "And he (Cormac), told his people not to bury him at Brugh (because it was a cemetery of idolaters); for he did not worship the same God as any of those interred at Brugh; but to bury him at Ros-na-Righ, with his face to the east. He afterwards died, and his servants of trust held a council, and came to the resolution of burying him at Brugh, the place where the kings of Tara, his predecessors, were buried. The body of the king was afterwards thrice raised to be carried to Brugh, but the Boyne swelled up thrice, so as that they could not come; so that they observed that it was violating the judgment of a prince to break through this testament of the king ; and they afterwards dug his grave at Ros-na-Righ, as he himself had ordered." And again, " The nobles of the Tuatha De Danaan were used to bury at Brugh."

From this it is evident that the place where the servants of Cormac endeavoured to cross the river with his body was

* See Petrie's Round Towers, p. 108. See also the Annals of the Four Masters, A. D. 285, with O'Donovan's note thereon. From the foregoing quotation it mould appear that Ogham inscriptions were used in the third century. With the exception of some markings upon the edges of one of the stones recently discovered at Dowth, which look like Ogham characters, we do not find inscriptions of this nature along the Boyne or Blackwater.

at the ford of Ros-na-Righ, in order to inter it in the cemetery of Brugh-na-Boinne. The Dagda, whose monument is
enumerated in this cemetery, was a king of the Tuatha De
Danaans, named Eachaidh Ollathair, whose reign for eighty
years, commenced (it is said in the annals) at the year of the
world 3371. He was styled Daghda-mor, the "Great Good
Fire," from his military ardour; and his monument in the cemetery of the Boyne was called Sidh-an-Brogha. May it not be
one of those great sepulchral mounds now in sight, which we
are about to describe? Several of the other personages whose
monuments are enumerated as being in this great cemetery
have been already mentioned.

About a mile and a half below Slane, and extending along
the northern bank of the river, we meet the great Irish cemetery to which we have just alluded. This consists chiefly of
a number of sepulchral mounds, or barrows, varying in magnitude, and occupying a space of about a mile in breadth, northward of the river's bank, and stretching from Knowth to the
confines of Netterville demesne, over a distance of nearly three
miles. In this space we find the remains of no less than
seventeen sepulchral barrows, some of these—the smaller ones
—situated in the green pasture lands, which form the immediate valley of the Boyne, while the three of greatest magnitude are placed on the summit of the ridge which bounds
this valley upon the left bank, and a few others are to be found
at Monk-Newtown, beyond the brow of the hill, towards Louth;
making upwards of twenty in all, including the remains at
Cloghalea, and the great moat on which the fortress of Drogheda
now stands, and known in the Annals as the mound of the
grave of the Wife of Gobhan. This latter, however, is on the
right or southern bank.

The three great mounds of Knowth, New Grange, and
Dowth, principally demand attention, not only on account of
their magnitude, but because one of them has remained open
for some years, and a third has been lately examined. Each of
these is situated within view of the other, and at about a
mile distant, and consists, at first sight, of a great natural
hill, rising abruptly from the surrounding surface; and this
idea is rather strengthened by the circumstance of one of these
having become covered with wood, and another having until
lately borne on its summit a modern stone building. An eye

practised to the forms of ancient structures at once recognises these vast pyramids as the work of man, and a closer inspection soon sets this point at rest. To follow in detail these magnificent Pagan monuments—for such they are—as they present themselves, in our downward course, we first meet with Knowth, an abrupt, hemispherical mound, with rather a flattened top, rising out of the sloping hill of the townland from which it takes its name. Some enormous masses of stone, arranged in a circular manner round its base, tell us, however, that it is evidently the work of design; and some excavations made into one of its sides show that it consists of an enormous cairn of small stones, covered with rich greensward, occupying in extent of surface about an acre, and rising to a height of nearly eighty feet. As far as we can judge by external appearances, although history is against us, it appears to be as yet uninvestigated ; but as there are no means of access to its interior, we can only speculate as to its use, and the mode of its construction, from an examination of similar structures in this vicinity. We therefore pass on to the next monument, that of New Grange, of which the accompanying illustration, taken from the road adjoining, affords a tolerably correct idea.

Like that just described, it consists of an enormous cairn or hill of small stones, calculated at 180,000 tons weight, occupying the summit of one of the natural undulating slopes which enclose the valley of the Boyne upon the north. It is said to cover nearly two acres, and is 400 paces in circumference, and now about eighty feet higher than the adjoining natural surface. Various excavations made into its sides, and upon its summit, at different times, in order to supply materials for building and road-making, have assisted to lessen its original height, and also to destroy the beauty of its outline ; but this defect has been obviated in part by a plantation, chiefly of hazel, which has grown over its surface.

A few yards from the outer circle of the mound, there appears to have stood originally a circle of enormous detached blocks of stone, placed at intervals of about ten yards from each other. Ten of these, three of which are here shown,

still exist on the south-eastern side. Such is the present appearance of this stupendous relic of ancient Pagan times, probably one of the oldest Celtic monuments in the world, which has elicited the wonder, and called forth the admiration of all who have visited it, and has engaged the attention of nearly every distinguished antiquary, not only of the British Isles, but of Europe generally; which, though little known to our countrymen, notwithstanding that it is within two hours' drive of Dublin, has attracted thither pilgrims from every land. It is said that a large pillar-stone, or *stele*, originally stood upon its summit. Before we speculate upon the date or origin, or offer any conjectures as to the uses of this vast cairn, we will conduct our readers into the interior, and point out the objects within most worthy of attention. This mound is hollow; it contains a large chamber, formed by stones of enormous magnitude, and is accessible through a narrow passage, also formed of stones of great size, placed together without mortar or cement; and, considering their bulk and the positions they occupy, exciting our astonishment how such Cyclopean masonry could have been erected by a people who were, in all probability, unacquainted with those mechanical powers so necessary in the erection of modern buildings. Moreover, although some of the stones, both within and without this tumulus, bear marks of being water-worn, and were probably lifted from the bed of the Boyne, others belong to a class of rock not found in the neighbourhood at all ; some are basaltic, and others must have been transported here from the Mourne mountains.

When this opening was *first* discovered it is now difficult to say. Sir Thomas Molyneux, who is generally, but erroneously, supposed to have first described this monument, states that the opening was accidentally discovered, by removing some of the stones to make a pavement in the neighbourhood. The earliest describer of New Grange was Edward Llhwyd, the Welsh antiquary, and keeper of the Ashmolean Museum, in Oxford, who, in a letter, dated Sligo, 12th March, 1699, and published by Rowlands, in his " Mona Antiqua Restaurata," gave the following account of it, which we quote, the more particularly as he evidently had examined it carefully, and in order that its present state may be compared with its condition 150 years ago.* " I also met with one monument in this kingdom, very singular; it stands at a place called New Grange, near Drogheda, and is a mount, or barrow, of very

---

* Although the *Mona Antiqua Restaurata* was published in Dublin, in 1723, the letter bears the date which we have mentioned above. In " the collection of such papers as were communicated to the Royal Society, referring to some curiosities in Ireland," we find a paraphrase of Mr. Llhwyd's Essay, printed here in 1726, but much less full, or explicit, than the original. Molyneux's account was printed in his Discourse concerning Danish Mounds, Forts, and Towers in Ireland, first published in 1725. It is, therefore, evident that the original describer was Llhwyd. See also Philosophical Transactions, vol. v. p. 694 ; Governor Pownal's Description in Archæologia II. ; Higgins's Celtic Druids ; Miss Beaufort's Essay, in Transactions of the Royal Irish Academy ; Petrie in Irish Penny Journal ; Sir R. C. Hoar's Tour in Ireland, &c. &c.

considerable height, encompassed with vast stones, pitched on end, round the bottom of it, and having another, lesser, standing on the top." When we first visited New Grange, some twelve years ago, the entrance was greatly obscured by brambles, and a heap of loose stones which had ravelled out from the adjoining mound. This entrance, which is nearly square, and formed by large flags, the continuation of the stone passage already alluded to, is now at a considerable distance from the original outer circle of the mound, and consequently the passage is at present much shorter than it was originally, if, indeed, it ever extended so far as the outer circle. A few years ago, a gentleman, then residing in the neighbourhood, cleared away the stones and rubbish which obscured the mouth of the cave, and brought to light a very remarkably carved stone, which now slopes outwards from the entrance. This we thought at the time was quite a discovery, inasmuch as none of the

modern writers had noticed it. The Welsh antiquary, however, thus describes it:—" The entry into this cave is at bottom, and before it we found a great flat stone, like a large

tomb-stone, placed edgeways, having on the outside certain
barbarous carvings, like snakes encircled, but without heads."

This stone, so beautifully carved in spirals and volutes, as
shown in the graphic illustration upon the opposite page, is
slighty convex, from above downwards; it measures ten feet
in length, and is about eighteen inches thick.   What its original use was,—where its original position in this mound,—
whether its carvings exhibit the same handiwork and design
as those sculptured stones in the interior, and whether this
beautiful slab did not belong to some other building of anterior date,—are questions worthy of consideration, but which we
have not space to discuss.

At the same time that this remarkable micaceous slab, which
is of a greenish colour, and quite different from the other stones
in the vicinity, was exposed, a few years ago, the edge of another very curious, and most exquisitely carved stone, was found
projecting from the mound, a short distance above and within
the line of the present entrance.   That figured beneath represents a portion of the carved edge of this lintel, which projects
horizontally above the entrance.

This stone, of which we can only perceive the edge, is five
feet eight inches long; its sculpture, both in design and execution, far exceeds any of the rude carvings which are figured,
apparently at random, upon the stones found within the cave;
and as it never could have been intended to be concealed from
view, it is most probable that it decorates the entrance into
some other chamber, which further examination may yet dis-
close. The largest of the Egyptian pyramids contains several
chambers, superincumbent upon the great sepulchral vault in
which the sarcophagus was placed. This sculptured stone is of

o

the same composition—a micaceous slate—as the great spirally carved slab beneath, and is not found at all in this neighbourhood; nor, indeed, are any of the great stones of the passage or the chamber of a rock found in the vicinity, while the small broken stones, which form the great bulk of the mound, were evidently gathered around.

We now enter the passage which faces the Boyne; it runs very nearly north and south, and measures sixty-three feet in length; it is formed of twenty-one upright stones upon the right side, and twenty-two on the left, and is roofed with flags of immense length, resting in some points upon the upright side-stones, but in other places chiefly supported by masonry external to them; one of these is seventeen feet long and six broad. The general height of the passage, for about three-fourths of its length, is about six feet: but from the accumulation of earth towards the entrance, it is scarcely so much at present. It then rises suddenly, and again, within seventeen feet of the chamber, it rises so as to slope gradually into its roof; and the stones of which this portion is composed are of gigantic size, many of them eight and ten feet high. Its average breadth is about three feet; but some of the side stones having fallen inwards, so as almost to touch; one requires to creep on all-fours to pass this point. Most of these side stones are remarkably smooth, even on parts where the rubbing of a century and a half could not have produced this polish, and appear to have been long exposed to the action of water or the atmosphere. Some have smooth transverse indentations, as represented by this drawing; and very many of the stones throughout this building, as well as others used for like purposes in the neighbourhood, have small sockets, or mortices, cut near or in their edges, of which we have an example before us. These appear to have been made for the insertion of wedges, either to split the stone, or to lift it.

The passage leads to a large dome-roofed chamber. As all is perfect darkness within this cavern, it is necessary to illuminate it in order to form any just idea of its figure or extent. When about half lighted up, and we begin to perceive the size and character of this great hive-shaped dome, and its surrounding crypts, formed by stones of such immense size, half revealed to us by the uncertain light of our tapers, an air of mystery steals over the senses,—a religious awe pervades the place; and while we do not put any faith in the wild fancies of those antiquaries of the last century, who would make the world believe that this was a great Druid temple, an *Antrum Mythræ*, in which the sacred rites of Paganism,

HANLON

with its human sacrifices, were enacted, we wonder less at the flight which their imaginations have taken. This cavern is nearly circular, with three offsets, or recesses, from it,—one opposite the entrance on the north, and one on each side, east and west, so that the ground plan, including the passage, accurately represents the figure of a cross.

The wood-cut on the last page, from a rough sketch by
Mr. Connolly, gives by far the truest idea of one of these
crypts, which we have yet seen. It shows the right or eastern recess, eight feet deep, nine high, and seven broad; it is
slightly narrowed at the entrance.

The basement of the great chamber, to about the height of
ten feet, is formed of a circle of eleven upright stones, partially
sunk in the ground, placed on edge, with their flat surfaces
facing inwards, and forming the sides of the cavern. From
this course springs the dome, formed by stones somewhat less
in size, placed horizontally on the flat, with the edges presented towards the interior; and by each layer projecting slightly
within that placed beneath, they thus, by decreasing the circle, form a dome, without an arch, and the whole is closed at
top, by one large slab: the stability of the mass is preserved
by the pressure of the surrounding material.

This form of roofing, which evidently preceded a knowledge
of the principle of the arch, is to be found in many of our early
buildings,—generally Pagan, and chiefly sepulchral, in this country,—in the interiors of some of the duns or raths, and in very
early Christian oratories; and not only in Ireland, but in Egypt,
Greece, and Asia Minor, in one of the pyramids of Sackara,
as well as in the remains of a temple at Telmessus. Pococke
had observed a similar structure in the pyramid of Dashour,
called by the Arab name of Elkebere-el-Barieh; and all the
visiters to the Cyclopean-walled Mycenæ are well acquainted
with the appearance of the great cavern, known by tradition
as the tomb of Agamemnon, and believed by some antiquaries
to have been the treasury of Atreus; between which and New
Grange comparisons have often been made; their resemblance,
however, consists in the *principle* on which the dome is constructed. That remnant of the early Hellenic people was
formed by an excavation scooped out of the side of a natural
hill; the gallery which leads to it does not appear ever to
have been covered in; the sides of the dome spring directly
from the foundation, like that at Clady, and not from a row
or circle of upright pillars. The interior is perfectly smooth,
and was originally covered over with plates of brass; some of
the nails which fastened them even yet remain; but these
latter circumstances merely show a greater perfection in art
among the early Greeks,—the architectural principle perhaps is

the same in both. The ground plan of the great Boyne monument also finds its analogue in the Orient; at Tyre and at Alexandria we find tombs carved out of the solid rock, of precisely the same cruciform shape, having three minor excavations projecting from the several chambers. But while we thus allow ourselves to draw upon our recollections of other lands, we fear our readers, and the visiters to New Grange, for whose use in particular we write, may require some further information as to the measurements, construction, and hieroglyphics of this remarkable monument. The top of the dome is nineteen feet six inches from the floor, which is now covered with loose stones and rubbish. From the entrance to the wall of the chamber opposite measures eighteen feet; and between the extremities of the right and left crypts, twenty-two feet. Each of the side chambers is nearly square, their sides being formed of large oblong blocks of stone; but they are not all of the same size ; that on the right of the entrance, the eastern, is very much larger than either of the others, and is also the most enriched with those rude carvings, volutes, lozenges, zigzags, and spiral lines, cut into the stones, and in some instances standing out in relief, to which we alluded in describing the passage.

In order to afford our readers some idea of these curious markings, we have introduced the accompanying illustrations.

Upon a careful examination of the spiral carvings, we find them nearly all formed of a double coil, commencing with a loop, and, in most instances, having seven turns.— Many of these spirals or scrolls look like the first drawings or markings for the subsequent engraving in relief, such as we find in the finished work of the great flag at the entrance.

The first wood-cut on the next page shows the projecting edge of the top stone in the southern wall of the great right hand recess. The lozenges, six in number, are cut in,

and are about three-quarters of an inch deep. Another specimen of this form of decoration may be perceived on the hori-

zontal slab at the meeting of the passage with the roof. A
few of those have carvings upon them of spirals, coils, and
zig-zag lines, cut, about half an inch in depth, by some sharp
tool.

Here again is a portion
of the device found upon
the roof of the eastern recess, carved upon a great
flag, twelve feet in length,
which spans the entire
breadth of the crypt.
Upon the back of the
same chamber we find,
and have represented in
the first wood engraving
on the opposite page, the
carving which is to be
seen on a projecting ledge,

which juts out from the back wall like a second roof. These
" scribings" appear to have been done with a tool like the pick
used in roughening mill-stones.

The chamber opposite the entrance affords, at first view,

but few specimens of this curious scroll-work. But that upon the left (the western), which is by far the shallowest, presents

us, besides some of the coil-marks, with two remarkable examples of the carving, cut into its right-hand jamb, totally different in form from all the others.

This, which we find low down upon the side of the stone facing the crypt, differs from all the rest, and has excited much mystical speculation among the followers of General Vallancey, who supposed it to be an undoubted piece of writing; but what the language is, or what tale it tells, they had not made up their minds; and as that school has now become nearly ex-  tinct, we fear the matter is not likely to be much further investigated at present. It is of a piece with Vallancey's speculation about the name New Grange (which is evidently of English introduction) having any reference to *Grian*, the sun, &c.

The following very remarkable circumstance struck us while investigating this ancient structure of New Grange, some years ago. We found that those carvings not only covered portions of the stones exposed to view, but extended over those surfaces

which, until some recent dilapidation, were completely concealed from view, and where a tool could not have reached them;
and the inference is plain, that these stones were carved prior
to their being placed in their present position; perhaps were
used for some anterior purpose.   If so, how much it adds to
their antiquity!

This carving, which is also in
the western recess, bears some resemblance to the palm-branch, or
to the impression of the male fern,
and is not cut so deep as the others.
The eastern jamb of the chamber
opposite the entrance has fallen inwards, and recently exposed a portion of the under surface of a great
flag, which is now, for the first time
since the erection of the building,
exposed to view. This flag has, like
most of the other stones here, a
sort of skin, or brownish outer polish, as if water-washed.   Now, in
all the exposed carvings upon the
other stones, the indentures have
assumed more or less of the dark
colour and polish around; whereas
in this one the colour of the cutting and the track of the tool is
just as fresh as if done but yesterday.   It must have been effected
immediately before the stone was
placed in its present position. The

question may well be asked, what was the purpose of those;
are they mere ornamental carvings, or are they inscriptions
from which the history of this monument, or whatever it
was originally intended for, might be learned?   Are they
ideographical, or hierographic, in the strict sense of that word;
that is, sacred carving?   To this latter we are inclined; and,
if we may be allowed to coin a word to express our meaning, we would call them Tymboglyphics, or *tomb-writing*, for
similar characters have as yet only been found connected with
the vestiges of ancient sepulchres, as here, at Dowth, and on
tombs of a like character in the counties of Down and Done-

gal. That the meaning of these scriptures, if any such they have, beyond being sacred to the dead, shall ever be brought to light from the haze of obscurity which now enshrouds them, is very problematical.

In each recess we find an oval, slightly dished, or hollowed stone basin, a rude primitive sarcophagus. This, upon the right-hand chamber, which is three feet long, is one of the most perfect, and differs from the others in having two minor indentations cut upon its upper concavity. It stands in another larger and shallower basin, while the western crypts contain but one such sarcophagus, as shown below.

Having conducted our readers thus far over the details, we think they are anxious to know what is our opinion as to the purpose for which New Grange was constructed. We believe, with most modern investigators into such subjects, that it was a tomb, or great sepulchral pyramid, similar, in every respect, to those now standing by the banks of the Nile, from Dashour to Gaza, each consisting of a great central chamber, containing one or more sarcophagi, entered by a long stone-covered passage. The external aperture was concealed, and the whole covered with a great mound of stones or earth in a conical form. The early Egyptians, and the Mexi-

cans also, possessing greater art and better tools than the primitive Irish, carved, smoothed, and cemented their great pyramids; but the type and purpose in all is the same. From Llhwyd's description we learn, that when New Grange was examined in 1699, it was found much in the same state which it now presents; that " under foot there were nothing but loose stones of every size, in confusion, and amongst them a great many bones of beasts, and some pieces of deer's horns." Neither in this account, nor in that published in Boate's Natural History of Ireland, does he make any mention, either that "the bones of two dead bodies, entire, not burned, were found upon the floor, in all likelihood the relics of a husband and his wife, whose conjugal affection had joined them in their grave as in their bed!" as related twenty-five years afterwards by Molyneux; nor of the "slender quarry-stone, five or six feet long, shaped like a pyramid," which the latter author states lay on the floor. That these rude bowls or typical urns originally contained human remains, we have little doubt; but from a careful examination of the authorities which refer to the accidental opening of New Grange, at the end of the seventeenth century, we feel convinced that this monument had been examined long prior to that date; and, therefore, we derive little information from modern writings as to what its original condition was. That the Danes were well aware that these tumuli contained caverns, and probably knowing that gold and treasure was to be found within them, rifled several of those ancient sepulchres, we have undoubted authority; for in the Annals of Ulster we read the following memorable account of an instance of this description; and although New Grange (which, as already stated, is a mere modern name, which gives no reference either to its use or locality) is not specified, it may fairly be inferred that it formed one of the group of the Boyne pyramids rifled by the plundering Northmen, A. D. 862. " The cave of Achadh Aldai, and of Cnodhba (Knowth), and the cave of the sepulchre of Boadan, over Dubhad (Dowth), and the cave of the wife of Gobhan (at Drogheda), was searched by the Danes—*quod antea non perfectum est*—on one occasion, that the three kings, Amlaff, Imar, and Auisle, were plundering the territory of Flann, the son of Conaing." The Annals of the Four Masters thus record the same circumstance: " The cave of Achadh Aldai in Mughdhorna-Maighen [Breagh]; the cave of Cnoghbhai; the cave of the grave of Bodan, i. e. the shepherd of Elcmar over Dubhath; and the cave of Gobhann at Drochat-atha; were broken and plundered by the same foreigners." All these sepulchres were in one territory, the land of Flann, son of Conang, one of the chieftains of Meath; and, in all probability,* the cave of Achadh Aldai,—that is, the field of Aldai,—the ancestor of the Tuatha De Danaan kings,—is that which is now known as New Grange? How far anterior to the Christian era its date should be placed, would be a matter of speculation; it may be of an age coeval, or even anterior, to its brethren on the Nile.

Were we to strip the chamber and passage of New Grange of the surrounding mound, to remove the domed portion of the cave, and to replace the outer circle, at those parts where it is deficient, we should have presented to us a monument not unlike Stonehenge.

Not only in the surrounding plain, but even on the hill of New Grange itself, do we meet small sepulchral caves and mounds. The whole is one vast cemetery. On the western side of the natural hill sloping from this mound, we some years ago were present at the opening of a small kistvaen, reached by a narrow stone passage,—a sort of miniature New Grange; in it were a quantity of human bones and those of small animals, pigs, sheep, dogs, and fowl; some burned, and some not bearing any marks of fire; but the most remarkable circumstance about it was, that the bottom of this little chamber was lined with stones, the upper surfaces of which bore evident marks of fire,—in fact were vitrified,—showing that the victim, or the dead body, was burned within the grave.

In the north-eastern margin of New Grange is a curiously constructed crypt, like a hermit's cell, but of comparatively modern date. It is, however, worth inspection.

Many years ago, a gold coin of Valentinian, and one of

---

* Mr. O'Donovan, in his note on Achadh Aldai, in the Annals, says: "This place is described by the Four Masters as situated in the territory of Mughdhorna-Maighen, now the barony of Cremorne, in the County Monaghan; but it is highly probable, if not certain, that Mughdhorna-Maighen is a mistake of transcription for Mughdhorna-Breagh, and that Achadh-Aldai is the ancient name of New Grange." It is also added in the same note, "that these mounds were first identified with these passages in the Annals, by Dr. Petrie, in his Essay on the Military Architecture of the Ancient Irish, read before the Royal Irish Academy, January, 1834." We sincerely wish, with every lover of Irish archæology, that Dr. Petrie could be induced to publish that Essay.

Theodosius, were discovered on the outside of the mound; and, not very long ago, a labourer, digging a little to the west of the entrance, discovered two ancient gold torques and a golden chain and two rings. Where are these? Are they in the great national collection of the Royal Irish Academy? Have they been recorded in the Proceedings or Transactions of that, or any other learned body in the kingdom? No; we regret to say, they were carried out of this country by an Irish noble-man, to exhibit at a learned society on the other side of the channel, in the Transactions of which body they will be found figured, together with a letter from their present owner, which, as he is our countryman, we will not quote!

Within view of New Grange, and about a mile distant, seated on one of the higher slopes upon the Boyne's bank, the third great cone of the group attracts our attention,—Dubhadh, or Dowth,—the accompanying view of which was taken prior to the examination of this rath in 1847. Although not so broad at the base as New Grange, it was more conical; the building on the top was a modern structure, a *tea-house* erected by the late eccentric Lord Netterville; and, certainly, although his know-ledge or love for antiquities may be questioned, there can be no doubt of his having chosen a spot from whence could be obtained one of the noblest prospects in Meath. A circle of boulder-like stones, some traces of which even still remain, originally surrounded the base of this mound, which is formed entirely of small loose stones; the external surface, however, has been covered with a thick and verdant sod.

We mentioned that Dowth, or Dubhadh, had been ransacked by the Danes, during one of their inroads in the ninth century; where they broached the mound, or whether they examined all its chambers, it is now difficult to say. A considerable gap existed in the western face of the mound, caused by large quantities of the stones of which it is composed having been removed at different times to erect buildings or to break up into macadamizing materials for the road which passes at its foot. It has been said, we hope without truth, that the grand jury of the county on one occasion presented, in form, for the stones of Dowth, to improve the condition of their roads. In this excavation, on the western side, a passage somewhat similar to that of New Grange had long remained exposed; but, from the falling in of its sides and roof, it was not possible to follow it for more than a few yards on either side. Whether this passage was that originally broken open by Amlaff and his plundering Danes, it is difficult to determine.

A desire having long existed to explore some of these monuments, the Committee of Antiquities of the Royal Irish Academy obtained permission from the trustees of the Netterville Charity, the present proprietors of the Dowth estate, to examine the interior; and funds having been procured, chiefly by private subscription, and afterwards aided by the Academy, the direction of the work was committed to the care of Mr. Frith, one of the County Dublin surveyors; and the Board of Works kindly afforded the tools, or "plant," for carrying on the excavations. Several excursions were made to the spot, for the purpose of deciding on the best means for gaining access to the interior, as, from the analogy to New Grange, it was supposed to contain a central chamber. Opinions were divided as to whether a perpendicular shaft should be sunk from the top by a well-borer, or a horizontal tunnel driven in from one of the sides towards the centre. The remarkably loose material of which the mound is composed presented such objections to both these plans, while the apparent feasibility of obtaining ingress through the passage already open on the western side, so far, at least, as it was possible to follow it, was so inviting, that this latter plan was adopted; and, although the examination has not been attended with the expected success, we have no hesitation in pronouncing it to have afforded the most valuable results. A catacomb, or series of chambers, not unlike those found beneath the great central chamber in the largest pyramid of the Sackara range, which we described some years ago,* has been fully explored and rendered accessible to the curious, and these we shall presently detail. Having made an open cutting into the western side of the mound, in following out these passages, it was certainly the most advisable, as well as the cheapest plan, to follow in the same course, till the centre was reached. In effecting this, the modern structure on the top was demolished; such, however, was indispensable, and it may act as a warning, and show all the future builders of tea-houses, in

such places, what may be the end of their labours. The upper portion above the lintel in this drawing, representing the mouth of the passage, is modern, the stones being replaced by the workmen, but the cut gives a very good idea of the appearance of this passage.

Following this exposed gallery, which runs eastward, and is formed of huge stones, set on end and slightly inclined at top, nine on the right, and eleven on the left, sunk in the ground, and roofed with large flags, similar to that of New Grange,—we are led into a chamber of a cruciform shape, and formed, with slight

* See Narrative of a Voyage to Madeira, and along the Shores of the Mediterranean.

exceptions, upon the type of that already described at page 196, in the great pyramid of New Grange. This passage is twenty-seven feet long, and some of its stones are carved with circles, curved and zig-zag lines. Both in this passage, and at the entrances of several of the minor crypts and recesses which branch from the chamber, we find sills, formed by large flags, projecting above the surface, placed there apparently for the purpose of preventing the external pressure driving in the side walls. The large central chamber is an irregular oval, nine feet four by seven feet, and the blocks of stone which form its upright pillars are fully as large as those found at New Grange, and several of them are carved like those which

we have already described in that place. Many of the carvings, however, at Dowth, which present great beauty of design, differ somewhat from those at New Grange. We find here, in addition to those already figured, a number of wheel-like ornaments and concentric circles, and others with lines radiating from a point; while some very much resemble the Ogham character, consisting of short, straight, parallel lines.* In some

* In A. E. Holmberg's "*Skandinaviens Hällristningar Arkeologisk Afhandgling*," there is a figure of a cromlech, with precisely similar markings.

instances we find the representation of a lotus, or lily-leaf, carved with such precision as to give it at first view the appearance of a fossil. And what adds to the interest of these sculptures, particularly that which we just described, is, that the leaf stands out about half an inch in relief, while all the surrounding stone, for many feet adjoining, has been picked away with infinite care and labour. We would direct the attention of the visiter to the great stone, immediately upon the right of the entrance of the central chamber; that, again, upon the right of the northern recess; and others, exposed lately, in the remains of a tomb, or sepulchral chamber, to the south of the present excavations. In the centre of the chamber stands a shallow stone basin, or rude sarcophagus, of an ovoid shape, much larger than any of those of New Grange, measuring five feet in its longer diameter. When the cave was recently opened, only a portion of this basin was discovered in its present locality, but all the fragments, nine in number, have since been recovered in the chambers and passages around, and now complete the entire. There are no basins in the three adjoining recesses. These recesses have narrow entrances, and are less open than those of New Grange; that upon the right and the one opposite the entrance are each five feet deep; the southern recess is six feet nine in length, and, at its western angle, leads into a passage, which opens by a narrow entrance into another series of chambers and passages, the most extensive of which runs nearly southward. The roof of the right hand chamber is nine feet seven inches from the floor. Creeping through these dark passages, and over the high projecting sills which we have already described, we come to two small chambers, one within another, running nearly south-west, and measuring about two feet six each in breadth. Following, however, the long, southern gallery, we find its floor formed by a single stone, ten feet six long; and, in the centre of this flag, we find a shallow oval excavation, capable of holding about one gallon of fluid, and apparently rubbed down with some rude tool, or another stone; it is not unlike one of the shallow, very early quearns in the museum of the Royal Irish Academy. Beyond this flag, and separated from it by a projecting sill, we find a terminal chamber, with a sloping roof, and capable of holding a man in the sitting posture.

The examination of this great catacomb, and the recent excavations at Dowth, have done good service to the cause of antiquarian research in this country.

No central chamber was discovered, although the centre was reached; it is possible, however, that there may be instead a number of minor crypts existing in the circumference of this great hill. In any future examination of tumuli in this great cemetery, we confess, we would prefer to open one of the minor mounds, situated in the valley of the Boyne: the expense would be much less, and the probability of finding them in their primitive condition very much greater. We hope to see the stones which formed the mound of Dowth replaced in their original position, as so interesting a monument should certainly be restored to the condition in which it was found by those who undertook the examination. This is due, not only to the trustees of the Netterville Bequest, who have permitted the works to be carried on, but to the country at large.

During the excavations some very interesting relics and antiquities were discovered. Among the stones which form the great heap, or cairn, were found a number of globular stone shot, about the size of grape-shot, probably sling-stones, and also fragments of human heads; within the chamber, mixed with the clay and dust which had accumulated, were found a quantity of bones, consisting of heaps, as well as scattered fragments of burned bones, many of which proved to be human; also several unburned bones of horses, pigs, deer, and birds, with portions of the heads of the short-horned variety of the ox, similar to those found at Dunshaughlin, and the head of a fox. Glass and amber beads, of unique shapes, portions of jet bracelets, a curious stone button or fibula, bone bodkins, copper pins, and iron knives and rings, the two latter similar to those found at Dunshaughlin, were also picked up. Some years ago a gentleman who then resided in the neighbourhood cleared out a portion of the passage, and found a few iron antiquities, some bones of mammals, and a small stone urn, which he lately presented to the Academy. Much might here be written upon the remains of the Fauna known to the ancient Irish, did our space permit; we can, however, merely specify some of the bones, and mention some of the articles which were discovered. In the beginning of the last century, a stone urn, somewhat similar in shape to "the upper part of a man's skull," was found in a kistvaen at Knowth; this, we believe,

is now in the collection of the Academy ; it is figured by
Molyneux.

The Council of the Royal Irish Academy have promised a
report upon Dowth, which is anxiously looked for: the plans
and drawings have long since been given in by the engineer.
Pending that report, which is in the hands of those best fitted
for its preparation, we forbear to enter into the further details
of this monument.*

We could point out many other curious structures and ancient remains, both Pagan and Christian, in this neighbourhood. Pillar-stones, probably monumental, stand all round in
the valley and on the sloping ground.

The accompanying woodcut shows
one of those in the circle of New
Grange; it is nine feet high and sixteen in circumference.

A few hundred yards to the south-
east of the moat of Dowth we have
St. Bernard's Well; some remains of
one of those structures denominated
Giants' Graves; the old castle of
Dowth; and the interesting little
church adjoining, which contains,
built up in its southern wall, a specimen of very early Irish sculpture,
concerning which there is at present
little known; it is similar in design
to the figure on the cross of St.
Adamnan, to which we alluded at page 123. Immediately adjoining are the ramparts, baths, walks, and ponds, made by the
late eccentric Lord Netterville, together with some of the finest
mulberry trees in this part of the kingdom.

The tourist should visit a small cave, formed with recesses,
similar to New Grange, in the pleasure grounds of Netterville;
and two other remains, a small circular moat and a fort, in its
vicinity. All these antiquarian riches occur within the space of
about half a mile; or if we were to extend our range to the mill

* The original sketches of the "Boyne" were commenced in the Dublin
University Magazine, several months before any examination of Dowth was
undertaken by the members of the Royal Irish Academy.

of Rossan, in Monk-Newtown, we could examine, with much interest, a ring fort and another New Grange, upon a minor scale, which was rudely torn asunder, and left in a dilapidated condition, in the spring of 1847, by some Goth, in order to convert a few of its stones into gate-posts: but we can now merely direct attention to the sites of these latter.

Within the demesne of Dowth or Netterville is to be seen one of the very largest ring forts or military raths in Ireland, except, perhaps, the Giant's Ring at Belfast. It is about 300 paces in circumference, round the top of the embankment, and has a large opening on the south-western side. This O'Donovan supposes was the fort of Dun-na-nGedh, where Domhnall gave his celebrated feast, to which we alluded at p. 176.*

In the same field, and immediately adjoining the road, and now forming the edge of a quarry, we meet Cloghlea, a portion of a stone circle, evidently a part of the side wall or basement of a sepulchral chamber similar to New Grange, than  which it was, perhaps, even larger. Four of these stones, of immense size (one twelve feet long), still stand, two others are prostrate, and two more are lying in the adjoining quarry,—eight in all. Human remains have, on more than one occasion, been found in the vicinity of this remnant of an ancient tumulus. On the edges of these stones will be found indentations similar to those in some of the stones of the passage of New Grange, one of which is figured at page 194.

* See Battle of Magh Rath, p. 7.

CHAPTER IX.

THE ETHNOLOGY OF THE ANCIENT IRISH.

MODES AND MEANS OF STUDYING ETHNOLOGY.—WHO ARE THE IRISH.—HISTORIC REFERENCES.—
WHAT REMAINS OF THE ORIGINAL STOCK EXIST.—THE CELTS.—THE FIRBOLGS.—THE TUATHA
DE DANAAN.—EARLY IRISH FORMS OF BURIAL.—TUMULI, AND THEIR CONTENTS.—CROMLECHS.
—KISTVAENS—SEPULCHRAL URNS.—INCINERATION.—SCANDINAVIAN RESEARCHES.—CRANIA OF
THE ANCIENT IRISH.—BATTLE FIELDS.—ADVICE TO TOMB OPENERS.

THE origin and early history of every nation is involved in considerable obscurity and doubt. As we follow up the stream of time towards its source, or trace back on the page of the world's history, the various people of the earth, we are accustomed to infer the antiquity of a nation from its monuments, or to receive as authority the tales and traditions of its existing inhabitants, when written records are defective. Thus, when we speak of that land of mystery, the offspring of the Nile, we point to its eternal pyramids, its regal tombs, and its solemn and majestic temples, as proofs of the magnificence of conception and design, the perfection in art, the illusive splendour of the religion, and the luxury and pomp of its early occupants.   In like manner, and with similar feelings, we view the Acropolis of Athens, or that of Corinth, as instancing taste and refinement among the early Greeks; but, long before the days in which these structures were erected, we turn for proofs of the arts and civilization of the earliest people of that classic land to the tomb and city of Agamemnon, or the Cyclopean-walled Tyrinthus. These, with the ruins of Persepolis, Petra, Baalbec, Hebron, and Palmyra, the palm-groved city of Solomon, together with the various monuments of India and the Americas, the Druid circle of Northwestern Europe, or the sepulchral pyramid of New Grange, all afford material to the speculative antiquary who takes architecture as his guide, whereby he may unravel the story of our race, or learn, by tracing the similarity in design and artistic execution, either in religious, warlike, or sepulchral monuments, the source from whence the various waves of population were originally given off.

Again, the philologist starts up and traces the origin, or,

if not exactly the origin, at least the connexion between different nations and people, by the study of language, and with
most extraordinary assiduity spends years, nay, a lifetime, in
investigating the subject of living speech, or the dead but
written tongues of various nations; and frequently, by the
derivation of some obscure term, traces such cognate affinities
—as they are termed—as lead him at once to conclusions often
as absurd as they are erroneous. At the same time there can
be little doubt that when such investigations are properly and
judiciously carried on by men of learning and ability, who
bring to the task an extensive acquaintance with the subject
of language generally, and who are able to read, or perhaps
speak, the tongues they treat of,—in fact, men who have something more than a mere dictionary knowledge of this interesting and hitherto neglected branch of science,—then, and not
till then, will any extensive progress be made towards that
entrance whereby the paths in the enchanted gardens of the
past may be trod with security, and through which the in-
vestigator of the natural history of man may yet hope to arrive
at the birth-place of nations.

The antiquary in language and the antiquary in architecture and artistic remains seldom agree; and the historian,
while he gathers what he can from both, generally increases
the maze of difficulty and perplexity under which the reader
of the works of the two former labours, by weaving a web
of his own, spun from the fables of old songs and imaginative romances, or the legends and traditions still living in the
mouths of the people of the country he is engaged in describing. Thus, conjectures the most improbable, and speculations the most absurd, are to be found in the writings of
historians on the subject of the early peopling of different countries; and the tenacity with which Irish writers have adhered
to the fables of the past has long since become proverbial. Let
this not, however, remain a matter of surprise; it has ever
been the feeling and the failing of mankind, individually and
collectively, to boast of their antiquity. The Tyrians did so
in the time of Ezekiel, who, in his graphic and glowing description of the downfall and destruction of their island home,
taunts them in these biting and sarcastic words, " Is this
your city whose antiquity is of ancient days?" and have we
not this feeling starting up in every-day society, and at every

turn, of people magnifying themselves by tracing back their pedigrees like the Hebrews and Phœnicians of old.

Of late years, to aid the investigations of the architect and artistic antiquary, the philologist, and the historian, a fourth science has been called into the field, which, while it in nowise detracts from the former ones, has even already, in its very infancy, done much to advance the proper investigation of the world's history, and promises to prove one of the most industrious and sure handmaids to history generally,—we mean the science of Ethnography, or the natural history of man, including his physical character; his from and stature; the colour of his skin, his hair, and his complexion; his physiognomy; his habits and moral condition, together with his geographical distribution; but more particularly than all the rest, the form of his skull. It sounds strange, but it is nevertheless true, that of all the living creatures that exist upon the surface of our globe, there is none whose zoological characters are, or at least were, until these few years past, so little studied or understood as man, in his animal character. This interesting inquiry, thanks to the labours of Blumenbach, Cuvier, Prichard, Morton, and others, has already become one of popular interest; and although it is rapidly progressing, yet the study of the natural history of man, in the present day, very much resembles the condition geology was in some few years ago, when men generalized from too few facts, and often propounded some wild and extravagant theory from the discovery of a single fossil. Yet, from the vast collections of minerals and organic remains that have been subsequently accumulated, more sober inquirers have drawn up rational and scientific systems. Now, wherever history extends her track, she carries with her, in addition to the traditionary and written records of a country, its antiquities and philology, an inquiry also into the physical characters of the human race or races, either living or extinct, that are to be found therein. Thus to the description left us in the ancient classic writings; to the written records in its hieroglyphic and phonetic writing, and the pictorial exhibitions either carved upon the monuments or imprinted on the walls of tombs and temples; and to those fanes and sepulchres themselves; we are now able, from the examination of the human remains found in that great necropolis of the ancient world, to add the physical characters of the ancient Egyptians; so that we have almost as lively a representation of the appearance, the warfare, the religious ceremonies, the arts, trades, manufactures and manufacturers, together with the social economy and the habits and manners of that extraordinary people, as any modern writer has afforded us of any country or people at present existing upon the face of the globe. But as other primitive nations were not similarly minded with the red-skinned inhabitants of Thebes, Memphis, or Heliopolis,—as they neither embalmed their dead, carved their sepulches out of the solid rocks, raised monuments like the pyramids, sculptured statues like the Sphinx or the Memnon, nor left us records of their deeds in a pictorial language preserved for upwards of three thousand six hundred years,—we have but scanty means whereby to found a probable theory as to their origin, habits, or condition, prior to the date of authentic written testimony. And as a country presents more or less of ancient monuments of art, or vestiges of language, even without the aid of written records, so will the antiquary or the historian possess in a greater or less degree the data whereon to found some rational theory as to the date of its first colonization, or the origin of its inhabitants, with their religion and their civil and social condition.

Having offered these brief remarks upon the best means for investigating the early history of a country, we now come to ask ourselves the questions, who we are?—from whence sprung the Irish race?—to what tribes of mankind did we originally belong?—at what period was this country first peopled, and what vestiges of that aboriginal race still exist amongst us to point out their physical characters, their habits, social, warlike, or domestic, their religion, or knowledge of literature, architecture, and the arts? The last inquiry is that most easily answered; we have still remaining in the island some relics of the early inhabitants, chiefly their sepulchral monuments, the cromlech and the kistvaen, the monumental pillar, the rude altar, the terracotta urn, a few bone and shell ornaments, and a variety of flint and iron weapons and implements, knives, arrow and spear-heads, and stone hatchets, together with that which it is our more immediate province to bring before the reader, their bones and skulls; and this may really be said to sum up all that is positively known about them. As to the inquiry of who they actually were, or from whence they first came, although it may be ungrateful to our national pride to acknowledge it, we must confess we are still wandering in the trackless fields of conjecture. But is this peculiar to the Irish nation? By no means. In Egypt, which for its antiquity and frequent mention in the earliest authentic writings, we have chosen for illustration, we see the monuments of the earliest date, we read the history of its people in characters which vividly bring before us their manners and customs; everything is there pourtrayed with the freshness of yesterday; the bodies of thousands upon thousands of its people still remain as they came from the hands of the embalmer, as if ready to start into a second existence; the arms of the warrior, the robe of the priest, and the toilet of the lady, are there ready for our inspection : yet, with all this, we positively know nothing certain as to who first peopled the valley of the Nile. So it is with the first people of America,—so with the Chinese,—so with the Irish: the certainty of origin cannot be traced back to any extent. There are, however, a few exceptions to this very general rule in those primitive nations against whom we read of certain direct and positive denunciations being issued by the great Disposer of the goings of man. Have we not still, after the lapse of hundreds upon hundreds of years, the " servant of servants" in the oppressed and enslaved sons of Africa? and do we not meet in the swarthy, sinewy child of the desert, the lawless Bedouin, who knows no law but his own will, and owns no master but his own appetite,—the man " whose hand is against every man?" But, above all, have we not that living miracle still before us, the Hebrew people, ever remaining distinct and separate, though outcast, scattered, and despised, with an unbroken descent, and an unaltered lineage from their forefather Abraham to the present day? These are nations, and we believe the only ones, where, in addition to their stereotyped physical characters and personal appearance, history has afforded a chain of evidence, as to their origin and descent, from the earliest period to the present.

To enumerate the various opinions, the crude hypotheses, the absurd and fanciful traditions of writers as to the origin of the Irish people, might, did space permit, or the subject we are about to treat of require it, afford us amusement, but certainly little instruction. Some assert that the early people of Erin were a Gothic race, but most writers seem to agree that we were a Celtic colony; but who the Celts were, from whence they sprang, what country they first inhabited, into what tribes they were divided, what was their original language, or what their physical characters or personal appearance, has not yet been decided by the learned; nor whether they existed coeval with, or how they differed from the Gothic, the Teutonic, or the Belgic races, in the early peopling of the western and south-western countries of Europe. And yet how learnedly, how frequently, and with what confidence, do we hear the term " Celts," or " of Celtic origin," or " Celtic Druids," or " the Celtæ and the Belgæ," with such like expressions, made use of in scientific as well as popular discourses! We believe that if the exact meaning of the persons who make use of these expressions was to be inquired into, it would be found to consist in neither more nor less than the original or primitive inhabitants of the countries under consideration. Having taken some trouble in inquiring into this matter,—having examined several authorities that allude to this race,—having traced them, as we thought, from country to country in Europe,—having sought after their remains in the collections of the curious, or in the writings of the modern learned, we found ourselves, like many others, although in possession of a large collection of facts and references bearing upon the origin of the Celts, and their connexion with Ireland, nearly as wise as when we commenced the investigation. In fact, we found we were running in a circle; and what one author put forward to-day, another contradicted to-morrow; so that the nearer we approach the age we live in, the more incongruous and uncertain become the opinions that are set forth. Herodotus informs us that the Celtæ were the primitive people that sprang from the borders of the Danube, yet we possess a skull found in an ancient tumulus on the confines of Hungary, which is evidently altered by artificial pressure, and in a remarkable manner resembles those compressed crania found in the sepulchres of the ancient Peruvians, particularly in the valley of Titicaca.* Similar tumuli, and containing similar re-

---

* See " Austria and its Institutions," p. 49, where there is a drawing of this very remarkable skull, for a cast of which we are indebted to Count Albert Thun, of Prague.

mains, stretch along the borders of the Danube, through both the Austrias, and extend in a north-western direction into Moravia, and even Bohemia.

Let us now turn to the immediate object before us. With the peopling of Ireland before the flood, as related in Irish manuscripts, or in the legends detailed by Keating, and, since his time, copied into all the popular histories of this country, we do not now deal. They may, or may not be fact, but they affect not the present subject. All authorities agree in according to this island inhabitants at a very early period, long prior to the Christian era: who those aborigines were, or from whence they came, is involved in the same mystery that hangs over the origin of the early people of Europe generally. In Irish they are generally denominated Firbolgs ; and it is reported that under them a settled form of government was first introduced into this island. In the mixture of fable and fact which relates to these people, either traditional or in our manuscripts, very little of their habits or physical characters has come down to our time. Of this people, says Dr. Petrie, in his learned Essay on the History and Antiquities of Tara,—" According to the Irish bardic traditions, the hill of Tara became the chief residence of the Irish kings, on the first establishment of a monarchical government in Ireland, under Slainge, the first monarch of the Firbolgs, and continued so till its abandonment in the year 563." In an Irish manuscript, the Book of Mac Firbis, written about the year 1650, an account of which, from a translation by Mr. Eugene Curry, has been laid before the Royal Irish Academy, by Dr. Petrie, it is said that "every one who is black, loquacious, lying, tale-telling, or of low and grovelling mind, is of the Firbolg descent." To this Firbolg race a Belgic origin has been usually assigned ; those Belgæ appear to have been of German or Gothic extraction; and as far as history has left us a trace of this people, they seem to have been followed, and subsequently subdued, by the Celtæ.

In the Irish version of the Historia Britonum of Nennius, we have some account of the early people of this country, from the time of the arrival of Partholan, whose descendants, the early colonists of Erin, were cut off by a plague, it is said, in one week, A. M. 2820. Then came Nemed, and "the Viri Bullorum, i. e. the Firbolg," so called, it is said, by Keating, from the leathern bags which they had with them in Greece, for carrying mould to lay it on the flat-surfaced rocks, so as to convert them into flowery plains; but as Dr. Todd, the learned editor of the work from which we quote, justly remarks, " Bullum, in the Latinity of the middle ages, signified, according to Du Cange, *Baculum pastoris*, which suggests a derivation of the name Fir-Bolg." Wherever they came from, it would appear that they were a simple pastoral people, who possessed little knowledge of art, science, or war, even according to the acceptation of these terms in the limited sense to which they may be applied in the very early ages. With these afterwards appeared the Fir-Gaileoin, the Viri Armorum, or Spearsmen, perhaps from their warlike propensities: and also the Fir-Domnann, who, as well as the Firbolg, seem to be a pastoral or agricultural people. "Afterwards the Plebes Deorum, i. e. the Tuatha De Danaan, took Ireland; it was of them the chief men of science, as Luctenus, artifex, Credenus, figulus [brazier], Dianus, medicus; also Eadon, his daughter, viz., the nurse of the poets; Goibnen, faber; Lug, son of Eithne, with whom were all arts. Dagda, the great son of Ealadan, son of Dealbaith, the king. Ogma, brother of the king; it was from him came the letter of the Scots"—Ogham.*

The Annals of the Four Masters inform us that the three last kings of this race who were in joint sovereignty over Ireland in A. M. 3471, were Mac Cuill, Mac Ceacht, and Mac Grein. Mr. O'Donovan has added the following valuable comment on this:

" According to an old Irish poem, quoted by Keating in his *History of Ireland* (See Haliday's edition, p. 212), the real names of these kings were Eathur, Teathur, and Ceathur; and the first was called Mac Cuill, because he worshipped the hazel tree: the second Mac Ceacht, because he worshipped the plough, evidently alluding to his wish to promote agriculture; and the third, Mac Greine, because he worshipped the sun as his god. For some fanciful disquisitions upon the history and names of these kings, the reader is referred to Vallancey's Vin-

* See " The Conquest of Eri, as recorded by Nennius," p. 45, *et seq.* We have given this account of the early Irish colonists from the volume recently published by the Irish Archæological Society, rather than extract from the more ancient but fanciful history of Keating, who must have drawn up his account of these people from this and similar other authentic documents.

dication of Irish History, p. 496. In Mageoghegan's translation
of the Annals of Clonmacnoise, it is stated that ' this people,
Tuathy De Danan, ruled in Ireland for 197 years; that they
were most notable magicians, and would work wonderful
thinges by magick and other diabolicale arts, wherein they
were exceedingly well skilled, and in these days accompted the
chiefest in the world in that profession.' From the many
monuments ascribed to this colony by tradition, and in ancient
Irish historical tales, it is quite evident that they were a real
people; and from their having been considered gods and magicians by the Gaedhil or Scoti, who subdued them, it may be
inferred that they were skilled in arts which the latter did not
understand. Among these was Danann, the mother of the
gods, from whom Ɗa ċiċ Ɗanainne (the two paps of Danan),
a mountain in Kerry, was called; Buanann, the goddess that
instructed the heroes in military exercises, the Minerva of
the ancient Irish; Badhbh, the Bellona of the ancient Irish;
Abhortach, god of music; Ned, the god of war; Nemon,
his wife; Manannan, the god of the sea; Diancecht, the
god of physic; Brighit, the goddess of poets and smiths,
&c. It appears from a very curious and ancient Irish tract,
written in the shape of a dialogue between St. Patrick and
Caoilte Mac Ronain, that there were very many places in
Ireland where the Tuatha-De-Dananns were then supposed to
live as sprites or fairies, with corporeal and material forms, but
indued with immortality. The inference naturally to be drawn
from these stories is, that the Tuatha-De-Dananns lingered in
the country for many centuries after their subjugation by the
Gaedhil, and that they lived in retired situations, where they
practised abstruse arts, which induced the others to regard
them as magicians."

Professor Rask supposes the aborigines of Western and South-
western Europe to have been an Euskarian race, from whom
sprang the Iberians; and his researches lead him to believe that
he can discover traces of the Euskarian language among the
French Basques and Spanish Bascayans, as well as in some of
the Finnish, Lapland, and Danish tribes; and it has been even
asserted that an inhabitant of Ireland and a Spaniard of the
Basque provinces, could understand one another. Mr. Borrow, who is probably better acquainted with the Euskarian
tongue than any other Englishman at present, asserts that
there is not the slightest affinity between them; but accu-

rate as Mr. Borrow's knowledge of the old Spanish may be, he does not appear to be sufficiently versed in the Gaelic, to offer as correct an opinion on it as on most other European tongues. In fact, to approach or handle this subject effectually, we should have scholars versed in the composition and construction of both languages, as well as possessing a fluency of speech in both, especially since mere sound is often the point of resemblance most relied on. From whatever examination we have been able to make, and from the communications with which we have been favoured from other countries, we find traces of the same aboriginal people spread over a large portion of the central and north-west parts of the European continent, together with Ireland, and probably Great Britain also. Whether this first wave of population arrived here from the East, having passed over to us from the South, as from Gaul and the littoral parts of Spain, or by the North, from Sweden and Denmark, is not so easy to determine. At all events, we find the remains of this people precisely similar, and the circumstances under which they are found accurately corresponding in every country where they have yet been discovered. Now, for distinction sake, we will call these the aborigines, and, in accordance with our traditions and histories, the Firbolgs. It is next related that the aborigines were overcome by another, and, evidently from the accounts in the manuscripts, a superior race, the Tuatha De Danaan. These hostile invaders, who are stated to have been skilled in magic, necromancy, and the like black arts, are supposed by some writers, even in the present day, not to be human beings at all, but fairies or sprites. There are, however, too many existing records of these fleshly inhabitants of our isle to doubt their identity; and we believe the very arts and magic assigned to them, particularly by the rude, simple, and comparatively ignorant aborigines of our country, arose from their knowledge of so much chemistry as related to the art of mining and the smelting of metals. Of the physical characters of this people we have but little knowledge. It is, however, related in the manuscript Book of Mac Firbis, to which we have already alluded, that "every one who is fair-haired, of large size, fond of music and horse riding, and practises the art of magic, is of Tuatha De Danaan descent." That these people were skilled in medicine we have elsewhere shown, and one of the oldest Irish manuscripts on record gives an account

of the celebrated battle fought on the plains of Moy Turey,
in the county of Sligo, when Nuada Airgeat Lamh, the king
of the Tuatha De Danaan, completely routed the Belgæ or Firbolgs, a vast number of whom are said to have been slain;
and on that battle-field, the Marathon of Irish history, we have
still remaining the tumuli or barrows erected over the remains
of our early Pagan progenitors.   Dr. Petrie detailed to the
Academy, in the year 1838, an account of a most remarkable
collection of cairns, cromlechs, and stone circles, at Carrow-
more, in the vicinity of Sligo, all containing human remains.
" Such monuments," he stated, " are found in all the battle-
fields recorded in Irish history, as the scene of contest between
the Belgians or Firbolgs and the Tuatha De Danaan colonies,
and he considers these monuments to be the tombs of the Belgians, who, after their defeat in the battle of southern Moy-
Thuree, had retreated to Cuil-Iorra, and were there again
defeated, and their king Eochy slain in crossing the strand of
Ballysadare bay, on which a cairn rising above high water
still marks the spot on which he fell."   To these Tuatha De
Danaan, or metal workers, we are inclined to assign a Celtic
origin, and to their art and ingenuity to attribute the workmanship of those beautiful bronze or antique-metal ornaments and
weapons, formed by a mixture of copper and tin, so generally
found over the face of the country, and now swelling our national collection at the Royal Irish Academy.

The Irish are said to be a Phœnician race, and perhaps these
Tuatha De Danaan were the Phœnician Cabiri. We are quite
willing to bow to those antiquaries who endeavour to show an
early connexion between Ireland and the Tyrian people, and
are personally willing to adopt, though we may not be able to
prove, the opinion expressed as to the Oriental commerce with
this country direct from Tyre and Sidon, or through their colonies in Spain and Tuscany; but it has not been proved that
the Phœnicians were the *original settlers* in Ireland. The Gaelic
is not the Punic tongue, although we believe the remains of
the latter are insufficient to determine the point; but we do
confidently assert that the earliest record of the Phœnician
people exhibit them to us in the highest state of civilization
of that day,—a great commercial and perhaps a literary people
also,—skilled above their fellows in all the arts of the time.
Sidon and its daughter Tyre, the cradle of Oriental art, are

mentioned by undoubted authority, as flourishing cities nearly sixteen centuries before the Christian era. More than a thousand years before that epoch, their inhabitants were the greatest artificers in the world, and were invited by the wisest and most gorgeous monarch of the East to construct the most splendid edifice that history, either ancient or modern, can point to; and from a people whom the great prophetic poet of the Babylonish court described as exceeding in power, luxury, and magnificence all surrounding nations, we cannot believe sprung the simple early inhabitants of Ireland, to whose handiwork we ascribe the rude cinerary urns, the cromlechs and kistvaens, with shell ornaments, bone pins and bodkins, and some stone weapons, found in tumuli, nor even to the people who lived in the early age of bronze that followed that period. It is a fact,—curious, but generally overlooked by Irish historians who bring hither colonies of different nations,—that there are but the remains of *one* language known in manuscripts, or spoken amongst us.

The Tuatha De Danaan were in turn overcome by the Milesian race [perhaps the Gaedhil or Scoti], but with this people our subject has little to do; for even if the Milesians did come to Ireland at the time and in the manner told in history, and that all the circumstances attending their invasion be as related by the Irish bards, still we believe they differed not in physical characters from their brother Celts who preceded them, although in civilization they were more advanced. After a long lapse of years, when Paganism had given place to Christianity, history becomes more definite in her terms, and more accurate in her descriptions. Probably about the year A. D. 900, those hardy, enterprising Northmen, who conquered wherever they trod, and found their way wherever there was a wave to carry them, landed upon our coast, and held sway for some time over the then existing inhabitants of our country. To this naval and warlike people, and to the age of their invasion, are generally attributed the iron weapons and implements discovered in this country. Dr. Prichard inclined to the opinion that the Romans assisted in the civilization of Ireland; but, with great deference to that eminent authority, we submit that there never have been any remains of that people discovered in this country, and we do not believe the Roman people ever had a footing in Ireland. With the various English invasions in more modern times every reader of Irish history is familiar.

We shall now demonstrate some of the human remains of the first or earliest inhabitants found in this country, and detail the circumstances under which they have been discovered. At the beginning of the last century, the distinguished physician, Sir Thomas Molyneux, was the first to investigate this interesting subject, which, from his day until the publication of the Proceedings of the Royal Irish Academy a few years ago, remained forgotten and neglected; and the very prejudices and superstitions of the lower orders of our countrymen who might accidentally open any of the ancient burial-places, led them to secrete or destroy any human remains found within them. Owing partly to this cause, and partly to the circumstance of their value not being understood from the days of Molyneux until within the last dozen years, there does not appear to have been any regard paid by antiquaries to the preservation or description of human remains. The following summary includes an account of the various forms of burial made use of by our aborigines, at least so far as we have any authentic account of them:—First and most notable is a dome-roofed stone chamber, containing the remains of one or more bodies, and approached by a covered way, the whole being enclosed in a large earthen tumulus or barrow, and generally surrounded by a circle of upright pillar-stones. This is the true pyramid, modify it as we please, of which the type is to be found in those great oriental monuments, with the characters of which all are acquainted. The most splendid specimen of this description, which we know of in Central or North-western Europe, is the magnificent mausoleum at New Grange, which may well be denominated the Great Pyramid of the West. When New Grange was first opened, a great many years ago, we are told that " two entire skeletons, not burnt, were found on the floor;" but what characters these bones presented, or with what emblems that might mark the date of their interment, we know not, as none of the remains discovered in this vault have come down to the present day. We only hear that the bodies were buried entire, and not burned. In 1839, the account of a tumulus of a similar character, found near Rush, in this county, was presented to the Royal Irish Academy by Lieutenant Newenham. This barrow, called Knochlea, consisted of a chamber about eight feet long and six wide, placed beneath an immense heap of earth and boulder stones. The chamber was approached by a stone-constructed passage, eleven yards long and one in width. "The lines of stones forming the sides of the passage appear to continue on through the mound towards the north side; and a few feet below the present surface of the barrow, a little to the north of the chamber, there is a bed of periwinkle shells, about eight inches thick, with some limpet and muscle shells intermixed; and beneath this bed of shells there was a quantity of dark, rich mould, with some reddish earth, which has the appearance of being burned. A few human bones, and some bones of small animals, were found in the earth beneath."

Professor A. Retzius, of Stockholm, and Professor Eschricht, of Copenhagen, two most distinguished northern philosophers,—and whose opinions in almost every particular correspond with and confirm the views which we have on two or three occasions ventured to put forward with regard to the characteristics of the aboriginal Irish heads, and the circumstances under which they are found,—have published accounts of the crania of the ancient people of Scandinavia, and the graves or tumuli in which they have been discovered.*

Eschricht informs us that two large tumuli, or "warriors' barrows," as they are popularly denominated, having been opened in the vicinity of Stege, "the position and the contents, which were almost the same in both, testified that they belonged to the barrows of the oldest period. Through a narrow aperture on the south side of each of the barrows ingress was given to a small passage, and thence to a chamber in the middle of the barrow, the proper sepulchral chamber." The passage and sepulchral chamber were constructed with large, flat, unhewn stones. It appears that the smaller tumulus of the two had previously been partially opened from above by some peasants,

---

* This communication was originally published in a small Danish periodical, the "Dansk Folkeblad," by Professor Eschricht; but his views having been questioned by Professor Nilsson, of Lund, who has also written on the Swedish crania and antiquities, they did not at first receive the acceptation which they undoubtedly deserve. We are much indebted to Professor A. Retzius for a copy of S. Nilsson's rare and most valuable work,—"Skandinaviska Nordens Ur-Inanare ett Försök I Komparativa Ethnografien," &c., Lund, 1838–1843,—where there are several lithographic representations of the northern crania. Nilsson asserts that the globular crania found in northern tumuli belonged to a Lapland people of the Mongolian race.

and no skeleton was found in it; but several stone weapons, clay urns, and a great number of amber ornaments, lay scattered throughout. In the larger barrow the passage was ten ells long, and the sepulchral apartment sixteen; the walls consisted of large oblong stones, the interstices between which were carefully filled up with slabs of split sandstone. The weapons, tools, and ornaments found in this barrow were all of stone, bone, shell, or amber; but what interests us most are the remains of nine or ten human bodies discovered in this sepulchral chamber, the heads of which were of rather a small size; and this wood-cut is a reduced representation of one of them.

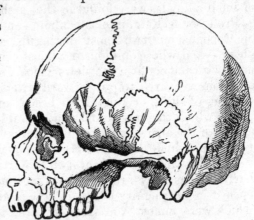

The description of head from which this was taken has many analogies with the remains of a globular-headed race found in ancient sepulchres in our own country, to be described presently. So small a head, says Professor Eschricht, is seldom found among the present Danes. It is the face, however, which appears small; the capacity of the skull is proportionably large. With regard to the peculiar tribe or race of people to whom this head belonged, all the conjecture that the learned Dane has ventured upon is, that these individuals belonged to a noble tribe of the Caucasian race; but whether Celts, Goths, or Lappons, he does not say. The facial portion of these heads being small, without doubt the whole body was not above the middle size. The traces of the facial muscles, on the other hand, were exceedingly strong; the play of the features was, therefore, during life, very energetic. The orbits or eye sockets are very small, low, and deeply hidden under the eye-brows. The nasal bones were particularly strong, prominent, and inclined towards the horizontal, with a deep groove or sulcus between their root and the margin of the brow. These people must, therefore, have had strongly marked, arched, prominent noses. In those casts and drawings which have been forwarded to us from Denmark and

Sweden the projections which support the eye-brows, or the superciliary ridges as they are styled in technical language, are remarkably prominent; and we are led to believe that the eyes themselves must have appeared small and sunken ; and, says our correspondent, " the small face, with the lively play of the features, the small eye set deeply under the eye-brows, and the large, aquiline nose, are characteristics which, taken together, imply a dark colour of the skin, eyes, and hair;" but the globular-headed Saxon Germans of the present day have generally light hair and blue eyes.

A second excavation of a barrow of great size was subsequently undertaken, in the island of Moen, at a place called Maglehaei. The sepulchral chamber in this contained twenty human skeletons, together with the skull and some bones of a dog, and the implements and ornaments were of the same character as those in the early excavations, consisting of bone, stone, and amber, but not the least trace of metal of any description. It is interesting to remark that upon one of the skulls found in this collection, a portion of dark brown hair still remained.

We now turn to another age in northern Europe, the bronze or metallic period. In the summer of 1821 there was dug up at Funen, in a gravel pit, two human skeletons, surrounded, it is said, by various metallic 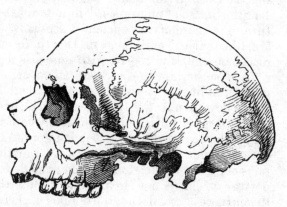 articles. A silver buckle lay on the breast, a spirally twisted gold ring, like our torques, surrounded one of the fingers, and a large metal pan or kettle lay at the feet. The skulls presented a totally different appearance from those found in the stone chamber, and in connexion with stone ornaments and weapons. This is a faithful representation of one of these long low skulls. The skeletons belonging to this race are said to be of a stature above the common. Subsequently to

Eschricht's communication, we were favoured with one from Professor A. Retzius, together with the cast of a cranium, of what he terms "an ancient Swede towards the end of the heathen era;" it is of the long-headed race, and he mentions that this is one of the common forms of head among the modern Swedes; and both he and Nilsson classify all the heads found in northern tumuli into—first, the oldest, with square-shaped heads like the Laplanders, found along with tools, and hunting or fishing tackle of stone or bone; second, the long-headed race, always accompanied with metallic implements, and which race they considered to be Celtic; and the third, an oval form, also accompanied by metals.

It would extend this ethnographical notice, which is intended chiefly for the popular reader, to too great a length, to detail the various other kinds of ancient burial found in northern countries, but we may remark upon one form of ancient grave found there, of which we have no example in this country, and that is the T-formed or hammer-shaped, of which it would appear there are a vast number, some of great size, and containing many skeletons, generally lying at full length, but sometimes placed in a doubled-up or sitting posture, like those of the ancient Peruvians. These sepulchres are, like that at New Grange or Dowth, formed of huge stones, placed on end, and roofed with immense flags, but not dome-roofed; neither are the basement stones arranged in circles like our's: the lines are nearly always parallel.

We now turn to the Irish heads again, and with them to the second form of burial, the cromlech, where the stone chamber under the centre of a mound is not approached by a passage as in the pyramidal structures at Grange, Dowth, or Rush, and contains one or more skeletons placed in a horizontal or recumbent posture. This is not the place to discuss the old question of the purpose of cromlechs; the opinion of their being altars seems to have completely given way to their sepulchral use and origin; and chiefly from the discovery and accurate investigation of a tumulus at Knockmaroon, in the Phœnix Park, near Dublin, by a committee of the Royal Irish Academy, in 1838.[*] Within this stone chamber two perfect male skeletons were

---

[*] The stone vault, or chamber, of a similar one, is now preserved in our Zoological Gardens.

found in a recumbent posture, and also the tops of the thigh bones of another, and a single bone of an animal, supposed to be a dog. Immediately under each skull was found collected together a number of small sea shells (the *Nerita litoralis*), which evidently formed a necklace; and a small fibula of bone, precisely similar to those found in Denmark, and a small flint arrow-head, were likewise discovered in this kistvaen. Within the mound which formed this sepulchre, but not within the tomb, were found four urns of baked clay, containing incinerated human bones. The two heads found in this sepulchre are, perhaps, the most perfect of their kind in existence; they are chiefly characterized by their extreme length from before backwards, or what is technically termed the antero-posterior diameter, and the flatness of their sides; and in this and most other respects they correspond with the second form of head discovered in the Danish sepulchres, but different from it; these long-headed aborigines of Ireland, and indeed we may say all our skulls discovered in sepulchres of un-doubted heathen times, are never found in connexion with metallic substances, but only with stone, bone, shell, or baked clay ornaments, weapons, or implements.

These skulls, one of which is ex-hibited in this re-presentation, pre-sent the same marked charac-ters in their facial aspect, and the projecting occi-put and promi-nent frontal sin-uses, as the Danish ones. The nose, in common with all the truly Irish

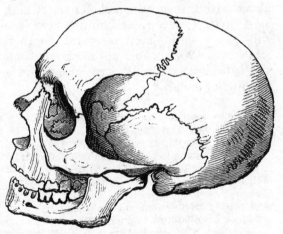

heads we have examined, presents the most marked pe-culiarities, and evidently must have been very prominent. With this we have evidences of the teeth having been slightly projecting, and the chin small, square, well-marked, and also prominent; so that on the whole this race must have possessed peculiarly well-marked features, and a shrewd, intelligent physiognomy. The forehead is low, but not retreating. The molar teeth are remarkably ground down upon their crowns, probably from long trituration of farinaceous food, and the attachments of the temporal muscles are exceedingly well-marked. It may be asked, do the characters exhibited in those skulls express the general appearance of a peculiar people,— were they not accidental varieties? No; we have already examined too many heads of a like character to be mistaken on this point; and, moreover, although we find every variety of head among the modern mixed races of civilised countries, when we come to examine primitive people, or savage tribes, we find the character of their crania and general physical condition more and more stereotyped as we recede from civilization.

Four years ago, while passing through the museum of Guy's Hospital, our eye lighted on a pair of heads lying in a remote corner, which we at once claimed, from their exceeding length, &c., as fellow-countrymen. Through the kindness of our friend, Mr. Dalrymple, we have received casts of these skulls, together with the following account of them. They were discovered, along with fifteen entire skeletons of both sexes and various ages, in 1821, in a great tumulus near Denley, in Gloucestershire; they were placed in several chambers beneath the cairn, which was 120 feet in length. Some bones of the wild boar, and two flint axe-heads, were also found in the tomb, but no remains of metals.*

---

* For an account of an ancient tumular cemetery recently discovered at Laurel Hill, near York, see Dr. Turnham's paper in the Proceedings of the Yorkshire Philosophical Society for June, 1848.

While examining the splendid collection of heads in the museum of anatomy in the Jardin du Roi at Paris, in 1840, along with the late distinguished Dr. William Edwards, two skulls, without labels or any marks to denote their locality or race, were presented to us. These, from their peculiarly long form, we at once pronounced to be ancient Irish. A laugh being raised at this surmise, and Mons. Laurillard, the Curator, not being able to give any account of them, Mr. Pentland, who presented them, was written to, and his answer informed us that they were found in Etruscan tombs of the very oldest date, which were opened in 1828, near Sarteano; and that with these heads were also found a number of antique vases. How far this supports the peculiar theory of Sir William Betham, we cannot take upon us to decide; but with the similarity of form which these skulls presented to the most ancient Irish and Norwegian, we were instantly struck.

Now we find conditions of head and feature similar to both the early Irish races still existing among the modern inhabitants of this country, particularly beyond the Shannon, towards the west, where the dark or Firbolg race may still be traced, as distinct from the more globular-headed, light-eyed, fair-haired, Celtic people who lie to the north-east of that river. Strange to say, the skull of Swift exhibits most of the peculiarities of this early race, though, as most people assert, he was not of Irish descent; and any one who has examined the old skulls found in the ancient burial-grounds either in Connaught or in Kerry, must have been struck with the appearances which we have now described.

We next come to the third form of burial, containing the relics of the second race of people; for of the first, or those found in the pyramidal structures with the stone passages, we have not seen the remains, and therefore cannot speak as to their form.   The vault in which the remains of this second race are generally found is usually beneath the surface, a kistvaen, or small stone chamber, roofed either with a single flag, or covered in with that form of arch resembling a bee-hive dome. There is no tumulus or heap of earth to mark the site of these sepulchres, several of which have been turned up with the plough. Within this small square vault the bones are generally placed in a regular manner, the small ones at the bottom, the long ones, as the legs and arms, at the top, and the whole is crowned with the skull.   One of these was found a few years ago in the neighbourhood of Dublin; it is much better proportioned, higher, more globular, and in every respect approaches more to the highest forms of the Indo-European variety of the Caucasian race, than either of the foregoing. It is said, but, we believe, upon very questionable authority, that metallic weapons and instruments have been found in connexion with this form of burial.

That most beautiful cranium figured upon the next page was presented to us by our friend Mr. O'Donovan, and we fear not to assert that in symmetry and general development it comes up to some of the finest Grecian models, though the general capacity of the head is small ; but it may have belonged to a small race or a small individual. The small stone chamber in which this skull was found, five years ago, was situated in the outer circle or breast-work of a rath, within 150 yards of the south side of the Rock of Dun-Masg, or Dunamase, in the Queen's County. Close by the side of the skeleton was found a cinerary urn, with one exception the most beautiful of its kind, either in design or execution, ever discovered in this country.*

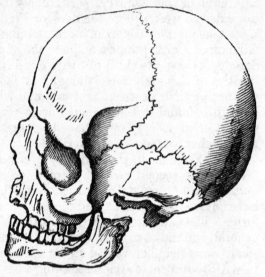

The fourth and last form of burial is what may be termed the urn sepulchre, in which we have manifest traces of the burning of the bodies having taken place; but to what age or to what people in particular we are to refer this ancient heathen rite, cannot, we think, be determined; for the cinerary urn, containing the remains of burned human bones, has been found not only as a separate and distinct form of burial, but also in connexion with the cairn, the cromlech, and the kistvaen or small stone chamber. Moreover, we have instances of bones being found partially or completely burned in some of the larger sepulchres, without any trace of the urn whatsoever. Urns containing human remains have been long known in this country, and were first well described by Molyneux, whose remarks upon them have since been copied by Harris into Ware's, and most of the publications that treat of the antiquities of Ireland. In June, 1842, Mr. J. Huband Smith communicated to the Royal Irish Academy a description of the recent discovery of a vast number of cinerary urns at the " Hill of Rath," within a few miles of Drogheda. In the progress of working a quarry at the foot of the hill a farmer discovered

---

* The most beautiful urn of its kind ever found in Great Britain, either in design or execution, is that small, echinus-shaped urn, with an ear or handle, lately found in the county of Carlow, near Bagnalstown, and which we described in the Proceedings of the Royal Irish Academy for January 10, 1818.

from 150 to 200 urns of unbaked clay, of various sizes, almost all placed in an inverted position, and each of them covering a considerable quantity of human bones. "They were placed, apparently without any regularity, about two or three feet asunder, and having been imbedded in yellow clay, without any flags or stones to protect them, had, in most cases, been pressed in and broken to pieces by the superincumbent earth." Some of the urns were very large. We have carefully examined the contents of one; they bear evident marks of fire, and consist of the bones of several individuals, as well as bones of birds, and a small animal of the dog kind. In another urn was found a flint arrow-head and a small bone needle.*

The second circumstance under which we find cinerary urns is in connexion with the cromlech; and the third, with the small stone kist: an example of the first of which was well shown in the tumulus in the Phœnix Park, where four sepulchral vases, containing ashes and burned bones, were found throughout the tumulus, enclosed in small separate stone chambers, but not within the cromlech itself; whereas in the third form, as in the kist at Dunamase, the vase is found in immediate connexion with the body, and within the chamber. To what period, or to what particular people these urns belong, it is difficult to determine, for we find them with nearly every form of burial among our ancient people. The condition of their contents determines the point as to the ancient people of this country burning their dead; but whether as a sacrificial or funereal rite we leave to the antiquarians to determine. This we may remark, that where found by themselves, as at the "Hill of Rath," they appear to have been funereal, while the circumstance of an urn containing human burned bones being placed within the tumulus or beside the body, the skeleton of which has been found perfect in all its parts, and therefore none of it subject to the action of fire, leads one to suppose that the person whose ashes the urn contains was sacrificed to the manes of the individual for whose body the tumulus or stone chamber

---

* It is said that a thin scale of copper was also found in one of the urns; but we think that the way in which this got there is very questionable, and by no means proves that the people who placed these urns in this ancient burial-place had any acquaintance with the use of metals. A somewhat similar collection of urns, occurring at Loughanmore, in the county of Antrim, has been described by the same gentleman, but the description of the former will here suffice. Why does not some industrious antiquary write a paper on our Irish urns? The materials for it are most abundant.

was originally erected. At all events we may safely assert, that burning the body and collecting the bones into an urn, was one of the earliest rites of the ancient Irish. It is also well established that both birds and dogs were interred, burned and unburned, with these remains, for their bones are constantly found with the human ones.

The Rev. Dr. Walsh has recorded an instance at Kilbride, in the county of Wicklow, where a stone coffin was discovered in a wild and solitary part of the mountain, and just large enough to contain a small urn, which was inverted over two small bones belonging to human fingers and toes, and no other part of the body! We are indebted to R. C. Walker, Esq., who has opened a great number of tombs in this country, for an account of a most interesting examination which he made of some tumuli in the county of Sligo, a celebrated locality for sepulchral remains, particularly those of the Firbolgs. Mr. Walker informs us that one kist or tomb, which contained the remains of a great number of skeletons, some evidently burned, and others exhibiting no trace of fire, occupied the centre of a large cairn. Some idea may be formed of the magnitude of this great kist when it is known that one of the stones which formed the side of it was sixteen feet in length, and about six feet in breadth. In this tomb were found six different human interments, which occupied the eastern and western ends, the centre part being unoccupied. The bones were not contained in urns, but were collected together into small heaps that rested upon the " freestone flag," which invariably formed the bottom or floor of the inner tomb. The large bones, such as the arms, legs, and thighs, covered the half-calcined remains of the smaller ones, and the skull surmounted the little pyramid thus formed. Round the margin of this heap was collected a quantity of the bones of birds, and some of the lower mammalia, together with a number of small shells, principally the land *Helix ;* and each of these six interments was kept distinct, and surrounded by small freestone flags. No weapon or ornament of any kind was discovered in this tomb. Here, then, in this very remarkable tumulus of the class denominated " giants' graves," we have remains of nearly every form of interment employed by the aborigines of this country.

A. N. Nugent, Esq., opened a sepulchral mound in the neighbourhood of Portaferry a few years ago. "There was," he writes to us, "a circle of large stones, containing an area of about a rood. Between each of these stones there was a facing of flat ones, similar to the building of our modern fences. The outer coating was covered with white pebbles averaging the size of a goose-egg, of which there were several cart-loads—although it would be difficult to collect even a small quantity at present along the beach. "After this was taken away we came to a confused heap of rubbish, stones, and clay, and then some large flag-stones on their ends,—the tumulus still preserving a cone-shape. In the centre we came to a chamber about six feet long, formed by eight very large upright stones, with a large flag stone at the bottom, on which lay, in one heap of a foot in thickness, a mixture of black mould and bones." These bones, some of which were kindly forwarded to us, are all human, and consist of portions of the ribs, vertebræ, and the ends of the long bones, together with pieces of the skull and some joints of the fingers of a full-grown person, and also several bones of a very young child ; none of these had been subject to the action of fire; but among the parcel forwarded to us were several fragments of incinerated or calcined bone, also human. Either these latter were portions of the same bodies burned, or they belonged to an individual sacrificed to the manes of the person whose grave this was; and we are inclined to think the latter is the more probable, from the circumstances under which similar remains have been discovered in other localities. This tumulus was evidently of very ancient date, long prior to the authentic historic period, and was, we should say, erected over some person or family of note in their day. There were no urns, weapons, or ornaments discovered in connexion with it; but our informant states that, in the field in which this barrow was opened, there have been, at various times, small stone chambers or kistvaens discovered, similar to those described at page 230; and in one of these a skull of the long, flat, and narrow character, was some time ago dug up. A farmer in the vicinity likewise told Mr. Nugent that, many years ago while ploughing in this same field, he turned up a stone chamber of the same kind, and that it contained a skull with a portion of hair of a deep red colour attached to it.

Mr. Getty, of Belfast, has been very industrious in the collection of ancient Irish remains; and the Belfast museum at present contains several specimens of old Irish heads. This leads to another locality in which bones of the ancient Irish people are said to have been found. We allude to the Round Towers, particularly to that lately excavated at Drumbo, in the county of Down, beneath which some bones were found. Interest was excited by this discovery, from the supposition that these human remains would offer some clue as to the origin and uses of these monuments, or assist in determining the probable era of their erection. The enchanted palace of the Irish round tower has, however, been opened for our inspection, and therefore all theorizing on the subject is at an end. We were presented at the time of the examination with a very beautiful cast of the skull found within the round tower of Drumbo; and the moment we saw it we felt convinced that, if it was of a contemporaneous age with the structure beneath which it was found, then the Irish round tower was not the ancient building it is usually supposed to be; for, compared with the other Irish heads, that skull is of comparatively modern date. Now, nearly all the round towers are in connexion with ancient burial-places, and that one in particular is so, and one need only dig around and without it to find many similar remains. We hear that the skeleton was found at full length, imbedded in the clay, within the ancient structure. Now, if the round tower was erected as a monument over the person whose skeleton was found within, the body certainly would not have been buried thus in the simple earth, without a vault or stone chamber, such as the enlightened architects who built the tower would be thoroughly competent to construct. Moreover, we do not believe that a skull thus placed loosely in the earth, without any surrounding chamber, would have remained thus perfect for the length of time which even the most modernizing antiquaries assign as the date of the round tower.

Here, however, is a drawing of a Danish head of undoubted authenticity, for which we are much indebted to the Rev. Dr.

Spratt, of this city. We believe it to be that of Donatus, the first Danish Archbishop of Dublin, who died (according to Sir James Ware) in 1074, and was buried in Christ Church; and it also has the peculiar length in its antero-posterior diameter to which we have referred.

At Larne, in the county of Antrim, a skeleton was lately discovered, which, from the iron sword and other weapons in connexion with it, appeared to have been that of a Templar; and similar remains were not long since discovered at Kilmainham. This Templar's skull, found at Larne, although it has an Irish physiognomy, and a Firbolg form of head, cannot be dated back farther than the eleventh or twelfth century.

We have two instances recorded of human remains found in the bogs of Ireland; one of these, the mummy of which is now in the Royal Dublin Society House, was discovered in a bog, nine or ten feet beneath the surface. When first exhumed the body was perfectly fresh, and enclosed in a dress not unlike that in the description given of Gurth in Ivanhoe,—consisting of a tunic of cow-hide, apparently tanned, but with some remains of hair still preserved on the side worn next the skin. This dress is joined in the most accurate and beautiful manner, exhibiting an extraordinary perfection in the art of sewing. The hair on the head, which is both long and fine, is of a dark brown colour, and the skull is compressed in a remarkable manner, owing to a portion of the earthy matter having been removed by the acid of the bog. The body of a man was found under precisely similar circumstances by Mr. R. C. Walker, but it is evidently of more recent date, perhaps not older than the time of Elizabeth; for the dress, which is of woollen texture, and still quite perfect, is precisely that represented in Walker's Irish Bards.

Of the modern race it is not our province here to speak; those of our readers who have followed us in the description of the ancient races will recognise among the true Irish of our own time distinct traces of the long-headed, dark-haired, black-visaged, swarthy aborigines or Gothic Firbolgs, and also (for they are very numerous) the oval or globular-headed, fair-haired, light-coloured, blue or grey-eyed Celtæ, or Tuatha De Danaan. But the present Irish race is very mixed; even those with genuine Irish names, the O's and Mac's, exhibit the greatest diversity. Finally, we may add that there can now be little doubt that the

same early race, whose heads exhibit the two forms which we
have figured at pages 229 and 231, inhabited, long before the
date of written history, Ireland and Great Britain, Sweden, Denmark, and the north-west of Europe generally, together with
the ancient Etruria, and perhaps the central parts of Germany
also; at least one or two specimens of ancient crania which we
examined at Halle and Berlin lead to these conclusions. We have
had an opportunity of examining some skulls of the Guanches or
ancient people of the Canary Archipelago, found by M. Bertilot
in Teneriffe, and they presented precisely similar characters.
In Denmark and Sweden, however, the order of these remains
appears to be reversed, for there the long-headed race is found
in connexion with metallic instruments ; and this appears to
go far to show that the first great wave of population passed
from this country towards the north, and that the original
people who, in Ireland, knew only the use of stone and bone
weapons, by the time they migrated into Denmark, carried
with them the knowledge of metals,—gained, perhaps, from
their Celtic conquerors.

To the skulls and human remains found in connexion with
sepulchral monuments alone can we assign a positive date, and
therefore it is that in the foregoing description we have confined
our remarks to those found under such circumstances, and have
figured them as typical forms. But we sometimes find human
remains in connexion with certain antiquities which serve to
fix their date, and sometimes upon battle-fields, the date of
the actions of which has been recorded in history; and the crania found under these circumstance have been partially preserved, and many of them we have had an opportunity of
examining. In that great collection of animal remains and
antiquities, found at Dunshaughlin some years ago, one
perfect, and fragments of two other human skulls were discovered. They partake of the characters of the long-headed
race, and the antiquities found in that collection would lead us
to believe that the persons to whom those skulls belonged
lived about the tenth century. And in the collection of bones
and antiquities found in the vicinity of Navan, which we have
described at page 135, and which must have belonged to a
much later period, as we know by an examination of the
antiquities, a skull which was there dug up evidently partakes of the character of the long-headed race, but it is

of a more globular form than those found in ancient Pagan
tumuli, as if intermixture of races had modified the peculiarities of the crania, from the elongated to the true globular or
Tuatha De Danaan. And again at the Ford of Kinnafad, we
have shown at pp. 38–40, that the skulls and skeletons of both
races, as well as the weapons which were probably employed
by each, were discovered. The fragments of heads found in
the great cairn at Dowth belonged to the long-headed race.
Last month (July, 1849), four skeletons were found in
the rocky cliffs above Redbay, near Cushendall, county of Antrim. Through the kindness of a friend we possess one of the
skulls of these skeletons; it partakes of most of the characters
of the long-headed race, but it is somewhat greater in capacity,
and approaches the globular form more than those found in
the ancient sepulchres of Pagan times. Now what adds particular interest to these human remains is, that a small stone
celt or hatchet, and two bronze celts, were found along with
them; these weapons enable us to form some conjecture of the
probable age of the skulls, and also show that the bronze and
stone weapons were used at the same time in this country: but
that which fixes the date of the interment of these skeletons
was the discovery of two small Saxon silver coins of the early
part of the ninth century.*

From the foregoing observations it is manifest not only that
two separate races, the earliest characterized by very long
heads, and who were probably the Firbolgs, or first colonizers,
and the other by more globular and capacious skulls, and who,
it would appear, were the Tuatha de Danaan, the conquerors of
the former, existed in this country prior to the Christian era;
but that both races subsequently existed together, and probably
amalgamated. Skulls exhibiting both characters may be observed among the present truly Irish inhabitants, but that the
more we approach the south and west the more do the former
predominate, both in the existing inhabitants, and in the crania
found in ancient burial-places.

It would not suit the present work to enter into a more

---

* Mr. J. Huband Smith, the kind friend who procured us this skull, informs
us that one of them is a coin of Berhtulf, engraved by Ruding (see vol. i. p. 120,
and vol. iii. plate 7, No. 3), who was King of Mercia, A. D. 839; and the other
is a coin of Ceolnoth, who is stated to have been Archbishop of Canterbury,
A. D. 830. See Ruding, vol. ii. p. 182, and vol. iii. plate 13, No. 7.

minute and anatomical description of these crania than that contained in the foregoing observations.

The subject of the ethnology or physical history of the early Irish people having been thus opened, we hope it will not be allowed to rest here, but that many investigators in this fertile field of research will appear. It is only from an examination of a great number of skulls the truth can be elicited, or proper inferences drawn; a single skull is of very little value to any person; and we therefore hope to see our national collection at the Royal Irish Academy increased from day to day by those persons who have become possessed of human remains.

To those who may be engaged in opening ancient tumuli, or who may be accidentally present at such examinations, we would offer the following word of advice. First, note accurately the bearings of the mound, grave, tumulus, or kistvaen, which has been accidentally discovered, or may be about to be opened. Find out the name of the townland, as well as the name of the immediate locality in which it is situated. Observe accurately the position of the skeleton, whether lying at length, placed in a sitting or crouching attitude, or whether the bones appear to have been collected together after they were denuded of the flesh, &c. ; and procure, if possible, drawings of the position of the bones. These bones are remarkably fragile, and should be handled with great care. Should urns be found in connexion with these remains, either in the sarcophagus itself, or in small stone boxes placed around it, their position should be noted, and their contents carefully examined. In many instances within our own knowledge, these urns have been wantonly destroyed by the people who found them. Their value should, therefore, be explained to the peasantry.

In conclusion, let us add, that if this essay may be the means of showing the value that ought to attach to our ancient human remains, and of saving such as may be subsequently discovered, from either the destruction or the oblivion to which they have heretofore been consigned, one of the chief objects of introducing it here shall have been obtained.*

---

* The description of the two forms of skulls, and the details of the various ancient modes of burial, were first broached at the Royal Irish Academy, and afterwards (in 1844) given at a lecture at the Irish College of Physicians; see page 41.

CHAPTER X.

THE BATTLE-FIELD OF OLDBRIDGE.—DULEEK.

THE BOYNE IN LOUTH.—THE CAMPAIGN OF 1690.—DESCRIPTION OF THE BATTLE-FIELD OF OLD-
BRIDGE.—POSITION OF THE IRISH ARMY.—THE HILL OF DONORE.—POSITION OF THE ENGLISH
ARMY.—THE KING'S GLEN.—PLAN OF THE BATTLE OF THE FIRST OF JULY.—THE SHOT AT
KING WILLIAM.—THE BATTLE OF ROSSNAREE.—TURNING OF THE LEFT WING OF THE IRISH
ARMY AT SLANE —POSITION OF JAMES.—THE PASSAGE OF THE BOYNE AT OLDBRIDGE.—DEATH
OF SCHOMBERG.—THE BATTLE.—THE FIGHT UPON DONORE.—THE RETREAT TO DULEEK.—CO-
LONEL BELLINGHAM'S JOURNAL.—STATE OF DUBLIN.—THE ROUT.—WHAT EFFECTS HAVE FOL-
LOWED.—NEW BALLAD OF THE BOYNE WATER.—THE ANTIQUITIES OF DULEEK.—FIRST IRISH
DAIMLIAG.—ST. KIENAN.—THE PRIORY CHURCH; ITS TOMBS AND CROSS.—ST. MARY'S ABBEY.

BELOW Dowth the banks of the river in many places rise high
and abrupt from the water's edge, particularly on the left side,
and the stream is, generally speaking, deep and sullen; but
although the scene along the river's brink presents much
beauty, it is not easy of access; so we must again follow the
high road to Drogheda, although, in so doing, we miss many
a beautiful view, which is presented below the wooded heights

of Dowth and the demesne of Farm, till we again join the
stream, at the confines of the county of Louth, near Oldbridge,
where the Mattock river enters the Boyne, and a short distance

R

beyond which we first catch a glimpse of the obelisk, and the battle-field of 1690. About a quarter of a mile above the "New Bridge" upon the Mattock rivulet, on the Meath side, stand the foundations of Proudfootstown Castle, but they scarcely deserve a visit.

We now enter Louth. Here the road approaches almost to the water's edge, and, following a graceful curve, which the stream makes at this place, continues so for about half a mile, till we pass the Boyne obelisk, which marks the site of the celebrated battle of " July the first." The last rapid upon the Boyne occurs near this. It is now the site of a salmon weir, and the tide comes up thus high, and occasionally even farther. As we pass into this defile the scene becomes truly picturesque. Upon the left, the rocky banks of Townley Hall demesne are clothed with the most splendid foliage; upon the right, the deep meadows and green inches are fringed by the woods of Oldbridge; and in the centre, upon a massive rock, which juts over the water, rises the obelisk raised to comme-morate the passage of the Boyne, when Stuart and Nassau con-tended for the crown of these realms. Grander battle-fields,— more extensive plains, as that of Waterloo,—or with the moun-tains looking upon the sea, as at Marathon,—may easily be found; but for inland sylvan beauty, the diversity of hill and dale, with wooded banks, and a shining river, this scene of action may well challenge competition.

We suppose our readers are already acquainted with the train of events which led to the "Battle of the Boyne," and of the details of the campaign, from the time of the landing of King William III. to the end of the month of June, 1690; and as we have neither space nor desire to discuss the various po-litical circumstances which led to this engagement, nor at all to enter into the general history of the country prior to this event, we shall here chiefly confine ourselves to a topographical description of the battle-field and a brief narrative of the fight, not only because they are more immediately connected with the object of this work, but on account of the discrepancies which, from their want of knowledge of those subjects, appear in the writings of various authors, historians, and tourists, heretofore considered authorities. And now as we approach the spot on which, for the last time in Great Britain, the crown of these realms was contested by kings in person, it is our duty to present our readers with a picture of the scene, and to point out to those who may visit the place, the most memorable and best authenticated localities.

After the Boyne passes the great monument of New Grange, it alters its course, turning towards the north, and, with various minor windings, forms a deep curve between that point and Drogheda, which is distant about five miles in a direct or bird line. Having reached Townley Hall, it again turns to the south-east, towards Drogheda, and thus completes the curve or elbow to which we have just alluded. Within this bend of the river, upon the right or southern bank, the ground rises by a succession of smooth and gentle slopes to the hill of Donore, a conspicuous elevation, crowned by a ruined church, and surrounded by a few straggling ash trees. Of this ruin nothing now remains but portions of the walls and the east window, beneath which, and within the enclosure of the church, we find the handsome altar tomb of one of the Synnots. It is probable that this church was a ruin in 1690. The view from this point commands the entire scene upon the north and east, including Drogheda and the mouth of the Boyne. It is a lone, deserted spot, seldom visited by the tourist, though memorable as marking the place at which the sceptre passed for ever from the last monarch of the royal line of Stuart. The Boyne winds round towards the north in front of this hill, from the summit of which it is distant not quite an English mile. To the right, or east, the hill fines off towards Drogheda, which is about a mile and a half distant. Its western side abuts upon, and is completely protected by the high precipitous banks of the river, now covered by the plantations of the demesnes of Farm and Oldbridge. Immediately behind this hill, towards the south, the way lies open to Dublin, along the sea-board line; and toward the south-west, situated about three miles from Donore, at the extremity of a long hill, is the village of Duleek. To the extreme north-west lies Slane, between which and Drogheda, a distance of about nine miles following the windings of the river, there was not at the time of the battle, nor is there yet, a bridge. Several shallows, however, occur between those two points; descending the stream, some weirs, about half a mile below Slane, point out the site of ancient fords, but the principal shallow is at Rossnaree, immediately beneath the monuments of Knowth and New Grange, about three miles lower down than Slane, and something more than that distance from the hill of Donore. At the weir, where the tide ends, near the entrance of the Mattock river, the Boyne is fordable in dry weather, but with difficulty, and the right bank rises rather precipitously immediately beyond its margin. Finally, the river turns towards the south-west, and just below the site now occupied by the obelisk, it enlarges considerably, and several islands occur in it; the most extensive of these are Grove Island and Yellow Island, the former containing more than five acres, and the latter about sixteen. The shallowest ford occurs here; an old road leads down to it, and it is passable for a carriage and horses, at low water, in summer-time. Immediately opposite this ford, upon the Meath or southern side, stood, in 1690, the little village of Oldbridge. From an old French bird's-eye view of the battle-field, published shortly after the action, as well as from the tapestry in the Irish House of Lords, still kept up in the Bank of Ireland, it would appear that there was, at the time of the action, a small church in the village of Oldbridge. There certainly was a large slated house, besides a number of small cabins.

The locality which we have here described may, properly speaking, be called the battle-field of the 1st of July; but a considerable portion of it, particularly opposite the fords, is now obscured by the plantations of Mr. Coddington's demesne adjoining.

King James's army, having fallen back towards Leinster, passed through Drogheda, and occupied the northern face of the hill of Donore, and the sloping ground between that elevation and the fords near Oldbridge, within the sweep of the river already alluded to. The Irish cannon, then consisting of twelve field-pieces, were planted upon two elevations commanding the fords, one a little to the south of Oldbridge village, which was here intersected by narrow lanes; the other nearly opposite the Yellow Island, on some projecting hillocks in advance of the right of the Irish lines; the latter place is now marked by a fir plantation. According to Story's map, a third small battery was placed opposite the ford, near the Mattock river. Some temporary, and it would appear very inefficient breast-works were also thrown up in front of the village, which was chiefly occupied by the Irish soldiery under Tirconnell.

James and his staff took up a position on the summit of the elevation of Donore, in the little church on which the deposed monarch, it is said, slept the night before the battle.

Upon the left, or Louth bank of the river, a bluff hill, sloping off upon its northern face, continues on from Townley Hall towards Drogheda, intersected here and there by deep, narrow defiles, which run down toward the water's edge; behind it is the rising ground of Tullyallen, where the site of King William's camp is still pointed out. At the end of Townley Hall demesne, a deep, narrow gorge, now generally known as King William's Glen, opens out upon the river, from which it is not more than three hundred paces distant, and, owing to the circumstance of a projecting brow of the hill through which it cuts, as well as its winding direction, the view up this valley is completely obscured, so that a whole army, of many thousand men, within it, might be screened from cannon-shot, and hid from observation, even from the eminences on the opposite side. On the high bank above, and to the east of this valley, was placed King William's chief battery, consisting of about fifty heavy guns and some field mortars.

William and his army marched in two columns from Ardee, upon the 30th of June. Having arrived within view of Drogheda, the position of the Irish encampment, stretching along the slopes of Donore, was at once recognised. A person standing upon any of the elevations in that neighbourhood, could with ease recognise every tent in the Irish camp; and, looking up the charming valley of the Boyne from this spot, over the scene which the celebrated tourist, Arthur Young, said, was " one of the completest landscapes he had ever seen," William may well have given utterance to the exclamation, " Well, it is a country worth fighting for!" The English army then turned slightly westward along the northern slope of the ridge we have described, and by which it was in a great measure concealed from the Irish, and took up its position nearly parallel with the Boyne; its right descending into the hollow of the King's Glen, and its left resting in another narrow ravine, at the eastern extremity of the hill, and very similar to the former. It had thus the advantage of being able to reach the Boyne in a few minutes through either of those two deep, narrow ravines; and William not only had this advantage of

position, but, while his own army was completely concealed
from view, every tent in that of his opponent was plainly
mapped before him, and many of them within point-blank
range of his cannon.   The English being encamped, and their
batteries erected, the firing commenced upon both sides, and
was continued during the greater portion of the day.   The old
ballad says, and perhaps truly:

> " King James he pitched his tents between
>   The lines, *for to retire,*
> But King William threw his bomb-balls in,
>   And set them all on fire,"

alluding, no doubt, to James's intention of retreating, and
to the murderous effect of the heavy English artillery, which
it is stated soon dismounted two of the enemy's guns.

It is related, that the Prince of Orange (William III.) rode
with his staff along the heights which run parallel with the
river.   George Story, a chaplain in the English army, and an
eye-witness of the scene, relates the following incident, which
we insert, principally because we have been enabled, from a
very careful examination of the locality, to decide upon the
exact spot where it occurred.

" His majesty rid on to the pass at Oldbridge, and stood upon
the side of the bank, within musquet-shot of the ford, there
to make his observations on the enemies' camp and posture;
there stood a small party of the enemies' horse, in a little
island within the river; and on the other bank, there were
several hedges, and little Irish houses almost close to the river,
there was one house likewise of stone, that had a court, and
some little works about it; this, the Irish had filled with
souldiers, and all the hedges and little houses we saw, were
lined and filled with musqueteers; there were also several
brest-works cast up to the right, just at the ford.   However,
this was the place through which his majesty resolved to force
his way ; and, therefore, he and his great officers spent some
time in contriving the methods of passing, and the places
where to plant our batteries.   After some time, his majesty
rid about 200 yards further up the river, nigh the west of all
the enemies' camp ;• and whilst his army was marching in, he
alighted, and sate him down upon a rising ground, where he
refreshed himself; whilst his majesty sate there we observed
five gentlemen of the Irish army ride softly along the other

side, and make their remarks upon our men as they marched in; those, I heard afterwards, were the Duke of Berwick, my Lord Tyrconel, Sarcefield, Parker, and some say Lauzun. Captain Pownel, of Colonel Levison's regiment, was sent with a party of horse and dragoons, towards the bridg of Slane; and whilst his majesty sate on the grass (being about an hour) there came some of the Irish, with long guns, and shot at our dragoons, who went down to the river to drink, and some of ours went down to return the favour, then a party of about forty horse advanced very slowly, and stood upon a plowd field, over against us, for near half an hour, and so retired to their camp ; this small party, as I have heard from their own officers since, brought two field-pieces amongst them, dropping them by an hedg on the plowd land undiscovered; they did not offer to fire them, till his majesty was mounted; and then, he and the rest, riding softly the same way back, their gunner fires a piece, which killed us two horses and a man, about 100 yards above where the king was; but immediately comes a second, which had been almost a fatal one, for it graized upon the bank of the river, and in the rising, slanted upon the king's right shoulder, took out a piece of his coat, and tore the skin and flesh, and afterwards broke the head of a gentleman's pistol."*

William took, it seems, but little notice of the affair, but rode quietly back into the glen, merely observing to those who came to render him assistance,—" There is no necessity: the bullet should have come nearer." The enemy were, however, so far deceived, that they raised a great shout, and an express was immediately sent off to the Continent, and bonfires, it is said, actually lighted in Paris to celebrate the fall of Nassau. James says in his memoirs that he himself ordered the guns to fire on this occasion.

The place where this accident occurred was on the side of a small hillock, by the water's edge, a little below the glen, and from which the stones have been taken to build the obelisk since erected just beside it. The real object of William's near approach to the enemy at this place was not, it seems to us, to reconnoitre their position, which he could have done more

* The torn buff coat William wore on this occasion was given to Colonel Thompson, and is still in the possession of the family at Ravensdale.

effectually from the hill behind him, but for the purpose of observing the tide and noting the proper time for crossing the river next morning.

In one of the editions of the Memoirs of the Duke of Berwick (son of James II.) there is related a curious account of what would appear to be the same story, of which the following is an outline. The day before the action a considerable number of the officers of the Prince of Orange were standing together in a group. As it appeared probable that the Prince of Orange was one of the number, the young Duke of-Berwick exclaimed: " 'Behold a splendid opportunity for putting an end to this war! We must attack that troop and destroy the Prince of Orange.' 'And who will dare to do it?' observed some one. 'I, myself,' said the Duke; and immediately, followed by a band of officers drawn on by his example, he attacked and defeated this very troop where he hoped to find the Prince. He looked about in search of him in defiance of every danger, but the Prince was not there."* This account of a piece of heroism, however, ceases to interest us when we remember the fact that at the time alluded to the Boyne at full tide was rolling between the belligerents! Of such tales, however, is history, and the history of battles in particular, often composed.

Thus ended the 30th of June, and thus stood the hostile armies upon the eve of the engagement. We have written the foregoing description of the battle-field from a careful examination of the scene, and the perusal of the most trustworthy documents within our reach. The exact position of each general's division in either army has not been ascertained with certainty, neither has any correct or veritable military plan of the battle ever appeared. The accompanying map we have had engraved from a plan of the battle, made about sixty years ago, by a Major Brown, for the Right Hon. John Foster, Speaker of the Irish House of Commons.† We present it to

---

* Mémoires du Maréchal de Berwick, Duc et Pair de France, et Generalissime des Armées de Sa Majesté. Tome Premier. A Londres, aux Depens de la Compaigne, 1758, pp. 64, 65.

† A copy of this document was presented by Viscount Ferrard to the Engineers' Library, Dublin, in 1829. It is now in the Ordnance Office. For the use of it we are much indebted to our friend Major Larcom, R. E., one of the Commissioners of the Board of Works.

our readers and the tourists to the Boyne, because it conveys to our mind a much better idea of the scene than either of the two older, ill-constructed plans of Story or Richardson.

Heretofore, the descriptions of the battle of the Boyne have been almost all one-sided, being, for the most part, written by violent partisans, pandering to the vanity of one party and exciting the sensitiveness of the other. The authorities from which the historians drew were nearly all Williamite; but within the last few years the gleaners in this department of Irish history have had access to documents written by officers in the Irish army and others in every way worthy of credit, and which must now induce the calm searcher after truth to very much modify some, and altogether reject other statements put forward by the former, and which have been generally received as facts. To give these latter their fair share of merit, and to weigh and discuss the adverse statements of both parties, would not suit the intention of the present work, and would require a more critical examination of the subject than our space would warrant.*

* We feel it the less necessary to enter into a very critical examination of the history of the battle of the Boyne in this place, because there is a work now on the eve of publication by the Irish Archæological Society,—" *Macariæ Excidium*, or the Destruction of Cyprus," by Colonel O'Kelly, edited by John C. O'Callaghan, Esq., a gentleman of literary acquirements and research, which will, no doubt, throw additional light on the subject. A portion of the *Macariæ Excidium*, edited by T. Crofton Croker, Esq., has been printed by the Camden Society.   In the mean time we may refer our readers to Harris and the various Lives of King William which have appeared : to a continuation of the impartial History of the Wars of Ireland, &c., London, 1793, written by " George Story, chaplain to the regiment formerly Sir Thomas Gour's, now the Earl of Drogheda's," from whom we have already quoted, and who was himself at the battle of the Boyne, and whose statements, until they are contradicted by irreproachable evidence, must, as far as mere matters of fact, be received as historic evidence.   A Captain John Richardson, who was an " eye-witness of the scene," published a plan of the battle, to which is appended a short account of the engagement.   The Memoirs of the Duke of Berwick, the Memoirs of King James II., and Dalrymple's Memoirs, should also be examined, and their statements carefully compared with writers on the other side of the question; and also with a manuscript copy of Count Lauzun's despatches, which exists in the library of Trinity College.   The Earl of Fingal possesses a manuscript account of the battle, written at Versailles, by one of the Plunket family, who followed James into exile.   In 1791 there was printed at Amsterdam a little work styled, "Histoire de la Revolution d'Irlande, arrivé sous Guillaume III.," which contains a description of the battle of the Boyne, some extracts from which we have

We should like, 'tis true, to fight this battle in detail, and record the gallant deeds of the O'Neals and Schombergs,—the Caillimottes and Sarsfields,—of Berwick, Sidney, Ginkle, Geraldine, Hamilton, and others who have left material for many a tribute to their fame. But this, at present, is denied us; perhaps some other day we'll try our hand at this " grievous battle," so bravely fought by a comparatively young, but experienced general,—gallant in the field and wise in council, with a highly disciplined army, a part of which had been trained in many a hard contested battle in France and Flanders, then the great battle-ground of European warfare,—against a weak and vacillating prince, advanced in years, and borne down by misfortunes, neither wise in council nor gallant in action, remaining in the rere of, but not commanding an army, which, however great its devotion, was totally unable to cope with its opponent.

The army of King William amounted, according to the most moderate calculation, to 36,000 men; some authorities make it upwards of 40,000; all well-disciplined soldiers; numbers of them tried veterans, whose prowess had been tested and their courage schooled in many a well-fought field in Europe; hardy warriors, well-appointed, and composed of the greatest number of nations that ever fought for or against the crown of England before or since—Danes, Dutch, Swedes, and Flemings, Swiss, French Huguenots, English, Scotch, Anglo-Irish, and Germans,—led by some of the most esteemed officers of the day, the two Schombergs, Douglas, Sidney, and La Mellionere, and commanded by one of the greatest generals of the age, personally brave, energetic, and well-skilled in war. The Williamite force, being chiefly composed of mercenaries, was less likely to be influenced by any feeling of loyalty towards the deposed sovereign than if it had been entirely English.

To this was opposed an army scarcely three and twenty thou-

given, because it has not as yet appeared in English, at least that we are aware of, while that by Story has been the principal ground-work for all modern writers. We are indebted for the use of this work to our friend Dr. Cane of Kilkenny. In the Royal Hospital there is a large oil painting of the Battle of the Boyne, and the scene is represented on the tapestry still remaining in the House of Lords (in the Bank of Ireland); there also exists an old mezzotinto engraving of the battle, from an original painting by Wyke, in the possession of the Earl of Leicester.

sand strong, a large portion of which, the French excepted, was composed of raw levies; undisciplined, and but ill supplied with arms or money; under generals no doubt brave and skilful, but whose interests were so constantly clashing that it was with great difficulty they could ever be brought to act in unison; and moreover commanded by a Prince whose weakness, imbecility, and bigotry, had already lost him a crown, who was totally unskilled in war, and whose heart was not in the country nor the cause of the men who fought for him. Either in order to secure a retreat, or fearing the issue of the engagement, James sent off all the baggage, and *six of his twelve guns*, to Dublin, the night before the battle, and dispatched a trusty messenger to the south to prepare a vessel for his departure.

In the " Irish Journal," a small quarto of thirteen pages, published in London, July 17, 1690, we find the best account of the condition of Dublin at the time of the engagement, as well as a very succinct and circumstantial recital of the battle of the Boyne. From this rare old tract we gladly present our readers with the following extracts:* " On Saturday, 21st (June), we heard the Irish army retreated, and the English were come towards Droghedah. We knew King James's design was to *avoid a battle* as much as he could, and to have walked the English army along the Boyne river, and so across the country to Limerick; but this day we were told from the camp that the enemy seemed to press towards Dublin, and King James was resolved to defend it, and that therefore they thought he could not be able to keep off a battle above ten days. On Sunday the Irish army came on this side the Boyne, and King James, as it would seem, distrusting the issue, Sir Pat Trant, First Commissioner of the Revenue, and another gentleman, were ordered to go from hence on Monday morning, to Waterford, to prepare ships.

"On Monday, the last of June, the English army, having had very little rest or victuals, drew to the Boyne; Lieutenant-General Douglas's horse were ordered to post themselves at a ford near Droghedah, upon a rising ground over against a bat-

* " A True and Perfect Journal of the Affairs in Ireland since His Majesty's Arrival in that Kingdom. By a Person of Quality. London, printed, and are to be sold by Randal Taylor, near Stationers' Hall, 1690." We are indebted to our friend Joseph T. S. Le Fanu, Esq., for this rare old tract.

tery of the Irish, of six guns, guarded by a party of their horse.
Here the English stood the shot of the enemy, every man on
foot by his horse, several hours, while there passed 200 shots;
the King, in the mean time, having rid between them and the
ford, where he received the hurt on his shoulder by a cannon
shot, which disabled him the next day from holding his sword.
At last, when the King had said, ' Now I see my men will
stand,' some guns were sent to them, upon the first discharge
of which among the Irish horse, they retreated from their
battery, and stood farther off."

There is one point in the battle of the Boyne (which we were
the first to point out, in the earlier edition of this work), on
which sufficient stress has not been laid, although it would appear to have had a greater influence on the issue of the fight than
historians are aware. The right wing of the Irish army was
completely protected by Drogheda, the Boyne, and the sea; its
left towards Slane was unprotected; and if this was once turned
or outflanked, the road to Duleek must be occupied, Dublin
would be cut off, and then the temporary refuge of the fortress of Drogheda afforded the only hope for the Irish army.
This could not escape the notice of a skilful opposing general,
neither was it unforeseen to some of the advisers of King James,
although he himself does not appear to have paid sufficient attention to it. At break of day upon the morning of Tuesday, the
1st of July, which was a remarkably clear, hot day, William despatched 10,000 men under the younger Schomberg, Generals
Douglas, Overkirk, and Lord Portland, to cross the river at the
fords, near Slane, of the existence and passability of which he
appears to have been well informed. Proceeding behind the hill,
now included in the demesne of Townley Hall, and crossing the
Mattock river at Monk-Newtown, they were concealed from the
Irish until they appeared on the elevated banks near Knowth,
above the ford of Rossnaree, where it would appear the cavalry
crossed with scarcely any opposition, except from the regiment
of Sir Neal O'Neale, who himself was killed in the skirmish. The
foot under Portland passed round by the bridge of Slane, two
miles farther off, but joined the English cavalry near a marsh
or bog which stood between them and their opponents, and
before a sufficient force could have been despatched by James
to oppose them. Here then was an army, nearly half the size
of that of King James, advancing upon the left wing of the

latter, and pressing to get between it and Duleek, and so cut off the retreat towards Dublin; and then it was (for William was informed, by express, of Douglas having made good his position) that the passage of the Boyne at Oldbridge was commenced, at half-past ten o'clock, A. M., while this left wing of the Irish army was already engaged two miles off with the division under Douglas and Count Schomberg.

" The Irish Journal," a Williamite authority, makes the amount of the army which passed at Rossnaree much more than what Story states. It says, " General Douglas was sent with 12,000 foot and 5000 horse, to a ford further up the river by Slane, where had been a battery of the Irish, but they were drawn off, and only 800 dragoons guarded the ford. The English were to go down a steep hill to the ford, and an uneven way, yet the Irish dragoons only once fired, and retreated to the body of their army, which lay towards Duleek."

That this manœuvre of William's, which so early decided the fate of the day, was not quite unexpected by the Irish generals, we learn from the fact that Hamilton had in council, on the preceding evening, advised eight regiments to be sent up the river to defend the bridge and passage at Slane; but James in reply, merely offered to despatch fifty dragoons to defend that important position! Soon, however, the error was discovered, when, at an early hour next morning, the advancing host of Douglas was observed crowning the heights of Knowth, and stretching westward towards Slane. Then, when too late, James, in the midst of hurry and confusion, despatched his *entire left wing and some of his centre*, chiefly foot, and the chosen French troops of Louis, under Lauzun, with *all his artillery*,—at most the remaining six field-pieces,—to oppose the army of Douglas, which must by that time have made good its ground, and had also been strengthened by the infantry of Portland. This must have occurred between 9 and 10 o'clock in the morning. The sudden withdrawal of this large body of the best disciplined troops, from the centre and left wing of the Irish, not only materially weakened but confused and disheartened the army at Oldbridge, which had been until that moment drawn up in battle array in two formidable lines to defend the fords of that place. It was at this moment, with the tide at its lowest ebb, and 10,000 picked men outflanking his opponent upon the opposite bank,—a cir-

cumstance of which he was then well aware, that William saw
was the most auspicious to cross the ford at Oldbridge, and
lead on in person his six-and-twenty thousand men against
that portion of the Irish army which remained upon the original battle-field. James himself, as we learn from his own
memoirs, was not at any time of the day at the battle of Oldbridge, and did not, as popular opinion and several histories
would lead us to believe, view the fight, a passive spectator,
from the church of Donore. The army of Douglas extended
its line to the right, to outflank the Irish, and cut off their retreat to Dublin, by getting before them to Duleek, and keeping
them behind the Nanny-Water; which Lauzun observing,
marched his army parallel with them, in order to prevent
such a disaster. "While this was doing," say the Royal Memoirs, "the King went to the right to hasten up the troops
to follow Lauzune, *believing the main body of the enemie's army
was following their right, which had passed at Slane. * * ** The
King took the reserve, consisting of Purcel's hors and Brown's
foot, with which he marched till he came up to the rear of the
foot, that follow'd Lausune, and there ordering Sir Charles
Carny, who commanded the reserve, to post himself at the
right of the first line of those foot, to make a sort of left wing
there, and then rid along the line, where he found Lausune
and the Enemie's right drawn up in battle, within half cannon shot, faceing each other: the King did not think fit to
charge just then, being in expectation of the troops he had
left at Old bridg, but while he was discoursing this matter
with Lausune, an Aid de Camp came to give the King an
account that the enemie had forced the pass at Old bridg, and
that the right wing was beaten; which the King wispering
in Lausun's ear, tould him, there was now nothing to be done
but to charge the enemie forthwith, before his troops knew
what had happen'd on the right, and by that means try if
they could recover the day; and accordingly sent Mons.
Hoguette to the head of the French foot, made all the
Dragoons to light, and placed them in the intervalls between
the hors, and ordered Lausune to lead on: but just as they
were beginning to move, Sarsfield and Maxwell, who had been
to view the ground betwixt the two armys, sayd it was impossible for the hors to charg the enemie, by reason of two
double ditches with high banks, and a little brook betwixt

them, that run along the small valley that divided the two armys, and at the same time the enemie's Dragoons got on hors back, and their whole line began to march by their flank to their right, and we soon lost sight of their van by a village that interposed; only by the dust that ris behind it, they seem'd to *endeavour to gaine Dublin road;* upon which the King (since he could not attack them) thought fit to march also by his left towards Dublin road too, to pass a small brook at Dulick, which was impracticable higher up by reason of a bog. The King was no sooner on his march, but the right wing's being beaten was no longer a mistery, for severall of the scattered and wounded horsemen got in amongst them before they rought Dulick."*

We have quoted this passage at length, because we believe it is the true history of the turning point of the battle. The retreat had already commenced; the best disciplined portion of the Irish were with the King himself, and also some of his most experienced officers, miles away from the field of Old-bridge, and hotly pursued by young Schomberg, thirsting to revenge his father's death, of which he was then aware. Even the repulse of the centre and left of the English army, at the ford at Oldbridge, would not then have saved the day.

Besides the authorities already quoted or referred to at page 249, we have become acquainted with a most interesting historic document, from which we have made the following extracts. It is a copy of the Journal of Colonel Bellingham of Gernonstown, now Castle Bellingham, " kept during the years 1688, 1689, 1690, including the whole of King William's campaigns in Ireland during the last year, when Colonel Bellingham attended the King and acted as a guide to the Army till after the battle of the Boyne."†

" The 30th, very hott, I called at Mr. Townley's in our march towards Boyne. I was for some time with the King on the hill of Tullahescar, from whence he view'd Drogheda, and

---

* Memoirs in Clarke's Life of King James II., vol. ii. p. 395, *et seq.*

† I am indebted to Edward Hardman, Esq., Secretary to the Royal Dublin Society, for the manuscript copy of these extracts, which have been carefully compared with the original in the possession of Sir Alan E. Bellingham. Some portions of this Diary have been published by Mr. D'Alton in his History of Drogheda, and also by the Rev. Mr. Graham. Why has not all this Journal been published ?

then went towards Oldbridge. On the south side of Boyne lay the enemy's camp, which the King going to view, he was hitt by a cannon ball on the shoulder, which putt us into the greatest consternation imaginable, but, blessed be God, it proved but a slight hurte; he went round his own camp and was received with the greatest joy and acclamations imaginable. The cannon fir'd att caste all the afternoon. We drew a great body of our horse up on the hills in sight of the enemy. We fir'd several bombs which did execution, and our cannon dismounted 2 of the enemy's batterye's.

"July the 1st, 1690, a joyfull day, excessive hott; about 6 this morning the King got on horseback and gave the necessary orders. Kirke ordered me to bring him some account from the enemy. I brought him a youth, one Fyans, who came that morning from Drogheda.* I carry'd him to the King, who was then standing att the battery, seeing his cannon play att the house of Oldbridge. He had sent early a strong detachment *of about* 15,000 men with Douglas towards Slane, who pass'd the river without any opposition, and putt the enemy to route who were on that wing."

We have already remarked upon the admirable position of the English army, protected by the immense battery immediately opposite the ford, and screened by the natural lie of the ground. The tide being out, the passage of the river was attempted in four different places. The Blue Dutch guards, the Irish Enniskilleners, and the French Huguenots, led by Caillimotte and the gallant old Schomberg, passed quickly out of the little glen opposite the principal ford, with drums beating, and dashing into the water both there and over the upper end of Grove Island, a little lower down, formed upon the opposite side, and carried the village and rude outworks at Oldbridge; not, however, without considerable opposition, some of the Irish soldiers rushing into the water to meet them. It was here the brave old Schomberg was killed,† and

---

* Sir Alan E. Bellingham writes to us : "The late Sir William Bellingham told me he was at a nobleman's house (I think the Duke of Portland's) who had a picture of the battle of the Boyne, in which an officer appears bringing up a young man to the King. The owner of the picture did not then know the object. The journal of Col. Bellingham explains it. The family of Fyans were at Dunleer within a few years back."

† Schomberg's body was immediately carried back, across the river, to the

also Dr. Walker, the gallant defender of Derry, and Caillimotte received his death wound.* The third crossing was made by the Danes and Germans, at a shallow between the two principal islands, where the water must have been up to their arm-pits, while the left wing, entirely composed of cavalry, consisting chiefly of Danes and Dutch, passed or swam across opposite the eastern valley which intersects the hill of Tullyallen, and effected a landing, apparently with little opposition, at a very deep and dangerous part of the river, nearly opposite the spot where one of the Irish batteries stood the day before, and where the margin of the stream is wet and swampy. Here it was, however, that, accompanied by the Prince of Denmark, William himself, with his arm in a sling from the effects of his wound, plunged into the stream, with Colonel Woolstey, and passed with great difficulty, " for his horse was bogg'd on the other side, and he was forced to alight, till a gentleman help'd him to get his horse out." Colonel Bellingham's Journal thus continues: " He sent another detachment of horse to the left to goe over at the Mill-foord, but the tide coming in and the foord bad, the passage was very difficult, most of them being forced to swim, insomuch that they could not come upp time enough to assist our foot who went over the foord att Oldbridge about 11 of the clock. The enemy had laid an ambush behind the ditches and houses on the other side of the water, who fir'd incessantly att our men as they were passing the river; who, as soon as arriv'd on land, immediately putt

English camp. His skull is still shown in the cathedral of St. Patrick's, where Dean Swift caused a monument to be erected to him. The family vault of the Schombergs is in the cathedral of Mayence. His sword is now the charter sword of the "Friendly Brothers."

Schomberg, it is said, was the person who advised the attack on the left wing of the Irish army. William having, in a council of war held at nine o'clock the evening before the battle, declared his intention of crossing the river next morning, "this was at first opposed by Duke Schomberg, as too dangerous an attempt; but finding His Majesty persist therein, he advised that part of the army should be sent *that night*, about twelve, to Stone Bridge (Slane) in order to pass the river thereabouts, and to get between the enemy and the pass at Duleek; but this advice was not followed, which would probably have ended the war in one campaign. It was opposed by the Dutch generals, which made the Duke retire to his tent." See the Life of William III., late King of England and Prince of Orange, &c. Illustrated with divers cuts, medals, &c. 2nd Ed. London, 1703. p. 270.

* Caillimotte is buried near the gate of Mr. Coddington's demesne.

s

those musqueteers to the route, and advanc'd farther into the field in battalia. Here the brave old Duke Shomberg was kill'd, and Dr. Walker and Coll. Callemott mortally wounded. The enemy advanc'd towards us and made a brisk effort upon us, but we soon repell'd them with considerable loss on theyr side. They made two other attempts on us, but were still bravely beaten back; and when our horse of the left came upp the enemy quite quitted that field, having left several dead bodyes behind them. 'Twas there we tooke Lieut.-General Hamilton. The enemye's horse of Tireconnell's regiment behav'd themselves well; *but our Dutch like angells.* The K. charged in person at the head of the Inniskilleners, and expos'd himself with undaunted bravery."

The royal memoirs thus confirm the view which we have taken of the admirable generalship of William in causing a diversion of the centre and left of the Irish army before he attempted to cross the Boyne. " As for what pass'd at Oldbridge it seems the enemie, perceiving the left wing and most of the foot had marched after Lauzune, attacked the regiment which was at the village of Oldbridge."

Thus, then, there were at least six and twenty thousand men, with a large battery, arrayed against fifteen or sixteen thousand, for we must subtract those already engaged, under Lauzun, Sarsfield, and James himself, towards Slane, fully three miles off, and *the Irish had not* (it would appear) *a single cannon at Oldbridge that day.** The right wing of the Irish army, chiefly composed of cavalry, was commanded by the Duke of Berwick, and the centre by Tyrconnel and Hamilton. Notwithstanding the very great disparity of numbers, their want of discipline,—the newly raised levies of Irish foot being nearly all at Oldbridge and immediately opposite the principal ford,— and their being unsupported by artillery, this portion of James's army behaved with great firmness, and parts of it with signal gallantry, some of the Irish rushing into the water to meet the Dutch, and others, the Royal Guards for instance, dashing through them as they were forming on the

---

* William had, it is said, a portion of his boot carried away by a cannonball during the action, but at what place or at what time is not specified. If the Irish had a park of artillery at Oldbridge, what became of it? They could not have taken it with them in the rout. If the English captured any guns, surely it would have been mentioned by some author.

Meath bank of the river, and being nearly all cut to pieces in their endeavour to return. Sir John Hanmer's brigade "were so valliantly attacked in front by Hamilton's horse that they were forced to retreat, and some of them to cross the river again."* As the Irish fell back, retreating up the hill towards Donore, they suddenly halted, and so furiously turned upon their opponents that the vaunted courage of the Enniskilleners quailed before them, although at the moment William himself led on that body, and His Majesty, being left upwards of a hundred yards in advance of his men, was thus exposed to most imminent danger. In the subsequent charge some of Schomberg's horse took those two standards of the Irish which are still preserved among the trophies in the chapel of the Royal Hospital of Kilmainham.† At another part of the field, in the lane or small bridle road (which still exists) to the left of the ford, Ginkle met with a serious repulse, "being over-powered there and also forced to retreat," till aided by the troops of Colonel Levison and Sir Albert Cunningham, who lined the hedge bordering the lane, and also possessed themselves of a farm-house adjoining, when a fierce conflict for some time took place, Ginkle, it is said, continuing "in the rear of his men, *endeavouring to make them keep their ground*."

The last rally made by the Irish on the slopes near the summit of Donore was under Hamilton, who being wounded in the head and taken prisoner immediately after, the action may be said to have ceased, and the retreat from Oldbridge then began. Upon being led up to King William, in whose very presence he was captured, and who regarded him as a renegade, and being asked whether he thought the Irish would fight any more, he pledged his honour that they would, where-

---

* Life of King William III. already cited, p. 270.

† Among the memorabilia of the Boyne may be mentioned, besides those already specified, King William's sword, which is at Townley Hall; his saddle and bridle are in the possession of Mr. Baker. His horse was brought to Connaught, and died at Mr. Mulloy's of Hewstown, near Carrick-on-Shannon. It was given to a Captain Mulloy, in return for one with which he supplied the King when his own was shot under him, at the time his pistol was broken and a portion of his boot carried away. The O'Mulloys were hereditary standard-bearers to the English Kings in Ireland. The kettle drums of one of the Irish regiments are in the Town Hall of Drogheda. The heart of James II. was embalmed, and is now in a shrine in a small chapel on one side of the Champs Elysees in Paris.

upon William turned upon him, and sarcastically repeated more than once, "*your* honour."

The natural consequences followed: the Irish centre and right wing fell back upon Donore, and finally, towards the close of the day, rapidly retreated to Duleek, towards which place the left wing, already beaten above Rossnaree, had previously retired.

It was now long past mid-day, the fierce conflict at Oldbridge, generally styled the "Battle of the Boyne," had raged for several hours, the sun waned in his path, and the victory already attained, almost without a blow, by the army of Douglas, was crowned by the retreat of the entire Irish force under the Duke of Berwick and Lord Tyrconnel. From Donore Hill to Duleek, a distance of about three miles, where the first natural obstacle presents in the deep sedgy stream of the Nanny Water, a succession of hills slope from the high grounds above the right or southern bank of the Boyne in a somewhat triangular form. The base of this triangle is the Boyne, between Oldbridge and Rossnaree, from which latter the retreat under James and Lauzun first commenced, and its apex, the little bridge which spans the Nanny at the village of Duleek. The sides of this triangle mark the two lines of the retreat. The high road from Duleek to Donore by the hill of Cruzrath (from which latter a good view of the whole scene may be obtained) marks pretty accurately the eastern line of the retreat. The left wing of the Irish, having succeeded in reaching the pass of Duleek "untouched," and bringing with them five of their six guns, long before the English right had come up, here stood, first upon the common which surrounds the village upon the north, where some stand was made, and then, falling back behind the river, they defended the bridge for several hours, until the centre and left wing, which had been beaten at Donore, rushed down upon them in confusion, hotly pursued by their opponents. While the pass of Duleek was retained by the Irish and French, King James, accompanied by a troop of horse, fled to Dublin, which he reached about ten o'clock, so that he must have left his army about five or six o'clock in the afternoon, probably when the retreating, or rather the flying army from Donore appeared in sight. Then, for the first time on that memorable day, the *entire* of the two armies stood opposed, but how different their situations may be gleamed from the foregoing details. Some skirmishing occurred at Duleek, but the bridge was soon gained, and William in person pressed on the victorious army in the pursuit, towards the Naul, a deep defile, at another small brook about six miles farther on. Here, night coming on, the pursuit was abandoned, and the English returned to Duleek, where they lay under arms during the night. The diary already quoted thus describes the circumstance. The King "pursued almost as far as the Naul, and left them not till near 10 o'clock at night. I was his guide back to Duleek. We killed about 2000 of theyr men, besides Lords Carlingford, Dangan, and several other officers of ranke killed and taken prisoners. We lost not above 200 in the whole action, many of which were killed by our own men through mistake. I returned to the camp at Oldbridge, having left the King in his coach at Duleek, where he stayed that night. I was almost faint from want of drink and meat."

All the Williamite authorities worthy of credit bear testimony to the "orderly" and "well-managed retreat" made chiefly by the Irish horse and French foot.*

The "Irish Journal" thus describes the state of Dublin upon the day of the battle. "Now as to us in this place, we were waken'd very early this Tuesday morning by an alarm, and the news that there would be a battel. The gates were kept strictly guarded, and the Protestants kept their houses. The issue we expected with the greatest apprehensions. Several reports were spread abroad every hour; one while that the French fleet was in our bay; another, that a French express was come from Waterford, with the news of taking the Isle of Wight by the French, and of their being gone to Dover; then that the English right wing was quite routed; then, that the Prince of Orange was taken prisoner; but at five that afternoon, some that had made their escape on tired horses told us the Irish were much worsted; and others at six, that they were totally defeated; from hence, till one that night, all the entries of the town were filled with dusty, wounded, and tired soldiers, and carriages perpetually coming in. We

---

* The "Boyne Water" has been a fruitful theme to the novelist, poet, and dramatist. Banim, author of "Tales of the O'Hara Family," has given a description of the battle; but by far the most graphic and unprejudiced is that related in Miss Boyle's novel of "The Forester;" London, Newman, 1842.

see several of King James's horse guards coming in straggling, without pistols or swords, and could not tell what was become of himself. Near 10 that night he came in with about 200 horse all in disorder. We concluded now that it was a total rout, and that the enemy were just ready to come into town, but were greatly surprized when an hour or two after we heard the whole body of the Irish horse come in in very good order, with kettle-drums, hautboys, and trumpets, and early next morning the French and a great party of the Irish foot." James departed for Waterford early the next morning, and none of the English army appeared until eight o'clock at night upon Thursday, the second day after the engagement, when an officer and one troop of dragoons arrived to take charge of the stores; the town having been previously evacuated of all the Irish force. King William arrived and encamped at Finglas, outside the city, upon Friday, the 4th.

With all their faults, the Stuarts elicited more loyalty than the world will ever witness again. We will not say that James II. was a coward,—he had previously shown his bravery upon sea,—but certainly he was no general. His defeat here was, however, inevitable. The King was then the palladium of his party, and his person was therefore of great consequence to his adherents, who may have forced him off the field. Under the circumstances he should not have delayed nor fought at the Boyne, where he had got into a most unlucky position, the apex of a triangle, one side of which was formed by the sea; and when William hemmed him round, defeating him at every point, not only by the superior discipline of his troops, which, after all, is courage, but by force of numbers and generalship, then retreat—flight, was the inevitable, the last resource. Looking back at this distance of time, it would appear to have been safer for James to have retreated with his small army, according to his original plan, and have garrisoned the principal fortified towns, and by laying waste the country, and destroying, as was intended, the English fleet in the Channel, thus cut off William's supplies; while a guerilla warfare would have greatly harassed and considerably diminished his forces. James cared nothing for Ireland nor the Irish, except so far as they could be made use of to restore to him his lost crown; he also hoped that a counter-revolution would have been got up in his favour in England, and that the King of France would have lent him further assistance. This, however, is not the place to discuss these subjects at greater length.

The numbers killed at the battle of the Boyne were not considerable, when we take into account the amount of the belligerents, and that the engagement and retreat lasted nearly twelve hours. On the Irish side it is stated to have been upwards of a thousand, and upon the English above four hundred. The orange and green have long been party words in Ireland; —are our readers aware of the fact, that while the Irish troops wore pieces of white paper in their caps, the livery of France, every English soldier was decorated with a branch of *green?* The English watchword was " Westminster."

Thus ended the battle of the 1st of July, 1690, the cause of so much subsequent party feud and so many heart-burnings in this country. To the one party it gave victory; liberty, civil and religious ; broad lands, power, and dominant sway : while the other suffered not only present defeat, but subsequent confiscation, penal laws, exile, death. Since then the fierce advocate of one party has cursed, " bell, book, and candlelight," the Williamite and the Orangeman; and the defender of the other has, upon bare, bended knees, pronounced a malediction (which, for sentiment and strength of language, is unsurpassed in the cursings of ancient or modern times) upon all who would not drink the " Battle of the Boyne," and the pious memory of the man who first robbed Ireland of her manufactures, and signed the warrant for the massacre of Glencoe !   Times, however, are changing, let us hope for the better; mutual asperities are softening down; prejudices of birth, of religion, so-called, of education and position, are happily being removed; men can now calmly discuss those subjects without passion or without offence. The memory of " The Boyne Water" must be dear to every Irish Protestant—every lover of Protestant liberty; let him drink it, if so minded; but ought he couple with it the idol of College-green ?

Had the Scotch Royalists and Lowlanders been allowed to celebrate the anniversary of the victory of Culloden, in processions, with flags flying, drums beating, fifes playing, " in the teeth" of the Highlanders, whose forefathers bled for Charles Edward, Scotland would not be the happy, prosperous country it is to-day.

As the little work already alluded to in the note at
p. 248, "Histoire de la Revolution d'Irlande, arrivée sous
Guillaume III.," is not generally known, we extract the following notice of some facts connected with the Battle of the
Boyne from it. It is evidently written in support of the Williamite side of the question, but it seems tolerably correct.

King William, it says, advanced at break of day towards
Drogheda and the River Boyne, along which King James's
army was encamped, in order to prevent the English crossing
the river. The infantry and artillery did not arrive until
very late, so that nothing could be done by King William
that day, except to reconnoitre the enemy's position, and to try
and find out the fords by which a passage could be effected,
for haste was now very necessary. This work then gives an
account of the wounding of King William the day before the
battle by a six-pound shot, but it adds little to the account of
that transaction already related: "As soon as the king's wound
was dressed, he again took horse, and acted for four hours more
before retiring to his tent, and resolved to cross the river with
his army the next day. On the evening of the same day on
which His Majesty was wounded, he ordered Count Menard de
Schomberg, with the cavalry of the right wing, two regiments
of dragoons of the left wing, the infantry brigade of Trelaw-
ney, and five small field-pieces, to go next morning to a ford
known to be about three miles higher up than the camp, to
try and pass it, and to take the enemy in flank, or compel them
to retire. The Count Schomberg having passed the night in
giving orders and disposing of the army for the passage, advanced early in the morning to this ford, and found on the
other side of it eight squadrons of the enemy drawn up to oppose his passage. He entered the river with his troops and
crossed to the other side, and attacking the enemy roughly,
routed them and disposed his troops in battle array, intending
to march against the enemy at the first order of the King, who
was immediately informed of his position, in order that he
should in other places attack the army of King James, lest all
the enemy should fall on him (Schomberg). The King then
sent word to the Count that he was going to cross over to the
other side with the rest of his army."

The account of the passage at Oldbridge is nearly the same
as that given by Story. Regarding the death of Duke Schom-

berg, he writes: " This brave general had crossed one of the first, being only preceded by the regiment of La Mellonniere, which had roughly repulsed the enemy. The Duke had crossed over to a village very near the river in order to pursue them. Unfortunately Tyrconnel's guards, taken by a desperate fury, charged this regiment with such impetuosity that they brake through it, and tried to prevent the crossing of those who were still in the water, but the greater part of them having been cut down, and the few remaining being unable to execute their purpose, they turned towards the village, where having met General Schomberg, they gave him two sabre cuts in the head, and, as many reported, a pistol shot. Nevertheless it is certain, as it is known to all those who belong to La Mellonniere's regiment, that when it was evident that Tyrconnel's guards were running towards that village, the officers commanded the fire to be directed that way, and that on all sides the words were heard, 'kill, kill'" [*tue, tue.*] So that it is probable some shots might have been unwittingly directed towards the Duke of Schomberg, who was killed by a ball which penetrated his throat, and he died soon after without being able to utter a word.

In years gone by, the Corporation of Drogheda paid an anniversary visit to the obelisk* erected to commemorate the first of

---

* The obelisk, of which we have given an engraving at page 241, bears the following inscriptions on the base :

" Sacred to the glorious memory of King William the Third, who, on the 1st of July, 1690, crossed the Boyne near this place to attack James the Second at the head of a Popish army advantageously posted on the south side of it, and did on that day, by a successful battle, secure to us and our posterity our liberty, laws, and religion. In consequence of this action James the Second left this kingdom and fled to France. This memorial of our deliverance was erected in the ninth year of the reign of King George the Second, the first stone being laid by Lionel Sackville, Duke of Dorset, Lord Lieutenant of the kingdom of Ireland, MDCCXXXVI.

" In perpetuam rei tam fortiter quam feliciter gestæ memoriam,
Hic publicæ gratitudinis Monumenti
Fundamen manibus ipse suis
Posuit Lionelus Dux Dorsetiæ xvii^mo die Aprilis, MDCCXXVI.

"JULY THE FIRST, MDCLXXX.

" This monument was erected by the grateful contributions of several Protestants of Great Britain and Ireland.

" Reinard, Duke of Schomberg, in passing this river, died bravely fighting in defence of liberty."

July, when they used to drink "the glorious, pious, and immortal memory" in the waters of the Boyne, and sing—

> "July the first, in Oldbridge town,
> There was a grievous battle,
> Where many a man lay on the ground,
> And the cannons they did rattle."

No—we'll not finish here, but present our readers with the following graphic ballad, which has been forwarded to us by some unknown correspondent, to whom we here offer our best thanks. As it is, on the whole, for a Williamite ballad, honest, spirited, and historically true, we insert it instead of the old party song.

THE BOYNE WATER.

THE OLD BALLAD RETOUCHED.

'Twas bright July's first morning clear,
　Of unforgotten glory,
That made this stream, through ages dear,
　Renown'd in song and story.
Yet, not her charms on history's page—
　For Nature's own I sought her;
And took my pleasant pilgrimage,
　To see the sweet Boyne water.

Here, musing on these peaceful banks,
　The mind looks back in wonder;
And visions rise of hostile ranks,
　Impatient, kept asunder:
From every land a warrior band—
　For Europe owns the quarrel—
His hand shall clench no barren branch,
　That snatches this day's laurel.

All-conquering William—great Nassau!
　Her crown a realm decreed him;
And here he vindicates her law,
　And champions here her freedom.
And ne'er let valour lose its meed—
　A foe right nobly banded,
Though changeless love for king and creed
　With treason's stain be branded.

Ah, wherefore cannot kings be great,
　And rule with man approving?
Or why should creeds enkindle hate,
　And all their precepts, loving?

Most of the little children in the cabins situate in the vicinity of the obelisk can repeat this inscription! The death of Schomberg took place immediately opposite the monument, on the other side of the river.

Here, on a cast, land, life, and fame,
    Faith, freedom,—all abide it :
A glorious stake !—play out the game,
    Let war's red die decide it !

Now strike the tents—the rolling drums,
    Their loud defiance beating,
Right for the ford brave Schomberg comes,
    And Sarsfield gives him greeting.
Grenade and musket—hut and hedge
    In flame unintermitting ;
I' the very sedge, by the water's edge,
    The angry fuse is spitting.

The banks are steep, the stream is deep,
    The cannon deadly knelling ;
On man and horse, o'er many a corse,
    Th' impeded tide is swelling ;
Yet firm, as 'twere some pageant brave,
    To their trumpets' notes advancing ;
And plumes and pennons proudly wave,
    And their eager swords are glancing.

With arms held high, and powder dry,
    Fast on the bank they're forming :—
Shame on those Kerne ! the steeps they fly,
    Should baffle England's storming.
But stand together—firmly stand !
    Down the defile, and crushing
Like loosen'd rocks, to the crowded strand,
    Come headlong squadrons rushing.

Gallantly done, bold Hamilton !
    The scared Dane flies before him ;
What can the Huguenot's pikeless gun
    'Gainst the sabres flashing o'er him ?
Their leader down—down in his blood—
    And William at a distance
Unhors'd, but toiling through the flood
    To back their brave resistance.

And back they go, the unsated foe,
    Still threatening, though retreating.
Away ! the Walloon broadsword's blow
    Will never need repeating.
And away together, hilt to hilt,
    Through the frighted hamlet going ;
The lavish blood, like water spilt,
    In its narrow street-way flowing.

The heights are carried : far and wide
    Are battle-lines extended ;
Morass and mound—on every side,
    And at every point defended ;
A moment well might William halt,
    In front a force so shielded ;
But prompt th' impetuous assault,
    And post on post is yielded.

But still the rattle and the roar,
    And flight, and hot pursuing ;
And Berwick rallies on Donore,
    The conflict fierce renewing.
No toil too great that wins renown :
    The fight seems still beginning ;
Proud valour's meed is fortune's crown,
    And that crown is William's winning.

But where is James ?   What ? urged to fly
    Ere quailed his brave defenders !
Their dead in Oldbridge crowded lie,
    But not a sword surrenders :
Again they've found the 'vantage ground ;
    Their zeal is still untiring ;
As slowly William hems them round
    In narrowing ring still firing.

O'Neill's upon the English front
    With whirlwind fury wheeling ;
And, flank or front, where'er the brunt,
    Their stoutest columns reeling :
Up, Brandenburg ! the bravest yield,
    The hoof they're trodden under :
On, Inniskillings ! and the field
    Shakes to their tramp of thunder !

And through and through the stubborn spears
    Such awful gaps they're cleaving—
Though Hamilton, still charging, cheers,
    The field's beyond retrieving.
Oh, Hamilton ! a hero now
    O'er prostrate foemen riding :
A moment more, and where art thou ?
    A foe thy rein is guiding.

Thy routed comrades crowd the pass :
    The weak impede the stronger ;
And terror strikes the yielding mass,
    And the brave are bold no longer.

Tis done : that beacon of the fight—
    That hope—the crown redeeming!
In heaven's sight, in victory's light,
    The English Banner's gleaming!

Now, Drogheda, undo thy gate—
    Saint Mary's bells are ringing;
The Mill-Mount captives, snatch'd from fate,
    Their grateful hymns are singing:
From dale and down, from field and fell,
    The sulphurous clouds are clearing;
The Boyne, with full but gentle swell,
    In beauty re-appearing.

But search the field, what friends are lost
    May claim our brief lamenting:
No victory wanting victory's cost
    Its scenic show presenting.
Schomberg, the silver-hair'd, is down—
    Caillemotte no trump awaketh—
And Walker, with his mural crown,
    His last, deep slumber taketh!

Well—honour'd be the graves that close
    O'er every bold and true heart!
And sorrows sanctified repose
    Thy dust, discrownèd Stuart!
O'er scenes like these our hearts may ache,
    When calmly we review them—
Yet each awake its part to take,
    If time should e'er renew them.

Here from my hand as from a cup
    I pour this pure libation;
And ere I drink, I offer up
    One fervent aspiration—
Let man with man—let kin with kin
    Contend through fields of slaughter—
Whoever fights, may FREEDOM win!
    As then at the Boyne water.*

---

* Next to the "Protestant Boys" and "Croppies lie Down," the most
popular tune amongst the Orange party has been "The Boyne Water;" but,
although descriptive of an historical event, which until very lately the Jaco-
bite party could scarcely bear to speak of, it seldom gave as much offence as
either of the former. The air is one of the most spirit-stirring in our Irish
music, and the ballad itself graphic, and for the most part historically correct.
We now allude to that commencing "July the First, in Oldbridge town," to
which we have already referred at page 266, and which we believe to be the
original ballad. Mr. Duffy, in his "Ballad Poetry of Ireland," has published

Having followed the victorious and retreating armies thus far, let us take a glance at this very ancient and memorable locality. Duleek is a long straggling village, four miles distant

this song, but asserts—upon what authority we know not—" that it is not the original written a century and a half ago," although " its plainness, vigour, and minute details argue it to be of an early date."

Some of the verses are so characteristic of the occurrences described in the foregoing text that we here insert them, referring our readers to the work already specified for the ballad in full.   The fourth verse begins :

> When we began the Boyne to cross,
>   The enemy they descended ;
> But few of our brave men were lost,
>   So stoutly we defended.
> The horse was first that marched o'er,
>   The foot soon followed after,
> But brave Duke Schomberg was no more
>   By venturing over the water.

Alluding to his hasty passage over the Boyne without his defensive armour upon seeing some of the French Huguenots give way when Caillimotte was cut down.   The following verse is more frequently in the mouths of the Ulster Yeomen perhaps than any other, and that which follows it gives us some idea of the damage done by the immense artillery of the English army upon the Irish, who had not a single gun at Oldbridge.

> When valiant Schomberg he was slain,
>   King William he accosted,
> His warlike men, for to march on,
>   And he would be the foremost.
> " Brave boys," he said, " be not dismayed
>   For the loss of one commander,
> For God will be our king this day,
>   And I'll be general under."

> Then stoutly we the Boyne did cross,
>   To give the enemy battle,
> *Our cannon, to our foes' great cost,*
>   Like thunder-claps did rattle.
> In majestic mien our Prince rode o'er,
>   His men soon followed after ;
> With blows and shouts put our foes to the rout,
>   The day we crossed the water.

The eighth verse rather strengthens an opinion put forward in Lord Fingal's manuscript, which we mentioned at page 249, giving an account of the engagement, in which it is endeavoured to be shown that King James's head-quarters were at Duleek, and that Oldbridge and Donore were but outposts.   The allusion to the French may have arisen from the fact of their having kept the

from Drogheda, and three from Donore. It is situated upon
the pretty stream of the Nanny Water, which is here deep and
sedgy, and crossed by a narrow bridge erected in 1587, by

pass so long during the retreat. The fields they set on fire must have been in
the neighbourhood of the Naul. It was probably a *ruse* to make it appear
that they were still ready for action, while we know that they were on their
way to Dublin.

> The cunning French near to Duleek
> Had taken up their quarters,
> And fenced themselves on every side,
> Still waiting for new orders.
> But in the dead time of the night
> They set the fields on fire,
> And long before the morning light,
> To Dublin they did retire.

Mr. M'Skinnan, the historian of Carrickfergus, supplied Mr. Duffy with
some fragments of " the old Boyne Water," which the latter has published in the
appendix to his " Ballad Poetry," acknowledging at the same time that the
poem was defective. About a year ago Mr. David Herbison of Dunclug, near Bal-
lymena, kindly furnished us with the following version, which he says " I have
collected from different parties within the last few years ; from among the *old
women* of the county of Antrim, and I think it will be the most complete copy
ever offered for publication." It contains the missing verses in Mr. M'Skinnan's version and several others. The length of the lines and the metre is
much the same as that in the so-called modern song.

> July the first, of a morning clear,
> One thousand six hundred and ninety,
> King William did his men prepare,—
> Of thousands he had thirty,—
> To fight King James and all his host,
> Encamped near the Boyne Water,
> He little feared, though two to one,
> Their multitudes to scatter.
>
> King William called his officers, saying,
> " Gentlemen, now mind your station,
> And let your valour here be shown
> Before this Irish nation.
> My brazen walls let no man break,
> And your subtle foes you'll scatter,
> See that you show good English play,
> When you go down to battle."
>
> His officers they bowed full low,
> In token of submission ;
> They said, " My liege, be not afraid,
> We'll follow your direction."

William Bathe and Genet Dowdall, as stated by an inscription
on a tablet inserted into the battlement, so that it is the very
bridge on which the cannon of James were placed at the time

He wheeled his horse, the hautboys played,
    Their drums did beat and rattle,
Lillibolero was the tune,
    That they played going down to battle.

Both horse and foot they marched on,
    Intending them to batter,
But the brave Duke Schomberg he was shot,
    As he crossed over the water.
When that King William he observed
    The brave Duke Schomberg falling,
He reined his horse with a heavy heart,
    On the Enniskilleners calling.

" What will you do for me, brave boys,
    See yonder men retreating,
Our enemies encouraged are,
    And English drums are beating."
He says, " My boys, feel no dismay,
    At the losing of one commander,
For God shall be our King this day,
    And I'll be general under."

The Enniskillen men did not know
    It was the King spoke to them,
But when informed of their mistake,
    They bowed full low unto him.
" We'll go before, stay you behind,
    And do not cross the water ;
Bold Briton's lamps will clearly shine,
    And our enemies we'll scatter."

King William he did first advance,
    Where bullets loud did rattle ;
The Enniskillen men bore noble hands,
    And soon renewed the battle.
So lion-like they made them roar,
    Like chaff they did them scatter.
King William pressed his way through blood,
    That day at the Boyne water.

We formed our bodies at the ford,
    And down the brae did swatter,
While each man grasped his fellow close,
    In the marching o'er the water.

of the battle, and the prolonged defence of which so materially
assisted the safe retreat of the Irish army, and the escape of
the last of the Stuarts. Insignificant as this place now ap-

> But oh! my stars, had you been there,
>   When we their trench came under,
> Sulphur and brimstone dark'd the air,
>   And the elements did thunder.

> Within four yards of our fore front,
>   Before a shot was fired,
> A sudden snuff they got that day,
>   Which little they desired;
> For horse and man fell to the ground,
>   And some hung in their saddles;
> Others turned up their forked ends,
>   Which we call coup de ladles.

> Prince Eugene's regiment was the first
>   In our fore front advanced;
> Great and gay, and in rich array,
>   Like princes' sons they pranced.
> In a whole body they came down,
>   Their captain was the contriver,
> With whip and spur, most Jehu-like,
>   As the devil had been their driver.

> Lord Cairmoile within a crack,
>   On our right wing advanced,
> Into a field of standing wheat,
>   Where Irish horses pranced.
> But the brandy which ran in their heads
>   Their senses all did scatter;
> They little thought to leave their bones
>   That day at the Boyne water.

> Both men and horse lay on the ground,
>   And many there lay bleeding;
> I saw no sickles there that day,
>   But sure there was sharp shearing.
> "Achree, achree," cried Gorman Roe,
>   "Come help, dear Lady Mary,
> Or by my faith we're a dead men
>   If we do longer tarry."

> I never saw nor never knew
>   Men that for blood so gaped;
> I'm sure there were not three in ten
>   Of them that day escaped.

T

pears, it bears a name of note, and one frequently mentioned
in the early annals of Ireland; and its history is intimately interwoven with some of the most remarkable events connected
with the introduction of Christianity, and of several circumstances highly characteristic of the state of the country during
the last six or seven hundred years.

Historic authorities assert that St. Patrick erected a church
here, and placed over it St. Kienan, whom he had baptized in
the year 450, and whom, moreover, he adopted as his son,
and as a further mark of his love, had bequeathed to him his
own copy of the Gospels. Kienan was high-born, having been
descended from the kings of Munster; and it is related that
when quite a youth he was one of the fifty hostages whom the
princes of Ireland gave to the tyrannical monarch, Loeghaire,
a personage already alluded to at page 153, &c. He was educated
at the monastery of St. Martin, at Tours, and on his return it
was that the learned Ware, in his History of the Irish Bishops,
when quoting from "the Office of St. Kienan, which is extant in
manuscript in the public library at Cambridge," says that he
"built a *church of stone* in this place, and that from thence it
took the name of Damléagh," from *Daimh*, in the old Gaelic,
a house, and *leag*, a stone; hence the term *Duleek*, " for before

> The Irish they ran first away,
>   The French they soon did follow,
> And he that farthest was away,
>   He was the happiest fellow.
>
> They threw away both fife and drum,
>   And firelock from their shoulder;
> The English they pursued them fast,
>   To smell the Irish powder.
> For aye the faster they did shoot,
>   The quicker they did scatter;
> And now the ford is a made clear,
>   You may pass over the water.
>
> Through France and Spain they did combine,
>   With Pope and Father Peter;
> They thought to steep a rod in brine
>   Wherewith to whip Great Britain.
> But Providence to us was kind,
>   Sent William to cross the water,
> Who broke their rod and black design,
>   And our enemies did scatter.

this time the churches of Ireland were built of wattles and boards." Thus it would appear that the original church here was the first stone ecclesiastical edifice ever erected in Ireland, being many years antecedent to the buildings at Armagh; and, by the early Irish annalists, the term *Daimliag* is used for " church" as well as *Tempull*. But although Kienan is said to have been, and probably was the first stone-church builder in Ireland, we read in an old poem, written by a monk of Monasterboice, usually called " Flann of the Monastery," in the eleventh century, that among the servants or attendants of St. Patrick there were three masons, whose names are specified, and who " *made daimliags first in Erin*."* A daimliag would evidently appear to mean not only a stone building, for such existed in Ireland prior to that date, of which the cloughans of Arran are examples (and perhaps some of the small stone oratories, and the buildings contained within the ancient cashels, might also be cited in proof of this), but a building of stones put together with lime, mortar, or other cement. Kienan died in 489, and his festival day is kept on the 24th November.† Duleek was the first bishop's see ever created in Ireland; and until the ambitious Simon Rochfort, shortly after the English invasion, suppressed it, or rather caused it to merge into another, on establishing himself sole Bishop of Meath, it was one of the seven which assisted to form that great ecclesiastical principality. From its exposed and maritime situation, the village of Duleek, with its rich abbey and church, offered an easy prey to the marauding Danes, by whom it was frequently plundered and burned, from 830 to 1037. After the battle of Clontarf in 1014, the bodies of Brian Borumha and his son Morough were carried to Swords, and next day conveyed by the monks of that abbey to Duleek, from whence they were afterwards transmitted to the abbey of

---

* This poem is preserved in the book of Lecan, one of our most ancient Gaelic manuscripts. See Dr. Petrie's reference to it in his History of the Round Towers, p 141.

† In the notes to the Irish Archæological edition of Nennius, p. 221, we read, " Cianan, of Daimhliag (Duleek) remains without corruption, without stinking, with his muscles perfect, and his hair and his nails grow." This curious tradition is mentioned in the notes to the Feilire Aenguis, at the 24th November ; it may, perhaps, be understood as communicating to us the fact that the whole body of the saint was preserved as a relic at Duleek.

Louth. Hugh de Lacy, the renowned Lord of Meath, established a cell here for canons regular of the St. Augustine order, subject to the priory of Lanthony, near Gloucester. After the Reformation, the extensive possessions of the priory of Duleek were granted to Gerald Moore.

Besides the cathedral church, Archdall has given the history and annals of two other erections, the priory of the Virgin Mary, founded by one of the O'Kelly family before the English invasion, and also an hospital called " Le Magdelyns." The borough of Duleek returned two members to the Irish Parliament.

The great object of attraction at Duleek is the remain of the priory which stands beside the modern parish church, and the handsome ivy-covered bell-tower of which very much resembles that at Slane.

This view of the ruins of the priory church is taken from the square or open space in the village, where stand two noble trees, an ash and a lime, in such close contiguity as to appear but one. The tower, which is still quite perfect, and about eighty feet high, is square, with a set-off on the western angle for the winding stair. From the parapet at top may be obtained a commanding view of the surrounding country, and the line of the retreat. A series of open arches occupy the northern side of the chancel, which is seventy feet long, and, except the eastern window, presents but little architectural beauty. Underneath the east window is a tablet, stating that it was built by Sir John Bellewe, Knight, and his wife, Dame Ismay Nugent, in 1587. Some handsome tombs stand in the upper end of the church. One in particular claims attention; it is that of a bishop, whose figure, in full canonicals, carved in high relief, lies upon the upper horizontal flag. Another of these intramural tombs, the position of which tells us that the church was a ruin, or at least unoccupied, a hundred and fifty years ago, is highly ornamented with heraldic devices, and was, we learn from the inscription, erected by Dame Mary Bermingham, to the memory of her husband, John Lord Bellew, who received a wound at the battle of Aughrim, of which he subsequently died in London in 1692. Some members of the Louth family, and also of the Barnwalls and Burkes, are likewise interred here.

The adjoining Protestant church is a much more modern structure. In the tower is a dumpy white marble statue of Judge Trotter; and in the surrounding graveyard, the upper portion, perhaps one-half, of a beautifully sculptured ancient stone cross, the arms being enclosed within a richly ornate circle. The cap, or shrine-like terminal, has been removed, but the tenon for the mortice on which it was placed still remains.

In the neighbouring demesne of the Earl of Thomond, which is pleasingly situated on the banks of the Nanny, and ornamented with some well-grown timber, we find the remains of the ancient abbey of St. Mary, in three detached portions, consisting of the ruins of the castellated gateway; a fragment of the eastern gable of the chapel, the windows of which must, from the scraps of stone mullions still visible, have been a splendid specimen of Gothic tracery; and a small bit of the refectory, or domestic part of the establishment; but these are all so completely surrounded by a thick grove, that, unless inquired for, the tourist could never find them out.

In the street of the village stands a remarkably formed, slender way-side cross, similar to that we described near Stackallan, at page 170, and, like it, was erected by one of the

Dowdalls, a family whose piety and ancestral reverence is marked in so many similar instances in this country. By an inscription on the side we perceive that

" THIS CROSS WAS BUILDED BY JENET DOWDALL, WIFE TO WILLIAM BATHE OF ATHCARNE, JUSTICE OF HIS MAJESTIES COURT OF COMON PLEES, FOR HIM AND HER, ANNO 1601. HE DECEACED THE 15TH OF OCTOBER, 1599. BURIED IN THE CHURCH OF DULEEK. WHOSE SOULES I PRAY GOD TAKE TO HIS MERCIE."

On the other sides are sculptured in relief figures of Saints Andrew, Catherine, Stephen, Peter, Patrick, Kienan, Magdelen, Jacobus, and Thomas.*

A bluff hill rises behind the village towards the south-east; but in all likelihood the retreating Irish army, in whose track we have wandered thus far from the " pleasant Boyne," followed the lie of the valley which winds round its base towards the south-east, leading to the Naul. The road thither passes over a portion of the high table land of the commons of Bellewstown, so famed in racing annals, and from which a most noble prospect may be obtained. The little hamlet of the Naul is charmingly situated in a deep gorge or defile, through which flows the water of the Delvan, a streamlet which divides the counties of Meath and Dublin. From Duleek to this point the road stretches along the sides of the succession of hills which lead up to Bellewstown, and commands all the way a view of one of the richest vales in Leinster, in the highest state of cultivation, and consequently teeming with fertility. The Black Castle of the Naul, one of the most picturesque ruins of its kind in Ireland, stands on a grey perpendicular rock that rises abruptly out of a most romantic little dell, through which the rivulet meanders with the most pleasing affect imaginable.

This, and other objects of beauty or antiquarian interest in the vicinity, would claim our attention, but that we have already (for the reason assigned) extended our researches beyond their prescribed limits.

---

* The parish priest and the villagers have lately had this cross repaired and re-cut.

CHAPTER XI.

DROGHEDA AND ITS ENVIRONS.

SUFFICIENTLY near the course of the Boyne, and of such para-
mount importance in an historic, scenic, and antiquarian point
of view, and, moreover, so intimately connected with the subjects discussed in the foregoing chapters, are the ecclesiastical
remains at Mellifont and Monasterboice, that we cannot bring
our wanderings to a close without paying them a visit. These
ruins can be reached either directly from Drogheda, from which
they are distant about four miles, or by passing up the by-
road leading through King William's Glen at right angles
with the river, and proceeding thus by Tullyallen, where the
site of the English camp is still pointed out, to Mellifont,
which is about two miles and a half from the river in a northern direction.

Of the ruins of Mellifont we see nothing until they spring
up, as if by enchantment, at our feet. There is no distant
prospect of them from any side, as they stand in the cup of a
small valley, approached by a narrow road ending in a *cul de
sac*. The Mattock river, a tributary of the Boyne, to which
we alluded at page 241, and which we crossed on our way from
Slane to Oldbridge, conducts us to the neck of a narrow gorge,
rich in planting, and its gracefully undulating sides clothed
with the most luxuriant herbage, relieved here and there, particularly upon the steeps to the left of the road, by grey massive rocks, which burst through the surface of the short dark
grass, and still darker furze,—the green tints of which contrast pleasingly with the light feathery ferns which are just

now unfolding their graceful tops to the gaze of summer. The water of the rivulet is here carried by a mill-race under the arch of the ancient gateway, a tall, dark, massive tower, square in shape and stern in aspect, and bearing an elevated turret at its north-eastern angle. This frowning portal, which still remains nearly entire, and was evidently the chief entrance to the monastic enclosure, is an historic evidence fully as authentic, and more truth-telling than books, of the state of the surrounding country at the time of its erection; and while the peaceful consecrated structures in the enclosure below are landmarks of learning and religion within, this bold castle tells a tale of the lawlessness and rapine which raged without. From this point we look down upon a confused mass of ruins,—arches, churches, solid blocks of ancient masonry, some standing, others prostrate,—several ivy-clad walls and grass-grown mounds, a few dirty thatched cabins, with an ugly, square, slated mill, and an adjoining farm-yard. But, fortunately, although the cabins and the mill sadly mar the general effect, neither of them is in immediate contiguity with the ruins.

Having passed the gateway, the next immediate object of interest, at least in point of position, is a small chapel, surrounded by a cemetery, now but little used, on the hill forming the north-eastern brow of the valley. It has little in itself to attract attention, but from it a fine panoramic view may be obtained of a great extent of country, spreading from the hill of Collon in the Oriel district to that of Slane. The building does not differ from the usual small Irish churches of the fifteenth or sixteenth century, and was probably the parochial church. The western gable, which rises at top into a double belfry, contains a pointed arched doorway; and above, but not immediately over this, is a small, double, round-arched window. One small narrow light occupies the eastern gable. A few paces in front of this building lie the remains of a very simple early cross, on the exposed surface of which is carved a circle containing a heart; and also a cross, the top and each arm of which end in a fleur-de-lis, or at least that form of terminal bearing some resemblance thereto, which is usual in such Irish crosses.

Descending into the valley, and before we proceed to examine the ruins in detail, we present our readers with a general view of the scene, taken from a spot beyond the river, and opposite the side at which we entered. The building in the centre is the gateway already described; that to the right is St. Bernard's Chapel, and on the left what is usually called the Baptistry; the structure in the distance is the chapel on the hill.

The history of this charming abode of the piety and learning of our ancestors is intimately interwoven with our national and social history. The story and the date of its erection, its annals and chronicles, recall many of the most romantic among the salient points in the authentic history of Ireland. The monastery of Mellifont (the Honey Fountain) was the first in point of time, and, we believe, as regards beauty of structure, design, and finish, also, ever erected in Ireland by the Cistercians, the great church-founders of the middle ages. So many circumstances bearing upon the conquest of Ireland appear in connexion with the foundation of this noble and extensive establishment, and so many distinguished personages and names of great interest present themselves in studying its annals, that we cannot forbear deviating from our usual course to dilate upon the history of a place much more intimately concerned in the introduction of foreign powers, ecclesiastical as well as civil, into this country, than the world is generally aware of. As true as that the Irish people were governed by their own kings and princes, and were amenable to their own laws and brehons only, up to the middle of the twelfth century, so sure is it that the Irish Catholic Church was independent of all foreign rule in either temporal or spiritual matters until the beginning of that period; and, indeed, according to the strict letter, until the bull of Pope Adrian sold us to Henry the Second for a penny. It is unnecessary to specify in what manner the Irish clergy were in spiritual matters obedient to their own hierarchy alone, nor is it requisite to enter here upon the subject of the celibacy which it appears, from good authority, the Irish parochial clergy at least did not observe for several hundred years after the mission of our patron saint. "At all events it appears certain that for 700 years after St. Patrick's arrival in Ireland, in 432, no Pope ever nominated, confirmed, sanctioned, or appointed, in any way, any one bishop or archbishop, or other dignitary, for any one see in Ireland; or gave a charter to any college, or school, or professor, or a license or dispensation of any kind for Ireland; or heard one cause connected with the Church of this country; or had the least hand in the canonizing, or blessing, or appointing of any single one of the ancient saints of Ireland, who lived before the twelfth century; or was allowed in any other way to interfere with the concerns of the Church of this island, until that time, i. e. 1132."*

Our bishops were appointed by synods, composed of both laity and clergy; and those cities and communities, such as Dublin and Limerick, &c., which did not ordain their own bishops, but sent them to Canterbury for that purpose, were all Danish; and although legates from Rome began to be received, it was not until the synod of Cashel was held, in 1172, three years after the English conquest, that the Pope's supremacy was fully acknowledged.

While the mass of the Irish people and all the petty kings and princes, with the great majority of the clergy, were well satisfied with this state of things, three powers were secretly but strenuously at work to subvert it. The Roman Pontiff wished to extend his sway over the whole christian world; the monarchs and nobles of England, then chiefly composed of the Norman stock, and but one generation removed from the conquerors themselves, desired to annex the neighbouring island to their own recently acquired dominions; and, no doubt, several of the Irish dignitaries, and some of the clergy, particularly of the higher orders, were anxious to curb the tyrannical power of

---

(a) The Little Red Book of the History of the Holy Catholic Church in Ireland. By Rev. Robert King. Dublin. James McGlashan. 1848.

their own nobles and the chiefs of the clans, by the introduction of a superior power, which, although exercising but a spiritual jurisdiction, would shelter them from the exactions of the laity, at that time very severe, if not unjust,—even as we know it long did Wolsey in a more enlightened age, when the feudal lordships and the serf system had begun to break up, if not before the face of the working man, at least before the power and intelligence of the merchant and the trader. Ample historic proofs evince all that we have here asserted. As yet, however, no ostensible movement or decided step had been taken by either party, although we may well suppose emissaries were at work, polemical and political, to gain these desired ends both here and at foreign courts, even as occurs in the ordinary diplomatic affairs of the present day. Always distracted and disputing among themselves, foreign influence must have spread rapidly through the Irish higher ranks of that day, particularly in Leinster and Munster. Let us now see how this topic bears upon the subject in hand.

Primate Malachy O'Morgair, the second Irishman canonized by the Pope, and who was a prelate of great natural endowments, exceeding purity of life, and remarkable for his learning and zeal, was, it seems, evidently in favour of the introduction of the Pontiff's power into Ireland in his time, when, in addition to the reasons already assigned, considerable laxity existed among the inferior Irish clergy, and the great bulk of the people were still in gross ignorance, or deeply imbued with the superstitious creed of their pagan ancestors. Celsus, the first Irishman canonized by the Pope, and who had made strenuous exertions to bring the Irish Church under the control of the Roman Pontiff, had, on his death-bed, appointed him his successor in the see of Armagh; but that office was usurped by another, so that he " dare not enter into the city of Armagh for fear of the tumults which the intruder would make on the occasion;" a circumstance which, no doubt, influenced him to favour the introduction of the Pontiff's superior authority here. In the year 1139 he undertook a journey to Rome, to solicit two palls or archiepiscopal cloaks for the Irish Church; one for Armagh, the other for Cashel; and on his way he spent some time with the renowned St. Bernard, at Clairvaux, then the most distinguished ecclesiastic in Europe, and who afterwards wrote St. Malachy's life. The palls were not granted at that time; however, the Pope showed him every mark of distinction, and, as an evidence of his special personal regard, took off his mitre, and placed it on the head of the Irish archbishop. The more immediate result of this visit to Innocent II. and Bernard was the subsequent introduction of the Cistercian order into Ireland.

There lived at this time a chieftain of great note, named Donough O'Carroll, King of Oirgialla, or Oriel,—a territory then comprising the present counties of Armagh, Monaghan, and Louth; he is memorable in history as the great church reformer of his day, and was the intimate friend of Malachy, in whose diocese his territory lay. In an ancient manuscript preserved in the Ussher collection in the library of Trinity College, we learn that it was he who " made the book of *Cnoc na n-Apstal* at Louth, and the chief books of the order of the year, and the chief book of the Mass. It was this great king who founded the entire monastery, both of stone and wood, and gave territory and land to it for the prosperity of his soul, in honour of SS. Paul and Peter. By him the church throughout the land of Oirghiall was reformed, and a regular bishopric was made, and the church was placed under the jurisdiction of the bishop. In his time tithes were received, and the marriage ceremony was assented to, and churches were founded, and temples and *cloigtheachs* were made, and monasteries of monks, and canons, and nuns, were re-edified, and nemheds (sanctuaries, or sacred enclosures) were made. These were specially the works which he performed for the prosperity of his soul and reign in the land of Oirgialla, namely, the Monastery of Monks on the banks of the Boyne, both as to stone and wooden furniture, and books, and territory, and land, in which monastery there are 100 monks and 300 conventuals."[*]

We can, without any great stretch of fancy, imagine these two great men, Malachy and O'Carroll, setting out to seek a spot sufficiently fertile, well circumstanced, calm and sequestered, on which to plant that great monastic institution, which afterwards bore so considerable a part in Irish church history, and being struck with the beauty and seclusion of the valley

---

[*] This extract from the ancient Antiphonarium of the Cathedral of Armagh was first published by Dr. Petrie in his inquiry into the Origin and Uses of the Round Towers of Ireland. The fact of the erection of cloictheachs or round towers, so late as the middle of the twelfth century alluded to in this manuscript, is highly confirmatory of that learned author's position with respect to the date of some of these curious structures.

whereon we now stand; its high banks, fringed with the natural wood which then overspread the country, and its bottom
watered by the rill, at which, perchance, in some of his hunting excursions, the Prince of Oriel had refreshed himself.
Here, in 1142, we learn that O'Carroll, at the instance of
St. Malachy, founded the abbey and monastery of Mellifont,
and that its first stock of monks were sent over by St. Bernard
from the parent convent of Clairvaux. A few of these were
Irish, but the great majority of them were Frenchmen, acknowledging the supremacy of the Pope, and decidedly
favourable to Anglo-Norman interests. Then was the underwood cleared away, the oak and the birch fell beneath
the woodman's axe, and the wolf and the wild boar were
scared from their lurking place, as the valley rang with the
clang of hammers and the sharp chip of the chisel. The bees,
for which the place was celebrated, and from which it was
named, no longer gathered their winter store from its sweet
flowers; and, where the crane and the bittern found their
resting place, arose the stately structures of the abbey and
surrounding monastic edifices, by far the most gorgeous which
had yet been seen in this country. There, where the cooing of
the wild pigeon, or the shrill whistle of the lapwing, alone were
heard in former years, the tolling of the vesper and the matin
bell spread in measured cadences over the surrounding wood-
lands, and the perfume of incense rose up from the depths of
the once solitary and uncultured valley of the Mattock.

Its first abbot was Christian O'Conarchy, who, in 1145, was
made Bishop of Lismore, and afterwards Legate, and the number of Irish bishops who were taken from the monks of this
establishment is quite remarkable. He it was who afterwards
presided at the Council of Cashel held by order of Henry II.,
and of which Roderick O'Conor, the Irish monarch, was totally ignorant. It was then and there the Irish Church
really became dependent on that of England, and consequently
of Rome; so that we may fairly trace the act to the influence of the first abbot of Mellifont. In 1157 a celebrated
synod was held here by Gilla Mac Liag, generally known
as Gelasius, Primate of Armagh, at which Bishop O'Conarchy and Cardinal Paparo, the Pope's legate, presided. At
this council there were seventeen bishops, and it was also
honoured with the presence of Murtogh O'Loughlin, one of
the royal family of Aileach, in Ulster, and then monarch of

Ireland, who presented to the abbey one hundred and forty oxen, sixty ounces of gold, and a townland near Drogheda; of O'Eochy, King of Ulidia or Down; Tiernan O'Rourke, Prince of Brefney;* and O'Carrol of Oriel, who endowed the abbey with sixty ounces of gold. The chief matter of consequence transacted at this convocation was the excommunication and deposition of Dunchad O'Melaghlin, King of Meath, and the election of Dermod, his brother, in his stead. It was upon this occasion that the abbey church was consecrated with great solemnity; and among the oblations made to it, besides those already specified, we read that Dervorgail, the ill-fated wife of the Leitrim chieftain, and whose so-called abduction is assigned as the cause of the English invasion, richly endowed this foreign monastery, having presented to it on that occasion sixty ounces of gold with a golden chalice for the high altar, and ornaments and holy furniture for nine other altars in the same church. And here, as we already stated at page 19, she afterwards retired towards the close of her life, and died in 1193. Whether she was present on the occasion of the consecration is not mentioned in the Annals, but the circumstance occurred during the seventeen years' interval from the period of her elopement to that of the first English invasion. In the same year (1193), the relics of St. Malachy, who died upon the Continent, were brought into Ireland and received with great pomp at this abbey. As might be expected from the foregoing recital, the house of Mellifont was patronized by the English on their first coming into Ireland, and accordingly we read that both Henry and John confirmed all its grants, and granted it several charters of great value. Upon several occasions the abbots of Mellifont were restricted from sending money to the original Cistercian settlement at Clairvaux; but, although originally so much devoted to foreign influence, the monks of Mellifont became, like other settlers, more Irish than the Irish themselves; and in 1322 "it was determined that no person whatsoever should be admitted into this abbey before he had taken an oath that he was not of English descent." This abbey is sometimes called Mell; in some

---

* Tiernan O'Rourke, the husband of Dervorgail, was slain at the hill of Ward by some of the English chieftains in 1172. They placed his head over the gate of Dublin, and his body was gibbetted with his feet upwards, at the northern side of the city.

places it is confounded with that of Drogheda, and in others it is styled the Monastery of the Monks. "Upon the dissolution of monastic establishments its extensive possessions were granted to Sir Gerald Moore, who fixed his residence here, making the abbey a magnificent and desirable seat, and at the same time a place of defence, as it bordered immediately on the Irish rebels, against whom the house constantly maintained itself until the 24th of November, 1641, when a strong party sat down before it. The garrison, which consisted only of fifteen horse, and twenty-two foot, made a vigorous defence, but, their ammunition being exhausted, the horse forced their way to the Irish camp at Drogheda, and were followed by the foot, who all effected an escape, eleven only excepted, which number the Irish sacrificed to the manes of 120 of their men who were killed on the field of battle."[*]

The existing ruins at Mellifont consist of the gateway and church already described; the outer wall of the enclosure of the abbey ground, which extends from near the latter, round the brow of the hill which bounds the valley upon the eastern side, until it approaches the river upon the south and west; the remains of St. Bernard's chapel; the Baptistry; the foundation walls of the abbey, with the crypts and arches beneath; and the well which is usually found within the grounds of a monastery.

St. Bernard's Chapel must have been one of the most elegant and highly embellished structures of the Norman or early English pointed style in Ireland, but from its size we never could imagine that it was the original church which held all the monks, nuns, and conventuals, which we read existed here shortly after the foundation of the monastery, nor that building, ten of the altars of which we learn were decorated and endowed by the princess of Brefney. It is a low crypt, with a groined roof, underneath another building evidently used for domestic purposes, and which was probably part of the apartments of the abbot. The upper room, which contains a chimney, but without any decoration, must have been a pleasant, cheerful abode, and its windows commanded a charming prospect

---

[*] Archdall's Monasticon Hibernicon. The family of Moore, from whom the present Earl of Drogheda is descended, possessed a large estate in Dublin; and hence the names of several of our streets, as Henry, Moore, Earl, Of (Off-Lane), Drogheda (now Sackville-street), and Mellifont (miscalled Elephant) Lane.

down the valley, with a view of the distant hills peeping up
from the south-west.   The chapel is only thirty feet long by
sixteen feet ten inches broad.   The altar and window above it
were not due east, but south-east, a circumstance not unusually
observed in some of our churches of the period at which this
was built.   There are no remains of the mullions or tracery of
the east window now existing.   At present there are two lights
upon each side, but upon a careful consideration of the ma-

sonry, both within and without the chapel, it is, we think,
apparent that, in the original plan of the building, the upper
window on each side alone existed, the others being evidently
subsequent innovations.   The original windows are still very
beautiful, deeply set, and though their stone mullions are
rather massive, each forms, with the tracery at top, a very
elegant figure.   The internal pilasters, which form an archi-

trave for the northern window, spring from grotesque heads, elaborately carved, and which appear as if pressed down by the superincumbent weight. A fillet of dog's-tooth moulding surrounds the internal sash. A projecting moulding courses round the wall of the chapel, about two feet from the ground, which, while it dips down to admit the splayed sill of the upper or original windows, continues unbroken by the lower ones, an additional proof that the latter did not exist in the first plan of the building. Three sets of short clustered pillars, four feet high, one in the centre, and one in each angle, spring from this course, and terminate in elaborately carved floral capitals, which differ slightly one from another. The centre rod of this cluster descends as far as the floor. From these spring the ribs which form the groining of the roof. The stone of which they are composed, as well as much of that used in the other buildings at Mellifont, is probably foreign, as were, very likely, the artists who carved them. Where the groins meet above the altar, we observe an aperture, surrounded by a star-fish ornament, from which the lamp which assisted to illuminate this sombre crypt was suspended. The grand architectural feature, and most elaborate piece of carving in St. Bernard's Chapel was the door-way, formed of a cluster of pillars, very deeply revealed on the inside, but apparently plain outside, which strengthens the idea that this beautiful little chapel was enclosed within the other buildings. Nearly the whole of the western end of the chapel has fallen, allowing the visitor to obtain from without the view given in the accurate illustration opposite, so that nothing but the foundations of this very splendid doorway now remain. A figure of it has, however, been preserved in Wright's Louthiana, published in 1755, where we read that it was " all of blue marble, richly ornamented and gilt;" but which, the author adds, " I was informed was sold and going to be taken to pieces when I was there." All the pillars and carved stone work of St. Bernard's Chapel were at one time painted in the most brilliant colours, the capitals light blue, the pillars themselves red; portions of this paint still remain in the crevices and among the foliage. Whether such decoration formed part of the original design, or was subsequently resorted to, it is not now easy to determine (see p. 305). There are three buttresses upon each side on the exterior of this building, and upon its

northern aspect may be observed some carved and hammered
stones, which had evidently been used in other buildings of
anterior date, worked into the wall, and which lend support
to the opinion we have already expressed, as to this not being
the great church at Mellifont, with its ten altars, the consecration of which is described at page 286, but perhaps one an
hundred and fifty or two hundred years later.

The oldest and by far the most interesting and curious
architectural remain in this place is that usually called the
Baptistry, an octagonal building, about one half-of which still
remains, and of which the accompanying internal view, taken

under our direction by Mr. Wakeman, gives, of the many attempts at illustrating this unique structure which we have
seen, by far the best idea. It consists of a colonnade or series of
circular-headed arches, of the Roman or Saxon character, enclosing a space of twenty-nine feet in the clear, and supporting a
wall which must have been, when perfect, about thirty feet high.
Each external face measures twelve feet in length, and was
plastered or covered with composition to the height of ten feet,
where a projecting band separates it from the less elaborate
masonry above. The arches are carved in sandstone, and

spring from foliage-ornamented capitals to the short supporting pillars, the shaft of each of which measures three feet five
inches. The chord of each arch above the capitals is four feet
three inches. Some slight difference is observable in the shape
and arrangement of the foliage of the capitals, and upon one
of the remaining half arches were beautifully carved two birds;
but some Goth has lately succeeded in hammering away as
much of the relieved part of each as it was possible. Whatever the original intention of this building may have been,
the arches were evidently open, and some slight variety exists in their mouldings. Internally a stone finger-course encircled the wall at about six inches higher than that on the
outside. In the angles between the arches there are the remains of fluted pilasters crowned by capitals at the height of
the finger course, from which spring groins of apparently the
same curve as the external arches, and which meeting in the
centre must have formed more or less of a pendant, which, no
doubt, heightened the beauty and architectural effect. Portions of this groining still remain, as well as some of the joist-
holes for the flooring above; and the narrow space between the
ceiling and the floor also proves that the groining was formed of
semicircular arches, similar to that at Coningsburgh Castle.
Like the pillars and stone carvings in St. Bernard's Chapel, the
Baptistry was also painted red and blue, and the track of the
paint is still quite visible in several places. The upper story,
which was lighted by a window on each side of the octagon,
bears no architectural embellishment which is now visible.

Archdall asserts that on the top of this octagonal erection
was " a large cistern from whence water was conveyed by
means of pipes to the different offices in the abbey." This
assertion, for which we cannot find any authority earlier than
the date of the Monasticon (1786), has since been copied by
all the subsequent describers of Mellifont. But an examination of this building will, we feel assured, dispel this conjecture. The windows would be quite inapplicable to a
cistern, and the roof evidently rose immediately above them.
Moreover, the walls, in parts of which we meet with brick,
would be quite too slight for such a purpose. So much of
the southern side of the building has been completely removed, that it is now difficult to say whether it was at
first joined to any part of the abbey or to any other build-

ing at all; certainly it would, like a round tower, have stood much better and more effectively alone. Nothing decisive can be said with respect to the use of this building. To the Temple Church in London it at first sight bears some resemblance in shape, but a more careful consideration of the two structures does not confirm this impression, nor indeed have we any warrant for supposing that this was a church at all. Probably it was, as has been conjectured, a Baptistry, and possibly it covered a well like the small octagonal structure at St. Doulough's, near Dublin. The accumulated rubbish within the site of the building precludes the possibility of making any search for the spring, if such ever existed. Had the arches been closed, or if doors were attached to the original building, one might speculate on its applicability for a chapter-house, but assuredly we cannot come to this conclusion by what now remains. It would have sadly marred its effect if it were mixed up with any other building.

The ancient well was discovered some years ago, and the arch above it has been restored. The foundations, and considerable remains of the monastery, still exist to the south-west of the Baptistry, and several low crypts, partially beneath the surface, are yet accessible. Above these, large portions of the masonry, though prostrate, still remain, held together by the ancient cement. These masses, thus preserved apparently by their own internal cohesion, resemble the true and invisible church itself, no matter how much shattered by internal schism or by external revolution, and its simplicity obscured by human craft or pride, is always capable of restoration, ever preserving enough of ornamental design, even in the fragments, to permit of repair, reconstruction, or reform. One cannot fail to be struck with the remarkable fact, that there is not a single characteristic emblem or element of true Irish ecclesiastical architecture at Mellifont; no round tower, no crosses, no inscriptions on tombs, no doorways with straight lintels and inclining jambs, and no knotted tracery, indicative of early Irish art. Everything we meet here is foreign.

The destruction and desecration going forward at Mellifont is perhaps greater than at any other place of the same note or beauty in Ireland. If the proprietor would clear away the accumulated filth and rubbish, and restore from the neighbouring gardens the heaps of carved stone accumulated

there, he would very much improve his property, confer a
boon on the tourist, and do good service to the country generally.

The little vale in which this group of ruins stands is not
above a quarter of a mile in length, and scarcely a furlong
broad. On a summer's holiday, when the clanking mill is at
rest, we know few spots more calm and sequestered; the breath
of the rude world sighs around, but rarely enters this peaceful
abode. We have now examined all the remains above ground
worthy of attention, but still we know that in the soil, deep beneath our feet, exist the consecrated graves of the brave and
pious, the chivalrous and beautiful, the worshipped and the wor-
shipper; those who in life ruled the hearts, commanded the
reverence, guided the fierce passions, or bent the weak wills
of others;—stern chieftains, subtle, intriguing politicians,
haughty ecclesiastics, and exacting churchmen;—fair women,
grave scholars, simple monks: but love and learning, avarice
and ambition, meekness and mercy, philosophy and ignorance,
as well as faith and scepticism, those innate gifts and defects,
all now mingle in one common clay. The swallows and martins
skimming lightly over the brim of the valley,—the cuckoo's
mocking note, which, in the season, is here almost invariably
heard,—the hum of the humble bee, as it roams in from the surrounding pastures to gather sweets from the fragrant apple
blossoms and snowy thorns which skirt the gracefully formed
hills, clad with their feathery purple grass that bound the eastern
slopes, and which contrast with the abrupt, grey, naked bank
of clay opposite; the myriads of midges in their aerial dances
o'er the gently murmuring streamlet,—for the Mattock is not
a brawling brook, but a quiet, gently running rill, such as
should ripple by a spot so sacred and secluded,—and the azure-
winged dragon-flies, flitting among the flaggers which mantle
on its margins; with the grey, distinct, but not glaring light
shed from the dappled sky (when the sun only gives its parting
kiss to earth in long, level rays at eventide), that we sometimes
meet with on days in early summer, and which gives a peculiar
effect to ruins such as these,—all combine to still the most
angry thoughts, and throw a sabbath air of the most bewitch-
ing calmness and repose over the mouldering walls of Mellifont.

We would fain linger longer here, but that time presses,

and that another object, totally different in its scenery and
architectural characters, but equally interesting to the archæological tourist, beckons us onward to a spot about three miles
farther, which we may reach by a hilly and indifferent road,
but sufficiently passable for an Irish car.

Upon the slope of a gently rising pasture-ground, lone and
solitary, rise the round tower, the simple, unostentatious
churches, with their guardian ash tree, the splendid crosses,
and the crowd of tombstones of Monasterboice,—the remains of
the ancient monastery of St. Buithe.

Very early in the sixth century St. Buithe or Boetius, son
of Bronach, from whom the place is named, founded a religious house here.

Within the enclosure of the cemetery of *Mainistir-Buithe*
stands one of our largest and, it is supposed, most recently
erected round towers. It is fifty feet in circumference at the
bottom, by 110 feet high; originally, however, it must have
been much taller; but the top has been shattered, apparently
by lightning. A rent also exists upon one side, and it leans,

or, more properly speaking, is bent several feet from the perpendicular. The circular-headed doorway, which is five feet six inches high by one foot ten inches broad, and stands six feet above the present outer surface, faces the south-east, and is decorated with a double band or moulding. There were originally five stories in this tower, each of the lower was lighted by an angular-headed window, and at top there were four oblong apertures, which permitted the toll from the *cloic-theach*, or bell-house, to reach the small Christian congregation which existed in early times around this establishment. From the great northern road which runs at a little distance from hence, this tall landmark, with the yellow lichens creeping over its grey sides, and the lowly churches and elegantly shaped crosses which nestle round its base, forms a conspicuous and pleasing object, no doubt well remembered by those who rolled by it on the top of some of the north-going coaches, before railways were established.

The annals of this monastic establishment are voluminous, but, with few exceptions, they consist of the obits of its abbots, and some account of the plunderings and conflagrations which it suffered. Among the latter is one worthy of recital, on account of its frequency or repetition in a number of ancient Irish authorities, as, for instance, the Chronicon Scotorum, the Annals of Ulster, and the Annals of the Four Masters, and because it lends considerable support to the theory of one of the uses to which the round towers were occasionally applied. It runs thus : " A. D. 1097. The cloictheach of Mainister, containing several books and valuables, was burned." It would appear from such fragments of history as have come down to the present time, that the monks of Boetius were distinguished for their learning, and that this monastery was long the repository of some of the most valuable literary and historic records of this country. The founder died upon the 7th of December, 522 ; and beyond the enumeration of his successors we learn little of the history of the establishment for some hundred years, until 1050, when Flann Mainistreach, a distinguished poet and historian, was abbot. Edward O'Reilly, in his account of Irish writers, published in the Transactions of the Iberno-Celtic Society for 1820, has given a catalogue of fourteen of his works, principally poems descriptive of the early history,

or relating some of the exploits of the later pagan and first
Christian kings of Ireland.   Some of these metrical histories
are preserved in our larger manuscript works, as the Book
of Lecan, and also the Book of Invasions, collected by the
O'Clerys, the monks of Donegal, who are generally known
as "the Four Masters."   In that account of the pagan cemeteries, to which we have already referred at page 184, we
find the following notice referring to the burying place of the
poets of Connaught, and to the grave of Dathi, one of the
early pagan monarchs of Ireland: "It was Flann and Eochaidh
Eolach O'Ceirin [O'Kerrin] that collected this account from
the books of Eochaidh O'Flanagan at Armagh, and from the
books of the monastery [Monasterboice], and from other select
books, viz., from the Libur Budi, which disappeared from the
Carcair at Armagh, and from the Libur Gerr, which was at
the monastery; and this was the book which the student took
with him by stealth across the sea, and was never found."*
The death of this distinguished man is thus related in the
Annals of the Four Masters:—"1056.   Flann of the Monastery, lecturer of Monasterboice, the paragon of the Irish in
history, poetry, eloquence, and general literature, died upon
the fourth of the calends of December [28th November], of
whom it was said:

"'Flann of the chief church of melodious Buithe,
Slow the bright eye of his fine head ;
Contemplative sage is he who sits with us,
Last sage of the three lands† is fair Flann.'"

There are the remains of two churches here, but evidently
of different dates.   That in the immediate vicinity of the round
tower, and which is probably of the twelfth or thirteenth
century, is thirty-six feet in length, by seventeen feet nine
inches broad in the clear. It runs south-east and north-west,‡
and is entered by a square-headed doorway in the western gable,

---

* See Petrie's Round Towers, p. 106.

† The three lands were Ireland, Mann, and Scotland.

‡ This fact, so frequently remarked in early Irish churches, may be owing
to the circumstance of the precession of the equinoxes; the alteration, with
respect to the earth, of the sun's rising and setting at particular times of the
year.   These churches were laid out, not by the compass, but by the sun.
We can thus generally tell, by taking its bearings, at what time of the year
the foundation of the church was sunk.

the architecture of which bespeaks its truly Irish character, and rather early erection. A large circular arch, bearing some similitude to that which we find in the chancel of some of our early churches, occupies the eastern gable; but from the present length of the church, and the obvious termination of the walls externally at that end, we are not inclined to attribute this purpose to it. A short distance within the door of this church stands a circular granite stone, like the fragment of a pillar. Upon this, each coffin which comes for interment to this much-used cemetery, is laid for a few minutes after it has been carried round the circuit of the graveyard, the churches, and crosses, according to a defined and well-known path. This circumstance would at once attract the attention of any person accustomed to observe the ceremonial of an Irish funeral, and, even if no further evidence existed, would be highly confirmatory of the antiquity of the church, and of the originally consecrated purpose of this stone. It was probably the shaft of the font. The second church, which stands at some distance from the round tower, and which is much more modern, is thirty-two feet long by thirteen feet six inches broad, and had a remarkably low roof. It is now nearly filled up with a luxuriant elder tree, and was entered by a low, circular-arched doorway.

The most attractive objects of antiquity here are those magnificently sculptured crosses, to which we have already made allusion, and which have been not only the great boast of Irish antiquaries, but which have so frequently, and in such glowing terms, elicited the admiration of foreigners. With the exception of the great cross at Clonmacnoise, and one which we ourselves recently exhumed near the cathedral of St. Brecan, in the great island of Arran, there is nothing of the kind in Great Britain, or perhaps in Europe, either in magnitude, design, or execution, to compare with two at least of the crosses at Monasterboice. Immediately in front of the round tower, and at the southern side of the adjoining church, stands the tallest of these crosses, and we believe the highest in Ireland; it measures twenty feet in the shaft, and is morticed into a base twenty inches high, but several feet of which are now hid beneath the surface. This beautifully slender cross, figured in the accompanying wood-cut, consists, independently of the base or socket, of three stones; the shaft is eleven feet; the central stone, consisting of the circle and arms, is six feet three inches; and the cap at top, representing a shrine or church, with a high pitched roof, sharp ridge, and fish-tail terminations over the gables, is two feet three inches high.* The shaft is two feet broad, and fifteen inches thick, but a considerable portion of its lower part has been hammered away, tradition says, by the soldiers of Cromwell, the usual scape goats, in Ireland, for every description of dese-cration or dilapidation. The figures were carved in strong relief, though now much worn by time and the elements. The sculptures are divided into tab-lets or compartments, each refer-ring to some portion of sacred, or of early church history, or some of the circumstances con-nected with the monastery and the cross itself. As is usual in all such monuments, a repre-sentation of the Crucifixion oc-cupies the centre of the prin-cipal side, which is always somewhat inclined, and which very frequently faces the west, that the rays of the setting sun might illumine the sculpture, and assist to brighten the story which these hieroglyphics (sa-cred representations) and pictorial writings taught the simple peasant that after his daily toil knelt at its base. In this in-stance the various compartments contain figures of the Apostles, the Virgin and Child, and some of our Irish saints and most ce-

* We lately measured this cross, by throwing a small stone, with a marked tape attached to it, over the ridge at top. For a person standing near its base to throw a stone over the round tower is considered one of the great feats of the rustics here. So is it at Glendalough, and wherever a round tower is to be found in Ireland.

lebrated ecclesiastics. It is not alone in the light, graceful form, or the sculptured figures, that this cross, in common with several of the same type, claims attention, but in the elegance and design of its details and ornaments, in the fillets and tracery elaborately wrought over each spot not occupied by figures, than which latter, as might be expected, they are very much superior. From the scroll-work upon the under side of the circle enclosing the arms, and which, owing to its protected position, is here, as in most crosses, particularly sharp and well defined, we give the accompanying figure.

Inferior in point of size, but eminently superior in artistic design and execution, is the second crucial monument, called by the people St. Boyne's, or Buithe's Cross, but which we know, from an Irish inscription on its base, was erected by the Abbot Muiredach.*

" oꞃ bo Muıꞃebach laꞃ Inbeꞃnab ın Chꞃoꞃꞃa."

"A prayer for Muredach, by whom this cross was made."

So that its erection is to be assigned to a period not earlier than the middle of the ninth, or later than the beginning of the tenth century. "The sacrilegious hands which attempted the ruin of the others appear to have spared this, and it stands almost as perfect as when, nearly nine centuries ago, the artist, we may suppose, pronounced his work finished, and chiefs and abbots, bards, shanachies, warriors, ecclesiastics, and perhaps many a rival sculptor, crowded round this very spot, full of wonder and admiration for what they must have considered

* As there were two distinguished abbots of this name, there is some uncertainty as to which is here referred to. The one was Muiredach, son of Flann, abbot of Mainister Buithe, who died in 844. The other, who was the " son of Domhnall, tanist-abbot of Armagh, and chief steward of the southern Hy Niall, and successor of Buithe, the son of Bronach, head of the council of all the men of Bregia, laity and clergy, departed this life on the fifth day of the calends of December," A. D. 924.

a truly glorious, and perhaps unequalled work."* This cross
is fourteen feet seven inches high, and the span of the arms
is seven feet, but the accurately diminishing shaft, and the
beautiful proportions remove, after we have quietly contem-
plated it for some time, the appearance of dumpiness, which at
a first view we might be inclined to attribute to it. It is only
when a tall man stands upon the pedestal, underneath the arms,
that its real height appears. The shaft and arms consist of one
stone, and the circle, as shown in the accompanying drawing,
is so narrow, as, with the
knobs projecting from the
graceful coverture formed
within it, to give an air of
lightness to the whole. The
top, or terminal stone, is
church-shaped, three feet
six inches high by two feet
two inches broad, and the
roof is carved in imitation
of tiling.

The crosses at Monaster-
boice, and this one in particular, are evidently monumental, erected to com-
memorate the virtues, the
piety, or the munificence of
distinguished personages by
whom the original churches,
the crosses, and, perhaps,
the tower itself were built.
Some crosses are purely
sepulchral; some mark a
memorable locality where some noted action or ceremony occurred, like the stele or pillar-stones set up by the oriental
patriarchs, and others, chiefly the simple, unadorned ones,
serve to mark the boundary of the Nemhedh, or sacred enclosure. Those, however, which were highly sculptured, were
no doubt intended to teach the rude and uneducated people
the rudiments of their faith: the story of the creation, the na-

---

* Wakeman's Archæologia Hibernica, p. 1.

tivity, judgment, and redemption; thus, some, as that at Clonmacnoise, were on this account styled in some of our Irish
Annals and monastic histories, *Cros na Screaptra*, the Cross
of the Scriptures. These monuments are also of general archæological interest, for in their carvings we have passages
of history represented, not only of value in themselves, but
of great importance in an ethnological point of view, by exhibiting the features, costume, weapons, and mode of warfare; the punishments, the games and ceremonies, as well as
the musical instruments; and also the dresses of the ecclesiastics of the time,—generally from the ninth to the end of the
thirteenth century. Several of these monuments bear bilin-
gual inscriptions, the pictorial or idiographic representations
already alluded to, and also writing, in the ancient Irish
character, generally round their bases. Indeed, a description
of our ancient crosses, their uses, by whom and for what
purpose erected, would form a volume, and a most interesting one too; and were all our other monuments effaced or obliterated, an outline of Irish history might be happily illustrated by them. They likewise exhibit the state of the arts
in this country at the time of their erection. Writers usually
style them "rudely sculptured," but this appellation is scarcely
warranted, The figures are not good, it is true, but they are
as well drawn as those of similar epochs elsewhere, and the
ornamental embellishments are quite unequalled in beauty
of design and artistic skill. Upon the western face of Muiredach's cross the central compartment represents the crucifixion,
with the Roman soldiers pointing spears at the pendant body,
and on each side of this a crowd of figures occupies the arm
of the stone. In both drawing and execution this representation is so like that figured on the front of the great cross that
we are forced to admit a synchronous era for their erection;
and, if not from the same hand, one is evidently a copy from the
other. The same is likewise to be seen upon the small third
cross near the north-eastern angle of the graveyard. The
wood-cut on the next page represents the two lower tablets
or compartments in the cross now under examination. The
upper one contains three figures, intended in all probability for portraits of some of the persons concerned in the history or the erections of Monasterboice, and the lower one an
ecclesiastic holding a bachall or pastoral staff, and stand-

ing between two soldiers with drawn swords. These swords are not shaped like the short, light bronze ones which abound in our collections, but bear the greatest resemblance to the long iron swords occasionally found of late years, a fine collection of which, turned up in the excavations for the Cashel Railway, near Dublin, now exists in the Royal Irish Academy. All these figures are highly illustrative of the dress of the period, and of the different ranks, military and religious, that existed here at the time. Beneath this, where the shaft rises out of the mortice, we see two dogs couchant, with long tails, probably the Irish wolf-dogs, or large rough-haired greyhounds, the animals most frequently represented in Irish ornamental emblazonry, both upon our monuments and illuminated manuscripts. Sometimes the animals are represented fighting, and in other  instances they form a curious scroll-work or interlacing one with another. Beneath this tablet is the inscription given at page 299. The eastern face of this cross is the most remarkable. In the top, above the centre, are two figures, one presenting a crozier to the other, who wears a long garment, and was probably Muiredach himself, the tanist-abbot of Armagh, and the successor of St. Buithe. Under this are figures representing the Trinity. The Judgment occupies the centre, and over the chief figure is an eagle with outspread wings. In the choir of angels which fills a portion of the space devoted to this representation, may be seen several figures holding musical instruments, among which we recognise the ancient Irish harp. To the right of the chief figure is a crowd of the doomed, flying before an armed fiend. In a small compartment beneath is a figure holding a scales or balance in which the souls are being weighed. The next tablet, which is the highest on this side of the shaft, shows the adoration of the Magi. The sculptures on the second compartment evidently refer to some historical event. They represent a double row of captive figures, several of them in a crouching or submissive attitude, before a single large figure, who holds a rod, and who is manifestly their conqueror. The whole greatly reminds us of some of the paintings on the early Egyptian tombs, and which have been so graphically and faithfully preserved by Rossellini in his magnificent work on that subject.

The third compartment is so remarkable, so full of meaning, and so ethnological, that we have had it engraved.

In the left hand corner sits on a chair a figure with a long gown or tunic, and a head-dress which falls over the shoulders. It is armed with a circular shield and a straight sword, and holds a horn in shape like the ancient drinking-horn, which is supported by the right hand. The second figure is standing,  dressed somewhat like the former, but with the addition of a short cloak hanging from the head and shoulders, and confined round the neck by a string. In the right hand is a sort of paddle, while the left grasps a *celt*, raised on high in the attitude of striking at the middle figure, apparently that of a captive, and, if we may judge by the difference of his costume, his pointed cap, and long beard, a foreigner and a warrior. The sword and shield are peculiarly Danish. This figure kneels, and seems to shrink from the impending blow of its adversary. The fourth figure resembles the second. This is, perhaps, the best exhibition of ancient Irish warfare extant.

In the fourth compartment the figures are in much better

preservation than in any other. It represents the Temptation in Paradise and the Expulsion. In the former subject are figures of Adam and Eve, the tree of knowledge, and the serpent. In the latter is the angel, with an ornamented tunic and long beard, driving our first parent from the garden, whose attitude, as he crouches into a corner, with the palms of his hands turned forwards, as if in entreaty and submission, is very characteristic, and, of its kind, the most expressive of utter helplessness we ever witnessed. On the base are two dogs fighting, one having hold of the other's ear. On other portions of the cross are various emblematic devices of little importance, with the exception of that beneath the northern arm, which represents a very well carved hand holding a paten. The neighbouring peasantry have a legend concerning this, to the effect that it was carved in commemoration of a woman who was impious enough to make a cake on a Sunday, and that it stuck to her hand. The lichen and moss which grow upon this cross are much sought after for the cure of various diseases, as is also the water which accumulates in

the mortice of the smallest or third cross, which stands near the north-eastern angle of the graveyard. This latter is the middle, and a part of the shaft of another, and probably unfinished cross, but of the same design as the two others. It measures six feet six inches, and the span of the arms is four feet seven inches. On the front is a representation of Christ with expanded arms, and beneath it two smaller figures, presenting spears, as in the cru-

cifixions carved on the two other crosses. On the reverse is a raised boss containing the ornamental scroll shown in the accompanying cut.

We find one early Irish tomb still remaining at Monasterboice, on the left of the path leading from the tower to the smaller cross just described. It bears this inscription: "Oꞃ ᴅu Ruaꞃcan," i. e. "A prayer for Ruarcan."

To those who have sufficient time to spare, after visiting Mellifont and Monasterboice, we would recommend an excursion to Termonfechen, a very noted locality, still containing some objects of antiquarian interest, within little more than three miles of Drogheda, upon the northern or Louth side of the Boyne. The ruins of its ancient castle are worthy of inspection, and there are many associations of historic value connected with its origin and annals. As its name implies, it was the termon or herenach land of St. Feichin, who flourished in the seventh century. Donough O'Carroll, the founder of Mellifont, also established "the first church of Termann Feichin." This place was long the country residence of the Archbishops of Armagh, and the last occupant of it was the learned Ussher, who died here in 1617. Originally there existed a considerable town here, situated on the small stream adjoining, and near which the Dundalk Railway now runs. The present church is crowded with monuments of the M'Clintocks, Brabazons, Pentlands, and other families that are or have been resident in the vicinity. In the churchyard is an ancient sculptured stone cross worthy of inspection.*

Leaving the field of Oldbridge, Mellifont, and Monasterboice, and passing down the left bank of the river, we now approach

---

* Since the description of Mellifont went to press we have received the following notice of the chemical composition of the ancient paint, alluded to at p. 289, from our friend Mr. Sullivan, First Chemical Assistant in the Museum of Irish Industry, to whom we submitted some portions of it for analysis:

"The priming of the walls was done either with an excessively rich ochre, or with colcother, or oxide of iron; over this were laid several coats of white lead, upon which the blue colour was laid on, consisting of a salt of copper, most probably the ordinary verditer blue. The menstruum employed was oil, but I could not say whether the colcother was put on with oil, or simply with water and size. The fact of oil having been used would tend, I think, to show that the painting could not have been very old, as it is not probable that the use of oil *in church painting* could have been introduced into Ireland for at least one century after its application to pictures by the Van Eycks. I may also add that the lead employed was 'genuine lead,' which is more than I could say for most modern specimens of church painting. In those days there was evidently little intercourse with the Dutch people, at least not as much as subsequently, or they would have learned the value of 'Dutch lead,' vulgarly called sulphate or carbonate of barytes.

"You will see from the account that I have given that there is nothing very peculiar in the case, except, probably, the priming of colcother, which, without expressing absolute certainty, I have every reason to suppose was put on with size, as in '*al fresco.*'"

the last remaining point of interest upon the Boyne, the ancient
city of Drogheda; if, indeed, our readers can feel much interest
in one of the dirtiest, worst sewered, and most ill-ventilated
towns in Ireland.   And yet, though we thus express ourselves,
Drogheda possesses many objects that peculiarly attract attention.   It is pleasingly as well as most advantageously situated;
abounds in ruins, and has been intimately associated with the
history of this country for many centuries.   Our excellent
friend, John D'Alton, has lately written a History of Drogheda
and its Environs, and to that work we must specially refer
those among our readers who seek further information upon
the subject than the limits of a guide-book can afford.

The early Irish name of this place was *Drochat-Atha*—the
Bridge of the Ford; but in after times the name was anglicised
Tredagh.   The grave of the wife of Gobhan, the smith, one of
those great sepulchral mounds which were rifled by the Danes
in the ninth century, to which we alluded at page 202, is the

Mill-Mount on which the fortress of Drogheda now stands,
on the right or southern bank
of the river.

We already remarked upon
the landing of St. Patrick in
432, at Inver Colpe, at the
Boyne's mouth, upon the
southern side of the river.
From that time to 1641, when
it was besieged by Oliver
Cromwell, and to 1690, when
it was occupied by James II.,
we could trace its annals from
year to year, almost without
a break.

Drogheda was a strongly
fortified city, and considerable portions of its walls, with
two of its gates, still remain.   St. Laurence's Gate, upon the
northern side of the river, is here shown from the outside.   It
consists of two circular towers, with a connecting curtain wall
over the arch, and, although built of small stones, it is one of
the finest specimens of its kind in Ireland.   "The walls of Dro-

gheda," writes Mr. D'Alton, "extended in their circumference, including the breadth of the river, somewhat more than a mile and a half, and enclose an area of about sixty-four acres of the old Irish measure, the general height being from twenty to twenty-two feet, and their thickness from four to six, diminishing toward the summit, so as to allow a space of about two feet, with embrasures for the soldiery to act from. In latter times, probably after the invention of gunpowder, this space was augmented by an addition of three or four feet, supported by columns of stone and elliptic arches, on and through which a passage led round the town, with doorways through the gates, castles, and turrets. The banks of the river were also fortified by walls and turrets, projecting into the water, as appears by a painting of Drogheda in the hall of Beaulieu House, taken in the reign of Charles II."* Upon the Meath or southern side, the West Gate forms a most pleasing and picturesque ruin. It appears to have been one of the flanking towers in the original town wall, and in one of the old maps of this place it is called the Butter Gate. The groove for the portcullis is still quite perfect. There

were also in ancient times several castles here, and the mound from which Cromwell battered the town is still shown upon the south-eastern side of the river, behind the present poorhouse.

Several Parliaments were held in this town; the most memo-

* See a History of Drogheda with its Environs, and a Memoir of the Dublin and Drogheda Railway. By John D'Alton, Esq., Barrister at Law. 1844. Vol. i. pp. 88, 89. To which work we must refer our readers for a more detailed description of Drogheda. In the Dublin Penny Journals there are also several accounts of this ancient city and its antiquities. See also Wright's Louthiana.

rable of these was that in which the bill of Sir Edward Poyning, since called "Poyning's Law," was passed, by which the
Irish Parliament was made dependent on that of England.

This town contained, according to the last Census, 17,300
inhabitants.   In its sunken position within the last defile of
the valley of the Boyne, with its narrow, tortuous streets, many
of which are ascended by steps, and the number of tall spires
and ancient ruins which rise out of the jumble of houses, it
bears a resemblance to many continental towns.   It is a place
of considerable trade; and in the river, below the narrow
bridge, the last upon the Boyne, and the only one in Drogheda,
may often be seen as many steamers as we find in the Liffey.
Up to a very recent period several wooden or bird-cage houses,
like those in Chester and some of the old English towns, existed
in Drogheda.   In one of these it is said Sir Arthur Aston, Governor of this town at the
time of Cromwell's siege,
resided, and in this house
tradition says King James
slept the night he arrived
in Drogheda, before he
encamped at Donore.

From time immemorial
Drogheda has been noted
for its ecclesiastical establishments, and the ruins
of several still remain; but
they are, generally speaking, scarcely approach-
able, owing to the quan-
tity of filth by which they
are surrounded. The most
remarkable of these ec-
clesiastical ruins is that
shown in the accompany-
ing illustration, the Abbey
or Church of St. Mary,
which spans a dirty lane,
now principally used as a stable-yard, behind the upper end
of West-street.

One of the most conspicuous objects in Drogheda is the

Magdalen Steeple, figured below, the only remnant of the church of the Dominican friary which once stood here. It occupies an elevated position upon the northern side of the city, near Sunday's Gate, and is immediately adjoining a series of arches pointed out as the remains of the town wall. It is now surrounded by the most miserable hovels, inhabited by the most wretched portion of the population, and not only is the adjoining locality a disgrace to the town, but the very site itself stands more in need of the efforts of a Sanitary Commission than any other place that we know of in the British dominions.

As soon as the Corporation of Drogheda cleanse their city, we hope to conduct the Boyne tourists round some of its other memorable ruins.

From Drogheda the tourist may visit Duleek, upon the Meath, and Termonfecken, Monasterboice, and Mellifont, upon the Louth side of the river. No visiter to this part of Ireland who has three hours to spare after examining the battle-field of Oldbridge, but should visit these two latter celebrated localities, which abound in ruins of the highest interest, consisting of ancient churches, some of the most magnificent sculptured crosses in Ireland, a round tower, and an ancient octagon church, or baptistry, similar to the Temple Church in London.*

Our pilgrimage is now nearly at an end. There is little further worthy of remark. Below Drogheda the Boyne spreads out into a broad estuary, which is shortly to be crossed by a

---

* By passing up King William's Glen, opposite the Obelisk at Oldbridge, the tourist can with great ease first visit Mellifont, then proceed to Monasterboice, and after that return to Drogheda.

bridge connecting the Dublin and Belfast Railways. As we sail down the river, several pleasingly situated villas range along the northern bank, and the fine old mansion-house of Beaulieu or Bewley particularly attracts attention. Upon the right or southern bank is Mornington, one of the earliest seats of the Wellesleys, and Colpe, the site of an ancient church, built, it is said, over the spot where the brother of Milesius was buried. Upon this southern shore of the Boyne's mouth stands an ancient square tower about eighty feet high, which has always been known by the name of the Maiden Tower; and at a little

distance from it inland is placed a small pillar of solid masonry, called The Finger. They are evidently landmarks, erected before light-houses were employed in this country. The tower, which is at least three hundred years old, may also have been originally used as a look-out station, for which purpose it is admirably adapted. There is a winding staircase in the centre, and the top, which is flagged, is reached by a small aperture, which could easily be covered with a large stone, so that it might, in case of siege, be rendered inaccessible from within. There are many "old stories" related about this tower,—tales of love, of maiden faith and knightly honour, and, in latter days, of mystery also. Tradition says it was erected by a fair lady, to watch the return of her betrothed from a far-distant country, whither he was obliged to journey upon the eve of their nuptials. It was agreed beforehand that, if the lover re-

turned successful, he should hoist a milk-white banner; but if
the contrary, a red flag should float from his mast-head. The
preconcerted signal was forgotten, and the knight, seeing the
tower,—which his true love had erected during his absence to
watch his return,—and mistaking it for the watch-tower of an
enemy and an invader, instantly displayed the blood-red flag,
whereon the disconsolate maiden precipitated herself from the
top of the tower, and was dashed to atoms. Not many years
ago a poor half-witted female recluse took up her abode on
the top of the tower, and was, like the hermits of old, supplied
with every necessary by the surrounding peasantry. It has
been conjectured that the tower was erected during the reign
of Elizabeth, and took its name from the Maiden Queen.

INDEX.

Y

THE END.